THE BALTIC ORIGINS OF HOMER'S EPIC TALES

THE BALTIC ORIGINS OF HOMER'S EPIC TALES

THE *ILIAD,* THE *ODYSSEY,* AND THE MIGRATION OF MYTH

Felice Vinci

Translated by Felice Vinci and
Amalia De Francesco

Inner Traditions
Rochester, Vermont

Inner Traditions
One Park Street
Rochester, Vermont 05767
www.InnerTraditions.com

Originally published in 1995 in Italian under the title *Omero nel Baltico,* by
Fratelli Palombi Editions, Rome

Library of Congress Cataloging-in-Publication Data

Vinci, Felice, 1946–
  [Omero nel Baltico. English]
  The Baltic origins of Homer's epic tales : the Iliad, the Odyssey, and the migration
of myth / Felice Vinci ; translated by Felice Vinci and Amalia Di Francesco.
     p. cm.
  Includes bibliographical references and index.
  ISBN 1-59477-052-2 (pbk.)
  1. Homer—Knowledge—Geography. 2. Homer—Knowledge—Baltic Sea Region.
3. Epic poetry, Greek—History and criticism. 4. Odysseus (Greek mythology)
in literature. 5. Trojan War—Literature and the war. 6. Troy (Extinct city)—In
literature. 7. Baltic Sea Region—In literature. 8. Geography, Ancient, in literature.
9. Civilization, Homeric. 10. Achaeans. I. Title.
  PA4037.V4513 2005
  883'.01—dc22
                                                                    2005028732

Printed and bound in Canada by Transcontinental Printing

10 9 8 7 6 5 4 3 2 1

Text design by Ginny Scott-Bowman
Text layout by Jon Desautels
This book was typeset in Sabon with Lithos as the display typeface

CONTENTS

ACKNOWLEDGMENTS

I offer my thanks and acknowledgment to all those who have helped with the English edition of this book. They believed a strange theory by an unknown Italian, and in so doing defied the dogmas of the conformists. I thank first Frederic (Fredo) Jueneman, who handled the huge task of improving my English translation and made many intelligent suggestions. (He modestly spoke of "a few things to benefit the cause.") Judith Davis has done "heroic service" at his side, correcting grammar, syntax, and typographical errors. I cannot forget Victor DeMattei, who gave the manuscript a preliminary reading and, like Fredo, spared no effort in spreading my theory.

I also acknowledge Laila Barr, Alfred and Amy De Grazia, Vine Deloria, Alberto DiPippo, Tom Van Flandern, Joscelyn Godwin, William Mullen, Leszek Wysocki, Dwardu Cardona, and many others who helped and encouraged me on this hard way.

I thank, on the other side of the Atlantic, Mrs. Soili Kuussaari (Finland), Erik Dahl (Norway), Tatjana Devjatkina (Russia), Karin Wagner (Germany), Peter Fletcher (England), and Finn Gemynth Madsen and Preben Hansson (Denmark). As for the help I received in Italy, I have many more people to thank than space allows. I must mention, however, Professor Rosa Calzecchi Onesti of Milan and Professor Giuliana Bendelli of the University of Pavia, who gave an extraordinary contribution in order to spread my theory in the academic world.

I particularly thank my son Vincenzo, the new Telemachus, who has cycled with me around Lyø (Ithaca), and my Pinina, who has been of incomparable moral support, always at my side in the correction of the English draft of the manuscript.

Last but not least, I thank the unforgettable chairman of Mensa Italy, the late Menotti Cossu, the first enthusiastic supporter of my theory: Right now, on his cloud in the sky, he must be chatting with Homer about the news concerning the poet and his work in this lower world.

FOREWORD

Homer's *Iliad,* which deals with the Trojan War, and *Odyssey*, the story of Odysseus's homecoming after the fall of Troy, are the earliest epic poems of Western literature. In a poll for the greatest books of all times and peoples, they would emerge near or at the top. It is no small matter, then, to strike at the roots of the received view of them: to claim that they are not Greek in origin, but rather describe peoples and events in ancient Scandinavia.

It is good to see those roots being attacked. Received beliefs are death to the mind, and minds that are alive and growing need to question them. It is itself a part of the historical process that history is in a perpetual state of revision, for knowing the past is not an exact science. Until someone invents a reliable time machine, the past can be seen only through the corrective lenses of the present, and these are sometimes very strong and distorting. For example, there are still people who wear the medieval spectacles of biblical literalism, for whom the entire past must be crammed into six thousand years. This book is an invitation to try on a new pair of lenses.

Often it is the experts who most resist new theories, but in this case the experts seem to have long been teetering on the brink of Vinci's conclusions. Moses Finley, a scholar second to none, demolished the orthodox view that Homer describes the Mycenean Age and that Heinrich Schliemann had excavated the real Troy on the Turkish coast. What, then, does Homer describe? Prehistorians such as Stuart Piggott and Georges Dumézil see the Homeric characters as part of a wider Indo-European culture. Karl Kerényi, the mythologist and friend of Carl Jung, finds repeated links between Greek and northern European themes.

Martin P. Nilsson, the Swedish historian of religion, comes out bluntly with a Nordic origin for the Mycenaeans. Then, after carbon-14 dating was recalibrated, in Lord (Colin) Renfrew's words, "The whole carefully constructed edifice [of prehistory] comes crashing down, and the storyline of the standard textbooks must be discarded." Stonehenge, it turns out, predates the Pyramids, and Balkan metalworking preceded that of the Aegean. The northern Europeans were not the inheritors but instead the ancestors of preclassical Greek culture.

According to Vinci, rereading Homer in this light "further erodes the thick wall between myth and history." But for the Homeric account to be read as the history of far-northern cultures, the lenses we see through must be recalibrated too, and preferably by an exact science. At this point we turn to climatology, which has as good a claim as any to being a genuine science of the past, and view the period in question through its findings.

After the last ice age ended in Europe, around twelve thousand years ago, the climate gradually became warmer, reaching a peak in temperature between about 4000 and 2000 B.C.E. Then, for five hundred years or so, the temperature fell in the Northern Hemisphere, glaciers advanced, rainfall increased, and the vegetation changed accordingly. The inhabitants of Scandinavia (Norway, Sweden, Finland, Denmark) and the Baltic coast could no longer sustain the way of life to which they had been accustomed. The death blow came with the eruption of the Thera volcano around 1630 B.C.E. and the cataclysmic weather that followed it. The northerners abandoned their homeland and headed south, probably along the Russian rivers. One tribe, called by Homer the Achaeans, reached the Peloponnese (the main peninsula of Greece) and there founded the Mycenaean civilization. Of course, they brought their myths and histories with them. As Vinci's theory goes, finding similarities between the Aegean region and that of the Baltic, they adapted to their new territory the names of their native towns, rivers, tribes, and so forth and resituated their epic stories there. But the two geographies did not quite fit, and that is why Homer seems not just to "nod," as the old saying had it, but to make blatant errors when he describes the Mediterranean world.

Generations of classical scholars have mapped and remapped the journeys of Odysseus / Ulysses, trying to find a plausible scheme for them somewhere in the Mediterranean. But if we assumes that "[t]he origin of the poem of Achilles, the *Iliad,* seems to be the regions of the

Gulf of Finland, whereas the first nucleus of the poem glorifying Ulysses, the *Odyssey*, likely originated in the area of what is now Denmark," then Homer had made no errors.

What is the evidence for this startling claim? Vinci offers one instance after another of similar names in the two regions. Of course, finding similarities in words from different languages is a habit of maverick prehistorians that we may mistrust with good reason. It needs strong corroborative evidence, which in Vinci's case comes from geographic parallels—river for river, island for island, and so on.

The reader must decide whether this carries sufficient weight, but the author's most persuasive argument comes from his fresh approach to the Catalog of Ships, that interminable account in Book 2 of the *Iliad*, which recounts the origins of all the contributors to the Greek fleet who will battle the Trojans. As Vinci explains convincingly, when set on Baltic geography, the catalog is brought into focus as a systematic, counter-clockwise tour of this northern coast.

At this point, another type of prehistorian enters, less respectable than those I have named here but strangely in accord with the ancient mythographers themselves: Bâl Gangâdhar Tilak was an Indian scholar and politician imprisoned in 1897 for agitation against British rule. In *The Arctic Home in the Vedas*, he situated his and his captors' common ancestors not in the Baltic, but rather even farther north. There are many enigmatic passages in Homer and in other examples of ancient mythology that make sense only if they are set in lands where the sun does not rise for days on end in the winter or set in the summer—that is, within the Arctic Circle.

In *The Baltic Origins of Homer's Epic Tales*, readers will discover how Vinci, working from the evidence of place-names and geographical features—of which those prehistorians knew nothing—comes to agree with these early social scientists and to conclude that "the original homeland of the Indo-Europeans lay in the northernmost part of Scandinavia, the sort of 'hat' atop the European continent that faces the Arctic Ocean . . . Five or six thousand years ago, when the constellation of Orion marked the spring equinox and the Dragon pointed out the North Pole, the primordial Indo-European civilization developed there, in the 'islands in the north of the world,' thanks to the most favorable climatic period ever experienced in the region."

Interestingly, this accords with an even less accepted body of writing, which began in 1888 with the publication of *The Secret Doctrine*, by

H. P. Blavatsky, founder of the Theosophical Society. She wrote on the early history of humanity, supposedly basing it on ancient Oriental sources, and situated its origins in the northern polar regions. Other Theosophists who claimed knowledge of the distant past, notably the clairvoyant Charles W. Leadbeater and the channeling writer Alice A. Bailey, took Blavatsky's scheme as their starting point, and Rudolf Steiner, the founder of Anthroposophy, retained its main outlines, adding many details of his own. The Traditionalist philosophers of the twentieth century, especially René Guénon *(The Lord of the World)*, and Julius Evola *(Revolt against the Modern World)*, presuppose a "Hyperborean" or Arctic homeland when they write of the earliest races of humanity. The idea of this northern origin, in short, has become a fixture of esoteric history.

As a scientist, Vinci sensibly ignores these currents. His work is not based on literature, except that of the ancient epics and myths themselves, and much less on any occult vision of the past. The inhabitants of his arctic homeland are not spiritual giants; they are ordinary people. They must have been more hardy than ourselves, however, for they forged a high culture in an extremely unfriendly climate. Surely they were more courageous, for when life became impossible where they had established roots, men, women, and children headed for unknown lands. Finally, they were without doubt more creative, for they went on to lay the foundations of Greek culture, which then "spread across the world, eventually by means of the Roman Empire, until this grand circle, which had begun many years before with the Achaean migration from the north, finally closed when the Romans came into contact with the Germans, eventually giving rise to modern European civilization." In fact, in case we think their gifts irrelevant to the present day, Vinci reminds us that "the most important value that Europe has given the world, the idea of democracy, is found both in the Greek *agorá* and the Viking *thing*, the public meetings held in Athens and Iceland, respectively."

The conclusion of the book hazards some bolder theories still: that the Egyptians and the Sumerians also have a northern origin, and that the migrants, expert seafarers, may even have reached Polynesia. The author's reasoning is worth following, but if readers reserve their final judgment on these theories, so too does Vinci, for he himself calls these "speculations," and merely a starting point for a greater search into the origins of humankind.

In this caution, he sends us an important reminder: The current revisioning of the past is an effort of major cultural import, but it has far to go. While some popular authors write as though they alone have discovered the key and answer to understanding our history, discerning readers know that no one researcher can be right or all completely wrong. Each has something to contribute, and it is far too early to declare the matter closed and all mysteries solved. Vinci points out, for example, that once the northerners settled in Greece, around 1500 B.C.E., they came into contact with advanced Mediterranean and Near Eastern peoples, and it was out of this blend that Greek culture emerged. The last significant work of historical revision regarding Greece was Martin Bernal's *Black Athena*, which addressed this very blend, showing how much Greek culture was influenced by Egypt. It would be illuminating to read her book and Vinci's side by side.

Vinci tells us of Homer's curious appearance in the ninth or early eighth century B.C.E., at the exact moment when alphabetic writing began to spread through Greece. Because the *Iliad* and the *Odyssey* existed only in oral form, each had to be transcribed and adapted to the language and the new invention of the time. As to what that adaptation might have involved, we may look at the evidence presented by Anne Macaulay *(The Quest for Apollo)*, David Fideler *(Jesus Christ, Sun of God)*, John Michell *(City of Revelation)*, and others who suggest that the Greek alphabet was an artificial creation and that the names of the gods as spelled in it were "rigged" so that their letter values, when added up, would produce significant numbers. With this, we are far from the epic poems of oral tradition that were recited around fires of mammoth bones during the long arctic winter. Yet constant through it all are the characters who, once encountered, are unforgettable: people such as the arrogant king Agamemnon, the constant wife Penelope, the proud warrior Achilles, and Odysseus, the "perfect incarnation of the Viking mentality, which is at the same time suspicious and daring and is endowed with an Odinic type of wisdom that is practical, curious, versatile, pragmatic and even unscrupulous, fundamentally based on a supreme control of language." It is these men and women and their stories that are truly timeless, wherever their origins may have been.

JOSCELYN GODWIN, TRANSLATOR OF
HYPNEROTOMACHIA POLIPHILI AND
AUTHOR OF *ARKTOS: THE POLAR MYTH IN SCIENCE,
SYMBOLISM, AND NAZI SURVIVAL*

THE KEY TO FINDING HOMER'S WORLD

Ever since ancient times, the geography in Homer's two epics, the *Odyssey* and the *Iliad*, has given rise to problems and uncertainty. Towns, countries, and islands described by the poet with a wealth of detail conform to specific places in the Mediterranean world only partially at best, but more often not at all. Indeed, the geographer Strabo (63 B.C.E.–23 C.E.) does not understand why, in the *Odyssey*, the island of Pharos, situated at the door of the port of Alexandria, inexplicably appears to lie a day's sail from Egypt. Likewise, the location of Ithaca remains confused: According to the precise descriptions in the *Odyssey*, it is the westernmost island in an archipelago that includes the three main islands of Dulichium, Same, and Zacynthus. But this does not correspond at all to the geographic reality of the Greek Ithaca in the Ionian Sea, which is located north of Zacynthus, east of Cephallenia, and south of Leucas. And what of the mountainous Peloponnese Peninsula that is described in both poems as a plain?

If Homeric geography was troublesome to Strabo, it is equally problematic for contemporary scholars. When the decoding of the Mycenaean writing "Linear B" (found on clay tablets and ceramic vessels in Greece and on Crete—that is, in the region of the eastern Mediterranean Sea, commonly considered to be the location of the events in the *Odyssey* and the *Iliad*) allowed us to compare the Mycenaean world to the Homeric one, the results were puzzling.

Professor John Chadwick, a British linguist and classical scholar famous for his work, along with Michael Ventris, in deciphering Linear B, states that there is a "complete lack of contact between Mycenaean

1

geography as now known from the tablets and from archaeology on the one hand, and Homer's accounts on the other."[1] In his turn, Professor Moses Finley, of Cambridge University, writes:

> I shall briefly illustrate how little remains of Homer today as a witness for the world in which the Trojan War is traditionally held to have occurred. . . . It would almost be enough to compare the relatively lengthy and optimistic list of Homeric-Mycenaean parallels in the material remains to be found in Helen Lorimer's *Homer and the Monuments,* published in 1950, with the paltry half-dozen or so that survived by the time Kirk's Songs of Homer appeared in 1962. Since then, the Homeric palace and the Homeric war-chariot have been jettisoned, together with their accoutrements. And, finally, the worst blow of all: the surrender of the last bastion, Homer's "Mycenaean geography."[2]

Professor John Chadwick has recently summed up his conclusions on this subject: "I believe the Homeric evidence to be almost worthless. . . . One major reason is precisely the The attempts which have been made to reconcile them . . . are unconvincing."[3] Similarly, University of Genoa (Italy) Greek literature professor Franco Montanari offers that "regarding the correspondence between Homeric geography and the Mycenaean one . . . people stress divergences now."[4]

In other words, when Homeric geography and topography are compared to the actual physical layout of the Greek world, glaring anomalies are revealed that are difficult to explain, especially given the consistency of Homer's descriptions throughout the two epics. For example, the description of the Peloponnese as a plain occurs not sporadically but regularly, and Dulichium, the "long island" (*dolichós* means "long" in Greek) located near Ithaca, is repeatedly mentioned in both the *Odyssey* and the *Iliad* but has never been identified in the Mediterranean. Despite its familiar names, the world described by Homer seems largely closed to us. How can we find it?

We can begin by reaching back two millennia to the words of the Greek biographer and essayist Plutarch (46–120 C.E.). It is he who provides a possible starting point to finally penetrating this puzzling world. In his essay "De facie quae in orbe lunae apparet" (The Face That Appears in the Moon Circle),[5] he quotes this line of verse from Homer: "A certain island, Ogygia, lies a long way off in the sea . . ." (*Odys-*

sey 7.244) and then adds that Ogygia—the goddess Calypso's island, where Ulysses lands after a long period of wandering and from which he resumes his journey to his homeland, Ithaca—is situated "five days' sail from Britain, toward the west."

In this passage, Plutarch unequivocally places Ogygia in the geographic reality of the North Atlantic Ocean. He goes so far as to state that beyond it, other islands are to be found and that farther on lies "the great continent, which surrounds the ocean." Plutarch offers another significant detail that confirms the reliability of his geographic understanding: In these "external islands," he says, the summer sun "disappears for less than an hour per night, over a period of thirty days, while twilight glimmers in the west," clearly a description of the way light lingers long in the sky during northern summer nights.

Plutarch's indications lead us to identify Ogygia with one of the Faeroe Islands, the northernmost and westernmost among the islands surrounding Great Britain (see fig. I.1). This is the key that allows us to discover the geographic reality of Homer's world, which has been elusive for so long. As we shall see in the pages that follow, many scholars through time have failed to find corroborating evidence that the world Homer presents to us is a southern, Mediterranean one, while an extremely strong case can be made for a northern Homeric world, one oriented around the Baltic Sea (see fig. I.2).

As we shall see in chapter 2, a series of precise parallels makes it possible to identify a group of Danish islands as corresponding exactly to all of Homer's descriptions regarding the archipelago where Ithaca can be found. Among these islands, Langeland, the "long island," finally reveals the solution to the puzzle of the mysterious island of Dulichium, Aerø corresponds perfectly to the Homeric Same, and Tåsinge corresponds to ancient Zacynthus. It is astonishing how closely Lyø, the westernmost island in the archipelago, coincides with the poet's description of Ulysses' Ithaca not only in its position, but also in its topographical and morphological features. Furthermore, the details reported in the *Odyssey* regarding the war between Pylians and Epeans, as narrated in Book 11 of the *Iliad*, have always been considered inconsistent with Greece's uneven topography, while they fit perfectly with the flat Danish island of Zealand, which stands in the same relation to Langeland as does the Peloponnese to Dulichium in Homer's descriptions.

A northern location also explains the huge anomaly of the great battle that takes up the central books of the *Iliad*, a battle that continues for two

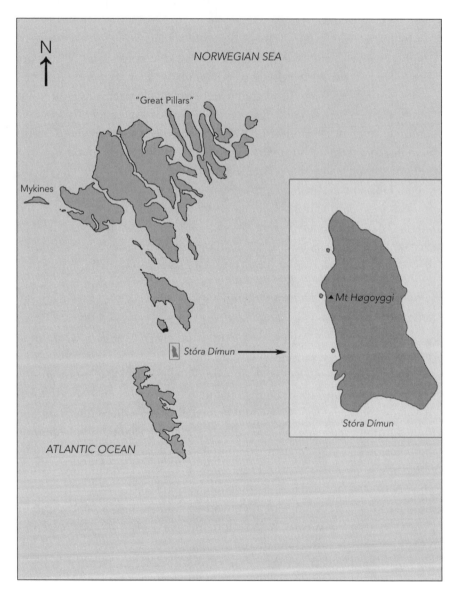

Fig. I.1. The Faeroe Islands and the island of Stóra Dímun (Ogygia). At the top
are located the "great pillars" of Atlas. The westernmost island is Mykines. Stóra
Dímun is enlarged at right.

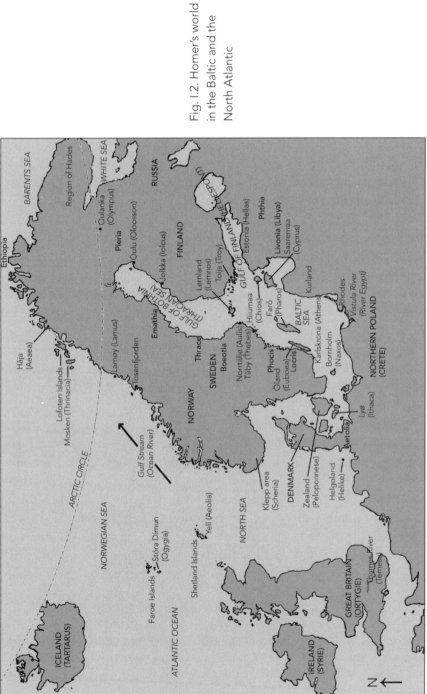

Fig. I.2. Homer's world in the Baltic and the North Atlantic

days and one night. It is incomprehensible that the darkness of night in the Mediterranean world would not put a temporary stop to the fighting, but the fact that the conflict continues unabated through these hours makes a good deal of sense in a Baltic setting: What allows Patroclus's fresh troops to carry on fighting through the night without a break is the dim, residual night light that is typical at high latitudes around the summer solstice. This interpretation—corroborated by the overflowing of the river Scamander during the battle that occurred two days after, a phenomenon that could certainly occur in northern regions in May or June due to the spring thaw—allows us to reconstruct the stages of the entire battle in a coherent manner, dispelling those perplexities and strained interpretations that have plagued readers and scholars to the present day (see chapter 7). To further strengthen this northern interpretation, we can even pick out from a passage in the *Iliad* the Greek term used to denote the faintly lit summer nights typical of the regions located near the Arctic Circle. This *amphilýke nýx* is a real linguistic fossil, which, thanks to the Homeric epos, has survived the migration of the Achaeans* to southern Europe.

But if Homer's world is indeed a Nordic one, how did it come to be so closely associated with the Mediterranean? Why would a southern Mediterranean people create tales whose geography, climate, place-names, and depicted culture so clearly hew to a northern reality? How, in other words, did the myths of the *Odyssey* and the *Iliad* find their way south?

As we shall see, the explanation lies in the journey of not only Ulysses but of whole peoples as well. Homer's tales embody what we might call the migration of myth. During the time from the sixth to the third millennium B.C.E. (overlapping the Bronze Age, which began between 4000 and 3000 B.C.E.), Europe experienced what is known as the *post-glacial climatic optimum*—that is, a period during which the northern reaches of the continent enjoyed significantly warmer weather and the variations of flora and fauna that accompany it. In fact, the climatic optimum lasted much longer and resulted in higher temperatures across Europe than

---

*Although they are more commonly termed "Greeks" in modern times, the protagonists of Homer's poems are referred to by the poet as the Achaeans (Achaioi) or, more rarely, Danaans (Danaioi) or Argives (Argeioi). Once settled in the Mediterranean area, they gave rise to what scholars call the Mycenaean civilization, which began about 1600 B.C.E. and fell four centuries later, when the Dorians invaded from the north. Ancient Greeks referred to themselves as "Hellenes" and their land as "Hellas." The term "Greeks" derives from Graeci, the name Romans gave to the populations living in Greece.

did the so-called warm medieval period (800–1200 c.e.), when Green-land actually was green and covered with meadows and when vineyards stretched north to Great Britain. Reaching its peak around 2500 b.c.e., however, the climatic optimum began to decline around 2000 b.c.e., likely impelling some northern peoples to migrate south in search of a more hospitable climate.

Considerable evidence has been found at Mycenaean sites to suggest that Mycenaean civilization came from the north. The distinguished Swedish scholar Martin P. Nilsson, in his *Homer and Mycenae*, reports archaeological remains uncovered in Mycenaean sites in Greece that corroborate this northern origin. These include the existence of a large quantity of Baltic amber in the most ancient Mycenaean tombs in Greece, which cannot be ascribed to trade because amber is very scarce in both coeval Minoan tombs in Crete and later graves on the continent (see chapter 9); the typically northern features of architectural remains (the Mycenaean *megaron* "is identical to the hall of the ancient Scandinavian kings"); the "striking similarity" between two stone slabs found in a tomb in Dendra and "the menhirs known from the Bronze Age of central Europe"; and the larger skulls more typical of northerners that have been found in the necropolis of Kalkani. This is why Bertrand Russell, in the first chapter of his *History of Western Philosophy*, claims that the Mycenaean civilization originated with fair-haired northern invaders of Greece who brought the Greek language with them.

Proposed in these pages is that the Trojan War and other events that have been handed down to us in Greek mythology were set not in the Mediterranean, but rather in the Baltic area, the primitive home of the blond "long-haired" Achaeans of Homer's *Iliad*. These events probably date back to the beginning of the second millennium b.c.e., a time when northern Europe was steadily growing colder. They may have occurred during the interval just before the people whom we know as the Achaeans found their way south to the Mediterranean, perhaps following the Dnieper River down to the Black Sea, just as the Vikings—whose culture is in many ways quite similar to theirs—did many centuries later. As they moved, the Achaeans took with them their stories, their gods and goddesses, their place-names, and other remnants of their culture, all of which can be seen in Homer's two epic poems.

While this book focuses on two important literary works, its means of exploration is essentially geographic, rather than literary, historiographic, or chronological. Yet to support the thesis that Homer's world is actually a Baltic one, we shall explore a variety of subjects: climate as it relates to the convergence of Homer's descriptions and a northern reality; etymology and morphology as they relate to the remarkable similarities between northern place-names and the locales in the *Odyssey* and the *Iliad;* chronology as it pertains to the Bronze Age and the postglacial climatic optimum; mythology as it reveals the parallels among Greek, Nordic, and other cultures; and, of course, the words of the two epics themselves, especially that part of the *Iliad* known as the Catalog of Ships, which, as we shall see in chapter 10, relates a verbal "map" nearly identical to the actual geography of the Baltic world.

Throughout our investigation, the specific language of Homer's work will be our guiding star: We will turn to it often to set our course, for it tells of a world that is far different from a Mediterranean one. For instance, the subject of climate arises frequently in the text of the *Odyssey* and of the *Iliad.* Returning to Ogygia, we can see from Homer's words that the temperatures on the island were not like those normally found in the Mediterranean: The fire burning in Calypso's dwelling—"a big fire was burning on the hearth" (*Odyssey* 5.59)—in a time of the year coinciding with the warm sailing season hardly fits with a southern setting, but is quite conceivable for the Faeroe Islands.

Likewise, Ogygia's vegetation (*Odyssey* 5.60–64)—that is, conifers (cedar, thuja, cypress), trees typical of those found near streams (alders and poplars), and "the soft meadows of violets and celery" (*Odyssey* 5.72)—seems to indicate a fresh and rather wet climate that is somewhat different from that of the Greek islands. The Faeroe Islands certainly could be characterized as wet, with an annual rainfall of more than sixty inches. While today the vegetation on the islands is extremely sparse, due, above all, to the strong winds prevalent there, conditions would have been very different during the postglacial climatic optimum. The high humidity levels of the archipelago would have been accompanied by warmer temperatures conducive to the growth of all kinds of vegetation—even the grapevines mentioned in the *Odyssey* (5.69).

But during the time of the setting of the *Odyssey* and of the *Iliad,* the climatic optimum had clearly begun its decline. In Homer's descriptions of unsettled weather, we see a world that—however mild it had been in the years before—is now distinctly northern. In the *Iliad,* for instance, the poet frequently mentions the "thick fog" that falls on those fighting on the Trojan plain, and in the *Odyssey* Ulysses' sea is never as bright as that of the Greek islands, but instead is always "gray" and "misty." There is mention everywhere of wind, rain, and cold temperatures, and snow falls both at sea and on the plains in the *Iliad*. Moreover, sun and warm temperatures are hardly ever mentioned. Homer seems to be telling us that we are far from the torrid Anatolian lowlands. Even the way in which his characters are dressed is in perfect keeping with this kind of northern climate: They wear tunics and "thick, heavy cloaks," which they never remove, not even during banquets. Interestingly, this attire corresponds exactly to the remains of clothing found in Bronze Age Danish graves, down to such details as the metal brooches that pin the cloaks at the shoulder.

Ultimately, it is not Homer's descriptions in these two poems but the very tales themselves that point to their genesis in the Nordic world and tell the tale of their migration southward. In our investigation, we shall look closely at the parallels between Greek and Nordic myth. From this comparison we will see how migrants from northern Europe carried south with them their tales and even members of their pantheon. Not least of the similarities we shall discover are those between Homer's Ulysses, who, Tacitus claims, sailed the northern seas,[6] and Ull, an archer and warrior in Norse mythology. In fact, along the coast and among the islands of the Norwegian Sea—which is crossed by a branch of the Gulf Stream identifiable as the mythical River Ocean (see chapter 13)—we find many tales that are similar to the famous adventures of Ulysses, indicating that Homer's stories may well have had their roots in northern sailors' tales and local folklore before being transformed by the art and imagination of the poet.

The remains of these ancient tales may well tell of the Greeks' distant Scandinavian past. Having survived that period in Greek history known as the Hellenic Middle Ages (or the dark ages that followed the Dorian invasion of the Mycenaean region and the subsequent fall of the Mycenaean world in the twelfth century B.C.E.), they may have eventually become crystallized as myths detached from temporal and geographic reality, so that any memory of a northern past was erased. Local northern folklore could, then, be the origin of Greek mythology, sustained by the bards who handed down such tales through the years.

But if these tales gradually became something apart from reality, their origins are evident in the many place-names in the Nordic world that have seeming counterparts in the south, for the migrants took the geography of their homeland along with them to the places where they eventually settled. No doubt spurred on by the similarity between Baltic geography and that of the Aegean and Mediterranean (a likeness that these seafaring peoples surely realized), they conferred on their new homes names that were familiar. They renamed with Baltic terms not only the new countries in which they settled, but also other Mediterranean regions, such as Libya, Crete, and Egypt, thus creating the enormous geographical misunderstanding of Homer's world that has lasted through the ages.

And so we find that the medieval Danish historian Saxo Grammaticus mentions in his *History of the Danes* (*Gesta Danorum*—see page 87) a region called Hellespont, located to the east of the Baltic Sea. Could this place be Homer's Hellespont? Likewise, there is the Finnish town of Toija, which may well be the original Troy (Troía in Greek). In the *Iliad*, the region of Troy is located along the Hellespont Sea, which is consistently described by Homer as being "wide" or even "boundless." From this description, this body of water hardly seems to coincide with the Strait of the Dardanelles in western Turkey, the location of the city brought to light on the Anatolian site of Hisarlik—the city that is, according to the German archaeologist Heinrich Schliemann's theory, the site of Homer's Troy. Yet the identification of this Turkish site with the Homeric Troy has always raised strong doubts. While it may coincide with the location of the Greco-Roman Troy—the Anatolian city so named by the Mycenaeans—Strabo claims that it does not coincide with the ancient Troy of Homer's work: "This is not the site of the ancient Ilium."[7] In reality, Strabo tells us, this plain in what is now Turkey was under the sea in Homeric times, a fact confirmed geologically in 1977.

So what of the northern Toija? In July 1992, I took a plane from Copenhagen to Helsinki and from there drove on Highway E18 toward Salo. The road, flat at first, gradually became more undulating as I approached the turn to Lake Suomusjärvi. From the lake I headed toward Kitula and then toward the town of Toija—Troy. It seems that this peaceful place, although unaware of its glorious and tragic past, maintains in its name a strong connection to it. What was plain to see was that the topographical features of Toija, a quiet Finnish village, with its gas station, post office, drugstore, and houses, correspond exactly to those Homer hands down to us (see chapter 6 for more geographical detail), including, near Toija in the direction of the sea, a place called Aijala, recalling the stretch of coast *(aigialós)* where, according to

Homer, the Achaeans beached their ships. Later, taking off from Turku airport in a small, single-engine craft, I was able to survey the entire area from far above: the two rivers to the north; the unmistakable elongated shape of the plain, now flooded (see chapter 6), where that famous fierce fighting took place; the hills around the village now called Kisko, but once the location of King Priam's city; and more. It is easy to imagine, as the craft swoops once again over the watery plain on its way back to Turku, that beneath us in the lake bed lie the remains of the tomb of Ilus, Priam's grandfather.

In fact, there are many examples of northern locales that are perfectly consistent with those places Homer describes—in many instances, much more consistent than the locations in the Mediterranean that have been traditionally considered Homer's settings. Indeed, west of Helsinki we find a number of place-names that bear an astonishing resemblance to the names of allies of the Trojans in the *Iliad:* Askainen (Ascanius), Reso (Rhesus), Karjaa (Caria), Nästi (Nastes, the chief of the Carians), Lyökki (Lycia), Tenala (Tenedos), Kiila (Cilla), Kiikoinen (Ciconians), and so forth. While these and other Scandinavian place-names do not have recent origins, it is very difficult to establish just how old they are. Unfortunately, not even the oldest written Scandinavian documents predate the year 1000 C.E. Before this date, there is no written evidence available for reconstructing the evolution of place-names. It is significant, however, when names that seem morphologically similar to those in the Mediterranean world are found in clusters—which makes accidental correspondence between the two worlds very unlikely—or when such names can be linked to specific geographic or mythological entities. Still, we use place-names mainly as traces or clues in the development of this theory, while essentially basing it on the amazing geographic, morphologic, descriptive, and climatic similarities between the Homeric world and the Baltic one.

If the Greeks migrated from the Baltic, we might ask why the Greek culture, even at the time of its height, did not seem to be aware of its northern ancestry. It is likely that over time, the memory of the migration of their ancestors from the Baltic began to fade from the collective mind of the Greeks, and that if there were any remnants, they were surely erased after the collapse of the Mycenaean world at the hands of the Dorians in the twelfth century B.C.E. After all, the migration had taken place almost five hundred years before, which represents roughly the same time lapse that separates us from the discovery of America and all the lore surrounding that period. The Greek people thus came to identify the Homeric Troy, Mycenae, Tiryns, Athens, Thebes, Crete, Egypt, and other cities with their Mediterranean namesakes and the people and places in their epics came to be conceived of as myth rather than as historical truth.

So it is up to us to recover this hidden history, to prove here the historical and geographic reliability of the information contained in the *Odyssey* and the *Iliad*. That both Strabo and Plutarch and many other scholars have established the inconsistencies encountered when Homer's world is grafted onto a map of the Greek world goes some way toward establishing the reality of Homer's world in a Baltic-Scandinavian locale. Further, as we shall see, once Homer's information is considered in this northern context, it becomes remarkably consistent and exact. Apart from the necessary archaeological corroboration, Homer's work thus can be seen as one of historicity, not merely mythology, and any new reading of his poems in this light further erodes the thick wall between myth and history. In fact, in the *Odyssey* and in the *Iliad*, the northern Early Bronze Age, wrapped in deep shadows until now, has most likely revealed not only a great bard, but also its first chronicler.

This should not be very surprising, especially if we consider the reminder given by the scholar Stuart Piggott in his book *Ancient Europe from the Beginnings of Agriculture to Classical Antiquity*:

> The nobility of the [Homeric] hexameters should not deceive us into thinking that the *Iliad* and the *Odyssey* are other than the poems of a largely barbarian Bronze Age or Early Iron Age Europe. "There is no Minoan or Asiatic blood in the veins of the Grecian Muses . . . they dwell remote from the Cretan-Mycenaean world and in touch with the *European* elements of Greek speech and culture," Rhys Carpenter remarked; "behind Mycenaean Greece . . . lies Europe."[8]

In part 1 of this book we shall travel the world of Ulysses, locating his home, tracing the path of his voyage and adventures geographically in the Baltic arena and beyond, and then compare his character and adventures to those of Norse mythology.

In part 2 we turn to Troy, discovering its geographic reality in the north as evidenced in Homer's *Iliad* and noting how it matches specific details of the Trojan War as narrated by Homer.

In part 3 we investigate the origins of the Mycenaeans in the Baltic-Scandinavian world at the time of the climatic optimum and explore the geographic reality of Homer's wider Nordic world as presented in the Catalog of Ships.

Finally, in part 4 we shall locate the primordial home of the Indo-Europeans and consider the decline of the climatic optimum that resulted in their southern movement, as well as the migration of their myths, with a close look at the fascinating solar, stellar, and lunar myths that bespeak a northern origin.

I am well aware that many hypotheses developed here radically contrast with certain current notions, some of which are thousands of years old. In response, we can recall an important and relevant reflection of Francis Bacon, the first great philosopher of modern empirical science: "One cannot restrict reality within the limits of human knowledge, as people have done until now. On the contrary, knowledge must be increased and widened to include the picture of reality as it is discovered." The historian of science Federico Di Trocchio expands upon Bacon's words:

> One must counter the ancients' statement *"Don't go beyond"* with modern science's *"Go the farthest beyond."* This is why he [Bacon] set the Pillars of Hercules on the title page of his most famous work, *Novum Organum:* They were a visible representation of the presumed limits of knowledge. He also set the words of the prophet Daniel as his motto between the Pillars: *Multi pertransibunt et augebitur scientia* (Many people will go beyond and knowledge will make progress).[9]

So we dedicate the following chapters to the memory of Francis Bacon. As we "go beyond" in our explorations, we shall find that we are able to feel and relive the true spirit of Homer's mythology not in the dry, uneven ground of Greece or in the sunny Mediterranean islands, but in northern Europe's immense forests and silent lakes; in its dark, misty seas and fickle skies and never-ending twilights. Echoes and memories of a distant Hyperborean past, lost but never completely forgotten, survived through these myths, later to be reflected in every expression of Greek civilization and, eventually, handed down to us.

PART ONE
THE WORLD OF ULYSSES

CHAPTER 1

Ulysses Homeward Bound: The Island of Ogygia and the Land of Scheria

OGYGIA

In the *Odyssey*, the island of Ogygia is the crucial turning point in Ulysses' wanderings: On the one hand, Ulysses' arrival there marks the beginning of his return journey to Ithaca; on the other, his time there marks an end to the fabulous adventures he tells in the Phaeacian court. It was Plutarch who has personally directed us to the North Atlantic by locating Ogygia there, which leads us to identify it with one of the Faeroe Islands at their high latitude just four degrees below the Arctic Circle.

Interestingly, there are many characteristic caverns along the coast of the archipelago that remind us of the "deep grottos" often mentioned in the *Odyssey* with regard to Ogygia. This setting likewise squares with the mention of the large number of seabirds that fly around Calypso's grotto: "Jays, sparrow hawks, and crows cawing with their long tongues / sea crows which love sea-life . . ." (*Odyssey* 5.66–67). The abundance of fish in northern seas does indeed lead to a greater number of seabirds there than in warmer waters such as the Mediterranean. In fact, one of the traditional activities of the Faeroese is gathering seabird eggs and feathers.

And what of Calypso herself? She may have been a local Faeroese deity: Homer actually calls her "goddess" *(theá)*. Is it mere chance that the root of her name is similar to the name of an island, Kalsoy, that lies inside the Faeroe archipelago?

Ogygia—where Ulysses lands after wandering across the open sea—must be an island lying to the east and directly facing the Norwegian Sea. In the southern part of the Faeroe archipelago lies the island Stóra Dímun, which corresponds to this position. Its highest peak is Høgoyggj. The similarity between this name and the name Ogygia (in Greek, Ogygíe) leads us to suppose that the ancient Bronze Age name of the island as a whole came to indicate the mountain looming up on the horizon. This little island could well be Ogygia, "far off in the sea," separated by an "immense abyss" *(méga laîtma)* from the mainland where, according to Homer, Ulysses was held captive by Calypso for seven years.

We can also find the headland where our hero, "sitting on the rocks of the seashore, / tearing his heart with tears, groans and distress, / looked at the tireless sea" (*Odyssey* 5.156–58): This refers possibly to the easternmost side of Stóra Dímun, Cape Raettartangi, beneath Klettarnir—the other peak on the island that rises a little lower than Høgoyggj—and facing the Norwegian Sea and the European continent.

Homer refers to Calypso as the daughter of Atlas, whose description fits perfectly with Ogygia's morphology:

> *A goddess lives there,*
> *terrible Atlas's daughter, he who knows*
> *all depths of the sea. He himself supports the great pillars*
> *[kíonas makrás]*
> *that support the earth and the sky.* (*Odyssey* 1.51–54)

The reference to the "great pillars" is not merely coincidental: The Faeroe Islands, especially those lying on the northern side of the archipelago, have a narrow, elongated shape and a peculiar layout (see fig. I.1, page 4). From above they almost look like the vertebrae of an enormous backbone, with narrow stretches of sea in between each. They tower over the sea, one next to the other, like a kind of grand colonnade. Here are the "great pillars" of Atlas.

Ulysses at last is able to leave Ogygia on a raft that he builds according to Calypso's instructions: "Come now, chop down some big trees with a bronze axe and make / a wide raft, then build on a deck / so that it can carry you across the misty sea" (*Odyssey* 5.162–64). The poet dwells for no fewer than twenty lines of verse on the various phases of this construction (*Odyssey* 5.243–62). The Italian scholar Adriano Romualdi makes an interesting statement on this subject: "The Mediterranean world has never seen anything like the raft Ulysses built upon leaving Calypso, and yet it is identical to those engraved on the rocks in Sweden."[1] In his turn, the German scholar Karl Schuchhardt says: "Homer's description of Ulysses' raft, built after Calypso's instructions, finally allows us to understand how the crafts which we see in the Northern engravings were actually made."[2]

After making his raft, Ulysses sails away (Book 5 of the *Odyssey*), watching the constellations, in particular the Bear, "which the bright goddess Calypso had told him / to keep on his left-hand [*ep'aristerá cheirós echónta*] while sailing across the sea" (*Odyssey* 5.276–77). We can easily deduce from these lines that Ulysses' return route lay in an *easterly* direction. Let us continue to follow the raft: "He sailed through the sea for seventeen days, / and on the eighteenth, the shadowy mountains of the Phaeacian land / appeared, which grew very close to him / and looked like a shield on the misty sea" (*Odyssey* 5.278–81). These lines undoubtedly suit the Atlantic Ocean much better than the narrow Mediterranean Sea, and those "shadowy mountains," which suddenly appear "like a shield" out of the "misty sea," cannot be anything else but the high Norwegian coasts (see fig. 4.1, page 52), likely the fjord area near Bergen. This is why Homer always refers to Phaeacia as "land" *(gaíe)* rather than "island."

Our lonely sailor nearly reaches the end of his long journey across the sea when "mighty Poseidon, on his return from visiting the Ethiopians, / saw him from the distant Solymi mountains; from there he watched him / sailing across the sea and flew into a rage" (*Odyssey* 5.282–84). The Solymi Mountains could be likened in name to Mount Sulitjelma, north of Norway, among the highest of the Scandinavian mountains, as well as to the town of Solum to the south, located in a mountainous region west of Lillehammer. At this point, Poseidon raises a storm, which ends up destroying the raft. However, Ulysses manages to straddle a log and save himself, thanks to the propitious aid of both a sea goddess—Ino Leucothoe, who gives him a magical "life belt," which we shall return to later—and the goddess Athena, his protectress:

> *She locked the ways of the other winds,*
> *told them to stop and go to sleep,*
> *then called for the violent Boreas [the north wind] and broke the*
> *   waves in front of him,*
> *so that he reached the Phaeacians, who are keen on ships.*
> (*Odyssey* 5.383–86)

SCHERIA

After Ulysses drifts southward for two days and two nights, the wind drops, but he finds it very difficult to reach the land: "There were no coves or harbors for ships, / only sheer cliffs, rocks and reefs" (*Odyssey* 5.404–405). By following the coast, he eventually manages to find a place to land "at the mouth of a fine river / which seemed to him to be the best place / as it was free of rocks" (*Odyssey* 5.441–43).

Here a sort of miracle occurs: The god of the river "stopped its current at once [*ho d'autíka paûsen heón rhóon*], halted its flow, / became still and drew him to safety / in the mouth of the river" (*Odyssey* 5.451–53). While a natural phenomenon like this would be very uncommon in a Mediterranean context, where the tides are almost imperceptible and the rivers' currents push unceasingly to the sea, it is quite normal on Atlantic shores, where the flood tide periodically washes up the rivers, allowing ships to come into the estuaries. This only adds to the line of reasoning that—starting from Plutarch's statement on Ogygia's location and following Homer's directions—has led us from the Faeroe Islands to the Norwegian coast, and this natural mechanism is how Ulysses reached Scheria, the land of the Phaeacians, who gave him a warm reception and then took him to Ithaca.

The above-mentioned passages provide us with a number of pieces of geographic information that help us to locate Scheria more precisely. After the storm took him by surprise off the Norwegian coast, Ulysses was blown southward by the north wind toward the land of the Phaeacians. Phaeacia can therefore be located in the southern part of the Scandinavian peninsula, where, beginning from the city of Stavanger and heading southward, the level of the coast becomes lower, beaches appear, and several rivers flow out into the sea.

Just a couple of miles south of Stavanger, in the area of Klepp, there flows a river known as the Figgjo, which is the first river of reasonable size to be found in the area south of the fjords. It is natural to identify it with the river mentioned in the *Odyssey,* especially because its name sounds rather like the term Phaeacians (Phaíekes in Greek). If we bear in mind that the city of the Phaeacians could not have been very far from the river where Ulysses landed and, as Homer says, a rock in the shape of a ship was situated at the entrance to the port (*Odyssey* 13.161–63), archaeology, perhaps with the help of some local tale or legend, might succeed in proving its location. In reality, about a half mile north of the mouth of the

Figgjo, at the entrance to the harbor of Sele, there lies an islet named Feis-
tein whose oblong shape is very similar to that of the keel of a ship.

The Homeric description of Phaeacia recalls the "picture postcard"
of a typical sea town of the Bronze Age:

> *A good harbor lies beside the city*
> *with a narrow entrance; the ships are ashore*
> *along the road and each has his own landing-place.*
> *The square lies round the beautiful temple of Poseidon*
> *and is paved with quarried stones thrusted into the ground.*
> *Here they prepare the equipment of their black ships,*
> *anchors and hawsers, and plane the oars. (Odyssey 6.263–69)*

Some of the most important Bronze Age remains in Norway lie in
the area of Klepp. They consist of a number of tumuli that are about
fifteen feet high and about a hundred feet in diameter and which contain
gold and bronze objects and jewels. There are also many rock engravings of the same age in which boats are often depicted, squaring with the
fact that Homer calls the Phaeacians "the famous seafarers"—*nausíkly-
toi ándres (Odyssey 8.191)*—though they, like Scheria, have no known
remnants in the Mediterranean.

It is also significant that the name Scheria, though having no meaning in Greek, is very close to the Old Norse word *sker,* which means
"sea rock" (*skjær* in modern Norwegian, similar to *scar* and *skerry*).
This suggests both the obstacles that Ulysses comes up against in his
landing—that is, sheer cliffs, rocks (*Odyssey 7.279*), and reefs—and the
morphology of the Norwegian coast, which "looked like a shield on the
misty sea" (*Odyssey 5.281*).

Interestingly, the word *misty* (*eeroeidés* in Greek) is frequently used
to describe the sea in both the *Odyssey* and the *Iliad*. Likewise, the
descriptor "wine-dark" *(oínops)* is often used. Neither evokes the sunny
Mediterranean during the sailing season; instead, both suggest the picture of a northern sea. Another adjective used by Homer to describe the
sea (although not quite so often) is *ioeidés,* "violaceous" or "violet-col-
ored," "gloomy," or "dark."[3] It is used in the *Iliad* to describe a stormy
sea (11.298), and is also used by Hesiod, an eighth-century-B.C.E. Greek
poet, for the same purpose.[4] This recurrent description moreover fits
perfectly with the entire meteorological picture in both of Homer's epics:
cold, wet, and generally unsettled, as we shall see later in more detail.

Mist is mentioned not only in reference to the sea: Ulysses is wrapped in a thick mist when he arrives in the Phaeacian town on his way to King Alcinous's royal palace (*Odyssey* 7.41–42).

Indeed, Scheria's climate, like that of Ogygia, is not mild, as a worried Ulysses notes as soon as he lands:

> *If I keep watch this troublesome night, here by the river,*
> *frost and moist dew together*
> *could finish off my painful gasping due to my exhaustion;*
> *an icy wind blows from the river before dawn.* (*Odyssey* 5.466–69)

Luckily, Nausicaa's maids hurry to provide our hero with "a cloak and a tunic" (*Odyssey* 6.214). Meanwhile, Arete, the Phaeacian queen, "sits by the hearth in the firelight" (*Odyssey* 6.305). Yet all these events are supposedly set in the warm sailing season!

Also of note geographically with regard to Scheria's location is Nausicaa's statement: "We live in seclusion, in the sea with many waves, / faraway, and no mortals are in contact with us" (*Odyssey* 6.204–205). This seems to fit perfectly with the position of Scheria on the southern coast of Norway, isolated from the Achaean world of that time, where, as we shall see, many peoples were settled around the Baltic coast. The *Odyssey* also tells us that the Phaeacians had not been living in Scheria for a long time; they had settled there after coming from another country known as "the vast Hypereie" (*Odyssey* 6.4). We could assume that their descent from the Hypereie to Scheria—that is, from northern to southern Norway—was linked to the decline of the climatic optimum, which had already begun in the period in which the Homeric poems were set.

Extraordinary Neighbors

Once Phaeacia is set in the geographic context of Norway, the other details that Homer reports about the Phaeacians and their neighbors not only reveal a strong consistency with the details of this locale, but also fit well with Norse literature. In their previous homeland, the Phaeacians had been subjected to harassment by some very unpleasant neighbors, the Cyclopes, described as "domineering people" (*Odyssey* 6.5) and "over-bearing and unfair" (*Odyssey* 9.106). As we know, the Cyclopes also made things difficult for Ulysses. As we shall see in chapter 4, traces of the Cyclopes exist along the high coasts of northern Norway. In addition, the name Hypereie, "highland," fits with the information that they lived "on the top of mountains" (*Odyssey* 9.106). Important evidence regarding the Cyclopes is found both in medieval Norse literature and Norwegian folklore, the last echoes of a tradition that is rooted firmly in the Early Bronze Age.

The Phaeacians, it seems, had a comfortable relationship with the gods, for, as King Alcinous says,

> *The gods appear visible in front of us*
> *whenever we offer them sumptuous sacrifices,*
> *they banquet with us, sitting where we are.*
> *Even if a lonely wayfarer meets them,*
> *they do not hide themselves because we are their neighbors,*
> *like the Cyclopes and the wild tribes of the Giants.*
> (*Odyssey* 7.201–206)

On the subject of the gods, Nausicaa confirms the words of King Alcinous: "We are most dear to the gods" (*Odyssey* 6.202). A little further on she defines the Phaeacians as "godlike": *antithéoisi* (*Odyssey* 6. 241). Zeus himself reminds Hermes that the Phaeacians are "related to the gods" (*Odyssey* 5.35).

Regarding the Giants, King Alcinous himself was a direct descendant of "the brave Eurymedon, / who once ruled over the bold Giants" (*Odyssey* 7.58–59). Norse mythology places the Giants in the north of Scandinavia (the trolls, legendary beings often depicted as gigantic and rather unpleasant in nature, play an important role in Norwegian folklore), and even from a geographic point of view relates the Giants to the gods, as does Greek mythology. In the *Edda,* the famous collection of mythological Old Norse poems written in the twelfth century (also called *Elder Edda* or *Poetic Edda* in order to distinguish it from the *Younger Edda,* authored by the thirteenth-century Icelandic skald Snorry Sturluson), the god Odin says: "The river that divides the Giants' area / from that of the gods, is called Ifing . . ."[5] A trace of the Giants' mythical home can be found today in the name of a region known as Jotunheimen, north of Bergen.

TALES OF THE SEA

The character of Ulysses, a great seafarer, fits splendidly with the skill for navigation that was thriving during the Norwegian Bronze Age due, in part, to the climatic optimum. Evidence of this navigational culture can be found in the lines of verse that Homer devotes to the Phaeacians' seafaring skills. In the context of such abilities, the length of the journey by raft from Ogygia to Scheria—seventeen days to cross the "fearful immense abyss"—is not at all unreasonable. When Captain Bligh was left in a boat following the mutiny on the *Bounty,* he managed to reach Timor after forty days and thirty-six hundred miles, which is almost ten times the length of Ulysses' voyage from the Faeroes to the Norwegian coast.

Later on, we shall learn specifically about the remarkable parallels between an Atlantic context and Ulysses' wanderings before reaching Ogygia. His adventures are probably what remain of ancient tales told by Bronze Age sailors, who undoubtedly spiced them up with exaggerations, paradoxes, and metaphors describing their routes across the Norwegian Sea at a time when the climate was much better than what we know it to be there today.

Even though the climate might have been more beneficent, we might well ask how these prehistoric sailors managed to keep course for hundreds of miles in open sea without the aid of a compass. Actually, a long time ago, Polynesian peoples traveled enormous distances from one archipelago to another over the immense Pacific Ocean using nothing but their thorough knowledge of the stars, acquired after many years of training. Ulysses is their perfect Western counterpart, sailing from Ogygia to Scheria while keeping a constant eye on the stars. Skill aside, the art of seafaring by means of the stars requires a certain number of clear nights to allow for sufficient visibility. It was the climatic optimum that made crossing the treacherous northern seas possible during the Early Bronze Age. In fact, after 1000 C.E., the Vikings managed to reach the North American coast from settlements in Iceland and Greenland thanks to a similar favorable climatic period.

Before we leave Norway and head for Ithaca aboard the Phaeacian ship taking Ulysses home, we should remember that thousands of years after the events related by Homer, the Vikings made their debut in history on the southern part of the Scandinavian peninsula—indeed, on the very spot where Ulysses encountered the Phaeacians. These Norsemen were extraordinarily skilled at goldsmithing, an art that can presumably be traced back to the splendid Bronze Age that had flourished in northern Europe and Norway ever since the second millennium B.C.E. We can find reference to this art in Homer's works—when, for instance, the smith god Hephaestus declares that he forged "many ornaments, / buckles, spiral bracelets, hair-bands and necklaces" (*Iliad* 18.400–401) in the vicinity of "the Ocean's Current," which is identifiable as the branch of the Gulf Stream that flows along the Norwegian coasts.

But the similarities between the Vikings and the Phaeacians extends even further: It is quite reasonable to assume a connection between the ocean-traveling Norwegian Vikings and the "long-oar Phaeacians" (*Odyssey* 8.191) who were "more skillful than any other man / at steering ships in the sea" (*Odyssey* 7.108–109). Nausicaa also states that the "Phaeacians do not care for the bow and quiver, / but for masts, ship oars and good ships; / being proud of them, they sail on the foamy seas" (*Odyssey* 6.270–72). A sentence from the Norwegian scholar Anton Wilhelm Brögger (quoted by Geoffrey Bibby in *The Testimony of the Spade*) is relevant here: "The Bronze Age in Norway was above all connected to the sea and navigation, much less to agriculture."[6]

Now that we have rediscovered and placed anew Ogygia and Scheria, it is time to leave the land of the Phaeacians and continue on our way in search of Ithaca and its archipelago. On this subject Homer has provided us with a wealth of detail, all of which makes a cohesive whole unto itself but does not correspond to the geographic and topographic context of a Mediterranean Ithaca. Yet, as we shall discover in the next chapter, it is extremely easy to detect Homer's archipelago in a new northern setting.

CHAPTER 2

ITHACA'S ARCHIPELAGO: DULICHIUM, SAME, AND ZACYNTHUS

I live in bright Ithaca; here there is the famous
Mount Neriton with its rustling leaves; many islands
lie hereabouts, very close to each other,
Dulichium, Same and wooded Zacynthus.
But Ithaca lies down there, the last in the sea
toward the night, whereas the others lie toward the dawn and
*   the sun. (Odyssey 9.21–26)*

Thus the *Odyssey* gives Ithaca's position exactly as being the westernmost island—"toward the night"—in an archipelago that includes three main islands: Dulichium, Same, and Zacynthus. Yet the comparison between these directions and the position of Greek Ithaca in the Ionian Sea—identified as being Ulysses' island from at least the fifth century B.C.E.—reveals unexplainable inconsistencies. The Greek Ithaca (see fig. 2.1) is not at all the westernmost island in its archipelago. Nor is there any trace of Dulichium among these Greek islands.

Dulichium, the "long" island (*dolichós,* "long," is a common adjective in Homeric language), is in both poems a significant geographic presence—it is mentioned twice in the *Iliad* and ten times in the *Odyssey.* Homer tells us that when the Greeks left for Troy, no fewer than forty ships went from Dulichium and the nearby Echinean Islands (*Iliad* 2.630), while only twelve ships, led by Ulysses, went from Ithaca, Same (called

25

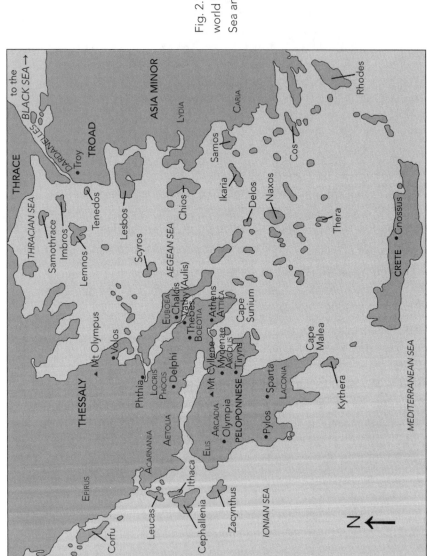

Fig. 2.1. The Greek world in the Aegean Sea and the Ionian Sea

Samos in the *Iliad*), and Zacynthus (*Iliad* 2.637), indicating that Dulichium was a relatively large island. This is confirmed by a precise detail in the *Odyssey:* Fifty-two suitors came from Dulichium asking for Penelope's hand, compared to twenty-four from Same, twenty from Zacynthus, and twelve from Ithaca (*Odyssey* 16.247–51). What is more, Homer always mentions Dulichium first when speaking of the islands. *Yet this island has never been identified in the Mediterranean world.*

Beyond the distinguishing features of Dulichium, one of the three main islands in Ithaca's archipelago—that it was probably the largest, judging by the number of ships and suitors that called it home, and that it was somewhat elongated in shape—the *Odyssey* provides us with other indications of the layout of the islands near Ithaca. Homer states that between Same and Ithaca there lay both a strait—*porthmós* (*Iliad* 4.671)—and another small island known as Asteris (*Iliad* 4.845–46), where the suitors lay in ambush for Telemachus. Thus we can deduce that Same lay near Ithaca, the westernmost island in the archipelago. All this information in the *Odyssey,* together with that in the *Iliad*—which verbally "photographs" Ithaca and the other islands in the Catalog of Ships—characterizes the layout of the archipelago. Yet no such precise location information exists for a Greek or even Mediterranean Ithaca.

Bearing in mind that we have located Scheria in southern Norway, from which Ulysses was taken by ship directly to Ithaca, we can now attempt to locate Ithaca in the archipelagos lying not too distant from the Norwegian coast. In examining the Danish islands, we immediately notice the island of Langeland, "Long Island," and the adjacent South Fyn archipelago, located close to the southern coast of Fyn. Besides Langeland, which, as its name implies, is very long, the archipelago has two relatively large islands that are much smaller than Fyn itself: Aerø and Tåsinge. Together with these three islands there are a series of smaller islands running roughly in a straight line from the southeast to the northwest, from Langeland up to little Lyø, which lies opposite the headland of Horneland, marking the western boundary of the archipelago.

In short, the layout of the South Fyn archipelago coincides exactly with the Homeric archipelago of Ithaca. We can therefore directly compare Dulichium, Same, and Zacynthus with Langeland, Aerø, and Tåsinge (see fig. 2.2).

Dulichium, the "long" island that has been a puzzle for thousands of years, is at once identifiable with Langeland, which looks like an elongated cudgel with its handle facing north. As we might expect, it is the largest

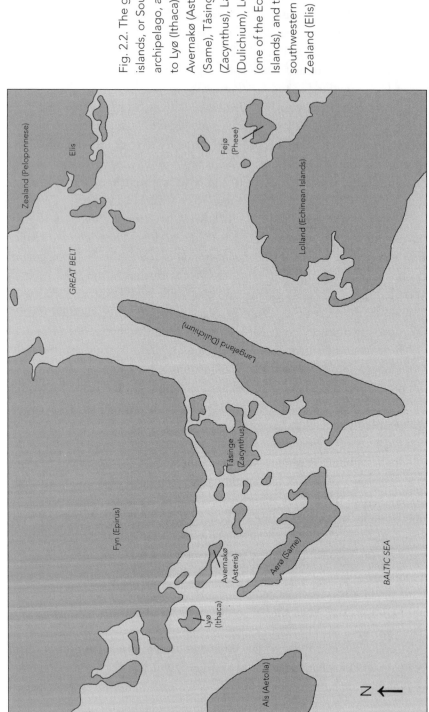

Fig. 2.2. The group of islands, or South Fyn archipelago, adjacent to Lyø (Ithaca): Avernakø (Asteris), Aerø (Same), Tåsinge (Zacynthus), Langeland (Dulichium), Lolland (one of the Echinean Islands), and the southwestern side of Zealand (Elis)

island of this group, stretching more than thirty miles in length with a maximum width of about six miles. The only other longish island in the Baltic is Öland, adjacent to the Swedish coast, though it is not part of an archipelago, and rather than being a suitable possibility for Dulichium corresponds to Homer's Euboea, as we shall see in chapter 10.

Same (Samos)—which, according to the *Odyssey*, is situated near Ithaca, the westernmost island of the archipelago—corresponds perfectly to the island of Aerø, which lies next to Lyø, the last island to the west. Further, in the small nearby island of Avernakø, located in the strait between Lyø and Aerø, we can identify the "not very large" island Asteris (*Odyssey* 4.846), "between Ithaca and Same [*messegýs Ithákes te Sámoió*]" (*Odyssey* 4.845), where Penelope's suitors tried to waylay Ulysses' son Telemachus.

If Dulichium corresponds to Langeland, and Same (Samos) to Aerø, then Homer's Zacynthus must correspond to Tåsinge, the third of the main islands of the group. Even the names of this Danish island and its Homeric counterpart sound somewhat similar, lending further credence to the correspondence among these islands of the South Fyn archipelago, not far from the Klepp area of southern Norway (Scheria), and those in Homer's Ithaca archipelago.

THE HOMERIC PELOPONNESE

Dulichium is the key both to the location of Ithaca and its archipelago and to the long puzzling whereabouts of the Homeric Peloponnese. In both the *Iliad* and the *Odyssey*, the Peloponnese—the home of several important Achaean kingdoms, such as those ruled by Agamemnon, Menelaus, Nestor, Arcadia, and Elis—is described as being a plain, while the Greek Peloponnese is distinctly mountainous. What is more, in spite of its name, meaning literally "the Island [*nêsos*] of Pelops," the Greek Peloponnese is not an island.

Using the geographic parameters we have established thus far, however, we can locate a more appropriate Peloponnese in the Baltic world: The *Iliad* states that Dulichium (Langeland) lay "beyond the sea opposite Elis"—*péren halós Élidos ánta* (*Iliad* 2.626)—the latter being a region of the Peloponnese. Given that Langeland faces Zealand, the largest island in the Baltic Sea, it follows that Zealand, as flat as Homer states in both poems, is candidate for the real Pelops Island. Interestingly, a map tells us that the Greek Peloponnese in the Aegean

Sea represents Zealand's geographic counterpart, for both of them lie
in the southwest of their respective basins—which is no doubt why the
Achaeans gave this place in their new southern home the same name as
the northern Pelops Island (despite the fact that it is a peninsula rather
than an island).

It was to Zealand that Telemachus came in search of news of his
father after sailing from Ithaca to Pylos, the Peloponnesian city of the old
king Nestor, who had taken part in the Trojan War. The wind that blows
his ship along, "the strong Zephyrus [the west wind] howling over the
wine-dark sea" (*Odyssey* 2.421), confirms Telemachus's eastward course.
The west wind, stirred up by the goddess Athena to lead his ship to its
destination (*Odyssey* 2.420), suits perfectly that which would accompany
a voyage from Ithaca to Pylos in this Danish setting, while in the Greek
world a north wind like the one Athena sent when she helped Ulysses
reach Scheria (*Odyssey* 5.385) would be more appropriate. As we shall
see in chapter 11, in a detailed examination of the regions of the Peloponnese and their northern counterparts, Pylos—whose geographic position
has been one of the most famous problems of Homer's geography since
ancient times—lies on the west coast of Zealand, to the east of the South
Fyn archipelago. This location provides an answer as to why Telemachus
chooses Pylos as his first stop on his journey to this Danish Peloponnese.

When Telemachus and his men return from Pylos to Ithaca:

> *They sailed along Crouni and Chalcis with fine streams.*
> *The Sun set and all the ways became dark.*
> *The ship, pushed by Zeus's wind, headed for Pheae*
> *and sailed along fine Elis where the Epeians rule.*
> *Then Telemachus directed it toward the islands . . .*
> (*Odyssey* 15.295–99)

We can still find the name of the island of Pheae—Fejø—in that sea
today. As for Chalcis, thanks to both its position and its name,* it could
be identified as the present-day Danish town of Halsskov, situated on a
headland on the west coast of Zealand, facing the northernmost point of
Dulichium-Langeland only ten sea miles distant. Telemachus, therefore,

---

*The initial aspiration *h* in Halsskov is identical to the initial *ch* of Chalcis. In Greek, *ch*
is the aspired consonant *x,* whose pronunciation corresponds to that of the *x* in Mexico.
Thus, the two words Halsskov and Chalcis sound rather similar.

must have passed in front of Halsskov, sailing first southward along the western side of Zealand on his way from Pylos before heading straight for the South Fyn archipelago and Lyø (Ithaca), the last island to the west.

RECONSTRUCTING A PUZZLING WORLD

The archipelago of Ithaca is one of the most important keys in the reconstruction of Homeric geography, for in it three elements converge and reinforce one another toward that new geographic reality of Homer's world: details found in the *Odyssey*, information found in the *Iliad*'s Catalog of Ships, and the geographic layout of the Baltic. By comparison, enormous inconsistencies arise if we attempt to locate Ithaca in a Mediterranean setting, not least of which are the facts that Ithaca is not the westernmost island of its archipelago, the "long island" of Dulichium does not exist, Same is located in the Aegean Sea rather than the Ionian, and the Peloponnese is anything but flat and is not an island, though its name explicitly tells us that it is.

By placing in their original northern context the extremely consistent geographic references found in the two poems, we can easily and accurately reconstruct a world that has represented a puzzle for thousands of years. In fact, the consistency between the world of Ithaca and the South Fyn islands is so exact that even if this correspondence had been discovered by mere chance, instead of by following Plutarch's indications, it would represent a very strong piece of evidence in favor of the northern location for Homer's world. As a matter of fact, there is no other group of islands in the entire world that corresponds so perfectly to the details provided by both poems as does this Danish archipelago.

Now let us turn our attention to Ithaca, "the last in the sea / toward the night, whereas the others lie toward the dawn and the sun" (*Odyssey* 9.25–26). The shape and layout of the South Fyn islands leave no doubt whatsoever: The last island to the west, the final island in the archipelago, beyond Aerø (Same) and Avernakø (Asteris), is Lyø. In chapter 3 we shall verify that not only the position, but also the topographical and morphological features of Lyø, fit perfectly with the descriptions of Ithaca provided in the two poems.

But before we confirm the accuracy of this northern location, let us first look at the situation of the Greek Ithaca, also called Thiaki, and determine why it does not tally with the place Homer so thoroughly describes. Moses Finley is extremely outspoken on the subject: "Even the topographical detail of Odysseus' home island of Ithaca can be shown to be in a jumble, with several essential points appropriate to the neighboring island of Leucas but quite impossible for Ithaca."[1] Moreover, the *Treccani Italian Encyclopedia* states: "Regarding the identification of the places described in Homer's poems, if the hypotheses put forward about Thiaki are puzzling, then those regarding Leucas are not convincing either."[2]

Quite simply, the poor island of Ithaca in the Ionian Sea is so different from the original described by Homer that all that remains as connection between the two is the name of Ulysses' glorious fatherland—for although the names of larger islands such as Same and Dulichium were lost or altered in their migration south, the Achaeans who moved to the Mediterranean probably made a point of preserving Ithaca's name, perhaps due to the fame it had achieved in a primitive version of the *Odyssey*.

It remains for us now to compare the features of Lyø with those described in the *Odyssey*. Because it would be far more beneficial for us to do this on Lyø, let us leave the islands we have explored thus far for this new island destination.

CHAPTER 3

ITHACA

A trip to the island of Lyø from the city of Fåborg on Fyn in Denmark certainly helps us to imagine that these waters were sailed by northern Mycenaeans in the Bronze Age. During the forty-minute ferry crossing from Fåborg to Lyø and Avernakø, the beautiful westernmost islands in the South Fyn archipelago file past. The geography here confirms how realistically Homer describes Antinous's plan to eliminate Telemachus on his way back to Ithaca from the Peloponnese: "Give me a fast ship and twenty partners / and I will go to lay an ambush for him / in the strait between Ithaca and rugged Same" (*Odyssey* 4.669–71).

Antinous and his cohorts lay in wait for Ulysses' son in Asteris (Avernakø), where "the observers were on the alert on the windy eminences, / taking turns" (*Odyssey* 16.365–66). Indeed, Avernakø has two heights, one on the western side of the island and one on east, from which it would be easy to watch the transit of ships in the strait between Lyø and the island of Aerø (Same) as well as in the inlet facing the adjacent coast of Fyn. From the configuration of these islands, we can readily see that if Telemachus were not to travel by night, as suggested by the goddess Athena—"Sail at night!" (*Odyssey* 15.34)—there would be no way out for him: His ship would be intercepted and the story of the *Odyssey* would be altered forever.

EXPLORING LYØ

Upon viewing Lyø and these waters, it is simple to envision the island as Homer's Ithaca. Far more than its Mediterranean counterpart, it resembles descriptions of that ancient island both geographically and topographically. Roughly shaped like a triangle, the island, which comprises about three square miles, has a radial network of paths and roads running from its coasts inland toward a small, pretty, typically Danish village (see fig. 3.1).

Lyø has many good beaches and fine views, and inland the island is quite agricultural, with wheat and vegetable fields and several farms raising livestock. There are many freshwater ponds and small lakes, where live happy families of ducks. Indeed, Homer mentions Ithaca's "perennial waterholes" (*Odyssey* 13.247) and the "spring Arethusa" (*Odyssey* 13.408).

The island does not rise far above the sea, which, unlike the mountainous Itacha in Greece, squares with Homer's description: *auté dé chthamalé,* "it's low" (*Odyssey* 9.25–26). Yet it is far from being flat, and an elevation in the eastern part of the island recalls "Mount Neriton with its quivering leaves" (*Odyssey* 9.22). Although this rise is only about eighty feet high and is covered by trees, it would not have gone unnoticed in the flat Baltic topography, especially viewed from the sea. By way of comparison, the Himmelbjerget (Mount of the Sky), one of the highest peaks in Denmark, has an elevation of 535 feet; the highest mountain on Fyn, the Frøbjerg, is 430 feet high; and a topographical feature in the southwest of Fyn produced by a morainal chain and known as the Fyn Alps is 131 feet high.

We can find confirmation of this rise by comparing the topography on the eastern coast of Lyø with the words of Homer: Here the land features include two points bounding a small cove that vaguely resembles a bird's beak—which corresponds to Homer's description that in "the port named after Phorcys, the old man of the sea, / on the island of Ithaca; two sheer points protrude / jutting out, and shield the harbor" (*Odyssey* 13.96–98). This is where the Phaeacians land and leave Ulysses asleep on the beach. Immediately on awakening, he recognizes "Mount Neriton covered by trees" (*Odyssey* 13.351).

On the western side of Lyø, there is evidence of ancient human settlement in the form of a dolmen made of stones placed vertically to support a larger stone placed in a horizontal position on the top. Dating back to the Neolithic age, it goes by the name Klokkesten, the "bell stone," which refers to the peculiar noise that issues from it when it is hit with a rock on a specific spot. It was already ancient in the Early Bronze Age of Ulysses and therefore must have also been an important landmark, which is perhaps born out in Homer's work: As soon as Ulysses lands

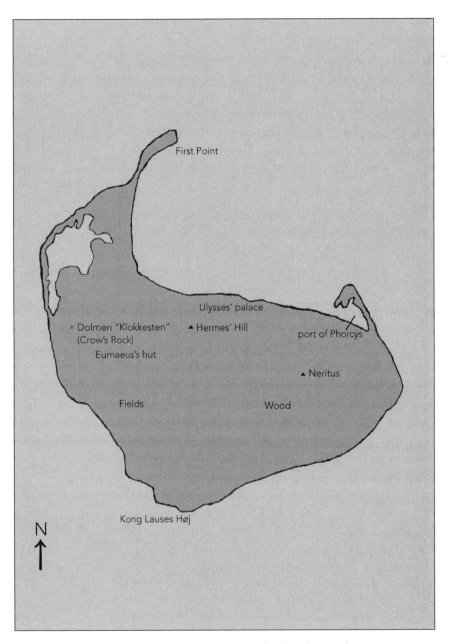

First Point

Ulysses' palace

✗ Dolmen "Klokkesten"
(Crow's Rock)

▲ Hermes' Hill

port of Phorcys

Eumaeus's hut

▲ Neritus

Fields

Wood

Kong Lauses Høj

N
↑

Fig. 3.1. Map of Lyø (Ithaca). This westernmost island in the South Fyn archipelago accords perfectly with geographical, morphological, topographical, and climatic descriptions of Ithaca in the *Odyssey*.

in Ithaca, he heads straight for his faithful swineherd Eumaeus, just as Athena had advised him to do: "You will find him sitting among the pigs; they graze / near the Crow's Rock" (*Odyssey* 13.407–408). Could this "Crow's Rock" be Lyø's ancient dolmen? Its Greek name, *kórakos pétre,* hints at both the name of the dolmen and, onomatopoetically, the sound it makes when it is struck. Locating Eumaeus on the western side of Lyø fits perfectly with yet another detail provided by the *Odyssey:* that referring to "the extremity of the fields [*agroû ep'eschatién*] where the swineherd has his home" (*Odyssey* 24.150).

This location may also help us identify the spot on Ithaca where Mentes, king of the Taphians, lands at the beginning of the poem: "My ship is over there near the fields [*ep'agroû*] out of the town, / in Rheithron port, under wooded Neion" (*Odyssey* 1.185–86). On that side of Lyø the southern coast bends, creating a sort of wide cove suitable for berthing. A little inland there is an undulating area that could be ancient Neion, and if we further follow Mentes' comments about his landing, in this same area, "near the fields" (*Odyssey* 1.190), we may locate the piece of land belonging to old Laertes, Ulysses' father.

Further comparison of ancient Ithaca's topography as described in the Homeric text with the physical reality of this small Danish island provides additional verification of the similarities between the two. Homer's Ithaca is wooded toward the east and in the middle—in other words, around Neriton and Neion, hence the mention of "a wood with all kinds of plants [*hýle pantoíe*]" (*Odyssey* 13.246). On the other side, facing west, where Lyø's land is farmed, are Homer's "fields." This area ends to the north in a point jutting out toward Fyn, "Ithaca's first point [*próte akté Ithákes*]" (*Odyssey* 15.36), where Telemachus lands alone after his risky voyage from Pylos by night while his companions sail on toward the town.

We can quite reasonably assume that Ithaca's main harbor was situated on the northern coast, somewhere near the "first point": It is the most sheltered spot and at the same time is accessible to the coast of Fyn. In fact, it is no accident that the present-day landing place for ferryboats on Lyø is situated here. The ancient "ferrymen"—*porthmêes* (*Odyssey* 20.187)—who connected the island with the mainland (Fyn) probably followed a course from this same landing place.

The town of Ithaca itself lay next to the port; indeed, it is likely that it and the harbor were one entity, as passages in the *Odyssey* like this one seem to indicate: "Telemachus was in the countryside and had made the ship / come back to the town [*astýd'apopleíein*]" (*Odyssey*

16.330–31). Homer tells us that after Telemachus landed on the "first point," his crew "sailed toward the town rowing backward [*anósantes*]" (*Odyssey* 15.553). If we look at the probable location of the town of Ithaca, in the center of the northern coast of Lyø (see fig. 3.1), we can see how backing up would be expedient for a ship that had initially come alongside the first point.

Interestingly, this curious detail regarding the crew of Telemachus's ship rowing backward is perfectly consistent with a peculiar feature in the structure of ancient Scandinavian ships, as reported by the Roman historian Tacitus (55–120 C.E.): "The shape of their ships is different from ours: both ends comprise a prow and are therefore ready for landing . . . and rowing can be reversed according to the circumstances" (*et mutabile, ut res poscit, hinc vel illinc remigium*).[1] This is confirmed by the most ancient northern craft found to date, "Alsen's ship," which dates to the fourth century B.C.E. The construction of this vessel is like that of Homer's ships, which are often referred to as being *amphiélissai* (*Iliad* 28.260; *Odyssey* 6. 264)—that is, "curved on both sides."

Eumaeus gives us yet another confirmation of the position of the town of Ithaca when, on his way home, he says: "I was on my way back, already above the town, / where Hermes' Hill lies, when I saw a fast ship entering / our port" (*Odyssey* 16.471–73). This suggests the closeness of the town to the port and allows us to identify Hermes' Hill with one of the island's small hills that rise above the northern coast. Because Eumaeus is heading to the west of the island, where his hut lies, after visiting Penelope in Ulysses' house, we can presume that Ulysses' home was located in the eastern part of town, to the right of the port—that is, near the area of today's ferry landing.

In the time of Homer's epics, the name of the town must have been the same as that of the whole island; thus, after landing at first point, Telemachus's ship "headed for Ithaca" (*Odyssey* 16.322). Like his father, Telemachus made a beeline for Eumaeus's hut (*Odyssey* 15.555), situated on the same side of the island—that is, near the dolmen. Ulysses himself, however, has to take a different route, for the Phaeacians leave him at the port of Phorcys, on the opposite side of the island. In order to reach Eumaeus's home, he thus has to cross the island from east to west rather than west to east, a walk of about two and a half miles that follows "the uneven track / through woods and rises, heading where Athena / had indicated the good swineherd" (*Odyssey* 14.1–3).

Slightly inland, just outside the town, is "the structure of the fountain with clear water / which the citizens drew" (*Odyssey* 17.205–206). There Ulysses, on his way home, meets Melanthius the goatherd, who, after a heated discussion with Ulysses and Eumaeus, "ran past them, as they were going slower, / went ahead and reached Ulysses' palace very quickly" (*Odyssey* 17.254–55). Wouldn't it be marvelous if archaeologists could find the remains of this Bronze Age fountain?

Even without such physical archaeological evidence, however, we can see that Lyø not only fits with the geographic position of the Homeric Ithaca, but that it also provides a topographical and morphological context that is completely consistent with the scenery described in the *Odyssey*, allowing us to actually reconstruct the routes and movements of different characters in these epics.

COWS AND GOATS, BUT NO HORSES: FURTHER EVIDENCE OF A NORTHERN ITHACA

The *Odyssey* never mentions chariots or draft animals being used in Ithaca; indeed, all the characters move from one place to another on foot, which makes sense given the island's modest size. At the same time, Homer often refers to Ithaca's topography as being "rough"—*trecheîa* (*Odyssey* 9.27, 13.242)—and when Ulysses is about to go down to the town, he asks Eumaeus for a stick, for "the path is slippery" (*Odyssey* 17. 196). Athena's description of Ithaca, which fits perfectly with this Baltic setting rather than with the dry Greek islands, similarly upholds this characterization of the island's topographical makeup and also sings its praises as a fertile and lush land in which to raise livestock:

> It is rough and unsuited to horses,
> it is not too narrow, but not even vast.
> Here wheat is very abundant and wine
> is produced, it always rains [aieí d'ómbros échei] and there is
>   plenty of moisture.
> It is excellent for goats and oxen, there is a wood
> with all kinds of plants, there are perennial waterholes.
>   (*Odyssey* 13.242–47)

We can note that the reference to wine production indicates a more temperate climate on the island than that of today, in keeping with the timing of the postglacial climatic optimum.

Overall, Lyø appears to be large enough for a king of the Early Bronze Age—Ulysses—whose name may still echo in the name of a place at the southernmost point of the island: Kong Lauses Høj, the "hill (or tomb) of King Lauses." Yet the island is small enough to justify the characterization of Ithaca in the friendly proposal of Menelaus, husband to Helen and ruler of Sparta and the surrounding region (called Lacedaemon by Homer and Laconia by the Greeks) to give one of his towns to his astute ally Ulysses: "I would have brought him here from Ithaca with all his wealth, / his son and his people, too" (*Odyssey* 4.175–76).

The small size of the island also explains why Telemachus refuses the horses Menelaus offers him as a gift: "There are no wide roads or grazing in Ithaca; / it is pastureland for goats, but it is dearer to me than a land suitable for horses" (*Odyssey* 4.605–606). Telemachus also stresses the gap between Ithaca's rural, unassuming world and

> *the sparkling of bronze, gold, amber,*
> *silver and ivory* in [Menelaus's] echoing home.*
> *The court of Olympian Zeus must be like this inside*
> *with such incalculable riches! I am astonished at the sight of it.*
> (*Odyssey* 4.72–75)

The poet repeatedly tells us that pigs and goats are reared in Ithaca. Ulysses himself owns "twelve herds of cattle in the mainland" (*Odyssey* 14.100), on the coast facing the island, as confirmed by the arrival of one of the cowherds at his palace: "Philoetius, the master cowherd, was the third to arrive, / taking a sterile cow and some fattened goats. / Ferrymen took them across, they who / take all men, whatsoever reaches them" (*Odyssey* 20.185–88). We are tempted to imagine that a direct ancestor of one of today's Fåborg ferrymen carried Philoethius and his cow more than a hundred generations ago on the morning of that fatal day when Ulysses slaughtered his wife's suitors.

The herds of cattle belonging to our hero illustrate one of the most curious aspects of Ulysses' multifaceted character: His mind-set, a precursor to our modern-day capitalistic mentality, deems it "the most profitable course / to accumulate wealth by going round many countries, /

---

*Amber was a typical Baltic product and ivory was traded by northern countries in the form of walrus tusks.

as Ulysses can make large profits among men. / Nobody else can compete with him" (*Odyssey* 19.283–86). This ancient Scrooge—indeed, Agamemnon contemptuously calls him "a man greedy for wealth [*kerdaleóphron*]" (*Iliad* 4.339)—

> *had incalculable goods, none of the other lords*
> *has as many, both they who lived on the dark mainland*
> *and in Ithaca itself. Not even twenty men together*
> *had as much wealth.* (*Odyssey* 14. 96–99)

Aside from revealing aspects of Ulysses' character, this passage and the reference to Philoethius allow us to deduce the proximity of Ithaca to a "dark mainland" (*épeiros* in Greek), which is, without a doubt, Fyn, a larger island next to Lyø—indeed, the largest by far of those islands in the South Fyn archipelago. The Catalog of Ships states that Ulysses' fleet included

> *the proud Cephallenians,*
> *those who had Ithaca and Neriton with its rustling leaves,*
> *those who lived in Crocyleia and rugged Aegilips,*
> *those who had Zacynthus and lived in Samos,*
> *those who had the mainland and lived on the opposite shores.*
> (*Iliad* 2.631–35)

Of the twelve ships that make up Ulysses' fleet, probably only one is actually from Ithaca, which we can deduce from the line that introduces the events surrounding Polyphemus: "Dear companions, stay here now / while I go with my ship and my companions / to realize who are these men" (*Odyssey* 9.172–74). Similarly, another passage from the *Odyssey* confirms that all sailors aboard Ulysses' ship come from "rugged Ithaca where they were born and grew up" (*Odyssey* 10.417).

But if the topography of Lyø, its nature as a hospitable home to livestock, and its proximity to the "mainland" of Fyn add even more credence to it being Ithaca, what can we make of its name in this regard? The name Lyø probably derives from *ly*, which means "shelter" in Danish. Yet it is the likeness between Lyø and *lys*, the Danish word for "light," that provides us with a starting point for a hypothesis regarding the name Ithaca (Itháke in Greek). Homer often links Itháke with the adjective *eudeíelos*, meaning "bright," "shining," "beaming," and "perfectly visible"—all the more reasonable if we consider that the meaning of Itháke can be traced back to the verb *aíthein,* "to glow," "to burn," or "to blaze." (The suffix *-ke,* as in Itháke, which is the feminine form of *-kos,* is a common ending for many adjectives in Greek.) Thus the name Ithaca probably means "the glowing (island)," and the expression "Ithaken eudeíelon" (*Odyssey* 2.167, 9.21) in the accusative case means something like "bright glowing" or "perfectly visible." We should note Homer's consistent use of the adjective for this prehistoric Île Lumière. Maybe its name originated from an ancient fire or the "perfectly visible" fires that were lit at night and seen by both the inhabitants of the opposite coast and any passing sailors.

Yet another confirming detail of Ithaca's Baltic location relates to Phemius, the bard of the Ithacan court who first sang of the glorious adventures of his king: he of the "disastrous return from Troy / Pallas Athena inflicted on the Achaeans" (*Odyssey* 1.326–27). Phemius's name can be found almost unchanged in the name of the island of Femø near Lolland, thirty sea miles east of Fyn. Because the distinctly Baltic setting of Homer's poems (except for the parts related to Ulysses' wanderings, which we shall deal with separately) suggests that their origin can be ascribed to local poets, it would be natural to suppose that the first bard to sing King Ulysses' feats was Phemius himself, the court poet who thus left his "signature" on the poem.

Yet another detail—or cluster of details—in both poems suggests that Ithaca's weather is far more similar to that of a northern climate than to that of the Mediterranean. For example, in the Homeric world, fog seems omnipresent. In the morning when Ulysses arrives in Ithaca, fog completely hides the island, so thoroughly, in fact, that "everything seemed foreign to the King, / the long paths, the good ports, / the steep rocks and the blooming trees" (*Odyssey* 13.194–96), until the goddess Athena "dispelled the fog and the land appeared" (*Odyssey* 13.352). The young man whom Ulysses meets immediately after his landing "was wearing a double cloak around his shoulders" (*Odyssey* 13.224). The night after his arrival is "bad, moonless; Zeus poured rain / and a strong Zephyrus wind, which brings rain, blew the whole night" (*Odyssey* 14.457–58).

This bad weather in Ithaca should not surprise us, however, for Athena has already informed us that there "it always rains" (*Odyssey* 13.245). When Ulysses goes to bed at the home of the swineherd Eumaeus, his host

> *set a couch for him*
> *by the fire . . .*
> *Here Ulysses lay down and he covered him*
> *with a large thick cloak, which served as a change*
> *he wore when a heavy shower pelted down.* (*Odyssey* 14.518–22)

Soon afterward, before he heads outdoors, Eumaeus dons "a very thick cloak to protect himself from the wind" (*Odyssey* 14.529). The next morning Ulysses complains: "I wear inadequate clothes and the frost at daybreak [*stíbe hypeoíe*] / might kill me" (*Odyssey* 17.24–25). Further on Eumaeus says: "Most of the day has already gone by / and soon it will be most cold this evening" (*Odyssey* 17.190–91). It is a fact that despite Ithaca's long-assumed Mediterranean location, throughout the entire fourteen books that the *Odyssey* dedicates to it, we never once hear mention of the sun or its warmth.

Of course, this makes it easier for us to understand Penelope's consideration for the respected guest whom she has not yet recognized as her husband: She orders her servants to "set a bed / with blankets, quilts and colored rugs / so that he may arrive quite warm at dawn" (*Odyssey* 19.317–19). Indeed, when Ulysses lies down, Eurynome "threw a cloak over him" (*Odyssey* 20.4).

Telemachus too sleeps "wrapped up in a sheep fleece" (*Odyssey* 1.443) and when he and one of his guests prepare for a banquet inside the palace, "after the maids bathed them and smeared them with oil, / they wore tunics and thick cloaks [*chlaínas oúlas*]; / then they left the baths and sat down" (*Odyssey* 17.88–90). And yet we have noted that all the events related to Ulysses' return take place during the sailing season, when warmer weather prevails! In short, it seems that the climate of Homer's Ithaca is not at all that of a Greek island and is instead that of the period in northern European when the climatic optimum was already in decline.

Now that we have outlined all the geographical, topographical, descriptive, and meteorological similarities between Ithaca in the *Odyssey* and the Danish island of Lyø, it is easy to see how closely the two match. If it took Ulysses twenty years to find his way back to his beloved Ithaca, it has taken us no less than three thousand! We can now only wait for archaeologists to confirm what careful readers and geographers can conclude.

ITHACA'S NEIGHBORS

Homer depicts Ithaca's neighboring peoples such as the Taphians, the Thesprotians, and the Phoenicians as carrying out seafaring activities in the form of trading or piracy. His descriptions contribute to modern-day attempts to reconstruct aspects of the Bronze Age in northern Europe, which, though it left many archaeological remains, did not hand down to posterity any written or literary works except for the first nuclei of the *Iliad* and the *Odyssey*. We have lost all traces of some of these peoples, but others, such as the Phoenicians, survived the collapse of the Baltic world and managed to keep their seafaring trade contacts with their original northern home, even after they moved to the Mediterranean. These peoples thus succeeded in creating giant and long-lasting cultural footprints.

In the beginning of the *Odyssey*, the Taphians are introduced by their king, Mentes, who lands in Ithaca on his way to Temesa, an overseas market for bronze. They are defined as being "seafaring" people (*philéretmoi*, literally "fond of the oars"; *Odyssey* 1.181, 419). In fact, we find several allusions to their vocation of piracy. In this regard, their stories are often intertwined with those of the Thesprotians and Phoenicians: For example, Penelope reminds Antinous, one of her suitors, that his father, "in agreement with the Taphian pirates / vexed the Thesprotians, who were bound to us" (*Odyssey* 16.426–27). This last detail suggests that the homes of both the Taphians and the Thesprotians are close to Ithaca. Another line of verse, in fact, confirms that the Thesprotians live near Ithaca: "Near here [*anchoû*] in the rich country of the Thesprotians" (*Odyssey* 19.271).

Another detail related to the origin of these Ithacan neighbors states that "a Thesprotian ship / heading for Dulichium rich in wheat" (*Odyssey* 14.334–35) "reached the fields of bright Ithaca in the evening" (*Odyssey* 19.407–409). If we assume that the Thesprotians, neighbors of the Taphians, set off from somewhere in the area between the northern coast of Fyn, the island of Samsø, and Jutland, then the most likely route to Dulichium (Langeland) is the one that traverses the western coast of Fyn, meeting with Lyø about halfway there. Ithaca, therefore, was an ideal place to stop. What is more, the distance from this part of Fyn to Lyø (about forty miles) tallies with the purported day's sailing that it took the zealous Thesprotian crew to reach Ithaca.

The *Odyssey* indicates that the Phoenicians' sphere of action was primarily local in that remote Baltic civilization and accords them the same level of recognition it gives the Taphians, yet the *Iliad* mentions them only twice (*Iliad* 6.290; 23.743) and on both occasions refers specifically to the city of Sidon. Corresponding to this, in the north of Zealand we come across both a Sidinge and a Sidinge fjord, which suggests that the Phoenicians had a settlement in that area. We also note that in the Bay of Tårs, which lies on the northern coast of the island of Lolland (south of Zealand), there is a small village also named Tårs, which recalls the mythical city of Tarsis. We must remember, however, that conclusions based on resemblances of names alone are less reliable than geographic and morphological evidence.

Finally, regarding Ithaca's neighbors, the *Odyssey* narrates that a friend of Telemachus was planning to sail for the nearby country of the Cauconians (Kaúkones; *Odyssey* 3.366), a coastal people of whom no trace has ever been found in the Mediterranean and who presumably lived not far from Ithaca. It seems quite reasonable to relate them to a Germanic tribe known as the Caucians, who lived along the coast of the North Sea during Roman times. The Homeric Kéteioi (*Odyssey* 11.521) could also be related to the Chatti tribe, which Tacitus mentions in his *Germania*.

FYN: "THE DARK MAINLAND"

Among Ithaca's neighbors is a certain king Echetus, nicknamed "the Ruiner of Mankind" (*Odyssey* 18.85, 116). This tyrant (whose imitators are still all the rage everywhere) ruled over the "mainland"—that is, the *épeiros* (*Odyssey* 18.84, 115). This Greek word *épeiros* is quite similar to the Anglo-German *ofer, over*, or *ufer*, meaning "shore" or "beach."[2] While in classical Greek it means "dry land" or "continent," in Homer it refers to "coast," "mainland," "shore," or "beach." For example, when the god Hermes arrives on the island of Ogygia after crossing the sea, he leaps "from the gray sea . . . onto the *épeiros*" (*Odyssey* 5.56). Likewise, upon landing, the Phaeacian ship "mounted the beach [*épeiros*] by a half-length of the keel" (*Odyssey* 13.114).

Again we come across *épeiros*—which is most likely the same *épeiros* as that of terrible Echetus—in old Laertes' recollection of a feat he achieved when he was young: "I took Nericus, a well-built town / lying at the point of the *épeiros*, when I was in command of the Cephallenians" (*Odyssey* 24.377–78). Nericus was probably situated in the area of the Bjerne Mark and Knolden peninsula, at the southeasternmost point of the headland of Horneland, facing Lyø.

As for references to épeiros in the *Iliad*, it is worth noting that in the entire Catalog of Ships—a lengthy list of coastal places and peoples—only one épeiros is mentioned, and it corresponds precisely to the mainland (Fyn) facing Ithaca: "Ulysses led the proud Cephallenians, those who had Ithaca and Neriton . . . those who had Zacynthus and lived in Samos, / those who had the *épeiros* and lived on the opposite shores" (*Iliad* 2.631–35). The verb *had* (*échon* or *eîchon* in Greek) appearing several times in this passage is included in a recurrent expression that indicates the name of the territory belonging to a single people—for example, "those who had holy Euboea" (*Iliad* 2.536) and "those who had Arcadia" (*Iliad* 2.603). The expression "those who had . . ." is always followed by the name of a place and appears some thirty-two times in the Catalog. Thus, it is difficult to believe that the term *épeiros*—which appears only once in the Catalog, where it is preceded by *had*—could be a reference to a common name. It is much more likely that, as for all the others, it is an actual place-name: that *Épeiros* here is not a generic *épeiros*, but rather a real name given to the land opposite Ithaca: "the Coast" or "the Mainland," or "the Dark Coast," as it is termed in the *Odyssey* (14.97). We need think only of Costa Rica or the Ivory Coast to understand this usage.

In short, present-day Fyn—or at least the southern side of Fyn that faces Ithaca and its neighboring islands, where King Echetus raged, where the town of Nericus lay, and where Ulysses' cattle grazed—was called Épeiros, or "the Coast *par excellence*." The Achaeans took this name with them to the Mediterranean, where we find the Greek Épeiros (Epirus in English), which, as it turns out, is nearly the southern geographic counterpart of Fyn—nearly and not perfectly because there are some distinct differences between the islands in the Baltic and those in the Ionian Sea. In the Baltic, Lyø lies between two large geographic entities: Fyn to the north and Jutland (ancient Aetolia) to the west. The Ionian islands, on the other hand, are not closed in between two lands but instead simply face the Greek coast. They lie opposite Aetolia and Acarnania, but are not exactly in front of Epirus, which is situated in a more northerly position. This is no doubt why the Greeks were obliged to change the meaning of the original Épeiros, the Achaean name of the area in front of Baltic Ithaca, to a generic épeiros or "mainland." Without doing this, a geographical paradox would have occurred, placing the Greek Ithaca right in front of Epirus—clearly a faulty location in terms of Ionian geography, though true in the Achaeans' previous Danish home. In this way they managed to preserve the consistency of Greek geography while inserting an anomaly in the structure of the Catalog of Ships, where the expression "those who *had* . . ." as we noted is always followed by the *proper name* of the corresponding region.

This concludes our resetting of Ithaca and Ulysses' "everyday" world, the focus of much of the *Odyssey*, which narrates, as much as heroic tales, the humble daily life of its ancient peoples. Their culture is frequently presented with subtle humor, such as when "Two men argue over a landmark, / having the rules in their hands, in the common field, / they quarrel over their right in a small strip" (*Iliad* 12.421–23); or when two women "who are enraged in the row which consumes the heart, / going into the middle of the street they reproach each other / with many things, some true, some not, but rage suggests these too!" (*Iliad* 20.253–55).

Sometimes the poet sums up a whole life in two or three lines: "Meges killed Pedaeus, Antenor's son, / who was illegitimate, but lady Theano brought him up carefully / like her own children, to gratify her husband" (*Iliad* 5.69–71); or paints a picture full of both realism and humanity: "a careful working woman with her balance, / who having the weight and the wool raises / and equalizes them, to earn a poor pay for her children" (*Iliad* 12.433–35). In lines like these we find the only literary evidence we have of everyday life in the northern Bronze Age.

What a pity that people remember Ulysses almost solely for his fairy-tale adventures. Though entertaining, these are not the most important part of the *Odyssey*. For those who have read and studied the poem, the parts taking place in the Ithacan setting have always seemed or been treated as somewhat extraneousness. Perhaps now we are finally able to understand why: There is an enormous contrast between the northern atmosphere we sense in the poem's Ithaca and the Mediterranean environment of which we are told it is a part. This could explain why Hollywood, with its unbelievable Circes and grotesque Polyphemuses, never did much for Ulysses' image. The right setting, however, could give back to Ulysses—a character whom Homer considered to be "as wise as Zeus himself" (*Iliad* 2.636)—a long-lost human dimension.

CHAPTER 4

THE ADVENTURES OF ULYSSES

The long-standing skepticism about the possibility of setting Ulysses' journeys in a real context is revealed by a rather ironic statement made by the Greek geographer Eratosthenes and reported by Strabo: "One could find the places where Ulysses wandered by tracking down the cobbler who sewed up the windbag." [1] He is referring to Aeolus, king of the mythical island Aeolia, who aided Ulysses by placing on board his ship a leather bag in which he had "locked the ways of the howling winds" (*Odyssey* 10.19–26). Yet the author of the *Odyssey* has, in fact, provided us with ample indications of a setting pointing to the "extra-Baltic world"—a world that stretches across the immense Atlantic Ocean up to the Arctic Ocean—through his fabulous (but also realistic) "reportage" of Ulysses' adventures.

The information contained in the *Odyssey* can be divided into two groups. The first includes the events Homer directly narrates. As we have seen with Ogygia, Scheria, and Ithaca, as soon as these events are set in their correct context, they find remarkable correspondences in real geographical places. The second group consists of the tales the poet attributes to his characters: Nestor, Menelaus, and of course Ulysses himself, who tells his Phaeacian hosts how he had made his way back to Ithaca after the Trojan War. In the account of his wanderings, which extend over four cantos of the poem, we can find folklore motifs and geographical references that are very relevant to a northern setting.

ATTACKS AND STORMS

The first adventure that Ulysses narrates—in fact the only one that contains considerable realism and very little fantasy—describes the attack his small fleet has launched on the town of Ismarus immediately after leaving Troy and the consequent counterattack of the Ciconians. Of all the peoples mentioned in his wanderings, the Ciconians are the only ones also mentioned in the *Iliad*, for they were allied with the Trojans during the Trojan War (*Iliad* 2.846).

As we shall see in more detail in part 2, the land of the Ciconians, an area that corresponds to a region between Helsinki and Turku, lay in southern Finland. The Ciconians' Greek name, Kíkones, recalls Kiikoinen, the name of a town situated inland near Tampere. This coincides perfectly with Ulysses' tale, in which the coastal peoples, after his attack, "fled and called upon the Ciconians / who were their numerous and brave neighbors, / living inland" (*Odyssey* 9.47–49). At first, the fact that Kiikoinen is located to the north of the Finnish "Troy"—that is, in a direction opposite from Ithaca—might seem contradictory, but the *Odyssey* itself provides us with an explanation for this: "Leaving Troy the wind carried me toward the Ciconians / and Ismarus" (*Odyssey* 9.39–40).

After an eventful flight from the enraged Ciconians, the fleet sails toward Ithaca, but close to Cape Malea they are caught in a storm: "Adverse winds carried me away for nine days" (*Odyssey* 9.82). As we shall see, Cape Malea can be located near today's Malmö, in the southernmost point of Sweden. This storm marks a turning point in the narration, because it catapults Ulysses' ships away from his familiar world into a completely fabulous one.

Let us reflect for a moment upon this and other storms that often carry Homer's heroes across incredible distances on the open sea. They last for many days and bear little resemblance to those in the Mediterranean, though they are typical of those in the Atlantic Ocean, as we can see in two accounts from the fifteenth century. In the year 1431 C.E., a terrible storm carried a ship belonging to the Venetian merchant Pietro Querini from the English Channel to the Lofoten Islands, which face the coast of northern Norway. The surviving members of the unlucky crew managed to land on the uninhabited rock of Sandö, where a few days later fishermen from the island of Röst in southern Lofoten rescued and looked after them until they were fit enough to return home.[2]

In 1484, the Spaniard Alonso Sánchez from Huelva was involved in a similar gale, the consequences of which left a significant mark on the history of humanity. According to Garcilaso de la Vega, a sixteenth-century Peruvian historian, Sánchez's small merchant ship was caught in a violent storm on a voyage from the Canary Islands to Madeira. He was dragged westward for many days, until he managed to land on what was probably the island of Santo Domingo. Alonso refitted his ship there, returned to Spain, then went straight to Christopher Columbus, "the great seafarer and cosmographer from Genoa," to tell him of his adventure. Columbus was extremely interested in his tale and, according to Garcilaso's authoritative opinion, "this was the first step and origin of the discovery of the New World."[3] Incidentally, this would explain why Columbus chose for his journey a southern course that actually took him to the Bahamas. He presumably had precise indications about the latitude but not longitude of the island where Sánchez had landed. He therefore chose to "be safe rather than sorry" and set his tiny fleet on the corresponding parallel, following it as far as his destination.

Returning to Ulysses, he was diverted from his world in the Baltic by a storm that left him roaming what we will recognize as the Atlantic Ocean. In this threatening world, though the narration becomes fanciful and fantastic, it is possible to identify references to real sea routes that were doubtless followed by fearless prehistoric sailors. The roots of Ulysses' adventures can be found in the legends and tales of northern Bronze Age seafarers, which the poet freely reworked and fitted to his main character. When these stories were later carried to the Mediterranean world, the peculiar geographic and descriptive details, such as the great Atlantic tides that are typical of the farthest north, became unrecognizable. Once these details are reconnected to their true context, they confirm the North Atlantic location of the adventures of the *Odyssey*.

In an article that appeared in the French magazine *Planète* in 1965, Professor Robert Philippe hypothesized a location for Ulysses' oceanic wanderings that was linked to Phoenician sailors' trade routes beyond the Mediterranean Sea. This article's theory is consistent with the daring "Atlantic" hypotheses about these wanderings that have been made since antiquity—for example, those by Cratetes of Mallus in the second century B.C.E. Philippe goes so far as to locate the land of the Phoenicians in southern Norway (though he does not dispute the classic Mediterranean location of the *Iliad* and the rest of the *Odyssey*). Given, however, that the Atlantic Ocean and the Baltic Sea are contiguous, Cratetes' and Philippe's hypotheses fit well with the northern location of the entire Homeric setting than with the traditional Mediterranean one.

THE LOTUS-EATERS

Ulysses' fantastic adventures begin when his ships are carried "beyond Cythera" by that terrible storm. Thus Cythera was likely the last familiar outpost in his world before the unknown. If we consider that when he was caught in the tempest Ulysses was trying "to reach the fathers' land" (*Odyssey* 9.79)—that is, Ithaca—lying near the entrance to Skagerrak Sound on the North Sea, we can infer that Cythera lay in the direction of the Skagerrak River, between the Baltic and the North Sea. Interestingly, in the southernmost part of Norway, directly above the mouth of the Skagerrak, there lies a region known as Agder[4] (Agdhir in Old Norse), the name of which could be compared with that of the Homeric Cytherians (Kýtheroi in Greek; *Odyssey* 9.81): Cythera and Agdhir have almost the same consonants. The initial *c* (*k* in Greek) is a guttural similar to *g*; *th* is close to *dh*; and both words share a final *r*.

Ulysses reports that on the tenth day, after nine days at the mercy of the winds, "we reached / the land of the Lotus-eaters" (*Odyssey* 9.83–84). Except, of course, to say that this land overlooked the sea (a characteristic common to all the lands Ulysses visits), this adventure—at twenty lines, Ulysses' shortest—is the only one in the *Odyssey* that does not provide us with any particular indication of its location. A slight hint might be found in the place-names Lote and Lotsberg, found adjacent to a fjord on the Norwegian coast near Nordfjordeid (about one hundred miles north of Bergen). No definite conclusions can be drawn, however, because we have no further evidence to support conjectures. Perhaps someday local folklore will be able to enlighten us as to the origin of the Lotus-eaters—and perhaps at some point we can find clues to the origins of these people by better understanding what it is that they ate.

Many people have wondered what the Lotus-eaters consumed. The Greek word for *lotus*—*lotós*—usually means "clover," a grazing plant that both the *Iliad* (2.776, 14.348, 21.351) and the *Odyssey* (4.603) stress as being good for horses. In fact, in the *Iliad* the expression *lotón ereptómenoi*, "browsing on clover" (*Iliad* 2.776), is used in reference to Achilles' horses. In the *Odyssey* (9.97) the same expression is used to refer to the Lotus-eaters. We could perhaps infer a link between the Homeric *lotós* and English oats, a typical grain for horses. The poet also includes that the Lotus-eaters used to eat *ánthinon eîdar*—that is, "vegetable food" (*Odyssey* 9.84)—where *ánthinon* derives from *ánthos*, "flower" or "shoot." Another line in the same book of the poem mentions a ram that crops *ánthea poíes,* "the shoots of the grass" (9.449).

Considering that the Homeric lotus is said to be "very sweet [*meliedéa*]" (*Odyssey* 9.94), much like clover blossoms, the "Lotus-eaters" could be surmised to be "clover-eaters"—that is, extremely primitive, vegetarian (herbivorous) people who were mild and friendly—while the uncivilized Cyclopes, who follow them in the narrative, are ferocious cannibals. Thus the poet could be emphasizing the differences between the civilized world of the Achaeans, a world in which people were used to eating bread, *sîton édontes* (*Odyssey* 9.89), as he underlines in the same passage, and the strange, sometimes savage, mythical and fantastical world where Ulysses undertakes his wanderings. In many mythologies, the image of bread marks the passage to civilization, bread itself requiring mastery of agriculture and baking. Interestingly, two fellows of Ulysses are tempted to join the Lotus-eaters and revert to a primitive state, but they are forced to go back to their ship. It seems that these early "flower children" are present in the story to indicate that even at such an early time in human history, some people wanted to refuse the ties of civilization.

THE CYCLOPES

In his next adventure, Ulysses meets the Cyclopes. These "arrogant men" appear as a real people located, as we have seen, next to the Phaeacians "in the broad lands of Hypereie" (*Odyssey* 6.4). This points us toward Norwegian territory, which, as we shall see, is the main setting for most of Ulysses' tales (see fig. 4.1). From the very beginning of the narration, when Ulysses' ships enter a port that is shrouded in fog, we can sense that these his wanderings take place in a northern context. In this passage, Homer's diction provides a wonderful medley of descriptive poetry and realism:

> We arrived in this port and some god guided us
> in the murky night, where nothing was discernible:
> a thick fog shrouded the ships, and the moon
> was not visible in the sky, but was covered by the clouds.
> Nobody saw the island with his eyes,
> nor did we see the long rollers breaking on the shore,
> before the ships leant on it. (*Odyssey* 9.142–48)

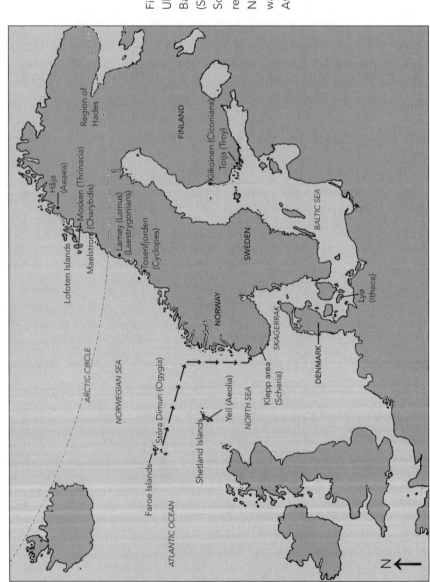

Fig. 4.1. A map of Ulysses' route in the Baltic from Ogygia (Stóra Dímun) to Scheria (near the Klepp region in southern Norway) and of his wanderings in the Atlantic Ocean

According to a map by Adam Bremen, an eleventh-century German historian, the "island of the Cyclopes *(insula Cyclopum)* lay along the coast of northern Norway, where, as Adam says in his *Gesta,* some Frisian sailors had come across one-eyed giants. There we can thus try to look for traces of Ulysses' adventure with the Cyclops Polyphemus, which immediately follows his encounter with the Lotus-eaters. Perhaps a trace of the Cyclopes can be found in the toponymy of this area. Along the central-northern Norwegian coastline, we find a fjord called Tosenfjorden, which does sound rather similar to the name of Polyphemus's mother: "Thoosa the Nymph, / daughter of Phorcys, Lord of the tireless seas, gave birth to him, / joined with Poseidon in the deep caves" *(Odyssey* 1.71–73). Near Tosenfjorden lies the mountain of Torghatten, whose characteristic bright "eye"—a large hole through the mountain—so visible to ships probably contributed to the birth of the legend of the one-eyed giant, whom Homer compares to "a woody peak of lofty mountains" *(Odyssey* 9.191). Erik Dahl, a writer and independent scholar from Trondheim, has made some interesting comparisons between the world of Homer's Cyclopes and the morphology of the Inderøya peninsula on the Trondheim fjord just south of Tosenfjorden. Although one place-name alone cannot provide reliable evidence of a location, it is tempting nonetheless to look among the islands lying near this fjord for the "flat island" *(Odyssey* 9.116) opposite the Cyclopes' port.

It is in comparing the *Odyssey* to northern legends, however, that we are provided with a consistent mytho-geographic picture, not least because of these myths' indications concerning the proximity of the Phaeacians, Cyclopes, and Giants. In fact, if we peruse the medieval literature of the north, we can glean traces of the Cyclopes that thousands of years of history have not managed to wipe out. Besides Adam of Bremen's mention, for example, there is a tale about a seafaring king who lands with his men in a faraway country where they face a sort of menacing ogre. They manage to defeat him by blinding him with a red-hot spear. This hero is not Ulysses but the Viking king Hjörleif, a character from the *Hálfs saga ok Hálfsrekka,* whose adventure is set in northern Norway. Gianna Chiesa Isnardi, professor of Scandinavian philology at the University of Genoa, notes that "its motif [of giants] reminds us of the myth of Polyphemus."[5] Moreover, according to the *Skáldskaparmál* (found in part 2 of the *Younger Edda*), the god Thor defeats the giant Geirrødh by throwing a red-hot iron at him, and among the small, toylike puppets displayed in Bergen's souvenir shops are those that depict the mythical trolls of Norwegian folklore, portrayed with only one eye in the middle of their forehead!

Even more astonishing is a Lapp tale—reported by Professor Roberto Bosi in his *Lapponi: sulle tracce di un popolo nomade* (Laplanders: On the Tracks of a Nomadic People)—about Stalo, who was a wicked giant, greedy for human brains, with only one eye in the middle of his forehead, exactly like Polyphemus. He lived in the farthest forests of Lapland. A tale narrates that he was blinded by a cunning guest in his hut; then he

> . . . stood up, realized that he had been blinded, and tried in vain to catch the Lapp. Then Stalo told him: "Push the goats out of the hut!" and stood in front of the door with his legs apart. The Lapp pushed the goats, which had to pass in single file and were felt by the giant, who said: "Let the he-goat pass last." While the goats were going out one by one, the Lapp killed the he-goat, put on its skin, and passed on all fours under Stalo's legs. "Well," the giant said, "you can pass now." But the Lapp was already outside, jumping for joy, and shouting: "I am already outside!" At this point, Stalo thought that only his sons could defeat such a cunning man and asked him his name. He answered: "My name is *I myself,*" and ran away. When Stalo's sons returned and discovered the killing of the big he-goat, of which they were very fond, they got angry and asked their father: "Who killed our he-goat?" "I myself," he answered. Then they killed Stalo.[6]

This tale not only replicates the details of Ulysses' flight from Polyphemus's cave, but also uses the famous pun, based on the false name of the cunning prisoner, that allowed him to fool his monstrous jailor and prevent the reaction of the other Cyclopes.

A peculiar characteristic of the Cyclopes, one that Homer repeatedly emphasizes, is their great strength, particularly their ability to easily move huge boulders:

> *Then [Polyphemus] reared and set a big, heavy*
> *slab; twenty-two good four-wheeled*
> *wagons would not have shifted it from the ground,*
> *so enormous was the stone he set at the entrance.*
> (*Odyssey* 9.240–43)

. . . after he had breakfasted, he let his fat flocks leave the cave,
easily removing the big slab, but immediately
he replaced it again, as if he were setting the lid on a quiver.
   (*Odyssey* 9.312–14)

He uprooted the top of a great mountain
and threw it in front of the ship . . .
then he reared an even bigger stone,
he whirled and threw it, giving it an immense force . . .
   (*Odyssey* 9.481–82, 537–38)

This unique ability has a significant parallel in Norwegian folklore, where "people say that the giants *threw* or *rolled* the huge erratic rocks of the land."[7]

Ulysses' adventure with Polyphemus can also be interpreted in terms of an oracle rite in which the prophecy regarding the hero's destiny is pronounced at the end of a sort of "fight" (*Odyssey* 9.532–35). Certain details such as the setting in a cave and the peculiar names of the protagonists—Polyphemus, meaning "he who talks a lot," and Nobody, Ulysses' false name—seem to reveal the ritual aspect of their encounter. The character of "Telemus Eurymides, who excelled at prophecy / and, prophesying, grew old among the Cyclopes" (*Odyssey* 9.509–10), fits very well with an interpretation of this kind, and with the shamanistic features of ancient northern cultures. The adventure of Hjörleif and the ogre, so similar to Ulysses' encounter, also reveals the motif of the oracle when the blinded giant predicts the destiny of the victorious king.

If these similarities point to a northern setting for these adventures, they also imply that the *Odyssey*'s first bard must have constructed them by using folklore, tales, and legends from the countries where he set them. How was it possible for him to know tales from such distant places? We can suppose that the great development of navigation during the Bronze Age, apart from leading to an increase in trade, led to cultural exchanges among different lands through sailors, merchants, pirates, bards, and so on. Homer probably drew inspiration from the adventures of the Argonauts and may also have received information and tales from the Phaeacians themselves, as certain references seem to suggest. Nestor sheds some light on this idea of "globetrotting" when he addresses his guest Telemachus to break the ice in conversation after their banquet:

O foreigners, who are you? Whence do you sail the wet ways?
Is this for a business, or are you wandering aimlessly
as the pirates on the seas? (Odyssey 3.71–73)

AEOLIA IN THE SHETLANDS

After the dramatic adventure in the land of the Cyclopes, "we arrived at the island of Aeolia, where Aeolus / Hippotades lived, a dear friend of the immortal gods" (*Odyssey* 10.1–2). Aeolus is one of the *Odyssey's* singular characters:

He gave me a leather bag made from the skin of a nine-year-old ox
where he locked the ways of the howling winds,
since Zeus had made him lord of the winds,
and he can drop and arouse the one he wishes.
He locked this bag in my ship with a shiny
silver chain to prevent the slightest leakage,
but he let Zephyrus' wind blow
to push the ships and us. (Odyssey 10.19–26)

We could suppose his island lay in the Atlantic Ocean, near the Norwegian coast, where, as indicated by Adam of Bremen, we might find traces of the Cyclopes. Before proceeding further, however, we can summarize the reasons why the setting of Ulysses' wanderings is likely the North Atlantic:

- Ulysses passes from his Baltic world to an apparently adjacent unknown and hostile world.
- The access to the Atlantic Ocean from the Sound of Skagerrak is not very far from Lyø, the Baltic Ithaca, to which Ulysses is headed when he is diverted by the storm that begins his wanderings.
- As we shall see, in this new world Ulysses comes upon phenomena that are typical of the North Atlantic, such as the great tide that produces the whirlpool Charybdis, and phenomena that are typical of the Arctic (which can be reached only by heading north from the North Atlantic), such as the very long days in the land of the Laestrigonians and the midnight sun on the island of Circe.
- At the end of his wanderings Ulysses reaches Ogygia, which, according to Plutarch, lies in the North Atlantic.

Let us, then, focus our attention on the Shetland Islands, off the coast of Norway at about 60° north latitude. Their cliffs correspond to the description of Aeolia, which, according to Homer, soars from the sea: "The cliff rises bare [*lissé d'anadédrome pétre*]" (*Odyssey* 10.4). This is a home suitable for "the lord of winds," for extremely violent storms occur here, with winds exceeding 130 miles per hour. And Zephyrus, the west wind, is exactly what Ulysses needs to get back home.

The Shetland Islands have been inhabited since prehistoric times—in fact, the Jarlshof archaeological site contains findings that go back as far as three thousand years. Even older remains have been found on the Orkney Islands, sixty-two miles to the southwest, and those found in Skara Brae date back to the third millennium B.C.E., testifying to human settlements in the Neolithic period. These findings also indicate that northern populations practiced oceanic navigations in very ancient times. The Shetlands lie in a central position between Scotland, the Faeroe Islands, and the Norwegian coast, and, therefore, must have been a particularly important reference point for Bronze Age seafarers. In particular, these islands were probably a port of call for merchantmen sailing between Scandinavia and the British Isles, at least during the climatic optimum, which made such a course relatively easy. It is no mere coincidence that the first Viking colonies arrived at the Shetlands in the ninth century C.E. during another favorable climatic period, the so-called medieval warm period. In fact, the mark of the Norse is still evident, despite the fact that the Shetlands have not belonged to Norway since 1472.

For our purposes, not only does the northernmost point of the archipelago have a curiously Greek-sounding name, Herma Ness, but also one of the larger islands is Yell, which could be the home of the powerful Aeolus (Aíolos). Did prehistoric seafarers perhaps have a shrine in Yell dedicated to the "lord of winds"? As we learned at the beginning of this chapter, Strabo reports the Greek geographer Eratosthenes' ironic comment: "One could find the places where Ulysses wandered by tracking down the cobbler who sewed up the windbag." Now we have good reason to believe that Eratosthenes' paradoxical "cobbler" had his workshop in these parts: the Shetland Islands. In *The Golden Bough,* James Frazer corroborates this idea: "Shetland Islands seamen even today buy winds in the shape of handkerchiefs and strings knotted by old women who claim to be able to control storms. People say that in Lerwick there are old witches who live by selling winds."[8] Additionally, there are copper mines on the Shetlands, which could explain "the bronze wall" (*Odyssey* 10.3) that existed in Aeolus's palace.

Some traces of Aeolus, whose Greek name means "variable," with clear reference to the sea's unpredictable nature, can still be found in Norse literature. We are referring to Njord, the god who rules both the winds and the sea. As Professor Chiesa Isnardi states, "[H]e must be invoked when setting out on a sea journey." The *Younger Edda* narrates that he lives in Noatun, "the city of ships," and his relationship with the sea is so close that his marriage is in jeopardy, for his wife prefers the mountains.[9] What is more, Njord is extremely rich—as is Aeolus, whose palace gives off "fumes of fat" *(knisêen)* and in whose home "there are countless delicacies" (*Odyssey* 10.9–10).

Njord is the main representative god among the Vanirs (the mythical seafaring rivals to the Aesir, the primary gods of the Norse pantheon). He has two children from an incestuous relationship with his sister, a common practice among the Vanir and similar to that seen in the family of Aeolus, who had "six daughters and six sons in their prime; / he had given his daughters to his sons in marriage" (*Odyssey* 10.6–7). We might even associate this with the fact that Aegir and Ran, the terrible couple who rule the seas in the Norse sagas, correspond in Greek mythology to Aegaeon and Rhea, *brother and sister*.

THE FAR NORTH

According to tradition, many of Ulysses' adventures were located west of Greece, in the area of the Tyrrhenian Sea—that is, on the Italian peninsula. This is probably due to the fact that the ancient Greeks still kept in their memory that the setting of these adventures was a fabulous, almost unknown western land, a sort of prehistoric, oceanic "Far West." Because the geographical southern counterpart of the Norwegian Atlantic coast is the Italian Tyrrhenian coast, it was there that the Atlantic adventures of the *Odyssey* were relocated. In this area, corresponding to the position of the Shetland Islands relative to southern Norway, the Aeolian Islands face the Calabrian coast in southern Italy. According to this model, then, the "vast Hypereie" was identified with Campania (the region of Naples); Circe's home with a headland called San Felice Circeo, which is sixty miles southeast of Rome; Thrinacia with Sicily; Scylla and Charybdis with the Strait of Messina; and so on.

Thus the unreal, dreamlike nature of the adventures' phenomena such as the Sirens, the deadly whirlpool named Charybdis, and the Dawn's dances—already mutated by the exaggerations of the sailors and the imagination of the poet—was emphasized still further. The transposition of Ulysses' tales to the Mediterranean, which probably occurred when the collapse of the Mycenaean civilization in the twelfth century B.C.E. erased the memory of the real location of the Homeric world, inevitably rendered them quite unrecognizable. Yet when we return these fantastic adventures to their proper setting, they become far more realistic.

After leaving the island of Aeolia, Ulysses' fleet

> *. . . sailed day and night for six days in succession.*
> *On the seventh we reached the high city of Lamus,*
> *Laestrygonian Telepylus, where going back the shepherd*
> *calls the shepherd, who replies going out.*
> *Here a sleepless man would earn two wages,*
> *the one for grazing cattle, the other for herding white sheep,*
> *since the paths of night and day are near . . . (Odyssey 10.80–86)*

These lines emphasize that the day is exceptionally long, indicating that this area lies at a very high latitude, probably to the north of the Shetlands—namely, Norway's northern coasts. Certain scholars such as Robert Graves have realized that the setting for the adventure with the Laestrygonians is Norway: "Telepylus . . . lies in the far north of Europe, in the land of the midnight sun, where the shepherds [come] in, exchange greetings with those going out . . . The Laestrygonians, 'a very fierce race,' were probably Norwegian."[10]

Adjacent to the Norwegian coast we come across an island—Lamøy—that reminds us of the Homeric Lamus. It is located not far from Tosenfjorden, in a setting that corresponds to the context of the adventures that follow. The imagination of the poet, backed by the information he no doubt heard regarding those remote sea courses, pushes the Ithacan ship farther and farther north after it alone survives the attack of the terrible Laestrygonians, who wildly destroyed the rest of Ulysses' fleet.

The seafarer's next adventure is set in the fabulous world of Circe, "the terrible goddess with human voice" (*Odyssey* 10.136), the lady of the island Aeaea. If the land of the Laestrygonians is located at a very high latitude, Aeaea must be even farther north, as shown by the words of a very worried Ulysses: "Here we can perceive neither where darkness is nor where dawn is / nor where the Sun shining on men goes down underground / nor where it rises" (*Odyssey* 10.190–92). Darkness *(zóphos)* and dawn *(eós)* here indicate the west and east, respectively (as we can clearly see in *Odyssey* 9.26 and *Iliad* 12.239–40). The reference to a place where the sun does not set during the summer months can only mean the far north, where this phenomenon occurs during the sailing season.

This setting is also perfectly consistent with an enigmatic passage concerning the island of Aeaea, "where early-rising Dawn / has her home and her dances" (*Odyssey* 12.3–4). What does the poet mean by these "dances *(choroí)* of the dawn,"which are mentioned nowhere else? We can find a parallel concept in the Vedas (the most ancient hymns of Indian mythology), in which Dawn, or rather the goddess Ushas (Eós in Greek), typically appears as a dancing figure. B. G. Tilak, an extremely learned Indian scholar (1856–1920), in his work *The Arctic Home in the Vedas*, demonstrates that Ushas's dance is a metaphor for a typical phenomenon of very high latitudes, beyond the Arctic Circle, where a "revolving dawn" appears toward the end of the long Arctic night, heralding the reappearance of the sun. Here is a charming description of this phenomenon from a nineteenth-century American writer, William F. Warren, quoted by B. G. Tilak:

> First of all appears low in the horizon of the night-sky a scarcely visible flush of light. At first it only makes a few stars' light seem a trifle fainter, but after a little it is seen to be increasing, and to be moving laterally along the yet dark horizon. Twenty-four hours later it has made a complete circuit around the observer, and is causing a larger number of stars to pale. Soon the widening light glows with the lustre of "Orient pearl." Onward it moves in its stately rounds, until the pearly whiteness burns into ruddy rose-light, fringed with purple and gold. Day after day, as we measure days, this splendid panorama circles on, and, according as atmospheric conditions and clouds present more or less favorable conditions of reflection, kindles and fades, kindles and fades—fades only to kindle next time yet more brightly, as the still hidden sun comes nearer and nearer his point of emergence.[11]

This is the explanation for Homer's metaphor "the dances of the Dawn." Let us remember that in ancient Greece (and also in contemporary Greece's Sirtaki, the "dance of Zorba"), the "circle choirs"* were round dances, and, as we have just seen, "the revolving dawns" are actually a sort of "ring-a-ring-o'-roses" of light in the background of the Arctic night. This is echoed by a peculiar ritual of the Samoyedic shamans called Medodè, which is performed at the end of the polar night:[12] On this occasion, boys continuously dance in a ring because "the rhythm of the unceasing ring-a-ring-o'-roses helps the rising sun to start its course again."[13]

In the *Odyssey*, Homer informs us that apart from the "dances of the dawn," another phenomenon takes place on the island of Aeaea: "the Sun rises [*antolaí Eelíoio*]" (*Odyssey* 12.4). Because this expression appears peculiar to this island (it is used by Homer only on this occasion), we can conclude that the poet is not referring to the usual sunrise. It seems quite reasonable to interpret, then, that the word *antolaí*, deriving from the verb *anatéllein*, refers to the sun "staying above" *(téllein aná)* the horizon. In other words, this appears to be another reference to the midnight sun, especially given that it comes after an allusion to the impossibility of using this sun as a means of orientation on the island. Again, these descriptions—both "the Dawn's dances" and "the Sun rises"—seem all the more significant as information to help us locate the action because they are mentioned only on this one occasion in the text of both poems.

Like the Lapps (Sami), who call themselves "the children of the Sun," Homer calls Circe "daughter of the Sun" (*Odyssey* 10.138), emphasizing her relationship with our star. Her shamanistic features are also evident, which is in keeping with the fact that Arctic shamanism is intimately connected to solar cults.[†] Circe is also "the sister of the terrible Aeetes," the king of Colchis, which, as we shall see, suggests the proximity between Colchis and Aeaea evident in another passage from the *Odyssey*. This information also squares very well with a passage

---

*It would be very interesting to compare the Greek *choroí* to the French medieval caroles, which were sacred dances performed by a number of people holding hands and going around and around accompanied by song. Traditional English Christmas carols, which in past times were circle dances, may also be part of this tradition, connected as they are to the winter solstice. This same "circle" principle applies to the blessed souls in Dante's *Paradise* (24.16–17) who go around and around "dancing these carols [*carole*] / in different ways."

†Solar cults are based on the worship of the sun god, the primary deity. For an extensive discussion regarding solar mythology and its origins in far northern European locations, please refer to chapter 15.

from the Greek writer Mimnermus (quoted by K. Kerényi) that suggests the midnight sun: "In Aeetes' golden halls the rays of the Sun used to rest during the night."

Following the Norwegian coast northward, continuing the direction indicated by Ulysses' previous stopping points, we come upon Lofoten and the Vesterålen Islands, beyond the Arctic Circle, where the midnight sun shines from the end of May until July. This area is therefore the most probable location for Circe's and Aeetes' enchanted kingdoms, which is corroborated by Circe's warnings to Ulysses about the dangers he will have to face after leaving Aeaea to return home: namely, the Sirens, the Wandering Rocks, Scylla, Charybdis, and the island of Thrinacia. All these "dangers" can be identified in the area of Lofoten.

DANGEROUS WATERS

As we have been establishing, the whole picture outlined in the Ulysses adventures in the *Odyssey* is consistent with the context of the northern coast of Norway, a world filled with innumerable islands with smooth granite cliffs that fall vertically to the sea; thousands of reefs that appear and disappear according to the tide; and tidal streams that run like rivers in sea channels, producing huge whirlpools.

Sailing in these waters, in particular off the western side of the Lofoten Islands, is extremely dangerous due to rocks and shoals (of which, as we shall see, the Sirens are a metaphor) that extend two to four miles offshore: As experts have observed, "This coast should be avoided."[14] Moreover, there are extremely strong tidal streams in the narrow passages between the four main islands of the Lofoten archipelago: Austvågøya, Vestvågøya, Flakstadøya, and Moskenesøya, which stand in a line from northeast to southwest, like the carriages of a train. At the southernmost point of Moskenesøya, off Cape Lofotodden, the tide periodically produces an infamous whirlpool known as the Maelstrom (*Moskenstraumen* in Norwegian), which we may relate to Charybdis. The *Odyssey* confirms that the episode of Charybdis involves just such a tidal phenomenon: "Charybdis absorbs the dark waters; / three times a day [*trís ep'émati*] she spews them, three times absorbs them / terribly" (*Odyssey* 12.104–106).

According to Homer, also in this vicinity there are "two rocks; the one reaches the sky" (*Odyssey* 12.73). This taller rock is doubtless

Scylla's rock. The second rock is "lower [*chthamalóteron*]" (*Odyssey* 12.101), and the two are situated "close to each other, within bowshot [*ken dioïsteúseias*]" (*Odyssey* 12.102). In actuality, at the foot of the steep, southernmost point of Cape Lofotodden (the rock of Scylla that "reaches the sky"), an oblong islet (the "lower" rock) called Rödöya lies parallel to the coast, separated from the cape by only a very narrow passage, Reidsundet, which is a mere 160 feet wide (see fig. 4.2)—making these two formations certainly within bowshot of one another!

Circe advises Ulysses to get through the "strait [*steinopón*]" (*Odyssey* 12.234) between the two rocks "by sailing quickly close to Scylla's rock" (*Odyssey* 12.108), so as not to be sucked under by the whirlpool, which extends beyond the islet (*Odyssey* 12.104). The instructions Ulysses gives the helmsman of his ship before passing through the strait conform to this scheme (*Odyssey* 12.217–21). It is worth noting that so many years after Circe's directions, the British Admiralty recommends the same course to sailors plying these waters: "It is advisable to keep near to Lofotodden."[15]

In fact, sailors have long feared the Maelstrom area for its legendary danger to ships, and it has long been a fixture on maps of the area. For years there have been tales of ships being swallowed by this whirlpool. The nineteenth-century writer Jules Verne, who was particularly interested in geographic details, includes this whirlpool in *Twenty Thousand Leagues Under the Sea* in a way that might seem rather exaggerated today, but effectively mirrors the fear experienced by sailors of that period:

> At high tide, the waters between the Faeroe Islands and the Lofoten precipitate with terrible violence, forming an eddy that no ship has ever fled. Huge waves surge up from all points of the horizon to form this whirlpool, which is known as "the navel of the Ocean"; its force of attraction stretches as far as 15 kilometers. These whirling waters swallow up even whales and polar bears![16]

The Odyssey also speaks explicitly of a "sea navel" when it introduces Ogygia, "the island in the middle of the waves, where the sea navel [*omphalós thalásses*] lies" (*Odyssey* 1.50). If we bear in mind that the archipelago of the Faeroe Islands lies in the open sea off the Maelstrom area, and that Ulysses landed on Ogygia after he fled Charybdis, it seems quite clear that the poet means to give a rough idea of the position of Ogygia by a geographical reference to the great whirlpool, which even at that time must have been well known. We should also note that Paul the Deacon, a Longobard medieval writer (720–799 C.E.), says with reference to the Maelstrom: "Not very far from the aforesaid coast, toward its western side, where the boundless ocean opens, there is the very deep water chasm that people call the sea navel [*umbilicum maris*]. They say that it swallows the waters twice a day, then it vomits them again . . . Virgil calls 'Charybdis' a similar whirlpool."[17] Significantly, no such "sea navel" exists in the Mediterranean.

As for Scylla, the dreadful monster that seizes some of Ulysses' companions during the crossing of the strait, he probably embodies a sailors' legend reexamined from a literary viewpoint: Who can forget the scene in *Twenty Thousand Leagues Under the Sea* of the octopus that uses its tentacles to pull a seaman away from the deck of the *Nautilus*?

To complete this picture, a little south of the Maelstrom, the small island of Mosken, with its distinctive shape of a three-pointed hat, corresponds to the Homeric island of Thrinacia—"the Trident" (see fig. 4.2)—home of the sun god's cattle and a place that proves fatal for Ulysses' companions. When visibility is good, its peculiar three-pointed silhouette is unmistakable on the horizon.

The Wandering Rocks "against which / the great waves of blue-eyed Amphitrite noisily break" (*Odyssey* 12.59–60)—in the *Odyssey* they are situated beyond the Sirens along an alternative to Charybdis (*Odyssey* 12.55)—probably refer to one of those dangerous passages between the Lofoten Islands that are infested with tidal streams and rocks appearing and disappearing according to the tide. Despite their threats, these straits allow seafarers to bypass the Maelstrom to reach Vestfjorden, which is the inlet between the Lofoten Islands and the mainland. The most dangerous is the strait between Moskenesøya and Flakstadøya. Going from north to south, ships first must pass Selfjorden, avoiding rocks and shoals, and then find the very narrow mouth of Sundstraumen Strait, with a navigable width of only seventy-two feet and an extremely strong tidal stream. Moreover, "Selfjorden is noted for its peculiar wind conditions. It is reported that, with a SW or W gale at sea, winds blow through the narrow mountain valleys with great force. During storms, spray is raised throughout the fjord."[18] This seems to fit with what we are told in the *Odyssey*: that at times even birds were dashed against the rocks (*Odyssey* 12.62–64) and that there was "a deadly fire storm" (*Odyssey* 12.68) in this vicinity (which perhaps hints at the spray that blinds the crew).

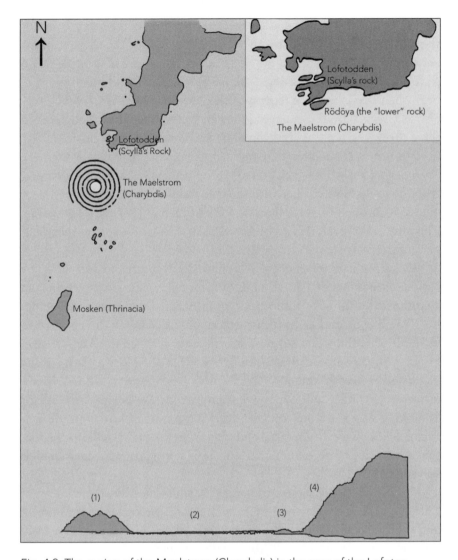

Fig. 4.2. The region of the Maelstrom (Charybdis) in the area of the Lofoten Islands, Norway. The whirlpool is found off the coast of the island of Lofotodden, between the southernmost point of the island (Scylla's rock) and the island of Mosken (Homeric Thrinacia). The inset map shows the strait between Lofotodden and the islet (the "lower rock") that Ulysses' ship passes through to avoid the whirlpool. Below is a side view of the topography of the area showing (1) the peculiar silhouette of Mosken (with the three points that accord with the name Thrinacia), (2) the expanse of sea affected by the whirlpool, (3) the "lower rock," and (4) the sheer headland of Helseggen at the tip of Lofotodden.

All of this—the gusts and the streams that hinder the safe passage of ships in that treacherous, stormy sea; the sheer cliffs; the narrow straits between rocky outcroppings; the difficulty sailors have in locating themselves or getting their bearings; the sea spray that can blind crew members—helps to create the legend of the "wandering rocks," which was also nourished by the exaggerations of the seamen who had escaped these threats or reported the appalling accounts of the survivors.

Homer also narrates that one ship managed to pass through the "wandering rocks: "the celebrated *Argo* on its way back from Aeetes. / It soon would have crashed into the enormous rocks as well, / but Hera guided it through because she was fond of Jason" (*Odyssey* 12.69–72). This confirms that the island of Aeetes' island, Aea, lay next to the island of Circe. (For more on Circe's land, see below.)

We can postulate that the Argonauts' adventures in search of the Golden Fleece, handed down to us by later poets, refer to a very ancient circumnavigation of Scandinavia dating back to the generation before the Trojan War and carried out in a counterclockwise direction from the Gulf of Bothnia. The Argonauts, it seems, reached the Arctic Ocean by land, then followed the northernmost coast of Norway toward the west, where Aeetes' kingdom lay. We note that in the traditional Mediterranean setting—contrary to what Homer states—Aeaea and Colchis are a long way from one another, the former being located on the Tyrrhenian Sea, west of Greece, and the latter in the Black Sea region. Once we place these islands in a northern setting, this inconsistency is solved.

Interestingly, the names of several islands found in the vicinity of Lofoten retain the stamp of the Greek language: Nesöya, Nykan, Myken, and a very small island called Trenyken, whose three peaks rise from the sea. This last, however, is too small and distant from the whirlpool (more than twenty-five miles) to be the Homeric Thrinacia. There is also an archipelago called Traena. On it signs of human life go as far back as the Stone Age and seamanship developed from extremely ancient times. Perhaps the Baltic Achaeans moved there, availing themselves of the climatic optimum before they were forced south.

Overall, the *Odyssey* provides us with ample evidence of in-depth knowledge of the Norwegian Sea. Regarding this, we should keep in mind the passage from "De facie" in which Plutarch mentions the Atlantic islands beyond Ogygia as being "inhabited by Greeks." These Atlantic islands opposite the area of the Maelstrom, in the middle of the Atlantic Ocean, are the Faeroe Islands, which Ulysses finally managed to reach after he fled the whirlpool a second time. Ogygia was their sanctuary after many days adrift at the mercy of the waves. But before they reached this island, he and his crew had several dangerous encounters, beginning with the sorceress Circe.

CIRCE'S ISLAND

The Greek name of Circe's island—Aiaíe—is formed by the suffix *aíe,* meaning "land" (it is often found in the Homeric poems as a variant of *gaíe*), and the prefix *ai,* also found in the name of Aeetes (Aiétes in Greek), and refers perhaps to the name of a people. It is possible that the Homeric Aiaíe is the island of Håja, northeast of Lofoten and about twenty miles west of Tromsø, Norway. Håja is a small island, only a little more than a mile wide, on which a peak rises about sixteen hundred feet. This squares with the "rocky peak" (*Odyssey* 10.148) Ulysses climbs on Circe to determine that he is on "an island encircled by the sea" (*Odyssey* 10.195).

While on Aeaea, Ulysses uses *môly* (*Odyssey* 10.195), a grass, as an antidote to neutralize the spell of the witch who has intended to transform him into a pig. Though Robert Graves points out in *The Greek Myths* that scholars have not been able to establish what this mysterious grass is, we should first of all note that the word *mûla* in Sanskrit means "root" and that, according to Giuliano Bruni, there is a typical expression related to this word—*mûla karman*—which, according to the *Sanskrit-English Dictionary,*[19] means "root machination, employment of a root for magical purposes." In other words, we find the same reference to magic that appears in the *Odyssey.* But exactly what kind of root is this? We find a plausible suggestion in the extinct language of the ancient Guanches, the primitive inhabitants of the Canary Islands before the arrival of the Spaniards, which the Austrian scholar D. J. Wölfel has reconstructed in his work *Monumenta linguae Canariae*: In that language the word *mol* means "wormwood" *(Artemisia absinthium)*. Perhaps the ancestors of the blond, dolichocephalic Guanches in ancient times were part of a "cultural community" that stretched as far as Norway, or perhaps they were a splinter group of a people coming from the north who landed in the Canaries due to ancient migrations.

Wormwood has an important role in European folklore, as we learn from James Frazer in *The Golden Bough*: It was reputed to protect people (in Bohemia) and animals (in Prussia and Lithuania) against witches and witchcraft. We also note that in Celtic mythology, Ceridwen (also Kerid-wenn) is a sort of witch who, in the *History of Taliesin,* distils a magic draft and fights someone who shapeshifts into various animals. Moreover, in an ancient Chinese tale, *K'ien's Myth,* the god Hiung gives wormwood to two animals in order to transform them into human beings.

Magic, sorcerers, and the metamorphoses they effect are the same elements that characterize the extremely archaic world of Circe, who is called *polyphármakos*—that is, "the one who knows many drugs" (*Odyssey* 10.276). That wormwood has psychedelic effects affirms its link to magic.

TO THE HOME OF HADES

From Circe's island, Ulysses makes a daredevil voyage to the "home of Hades* and terrible Persephone" (*Odyssey* 10.564) before heading past Charybdis's whirlpool. In this episode, which we might well expect to be completely fantastical, we can instead discover some remarkable geographic correlations to this Scandinavian part of the world that also corroborate Aeaea's location in the far north of Norway.

So, let us follow Ulysses' ship, which sails from Circe's island toward

> *the end of the deep-streamed Ocean,*
> *where there are the Cimmerians and their city,*
> *shrouded in fog and clouds. Never*
> *does the bright Sun look at them with its rays*
> *. . . but a dreadful night burdens those wretched mortals.*
>   (*Odyssey* 11.13–16, 19)

Robert Graves unhesitatingly locates the Cimmerians in the far north: "[They] also belong to the cold region that enjoys the midnight sun in June, but it is dark at midday in winter."[20] We should also note that the name Cimmerians is probably Indo-European, judging by the Latvian *ziemeli,* meaning "northerners."[21]

---

*It is correct to translate the Greek "Aídao dómous" as "home of (the god) Hades." In the Homeric poems, Hades is not a hellish *place;* it is always presented as a being, a god—that is, Persephone's husband and Zeus's brother.

In chapter 13 we shall identify Homer's "deep-streamed Ocean" with the Gulf Stream, which moves from southwest to northeast in the Norwegian Sea. Here we see, though, that Homer's directions are consistent with the course of the northernmost branch of the Gulf Stream, which turns eastward after following the length of the Norwegian coast and ends up in the Arctic Ocean, where it meets deserted and even more inhospitable regions. That's why Ulysses despairs when Circe tells him he must go and visit the "home of Hades" before he can return to Ithaca: "My heart broke, / I cried sitting on the bed and my heart / no longer wished to live or see sunlight anymore" (*Odyssey* 10.496–98).

It is significant that Saxo Grammaticus, in his tale of the expedition of the Icelander Thorkillus, locates in the same area a land of the dead amazingly similar to the Hades that Homer describes. He places it in Biarmia, a region stretching from the Urals to the White Sea, which was known as Gandvik in Norse, derived from *gandr,* meaning "magic," because those far northern peoples were considered the guardians of a particular kind of shamanism known as *seidhr* in Norse sources. Although Saxo's tale is quite similar to Ulysses' adventure, it originates from Norse sagas. In fact, the protagonist's name—Thorkillus—calls to mind Thor, the famous Norse god.

Interestingly, in the same area where Saxo locates the world of the dead, a character called Guthmundus has a paradisiacal "garden of delights," corresponding in Norse literature to the kingdom of Godhmundr known as Glaesisvellir (meaning "glass fields" or "shining plain"), or Odáinsakr (Field of the Immortals). This recalls "the Elysian plain at the ends of the earth," where "blond Rhadamanthus lives" (*Odyssey* 4.563), which Homer describes as being somewhat similar to the Garden of Eden.*

Saxo tells us:

Icelanders used to tell incredible stories of enormous riches piled up there, but the way to this place was full of dangers and almost inaccessible to mortals. According to the experts of this route, one had to cross the Ocean that surrounded the Earth, leaving Sun and stars

---

*We should also note the curious similarity between Guthmundus and Rhadamanthus, not withstanding the different initial consonants g and rh, for in Greek the r is marked by the "spirit"—that is, the sign that marks initial vowels; in the Sicilian dialect, which probably still reflects an ancient Greek influence, this initial r is pronounced almost like j, which, in turn, is not far from g. Interestingly, Rome is pronounced as *jym* in Polish.

behind, traveling through the kingdom of chaos and finally moving into places without light, shrouded in perpetual darkness.[22]

This "perpetual darkness," similar to the one that afflicted the Cimmerians, presumably refers to the dark winter solstice in the north.

The far northern location of the Cimmerians suggests that Ulysses' journey "along the Ocean's stream" takes place in the inlet of the Arctic Ocean known as the White Sea, which lies east of the northernmost part of Scandinavia. As we continue to follow our hero, he reaches "the rotten home of Hades; / here the Pyriphlegethon flows into the Acheron, / with the Cocytus, which flows from the waters of Styx" (*Odyssey* 10.512–14)—the most mysterious and sinister geographic entity in Greek mythology. The Styx, which means "hateful" (its root, *styg-*, is very similar to the Norwegian adjective *stygg*, meaning "ugly"), is also a clue to the location of the "home of Hades" in a place that is corroborated in the *Odyssey*, the *Iliad*, and the *Gesta Danorum*, as we shall see very soon.

First, though, we should note that Homer never talks of "a river" when he refers to the Styx. On the contrary, he uses the expression "the waters of Styx" *(hýdor Stygós)*. In the *Odyssey*, Homer tells us that the river Cocytus flowed from the Styx toward the Acheron, and in the *Iliad* he states that the Styx had another effluent known as the Titaresius, a tributary of the river Peneus, flowing through the country of the Peraebians and Enienes (*Iliad* 2.749–55). As we shall see in chapter 10, the Catalog of Ships places the home of the Peraebians on the northernmost side of the Gulf of Bothnia, on the river Peneus. In other words, the Homeric Styx's two effluents, the Cocytus and the Titaresius, flow in opposite directions, into the White Sea and the Baltic Sea, respectively. We should note that this is the only point of contact between the "oceanic" adventures of the *Odyssey* and the world of the *Iliad*, and both are easily identifiable in the northern world, while no such corroboration exists in the Mediterranean region.

At this point, we have only to examine a map of northern Finland to find "the waters of Styx." Here there is an area abundant in lakes and rivers lying between the White Sea and the Baltic, which are about 220 miles apart. At the center of this region an area of high ground, called Maanselkä, is the watershed between these two bodies of water on either side. Here, just below the Arctic Circle, not far from the Finnish border with Russia, two adjacent lakes, called Lake Kitka and Lake Livojärvi, rise several hundred feet above sea level. Their respective effluents on one side are connected to the hydrographic system flowing northeast into the White Sea and on the other to the system flowing into the Baltic (see fig. 4.3). This explains why Homer refers to "the waters of Styx" as "overflowing [*kateibómenon*]" (*Iliad* 15.37, *Odyssey* 5.185). According to the literal meaning of this Greek term, these waters actually "flow down" from Lake Kitka and Lake Livojärvi to feed their respective effluents, the rivers Kitkanjoki and Livojoki, which flow into the White Sea (in the case of the Kitkanjoki) and the Gulf of Bothnia (in the case of the Livojoki). This territory lies next to the mountainous area we shall identify in chapter 13 with Olympus, the home of the gods. Tellingly, Homer considers the waters of Styx to be the "terrible oath" of the gods (*Iliad* 2.755, *Odyssey* 5.186), which corroborates the close relationship between Styx and the pantheon.

After identifying the Styx, it is easy to locate the Homeric Hades. The Kitkanjoki—that is, the effluent of Lake Kitka flowing into the White Sea—runs eastward and flows into the Oulankajoki (the Oulanka River) near the border with Russia. Its waters continue into Russia as the Olanga River and flow into Lake Kouta after passing through the complex hydrological system of Karelia. From here they flow into the western part of the White Sea—to be precise, the Bay of Kandalaksha, lying at 66°40' north latitude. Here lay the "Home of Hades," where "the Pyriphlegethon flows into the Acheron, / with the Cocytus."

We note that the name Kouta sounds similar to Cocytus, known as Kokytós in Greek (curiously enough, Dante in his *Inferno* considers it an icy lake). Moreover, there is another river found in the same hydrological system, the Kuma, which is an effluent of the lake into which the Olanga flows. This name, Kuma, recalls the root of the name of the Cimmerians, "the wretched mortals" who, according to the *Odyssey*, live in the region of Hades. Another lake in Karelia, Lake Keret, recalls the Kere, Greek mythology's demonic announcers of death. As we can see, the complex hydrography of this area surrounding the White Sea perfectly coincides with the passage of the *Odyssey* that mentions the various rivers of Hades.

The high latitude of this area and the long winter solstice night explain the references to the darkness made so frequently by Homer and Saxo. The *Iliad* directly associates Hades with "the foggy darkness" (*Iliad* 15.191), while the specific reference in the *Odyssey* to these peoples "shrouded in fog and clouds" can be accommodated by Karelia's climate, where lakes and immense marshlands alternate with vast stretches of woodland. Here "surface waters and forests maintain an extremely high level of

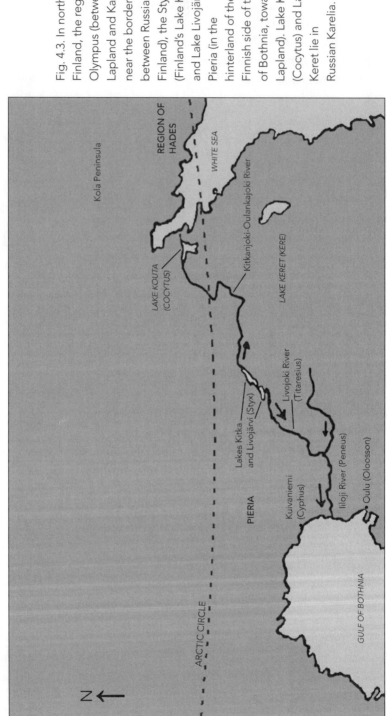

Fig. 4.3. In northern Finland, the region of Olympus (between Lapland and Karelia, near the border between Russia and Finland), the Styx (Finland's Lake Kitka and Lake Livojärvi) and Pieria (in the hinterland of the Finnish side of the Gulf of Bothnia, toward Lapland). Lake Kouta (Cocytus) and Lake Keret lie in Russian Karelia.

humidity in the atmosphere; therefore, cloudless days are very rare."[23] The *Odyssey* also states that in this area "there is a low beach and the woods of Persephone, / with tall poplars and fruitless willows" (*Odyssey* 10.509–10)—trees that usually take root in humid woods or that line the edges of rivers. Willows in particular are one of the few species that can live along the banks of the rivers of the tundra, that icy Arctic desert.

What probably preserved the memory of such a distant world that was so difficult to reach was the ancient shamanistic magic *(seidhr)* practiced by the northern peoples of these regions. Interestingly, the conjuring of the dead narrated in detail in Books 10 and 11 of the *Odyssey* seems to recall the traits of a primordial shamanistic rite performed in the dark Arctic winter in a far-off marshland in Karelia at the foot of "the rock where two sounding rivers meet" (*Odyssey* 10.515). Maybe the rock was a dolmen or the tumulus of a king, ancient even in Ulysses' time.

> *When you, hero, land there, as I tell you,*
> *dig a pit one cubit long and wide,*
> *and around it pour out the libation for all the dead:*
> *firstly with honeyed milk, then with sweet wine,*
> *thirdly with water, and sprinkle white flour . . .*
> *After invoking the illustrious ranks of the dead with vows,*
> *sacrifice a ram and a black ewe,*
> *turning them to the Erebus, but you must turn elsewhere*
> *to the river stream. There many / of the dead's souls will come . . .*
>   (*Odyssey* 10.516–20, 526–30)

Besides the mysterious, archaic charm of these lines, we cannot help being piqued by that "pit" *(bóthron)* around which the rite was held: It is not difficult to recognize it as the equivalent of the ancient Roman *mundus,* a well or "mouth" (*Mund* in German) that acted as the entrance to the Underworld. This was also the pit Romulus dug when he founded Rome, the hole into which he threw the sacred first harvest. Georges Dumézil, noted French scholar of Indo-European populations and cultures, points out that it

> . . . corresponded remarkably to an archaic Vedic rite where the square sacrificial fire place was marked out . . . In the middle of the quadrilateral, exactly where the diagonals met, in a spot called "mouth," the priests placed a tuft of grass called *darbha* onto this

symbolic equivalent of a mundus; then they poured twelve jars of water and sprinkled all kinds of herb seeds over it. This rite is surely very ancient.[24]

The connection to Vedic rites tallies with Tilak's theory that his ancestors, known as the Aryans—who spoke a language that belonged to the same family as the Greek and Norse languages—originated from an Arctic land. Although he was not able to locate it exactly, in chapter 14 we shall come across significant traces of the primitive Vedic world in the northernmost part of Scandinavia, not far from where we are locating Homeric Hades and where Ulysses carries out the extremely archaic rite of the *mundus*.

In Book 11 of the *Odyssey*, the ghost of the prophet Teresias, raised by the rite, goes near the pit and tells Ulysses he has to offer "a ram, a bull, and a boar" as a sacrifice (*Odyssey* 11.131). This is identical to the Roman sacrifice called *suovetaurilia,* which, according to Dumézil, "was very ancient. . . . It was similar to a Vedic rite—that is, the sacrifice of three animals, called *sautramani.*"[25] The recurrence of the relation among the Homeric Hades, ancient Roman rites, and Vedic rites in the same episode is further evidence that Homer drew inspiration from an extremely ancient source dating back to a primordial, undivided Indo-European world. Further, all of this indicates that in very ancient times, when the climatic optimum was at its peak, an Arctic civilization flourished in the far north and that after the climatic collapse destroyed it, this world became the "land of the dead"—that is, a land of ancestors that was idealized in the memory of their descendants. Ulysses' journey to the Home of Hades can be seen, then, as a backward trip, in both space and time, to the original home of the Achaeans' ancestors.

The rites connected to the journey to Hades' home, told by a "shamanistic" character such as Circe, could be the meeting point between very ancient forms dating back even to Neolithic and Indo-European rites. The descent into "hell" is a typically shamanistic theme: Mircea Eliade writes that, according to Altaic shamans, it occurs by passing through "a hole which is the entrance of the other world, called *yer mesi* [earth's jaws]," while the Indian Tuanas "make a hole in the ground . . . and mime energetically the fight with the ghosts."[26] This is echoed by the attitude of Ulysses, who repeatedly menaces with his sword the ghosts gathered around the pit (*Odyssey* 10.536; 11.49, 95, 231). A modern counterpart of Ulysses is the old Eskimo woman who, as James Frazer reports, after throwing a ghost out of the house, "was whirling a big knife in front of the entrance to prevent him from returning."[27]

On his return from Hades, our hero sails upstream on the River Ocean, using "first the strength of the oars, then a beautiful breeze" (*Odyssey* 11.640), whereas on his journey to Hades, he had followed the "Ocean's current [*róon Okeanoîo*]" (*Odyssey* 11.21)—that is, the Gulf Stream's Arctic branch. In fact, in order to navigate from the White Sea to Circe's island, along the coast of northern Norway, we must sail upstream: yet another realistic detail within a tale replete with mythological references that when transposed to its real geographic context turns out to be much less imaginary than previously supposed. The location of Homer's Hades perfectly coordinates Homer's data, Norse tradition, the geographic and morphological features of this northern area, and the shamanistic tradition of Laplanders.

In conclusion, even the most "fantastic" of the *Odyssey*'s itineraries—Ulysses' journey from Circe's island to the land of the dead—finds a plausible location and precise correspondences once it is placed in northern Europe. It also provides us with what may be the last trace of remote prehistoric routes (probably considered mythical as long ago as Homer's time) to the lost ancestral homeland, at the "ends of the world" as understood at that time. It is a good omen that the key to its identification lies in the Styx, symbol of the supreme pledge of truth in the ancient world.

SONG OF THE SIRENS

After visiting the "Home of Hades," Ulysses' ship at last leaves Aeaea for Ithaca. Before passing Scylla and Charybdis, however, he must undergo another fearful test:

> *First you'll reach the Sirens, who*
> *bewitch all men, whoever reaches them.*
> *Whoever out of ignorance approaches and hears the Sirens'*
> *voice, never again meets his wife and children*
> *nor rejoice they at his returning home,*
> *but the Sirens bewitch him with their musical song,*
> *sitting in the meadow; there lies a big heap of bones*
> *of putrescent corpses, their skins wrinkling on them.*
> (*Odyssey* 12.39–46)

This tale—which through the ages has produced several interpretations, images, and elaborations—certainly derives from a sailors' legend. The northern location for these adventures now provides us with a rational explanation and a precise geographical reference for the Sirens: the shoals and shallows off the west coast of the Lofoten Islands, an area made even more dangerous by the fog and the size of the tides. Sailors could be deceived into believing land was at hand by the noise of the backwash (the Siren Song) on the half-hidden rocks, only to wreck on the reefs as they attempt to make "landfall."

Homer's "Siren Song" has a counterpart in Norse literature, in a passage that mentions the burial of the Swedish king Yngvarr on the seashore after his death in battle against the Estonians: "So the Eastern Sea takes pleasure in singing *Gymir's song* for the King of the Sviars."[28] Gymir is the name of a marine giant who, in these lines, represents the sea itself. His "song," which is exactly like that of the Sirens (apart from their malice), is the roar of the rollers that break incessantly at the foot of Yngvarr's tumulus.

Finally, we can note that the Greek word *seirênes* seems to echo the name of a Norwegian island called Sjernarøy as well as certain shoals off the coast between Egersund and Flekkefjord that are called Sire-grunnen (*grunnen* means "shoals"). We can also match this name with the root of the Greek term *xerón,* which appears in the dramatic account of Ulysses' landing on the coast of Scheria during the storm: "The big rollers noisily broke on the shoreline [*xerón epeíroio*] / frightfully roaring" (*Odyssey* 5.402–403).

It is thus very likely that some tales of the Sirens narrated by Bronze Age sailors referred to the tempting but deadly sound of waves crashing on rocks. In the taverns of that time, the content of these tales was probably far more fearful and raw than the features attributed to the Siren Song aimed at bewitching a high-ranking character like Ulysses. The poet, of course, has tailored these tales for his hero, and the images he uses seem to hint at initiation rites. The context of Ulysses' experience is somewhat similar to that of Oedipus, with dangerous, polymorphous creatures analogous to the Sphinx, symbol of the inexorable passing of Time that devours everything. Here is the deep sense of that lugubrious "big heap of bones / of putrescent corpses, their skins wrinkling on them." The words with which the Sirens lure Ulysses—"We know everything that happens on the fruitful earth" (*Odyssey* 12.191)—remind us of the solar myths in which the sun god "knows" everything because he can see everything. They also recall the biblical Adam and Eve and the temptation of the snake, yet another symbol analogous to the Sirens and the Sphinx.

It is interesting to note that in order to endure listening to the Sirens, Ulysses is tied not to the mast, as is usually represented, but to the "wedge of the mast [*histopéde*]" (*Odyssey* 12. 179)—that is, to "the beam where the mast was driven."[29] If we consider that the mast of the Achaean ships was removable—it was put on a trestle (*Iliad* 1.434) when the sail was stricken—we are presented with the rather peculiar scene of a man standing in the center of the ship, in the place of the mast. It is realistic, however: On that treacherous sea full of rocks and reefs, hoisting the sail would be very daring, which is no doubt why the mast is lowered. In fact, as can be seen in line 180, Ulysses' ship was using the oars.

The Sirens, as *margygr,* are creatures of Norse legend as well as Greek. As Chiesa Isnardi writes, a margygr was killed by the Christian king Olaf:

Her singing was so soft that the crews fell asleep, and then she overturned the ships, but sometimes she shouted so loudly as to drive people mad. She had a snake-like body and a horse-like head; her eyes were green and her body was hairy and grey like that of a seal.[30]

In another episode, the sea monster is described as "a fish or whale down to the waist, a woman up from the waist."[31]

SCYLLA AND CHARYBDIS

After his encounter with the Sirens, Ulysses' ship draws nearer to Scylla and Charybdis: "All at once / I saw surf and huge waves and heard a rumble; / the oars fell from the hands of my frightened men" (*Odyssey* 12.201–203). They were nearing "the two rocks, the one reaches the sky / with its sharp top [*oxeíei koryphêi*]; a dark cloud [*nephéle kyanée*] / shrouds it and never leaves it . . . / The rock is smooth [*pétre lís esti*] as if polished" (*Odyssey* 12.73–75, 79).

This is the description of Scylla's rock, which we can compare to the portion of the tale "A Descent into the Maelstrom" by Edgar Allan Poe in which he describes the precipice situated at the southernmost point of

Cape Lofoten, on the island of Moskenesøya, facing the area where the great Atlantic tide generates the Maelstrom:

> A sheer unobstructed precipice of black shining rock, some fifteen or sixteen hundred feet from the world of crags beneath us . . . The mountain upon whose top we sit is Helseggen, the Cloudy . . . I looked dizzily, and beheld a wide expanse of ocean . . . A panorama more deplorably desolate no human imagination can conceive. To the right and left, as far as the eye could reach, there lay out-stretched, like ramparts of the world, lines of horribly black and beetling cliffs, whose character of gloom was but the more forcibly illustrated by the surf which reared high up against it its white and ghastly crest, howling and shrieking for ever.[32]

This sinister crag of Helseggen, "the Cloudy," perfectly matches Homer's description of Scylla's threatening rock, which was extremely tall, falling in a sheer drop to the sea, and always covered by that "dark cloud." Furthermore, the word Scylla, Skýlle in Greek, can be heard in the Norwegian term *skjell*—that is, "shell"—related to Old Norse *skel*.

Edgar Allan Poe continues to describe the whirlpool under the crag, the fearsome Maelstrom:

> When it is flood, the stream runs up the country between Lofoden and Moskoe with a boisterous rapidity; but the roar of its impetuous ebb to the sea is scarce equalled by the loudest and most dreadful cataracts, the noise being heard several leagues off; and the vortices or pits are of such an extent and depth, that if a ship comes within its attraction, it is inevitably absorbed and carried down to the bottom, and there beat the pieces against the rocks.[33]

It is remarkable that Poe's words "inevitably absorbed" echo those that Homer repeatedly uses: "Charybdis absorbs [*anarroibdeî*] the dark waters; / three times a day she spews them, three times absorbs them / terribly; may you not happen to be there when she absorbs!" (*Odyssey* 12.104–106); and, "when she absorbed the salt water of the sea / she appeared to be all upset inside; the rock around / rumbled terribly; at the bottom the ground appeared, / dark for the sand" (*Odyssey* 12.240–43). According to these lines, the sea is not very deep, which squares perfectly with the Maelstrom area. The morphology of the Strait of Messina in the Mediterranean, however, the area there typically identified with the location of Charybdis, is completely different: Aside from the fact that the water is deep there, neither the rock that "reaches the sky," with its "dark cloud" that "never leaves it," nor the lower rock "within bow-shot" exists there.

Also of note is that in Olaus Magnus's *Sea Chart*, which goes back to the sixteenth century, the Maelstrom is called (in Latin) *"horrenda"* (horrifying) Charybdis. What is more, the early-eighteenth-century Norwegian writer Jonas Ramus located Scylla and Charybdis near the Maelstrom.

ISLAND OF THE SUN GOD

As soon as we fled the rocks, the terrible Charybdis
and Scylla, we immediately [autík'épeita] reached the wonderful
*   god's island.*
Here there were the fine wide-foreheaded cows
and the many fat sheep of the Hyperion Sun. (Odyssey 12.260–63)

These lines help us to identify Thrinacia, the mythical island of the sun god. The area where the tide triggers the Maelstrom is bounded to the south by the island of Mosken (fig. 4.2), which lies in the path of Ulysses' return route, given that it was the south wind that blew Ulysses' ship back toward Charybdis after he left the island of Thrinacia (*Odyssey* 12.427–28). What is more, the meaning of Thrinacia comes from the term *thrínax*, meaning "with three points"[34] and, as we have learned, Mosken is shaped like a three-cornered hat.

On Thrinacia, "many / of the cattle and the fat sheep of the Sun graze, / seven herds of cows and as many fine flocks of sheep, / fifty to each herd" (*Odyssey* 12.127–30). These animals are connected with the terrible taboo that both the seer Tiresias and the sorceress Circe solemnly utter:

If you do not touch them, if you care about homecoming,
you will get to reach Ithaca, although suffering misfortunes;
but if you steal them, then I foretell the ruin
of your ship and your companions.
*   (Odyssey 11.110–13, 12.137–40)*

These cattle are very strange, for "Births never occur between them / nor die they" (*Odyssey* 12.130–31). This type of language indicates that the poet is speaking metaphorically, but what could be the hidden meaning of "the cattle . . . of the Sun"?

B. G. Tilak, whom we have already mentioned with reference to the "revolving dawns," supplies us with the key to this mystery. After an extremely thorough analysis of the ancient sacred Indian hymns, which includes a study of Greek mythology, he identifies the 350 puzzling cows with the days of the year. This relationship, which we shall find again later in the *Homeric Hymn to Hermes,* in which the cows of the sun god Apollo are mentioned (chapter 13, page 288), is hidden in two lines at the beginning of the *Odyssey:* "They ate the *cows* of the Hyperion Sun / and he destroyed the *day* of their homecoming" (*Odyssey* 1.8–9), as well as in the angry words the sun god himself utters after the death of his cows:

> *O Father Zeus and all of you blessed immortal gods,*
> *punish the companions of Laertiades Odysseus,**
> *who arrogantly killed my cows, in which*
> *I delighted when I was rising into the starry sky*
> *and then returned down to earth again!* (*Odyssey* 12.377–81)

These lines clearly outline the sun's progressive rising into the vault of heaven, day after day, until the arrival of the summer solstice, when it begins its slow descent. The sun follows a spiral path, portrayed in many decorations dating back to the Bronze Age, a phenomenon that the high latitude accentuates. Mosken is situated above the Arctic Circle and the words attributed to the sun god—"If they do not pay the fair penalty for my cows / I will go down to Hades and give my light to the dead men" (*Odyssey* 12.382–83)—could reflect the fear that the sun might never appear again after its disappearance during the solstice night.

The fact that Thrinacia, the "three-pointed" island, was dedicated to the sun god reminds us that certain solar cults in Egypt, as in India and

---

*Ulysses' name appears in the Homeric poems as Odysseús or Odyseús. The *Odyssey* states that it derives from the word *odyssámenos,* meaning "he who hates," referring to his grandfather Autolycus (*Odyssey* 14.407–409). It is also found as Olysseus and similar forms in Corinth, Athens, and Boeotia, at least up until the sixth or seventh century B.C.E. Philologists believe that this name could have been of pre-Greek origin,[35] perhaps a variant of Ulysses. As regards examples of the varying use of *d* and *l* in the name, such variance can be found in the Sicilian *addumari,* meaning "to light," which may be a corrupted form of the French *allumer,* and in the Greek *dákryon,* that is, "tear," which is similar to the Latin *lacrima.*

elsewhere, were based on "trinities" that may have expressed the three-fold appearance of the sun, which is *red* when rising, *white* at the zenith, and *black* during eclipses and by night. The link between sun worship and Thrinacia—which accords with its high latitude, where the phenomena of the annual solar cycle are extremely intensified—is stressed by the names of its shepherdesses, two nymphs who are children of "the Hyperion Sun" (*Odyssey* 12.132–33): Lampetie (shining) and Phaethusa (bright), which are very similar to Lampus and Phaethon, "the two horses that carry Dawn" (*Odyssey* 23.246). Tellingly, these two horses are found in Bronze Age engravings in Scandinavia and are mentioned in the *Poetic Edda*: "Skinfaxi is the horse which brings the shining / day to men. . . . His mane is always shining." Another remarkable analogy is found in an episode of the *Gesta Danorum*, derived, as we have learned, from a Norse saga, in which are mentioned the names of two swords, Liusingus and Hvitingus (Lysingr and Hvitíngr in Norse), "the Shining" and "the White."[36] The meaning of the names of these ancestral weapons forged by mysterious smiths are virtually the same as the Homeric Lampetie and Phaethusa. There is also a passage from the *Skáldskaparmál* (of the *Younger Edda*) that shows a remarkable relationship between the light and the swords of the gods: "At nightfall, when it was time to drink, Odin had swords brought into the hall: they shone so much that other lights were not necessary when drink was offered."[37]

But what of the Hyperion Sun—that is, the father of the two nymphs living in Thrinacia? The term *hyperion* translates as "over-going,"[38] *hypér* being a Greek adverb meaning "over" or "above" and *ión* being a participial form of the verb *iénai,* "to go." Given the location of Thrinacia above the Artic Circle, it follows that the Hyperion Sun very likely refers to the phenomenon of the midnight sun, which actually remains permanently *above* the horizon during the Arctic summer. This assumption is supported by the fact that all of the references to the Hyperion Sun in Homer's poems—two in the *Iliad* and seven in the *Odyssey*—are in settings that, like Thrinacia, are clearly in northernmost Europe. The Hyperion Sun, it seems, is thus a concept strictly linked with the farthest north.

Ulysses and his companions reach Thrinacia after they escape Charybdis, but they cannot leave the island because "for a whole month the south wind was continuously blowing and no other / wind rose but the south and east winds" (*Odyssey* 12.325–26). This too fits perfectly with the northern geography we have been establishing: The south and east winds blow in the opposite direction from their return home. The sailors' stalemate was resolved when the south wind "stopped raging violently; / we immediately boarded and sailed on the broad sea" (*Odyssey* 12.400–401).

AFTER THE WRECK

At this point the gods begin their punishment for the misdeed Ulysses' companions committed on Thrinacia, for after running out of food, they capture and devour the "untouchable" cows. A sudden storm with terrible winds takes down the mast of their ship, then

> *Zeus thundered and threw a lightning at the ship at the same time:*
> *the whole ship, struck by Zeus' lightning, spun*
> *and was filled with sulphur smoke; my companions were hurled*
>   *from the ship*
> *. . . The god took away their homecoming!*
>   (*Odyssey* 12.415–17, 419)

Ulysses is thus left alone on the wreck: "All at once the West Wind stopped raging violently, / but the South Wind rose immediately, distressing my heart, / since I was returning to the dreadful Charybdis" (*Odyssey* 12.426–28). The interplay of these winds is consistent with the geographic layout of this northern region: The west wind finally allows the ship to set sail from Mosken toward the Norwegian coast, but, after lightning strikes the vessel, the south wind drives it back again toward the strait between Mosken and Lofoten, where the Maelstrom awaits.

The whirlpool finally sucks down the ship:

> *She was absorbing the sea salt water,*
> *but I stretched up toward a big wild fig-tree,*
> *which I clung to like a bat . . .*
> *I clung all the time until she spewed up*
> *mast and keel again; I was longing for them and they eventually*
> *arrived! At the time when the man who settles*
> *many quarrels between fierce opponents leaves the square for dinner,*
> *then my timbers emerged from Charybdis.*
>   (*Odyssey* 12.431–33, 437–41)

The image that Ulysses uses in this final metaphor—that of the judge heading home for dinner after settling "fierce" disputes—is a welcome touch of humor after the climax of the dramatic action. The details of the emergence of the remains of his ship from Charybdis are based on actual facts of the action of such a whirlpool: As Poe tells us in his "A Descent into the Maelstrom," "when the water relaxes, the fragments thereof are thrown up again."

As regards the providential fig tree *(erineón)* that allows Ulysses to survive the whirlpool, Professor Giacomo Tripodi, a botanist at Messina University, claims:

> Although Sicily is rich in figs, the coast off Charybdis is sandy and the beach is very broad, thus reaching fig-trees from the sea is impossible. On the other hand, the rocks in the Maelstrom area are very rich in seaweed *(phykia)* belonging to the species *Ascophyllum nodosum* that lives where it is wetted by the tides, waves, and spray. These are able to support the weight of a man; their size is almost two feet. Therefore, these lines of verse could refer to the fact that Ulysses clung to this seaweed, which thrives on North Atlantic rocks, not in the warm Mediterranean sea.[39]

Tripodi also notes that the term *erineón,* which is usually translated as "fig tree," probably originates from the adjective *eríneos,* meaning "woolly," deriving from the word *érion,* "wool" (*Iliad* 12.434, *Odyssey* 4.124). "Woolly" is an accurate adjective to describe *Ascophyllum,* which covers the surface of the northern rocks like a fleece.

Having survived the whirlpool, Ulysses is driven toward the center of the Atlantic on the wreck of his ship: "I drifted for nine days, at the tenth night / the gods let me approach the island of Ogygia" (*Odyssey* 12.447–48). At the end of his wanderings far and wide across the Norwegian Sea, Ulysses lands on Calypso's island, in the middle of the ocean, "five days' sail from Britain." If Plutarch has given us the clue to Homeric geography, Homer's words corroborate Plutarch's daring statement, the clue that set us on our journey.

COMPLETING THE CIRCLE

In order to return to Ithaca, Ulysses must overcome yet another difficult test: the interminable crossing by raft from Ogygia to Scheria, which ends with his troubled arrival on the Phaeacian land. We have verified that the description in the *Odyssey* corresponds perfectly to the geographical reality of the Norwegian coast, with its "shadowy mountains," its sheer coast "like a shield" near Bergen, its rocks, its steep coastline that becomes more gradual toward the south, and so on. From these details, we get the distinct impression that the poet is familiar with the Phaeacian world and that he must have known Ulysses' landing place particularly well. As we have seen, this landing place corresponds to the mouth of the Figgjo, the first river lying to the south of the fjords in the area of Klepp—interestingly, one of the richest in Bronze Age remains in the whole of Norway.

Along the quiet byroads of the area of Sola, there are a number of Bronze Age tumuli and some rupestrian (rock) engravings that often portray pictures of ships. Beside the road to Sele is a beach where the Figgjo flows into the sea. The river here is a small stream about thirty feet wide and not very deep The area behind its mouth is slightly raised and covered with vegetation and trees. Although it is highly unlikely that the Bronze Age coastline has remained unaltered all these years, we may imagine that it is here that beautiful Nausicaa washes her clothes in the river, eats, and begins playing ball with her maids (*Odyssey* 6.100) shortly before Ulysses appears from behind a bush. He had managed to land in mouth of the river the day before, after his long, lonely, troubled crossing by raft. At once he looked around for some place to lie down and rest and decided that the best solution was to "climb up the hillock [*es klitýn*] into the dark wood" (*Odyssey* 5.470): "[H]e found it close to the water, / in a raised area, and he crept under a twofold bush" (*Odyssey* 5.475–76), where he finally managed to sleep until the cries of the maids awaken him the following day.

From this examination of the wanderings narrated in the *Odyssey,* we can see that Ulysses' adventures represent the sole recollection of the sea routes the fearless Bronze Age sailors followed—being favored by a climate far milder than today's—from Norway to the Shetland Islands, from the Lofoten to the Faeroes, and maybe even farther, as we shall soon see.

CHAPTER 5

ULYSSES AND NORTHERN MYTHOLOGY

Some people believe that Ulysses too, in his long and fabulous wanderings, arrived at this Ocean and visited the lands of Germany *(in hunc Oceanum delatum adisse Germaniae terras).*[1]

We may now read this passage from Tacitus in a new light. Here he uses the common name Germania to indicate all the regions of northern Europe up to the Baltic and Scandinavia. Even if Tacitus belongs to a time halfway between the events Homer narrates and the present day, his reference to a northern Ulysses, which appears to be an ancient recollection rather than merely a literary hypothesis, tallies with what his contemporary Plutarch says regarding the North Atlantic position of the island of Ogygia. In short, it seems that both historians are linked by an uninterrupted tradition that began in the early Bronze Age and spanned millennia. It is likely that these tales reached Rome in the first century C.E., owing to the expeditions the Romans undertook in Great Britain at that time. In fact, Tacitus's father-in-law, Iulius Agricola, was governor of Britain for seven years, beginning in 77 C.E. Of course, we can continue to factor in details to support our conclusion of a northern origin for these epics, such as the fact that the *Odyssey* calls Ulysses "fair-haired [*xanthás tríchas*]" (*Odyssey* 13.399, 431) and that he is traditionally portrayed with a cone-shaped cap that is identical to the traditional Viking cap.

Additional support for our contention that Homer's Achaeans were a northern European people before they moved south to start the great Mycenaean culture of Greece comes from the realm of mythology. A comparison of the myths of that southern culture and those of the north reveals many similarities between the world and the character of Ulysses and those of northern mythical heroes.

THE CHARACTER OF ULYSSES IN MYTH

Let us first turn our attention to the *Poetic Edda,* the famous collection of mythological Old Norse poems written in the twelfth century. Its name is believed to be derived from the word *ódhr,* meaning "song" (perhaps connected to the Greek term *aoidé*). Here we meet the heroic figure of the warrior and archer Ull, who must have been a very important character in the distant past, judging by the recurrent use of his name in the toponymy of Sweden, Norway, and Denmark. "By the ring of Ull" were also the words of a solemn oath. It is a rather curious coincidence that the Norse Ull was the son of Sif and that Ulysses was called "the son of Sisyphus" by some Greek authors, including Euripides in his *Iphigenia in Aulis.* We also note that the *Grimnismal*—one of the most ancient poems in the *Edda*—mentions Ull's residence: "Ydalir is the name of the place / where Ull built his home."[2] According to the *Odyssey,* Ulysses also built his own home; there are a number of occasions in the poem when Ulysses is described as "he who has home in Ithaca [*Ithákei éni oikí'échonta*]" (*Odyssey* 4.555, 9.505, 9.531).

The figure of Ull the archer, found also in the *Younger Edda,*[3] matches the character of Ulysses very well. In the *Odyssey,* Ulysses demonstrates his skill in archery both in the famous competition and in the subsequent massacre of Penelope's suitors. Even before these events, he boasts to the Phaeacians of his ability as an archer: "I can handle the polished bow well; / . . . only Philoctetes beat me with the bow / in the Trojan country" (*Odyssey* 8.215, 219–20). Book 10 of the *Iliad* corroborates this when Ulysses, with Diomedes, arms himself with "his bow and quiver" to reconnoiter the enemy camp.

THE *GESTA DANORUM*

In order to look more closely at the parallels between the Homeric epics and Norse myth, we next turn to a crucial text known as the *Gesta Danorum* (The Feats of the Danes), a monumental literary work written in Latin by Saxo Grammaticus, a learned Danish scholar who lived in the second half of the twelfth century. This work is well known as

Shakespeare's inspiration for the character of Hamlet. In the *Gesta,* Saxo reconstructs his people's history and legends that had been interwoven with those of other northern peoples starting from a very remote period. Naturally, he includes numerous facts and details that can also be found in Norse poetry. In the *Gesta* we can recognize many of the myths and motifs found in Greek mythology and the work of Homer, but these often cannot be traced back to classical—that is, ancient Greek or Roman—models. The roots of the myths and motifs collected by Saxo in the *Gesta* usually lie in Norse and especially Icelandic literature.

Despite the thousands of years separating the Homeric poems and the *Gesta,* Saxo's work is pervaded by an atmosphere that surprisingly recalls Homer. For instance, the words of praise sealing Hamlet's biography at the end of Book 3 of the *Gesta* remind us of Ulysses: "What a strong man, worthy of eternal glory! By feigning foolishness, with great sagacity, he concealed perfectly his intelligence . . . Since he cleverly defended himself and courageously avenged his father, one is undecided whether he is worthier as a model of strength or as an example of sagacity."[4]

The characteristic of sagacity, cleverness, or astuteness is extremely appreciated in the *Gesta,* where it often plays a crucial role in solving conflicts and sieges, such as the siege of London undertaken by King Frothon of Denmark: "The strength of its walls was preventing him from storming it, therefore he resorted to astuteness to reach his aim . . ."[5] Another example is the very unusual trick that allows the Danes to defeat Andvanus, king of Hellespont, "who had barricaded himself in the city of Duna, behind impregnable fortifications and defense stonework."[6] In order to storm these bulwarks, the Danes place lighted fuses under the wings of the birds that nest there.

This reference to Hellespont and to the "Hellespontians," which is extremely pertinent to our theory regarding the northern origins of the Mycenaeans, is not the only one we come across in the *Gesta Danorum.* Saxo portrays the Hellespontians as being an eastern Baltic—*not* Mediterranean—people, and as having frequent contact with the Danes, especially in the form of armed conflicts. Their city Duna probably corresponds to today's Daugavpils, lying along the course of the western Dvina in Latvia. These rather strange people, whose northern origin puzzles scholars, can be connected to the "Broad Hellespont," where, as Homer states, lay Troy. As we shall verify in chapter 6, this area is identifiable with the Gulf of Finland rather than the narrow Dardanelles. We can see from the *Gesta* that this ancient name dating back to the Bronze Age persisted up to Saxo's time. When the Achaeans moved to the south of Europe, they used the same name for the sea that seemed to represent the northern Hellespont's southern geographic counterpart, even if it was anything but "broad"! As we shall see in the sequence of the Catalog of Ships, the Homeric Hellas, whose name is obviously linked to Hellespont, corresponds to today's Estonia, on the shores of the Gulf of Finland, while in the Greek world Hellas and Hellespont are not adjacent. Yet again, two mysteries—in this case, Saxo's "northern Hellespont" and Homer's "broad Hellespont"—are immediately solved once they are associated.

There are other telling geographical clues in Saxo's work. He identifies an area in the eastern Baltic called Curetia (now Kurland, a district of Latvia), whose inhabitants were called Curetes. It seems more than natural to associate them with the Homeric Curetes (*Iliad* 9.529–89), who are also found in Greek mythology, though they cannot be located in the Greek world geographically.

Themes found in the *Gesta* and Homer's work also echo one another. There is the very familiar theme in the *Gesta* of a prince abducting a queen with all her riches, which, of course, results in war. While it seems as though Saxo is referring to Helen and Paris, he is instead telling the story of Snion, the son of the king of Denmark, who abducted the beautiful queen of Sweden (once again using "astuteness"):

> He managed to take the Queen aboard—who had left her palace on the pretext of bathing—with all her husband's riches. In consequence of this, a war broke out between the King of Sweden and Snion . . . since the former wanted to take back his legitimate wife, and the latter wanted to keep the woman he had unlawfully got.[7]

In the *Gesta Danorum* (which is set not only in the Baltic Sea, but also in both the North Sea and the Norwegian Sea), the sea itself is of primary importance, just as it is in Homer's poetry. The description of the great naval battle of Brávellir, fought between the Danes and the Swedes in the waters of the Sound (the strait between the island of Zealand and southern Sweden), offers a significant parallel to Homer's work, preceded as it is by the list of fighters who constitute the two opposing fleets, as well as their places of origin,[8] very like the Catalog of Ships in the *Iliad*. The list makes it clear that those ancient seafaring peoples managed to round up an astonishing number of ships when necessary: Apart from the battle of Brávellir, in which one of the two fleets was made up of a total of twenty-five hundred ships, Saxo reports fleets of nine hundred,[9] seventeen hundred,[10] and even three thousand ships.[11] These numbers make Homer's catalog numbers very credible and confirm the feasibility of gathering the twelve hundred ships the Achaeans used in the expedition against Troy. Tacitus confirms that the Suions (or Svions, who correspond to today's Swedes) "stand out, apart from men and weapons, also for their fleets" *(praeter viros armaque classibus valent)*.[12]

Another curious detail in the *Gesta* is that the Danes make use of "bronze horses fitted with wheels."[13] According to the *Gesta,* these bronze horses are thrown at enemy troops with the aim of breaking their lines, and although this is not exactly the same way in which the famous wooden horse was employed in the battle with Troy, it is nonetheless evocative of that episode in the Trojan War. Added to this is the fact that the Vikings also resort to trickster devices to conquer cities. For example, they manage to enter the city of Luni, near the mouth of the Magra River in northwest Italy, by feigning the conversion and the subsequent death of their leader. This imitator of Ulysses, after being taken with much ceremony to the church for his funeral, jumps out of the bier (which Pörtner calls "the coffin of Troy"!) with his sword. He and his followers subsequently slaughter the congregation, lay waste to and sack the town, and depart with their fleet, which awaits them on the shore.

Disguises and Banquets

Just as in the *Odyssey,* in which Ulysses disguises himself upon returning to Ithaca, there are many cases in the *Gesta Danorum,* often on the occasion of banquets, when kings or princes disguise themselves as servants or old beggars in order to fool their enemies. For example, Hiarnon, a runaway king who plots to use trickery to take revenge on his rival, manages to be admitted to the court by disguising himself as a salt-refining slave, but a scar on his body reveals his identity.[14] This reminds us of Ulysses, whose scar causes him to be recognized by his old nursemaid (*Odyssey* 19.467–68). Another character in the *Gesta,* Olon, manages to free his father's palace from a usurper by arriving there "disguising himself as a weak old man."[15] And then there is Grep, who, after his sweetheart refuses him, takes revenge by gathering all her suitors at a banquet and killing them.[16] Similarly, King Haldan attends a wedding banquet incognito, where "he cancelled every sign of regal dignity, by horribly masquerading" and then killed the bridegroom. Thus, Saxo concludes, "he transformed the wedding into a funeral."[17]

Apart from the massacre of the suitors that Ulysses carries out at the end of the banquet in Ithaca, these tales remind us of Agamemnon's tragic fate after his return from Troy:

> *Aegisthus immediately plotted a fraudulent plan.*
> *He chose twenty strong men in the city,*
> *laid an ambush and prepared a banquet elsewhere.*
> *Then he went to invite King Agamemnon*
> *with horses and chariots, scheming an infamy.*
> *This way he led him to death and killed him*
> *at the banquet, as one butchers an ox at the manger.*
> (Odyssey 4.529–35)

Banquets, however, were not always linked to such cruel events. They normally represented the initial stage of receiving a guest. Usually, the reason for the visit was discussed after the festivities. Saxo is keen to underline that "in ancient times this was the way in which guests were received,"[18] which fits perfectly with the custom represented in the Homeric poems. This is how Nestor behaves toward Telemachus after the latter arrives at Pylos:

> *After they ate and drank,*
> *the old charioteer Nestor began to speak:*
> *Now it is the right time to ask and inquire*
> *about our guests, after they enjoyed food.*
> *Oh foreigners, who are you?* (Odyssey 3.67–71)

Another custom existed that was much less inspired by *bon ton* but, alas, was rather frequent. This consisted of ridiculing a guest by throwing the banquet leftovers or other objects at him. Saxo narrates: "During the party the champions ran wild and started to throw bones and cartilages at someone."[19] Sometimes this habit went seriously amiss, as with the archbishop Elphegus in the year 1012: During a rather lively party, he fell victim to drunken Vikings who enjoyed pelting him with oxen skulls. This story reminds us of Ctesippus's act of bravado narrated in the *Odyssey*. During the last banquet before the massacre, this suitor of Penelope "threw an ox-hoof with his strong hand, / taking it out from a basket; Ulysses avoided it / by slightly bowing his head, and smiled scornfully / in his mind" (*Odyssey* 20.299–302). Ctesippus pays dearly for his action, for soon after he is ingloriously killed by Philoetius the cowherd, who, after hitting him, reminds him of the blameworthy act he has committed.

Eloquent Heroes and Gods

Another point of contact between the northern world as depicted by both Saxo and Homer is the high esteem in which both authors hold poetic and musical art and achievement. The *Gesta* often expresses appreciation for poetry, emphasizing the fact that the bards were particularly honored. Moreover, heroes such as young Otherus, who is extremely strong and bold, excel in playing string instruments.[20] Similarly, the *Odyssey* states that "for all men on earth, the poets / are worthy of honor and respect, since the Muse / taught them her songs; she loves the guild of the poets" (*Odyssey* 8.479–81). Likewise, the *Iliad* portrays Achilles in a moment of idleness: "They caught him taking delight in a tuneful cithara . . ." (*Iliad* 9.186). We can consider that *guitar* derives from the Greek *kíthara*.

Ancient northern people thought as highly of oratory as did those in the Greek world. Indeed, there was a particular type of tale, known as *tháttr*, centered on the arrival of a foreigner at the Norwegian court and the oratory performances he was bound to carry out. Similarly, the excellent speeches Ulysses makes at the court of Alcinous earn him not only the benevolence of the king and many precious gifts, but also assistance on his way back to Ithaca.

Several important characters mentioned in the *Gesta* excel in the art of public speaking. Two such examples, Ericus and Starcatherus, are also extremely skilled in punning and double meanings, a talent with which Hamlet himself was endowed. Ericus says of himself: "My distinctive feature is my eloquent language . . . I have no other aim than gaining knowledge and I have studied different customs by traveling through many countries."[21] According to what Ludovica Koch, professor of Scandinavian philology at the University of Rome, claims in her introduction to the Italian edition of the *Gesta Danorum*, Ericus represents "the perfect incarnation of the Viking mentality, which is at the same time suspicious and daring and is endowed with an Odinic type of wisdom that is practical, curious, versatile, pragmatic and even unscrupulous, fundamentally based on a supreme control of language."[22] These are all characteristics of Ulysses, whom Homer introduces in the beginning of the *Odyssey* as "the resourceful man . . . / who saw the cities of many people and knew their minds" (*Odyssey* 1.1–3). Besides outsmarting the Cyclops with the famous pun about his name, Ulysses often shows off his eloquence in the *Iliad*, in which it is said that his words fall like "flakes of snow in the winter" (*Iliad* 3.222).

Some scholars underline a number of significant similarities between the figure of Ulysses and that of Odin, who, in Norse mythology, is not only a great warrior but also exceptionally astute with a refined eloquence. For example, chapter 6 of the *Ynglingar Saga* praises his talents. Saxo also introduces a character called Ollerus (corresponding to Ull) who acts as Odin's alter ego during the latter's period of exile, even going so far as to adopt his name.[23] Further on in the tale, the writer refers to Ollerus as being a gifted sailor: A spell is cast upon him that enables him to cross the sea on a bone[24]—a detail that rounds out the collection of similarities between Ull and Ulysses on the one hand and between Ulysses and Odin on the other.

Many of Ulysses' adventures also parallel those of Hadingus, a legendary Danish king and great-grandson of the mythical progenitor Dan, whose exploits are narrated in the first book of the *Gesta Danorum*. This great warrior resorts to a stratagem to conquer a city, is seduced by a sorceress skilled at shapeshifting, is recognized by a woman because of a scar in the calf, kills a sea monster and is thus persecuted by the gods (Ulysses was persecuted by Poseidon, the sea god, because he had blinded his son, Polyphemus), and visits Hell. He is also fond of the sea and ships—in fact, his passion is "to test the waves with the oars, / to enjoy the fruits of the sacks, / to pursue other people's money, / to long for profits wrung out of the sea."[25] Moreover, Odin gives advice and helps him, exactly as the goddess Athene does for Ulysses. There are other characteristics of Odin and Athene that make them curiously alike: their wisdom, their connection with warfare, their spear, their birds (the rook and the little owl, respectively), and even their names (Odin can be written Othin, which is very similar to Athene).

Blood and Honor

The character of King Haldan brings us to another theme found in both the *Gesta Danorum* and Greek mythology: that of family feuds. Haldan's father, Harald, has been murdered by order of his own brother Frothon, with whom he alternated sea and land rule every year. The evil uncle then tries to do away with his two nephews, who manage to flee. Once grown, they return to seek revenge and reconquer their kingdom.[26] Here Saxo seems inspired by an ancient Norse poem called the *Hrolfssaga Kraka*. The parallels between this story and the tragic events of the Atreids, Agamemnon and Menelaus, is astonishing: The father of Agamemnon and Menelaus, Atreus, is slain by his brother, Thyestes, who tries to kill the sons as well. They, however, manage to flee and later return to avenge their father's death.

Interestingly, the yearly alternating of rule by the brothers Harold and Frothon reminds us of another famous mythical pair, Eteocles and Polynices. Even the way in which these later two kill each other—at the end of a tragic duel—seems echoed in the *Gesta:* "His sacrilegious sons dared to fight a duel using cruel weapons which killed both of them . . . they were struck by mortal misfortune because of their thirst for power . . . they went down together to see the Styx . . ."[27] We should not be misled by this seemingly "classical" (implying ancient Greek or Roman) reference to the Styx, for here Saxo is inspired by a Norse poem called *Asmundar Saga Kappabana.* (It would be tempting to imagine that *Asmundar Saga Kappabana,* in turn, derives from some tradition going back as far as the lost *Thebaid,* which some scholars believe was created by Homer.) In her introduction to the *Gesta dei re e degli eroi danesi,* Ludovica Koch underlines that this episode "echoes an ancient Germanic heroic theme—that is, the conflict between the voice of blood and sense of honor, which ends with a tragic encounter between relatives."[28] The same theme inspires many events in Greek mythology.

Along with the action itself, there are details regarding objects in the *Gesta* that echo those in Homer's work: The shield Haldan uses in his duel "is decorated with different engravings in its shining surface and encircled by panels with admirable figures."[29] Saxo also dedicates an entire chapter to describing those images that "a skilled craftsman had represented with extremely refined art on Hamlet's battle shield, imitating things with figures and describing events with pictures."[30] In this case too, Koch writes that the inspiration comes not from a classical Greek model but "from the most ancient skaldic genre: 'the description of the shield' Bragi Boddason excellently inaugurated in his *Ragnarsdrápa.*"[31] All of this corresponds to the shield that Hephaestus, the smith god, creates for Achilles, on which "he made many decorations with his wise mind" (*Iliad* 18.482). Likewise, Agamemnon's shield is

> . . . *wonderfully decorated*
> *and fine; there were around ten rings of bronze,*
> *inside twenty white bosses of tin,*
> *and one of dark enamel was in the center.*
> *A terrifying Gorgon adorned it,*
> *gazing grimly, together with Terror and Rout.* (*Iliad* 11.32–37)

Decoding Prophecies

Other parallels between the *Odyssey* specifically and the *Gesta Dano-rum* are related to prophecy. Part of the prediction of Ulysses' destiny uttered by the blind prophet Tiresias is:

> *You will set off, taking a well-cut oar;*
> *. . . when another wayfarer who meets you*
> *tells you that you are carrying a winnowing fan on your strong*
> *   shoulder,*
> *then stick your well-cut oar into the ground*
> *. . . and return home.* (*Odyssey* 11.121, 127–29, 132)

In the *Gesta*, Saxo tells us regarding Hamlet: "While they were walking along the beach they ran into the rudder of a wrecked ship. Then his companions stated that it was a knife of extraordinary size and he said: 'this would be suitable for slicing an enormous ham,' obviously referring to the sea, whose immensity was in proportion to the size of the rudder."[32]

Both of these pieces employ the same kind of poetic play. These objects, meant for *sea* use—the oar reverses the waves and the rudder cuts through the sea—are described in terms of *land* metaphors—that is, the shovel used for winnowing wheat and the knife for slicing ham. This is the typical mechanism of a kind of metaphor known as a *kenning*, a poetic device used very commonly in Norse poetry and, as we see here, in Homer's work. The above episode in the *Gesta* contains another kenning introduced by Hamlet: "the sand which is called flour since it is milled by the frothy stormy sea." It is a metaphor Saxo borrowed from the tenth-century Icelandic skald Snaebjorn. In another example, the phrase "the horse of the waves" is used to indicate a ship (*vágmarr*, from *vágr*, meaning "wave," and *mar*, meaning "steed") and is identical to the Greek expression "sea horses [*halós híppoi*]" (*Odyssey* 4.780) used by Penelope to describe ships. Just after the reference to the winnowing fan, the *Odyssey* includes another similar kenning—"the well-cut oars which are the wings of the ships" (*Odyssey* 11.125).

It is the direct comparison of Norse mythology in the *Gesta* and the works of Homer as well as the identification of the kenning mechanism in Homer's poetry that allow us to decode Tiresias's prediction, with its reference to both the "oar" and the "winnowing fan."

The parallels between Greek mythology and Norse literature, which both incorporate many themes on the sea and sailing, could also help to interpret a rather obscure passage by Hesiod. This ancient Greek poet, who narrates the myth of the creation marked by a sequence of human races (each associated with a particular metal—gold, silver, bronze, and iron), states that the third race, linked with bronze, was "mighty, terrible" and warlike. These men were "children of the ashes" who "came from the ashes" *(ek meliân)*.[33] What does this expression mean? The eleventh-century historian Adam of Bremen unintentionally supplies us with a plausible explanation: He calls the Vikings "Ascomans"—that is, "ash men (*esche* means "ash tree"), because, as the German scholar Rudolf Pörtner tells us, "they preferred this kind of wood for their boats."[34] Moreover, Norse mythology holds that humankind is descended from Ask, an ash that was changed into a man. In light of what we discover here about the origins of the Bronze Age, there is a remarkable parallel between the medieval northern Ascomans and "the children of the ashes," those terrible Bronze Age warriors mentioned by Hesiod.

THE *KALEVALA*

My brother's old dog, which I fed as a child and trained as a young girl, will mournfully bark behind the manure heap, inside the cold winter pens; he will surely recognize me as the daughter of the house.

These lines of verse are taken from Rune 24 of the *Kalevala*, Finland's national epos. In the nineteenth century, Elias Lönnrot arranged the large number of miscellaneous traditional poems he himself had collected— mainly in the region of Karelia—into fifty runes, or cantos. Rune 24 tells of a married woman who returns to her paternal house after many years and expects her old dog to recognize her. This, of course, recalls this famous scene from the *Odyssey:*

A dog was lying there who pricked up his muzzle and ears,
Argus, the dog of firm Ulysses, who once
himself had fed him . . .
but now, after his owner's departure, he lay neglected
on a manure heap of mules and cattle . . .
There Argus the dog lay full of ticks,
but when he felt Ulysses coming near,
he wagged his tail and dropped his ears.
      (*Odyssey* 17.291–93, 296–97, 300–302)

This similarity could be merely accidental, especially given that the *Odyssey* frequently mentions dogs, including the episode when Telemachus goes to the public assembly convened in Ithaca and two "fast dogs followed him" (*Odyssey* 2.11) and the detail of the dogs guarding Eumaeus's hut. But the *Kalevala,* too, often includes dogs: Musti the dog, for example, is mentioned on a number of occasions.

Yet there are other parallels between Homer's works and the *Kalevala.* We learn in the *Odyssey* that young Ulysses was wounded in the knee by a wild boar when he was hunting with his grandfather Autolycus: "Autolycus's dear sons immediately took care of him, / they skillfully bandaged the wound of the noble / godlike Ulysses and with a magic song stanched / the dark blood" (*Odyssey* 19.455–58). The "magic song," (*epaoidé* in Greek, corresponding to the Norse *galdr*) used to stanch bleeding is also found in Rune 8 of the *Kalevala:*

O blood, stem your flow! . . . Keep still as a wall, remain motionless as a hedge! . . . Flow through the flesh and slide among the bones! You were better to remain inside, living under the skin, throbbing in the veins and sliding over the bones, instead of spilling out onto the ground. . . . Precious blood, slow your trickling! Red fluid, calm your flowing![35]

Here the victim is old Väinämöinen, one of the poem's heroes, and, as for Ulysses, the wound is in his knee. We are tempted to surmise that the verses of the *epaoidé* chanted by the relatives of young Ulysses were similar to the magic song in the *Kalevala.*

A SHAMANISTIC BED

A famous passage in the *Odyssey* in which Ulysses describes his bed built around an olive trunk also has connections to the archaic northern world: "I built my bedroom around it with thick stones / till I finished it, then I suitably covered it above properly / and built sturdy doors" (*Odyssey* 23.192–94). According to Mircea Eliade, a central pillar is typical of the homes of many primitive peoples (particularly those of the Arctic and North America), and represents the Axis of the World or the Cosmic Pillar, which is a very important image in shamanistic ideology and experience. According to this concept, three levels—heaven, earth, and hell—make up the whole universe and are connected by a central axis.

The hole made by this axis allows the shamans' souls to rise or descend in their journeys toward heaven or hell. This cosmology is perfectly portrayed in our world, a microcosm of the universe: The World Axis is represented by the pillar that supports the home. (Inuits consider the pole in the middle of their homes to be identical to the heaven pillar.)

Eliade also claims that

> . . . the Cosmic Tree is essential for the shamans . . . In many primordial traditions the Cosmic Tree, which expresses the very sacredness of the world, its fecundity and perennial stability, is correlated to the ideas of creation, fecundity and initiation . . . The Cosmic Tree always appears as being the receptacle of life and the master of destinies."[36]

These concepts are perfectly consistent with Ulysses' idea—which could otherwise seem to be eccentric—of building a bedroom upon and around a tree.

The concept of the Cosmic Tree is also very important in the Norse world: The legendary ash tree called Yggdrasil, according to Chiesa Isnardi, "stands in the center of the universe and supports it . . . assumes the concepts of Power, Divine Wisdom, and Sacredness, and symbolizes the three spatial layers of existence (Earth, heaven, hell) as well as their interrelation."[37] This is why "in Scandinavian folklore we find the image of a tree, growing by a farmhouse, whose life is linked to the prosperity of the people living there."[38]

It is remarkable that a very striking counterpart to the tree inside Ulysses' home is found in the legend of the Nordic king Völsung, an ancestor of Sigurdh, the Nordic hero par excellence who corresponds to the Germanic Siegfried). According to Chiesa Isnardi: "King Völsung built a wonderful home. There was a big apple tree in the hall, whose branches with their fine flowers spread out on the roof; though its trunk was inside the house."[39]

Inside Ulysses' home the bedroom and the nuptial bed were "upstairs [*hyperóia*]" (*Odyssey* 18.206). It follows that the trunk supporting them, which is compared to a "column [*kíon*]" (*Odyssey* 23.191), passed through the banquet hall, situated downstairs on the first floor. It is probably the "pillar" (*Odyssey* 1.333, 18.209) by which Penelope stands (perhaps to make herself feel more protected and allow her to proudly emphasize her position in "her" home) after coming down from the bedroom to the hall where her suitors wait, and may also be the "column [*kíona*]" (*Odyssey* 23.90) beside which she finds Ulysses after the massacre, when she comes down to the hall to ascertain whether he is the husband she has been awaiting for the past twenty years. We should also note both the narrative and the psychological subtlety of the positioning of the two main characters of the poem, who are both found next to the central pillar of their home at different but significant moments.

The kind of tree chosen by Ulysses remains somewhat puzzling, however: Olive trees have a very contorted shape and are therefore not at all suitable to represent an axis or a straight pillar. This leads us to suspect a misunderstanding caused by the antiquity of the two poems and the change of environment that may have affected them. In fact, another passage of the *Odyssey* contains a very obvious misunderstanding referring to an olive tree: It is clear from the story that the "big stick" (*Odyssey* 9.319) Ulysses uses to blind Polyphemus is the log of a straight tree, though the text absurdly states that it is an olive log *(elaíneon)*, which would be absolutely unfit to serve as a stick or a punch. Moreover, this stick is "so long" that Homer compares it to "a mast" (*Odyssey* 9.324), which confirms that it was not an olive log and suggests a plausible solution to the confusion. Masts were usually made of fir logs, for the fir tree is straight and slim. In fact, masts and fir logs are so identified with one another that the former are also referred to poetically as "firs" in various sources. The *Odyssey* itself describes the mast of Telemachus's ship as a "fir log" *(elátinon; Odyssey* 2.424).

So how did the straight log found in the cave of the Cyclopes, most likely a slender fir log, become an olive branch? This detail is probably one that was altered when the Achaeans' environment changed. In the northern world fir trees are widespread, even near the coast, while at the Mediterranean latitudes coniferous trees grow only in the mountains. Perhaps a Greek bard, puzzled by that fir log in Polyphemus's cave near the sea, thought it better to refer to it as an olive tree, even though the contorted shape of the an olive is absolutely discordant with the rest of the narration. The Greek bards could also have been misled by the similarity between the Greek terms indicating "fir tree" *(eláte)* and "olive tree" *(elaíe).*

If we substitute "fir" for what has always been read as "olive," the otherwise incomprehensible work of the Homeric hero gains a powerful symbolic value: The image of the fir tree towering toward the sky recalls the World Axis, thereby corroborating the extreme antiquity of the Homeric poems as well as the archaic concepts on which they are founded, and likewise revealing a connection between the shamanistic nature of their northern context and the character of Ulysses himself.

THE CELTIC CONNECTION

In *The Druids,* Stuart Piggott claims: "Celtic literature was orally created and handed down by a barbaric society, just like the original version of the Homeric poems and the Sanskrit Rig Veda." Still on the Celts, he writes: "It was a barbaric civilization . . . From the archaeological evidence, we deduce that it was a model of society going back to barbaric Europe of the second half of the second millennium B.C.E. at least. This was a heroic age, similar in one way to [that of] Homer and the Rig Veda, in another to [that of] *Beowulf* and the Norse sagas."[40]

In his turn, the mythologist Robert Graves makes the following observation regarding a passage in the *Mabinogion,* a collection of stories of Celtic origin told in and around Britain:

> In [the] *Mabinogion,* Gwidion (King Odin or Wotan) uses the same shrewdness in similar circumstances as Odysseus did to unmask Achilles. In order to take Llew Gyffes away from the protection of his mother, Arianrhod, Gwidion feigns the uproar of a battle outside the castle walls and frightens the Queen to the point that he succeeds in convincing her to give Llew Llaw spear and sword. The Celtic version of this myth is probably the most ancient.[41]

The Odyssey *and Celtic* Immram

Celtic poets, known as *fili,* entertained the court's noblemen, just as the Homeric bards did. Their favorite themes included adventure *(echtra)* beyond human bounds and wanderings *(immram)* from island to island over far-off seas. This, of course, reminds us of Ulysses' tales in the palace of Alcinous about his fabulous adventures and wanderings.

What is more, one of the favorite destinations in Celtic tales such as "Immram curaig Máele Dúin" (The Voyage of Máel Dúin's Ship) and "Immram Brain maic Febail" (The Voyage of Febal's Son Bran) are the paradisiacal islands situated in the middle of the ocean, toward the far west, where divine women refresh and make love to the heroes who arrive there, offering them immortality and everlasting youth. According to Jean Markale, the French scholar of Celtic culture and literature, this is how the queen of one of these fabulous islands addresses a hero after he goes ashore: "If you remain here, old age will not catch you. You'll be young as you are now, and will live for ever."[42] All of this is identical to the remote ocean island of the goddess Calypso, who promises to make

Ulysses "immortal and ageless [*athánaton kaí agéron*] forever" (*Odyssey* 5.136, 7.257). Incidentally, we might note a similarity in the name Ogygia and the Celtic island of everlasting youth, which is called Tir-na n'Og. Perhaps Ogygia means "the Land of Youth."

Lughnasa

We can also find a very specific connection between the story of Ulysses and the Celtic summer festival known as Lughnasa, dedicated to Lug, a god and hero of Irish sagas whose name is echoed in place-names such as Lugdunum, present-day Lyon. Of the four main feast days in the Celtic calendar (one for each season), Lughnasa, on August 1, which became largely a harvest festival, was originally dedicated to the king, good government, family and marriage, social welfare, and political matters, according to the French scholar Françoise Le Roux.[43] Its name, which seems to mean "Lug's Meeting," has also been interpreted as "Lug's Wedding." The fact that this feast is celebrated in summer emphasizes Lug's solar, or Apollonian, features, which Jean Markale claims have been "far too ignored: his name means whiteness, light; in Irish epos he is referred to as a solar, radiant hero, who never really dies, but rises every morning; the crow is his symbolic animal, just like Apollo's."[44] His name also could be linked to Lykegenés, an epithet of Apollo the Archer (*Iliad* 4.101).

Lughnasa owes its origin to the final defeat of the fierce Fomors and Fir Bolg, enemies of the Celts, and the return of Lug, who marries Erinn and grants the country peace and prosperity. It is the celebration of the victory of the sun over darkness and death, when the heat from its rays quickly ripens the harvest after the cold and the rain. This corresponds to Ulysses' return and his victory over Penelope's suitors, which is sealed by his symbolic "wedding"—*gámon* (*Odyssey* 23.135)—to Penelope.

This parallel is not accidental. On the contrary, it is confirmed by the concurrence—which is repeatedly underlined in the *Odyssey*—between the date of the archery contest (the bride being the prize) and the feast day dedicated to Apollo the Archer (*Odyssey* 21.267). On that festival day "the heralds took the sacred hecatomb to the town / and the long-haired Achaeans gathered / in the shady grove of Apollo the Archer" (*Odyssey* 20.276–78). The contest is unequivocally dedicated to the god: "Today the town celebrates the solemn feast / of the god; who will stretch the bow?" (*Odyssey* 21, 258–59); and, Penelope says, "If he stretches the bow and Apollo gives him the honor" (*Odyssey* 21.338). After Ulysses wins the archery contest,

He said to the suitors:
"This fatal contest has ended;
now I am aiming at another target that no man has ever shot,
if I can hit it and Apollo grants me the honor."
Then he pointed a deadly arrow straight at Antinous.
   (*Odyssey* 22.4–8)

In all of these details we must not forget that the greatest feat attributed to Apollo the Archer—the sun god and Lug's counterpart—is his use of bow and arrow to kill the dragon of darkness, the snake Python.

There is precise reference to the god Apollo in another archery contest, narrated in the *Iliad,* which takes place on the occasion of Patroclus's funeral. The poet stresses that Meriones, a Cretan hero, wins because "he promised a hecatomb of lambs / to Apollo the Archer" (*Iliad* 23.872–73). Another link between the two contests concerns the axes found in both episodes (and which are also found as a common element in Scandinavian graffiti). In the *Iliad* they are the prize, while in the *Odyssey* they mark the course to the target: Twelve axes are lined up, with the object being that the arrow is to go through all twelve of them. The *Odyssey* repeats this number three times (*Odyssey* 19.574, 19.578, 21.76) to emphasize its importance. Could it be that these twelve axes are related to the twelve months of the year? If this is the case, then the archery contest coinciding with Apollo's feast day has a potent symbolism hidden in a sophisticated astronomical-calendrical metaphor, in keeping with the kenning logic found in both the *Odyssey* and Norse myths: The arrow shot by the solar archer, with whom the contest winner identifies himself, goes through all twelve axes, which alludes to the passing of the year, marked by the sun that intersects the twelve months. Additionally, the curved line of the ax blade recalls the moon, the lady of the monthly cycle. As we shall see later in more detail, a Swedish graffito engraved on a stone slab of a huge tomb near Kivik corroborates the identification of the moon with the ax symbol.

The connection between the *Odyssey* and Lug is further born out in Lug's peculiar nickname, *samildanach,* translated as *polytéchnicien* in French, which parallels certain names given to Ulysses, such as *polýtropos,* as he is called in the *Odyssey*'s first line, and *polyméchanos,* meaning "resourceful," "ingenious," or "versatile." Ulysses indeed demonstrates these qualities: Not only does he think up the stratagem of the wooden horse, but he is also capable of building his own house (*Odyssey* 23.192–94), as well as the raft he uses to return home after his ship is destroyed by Charybdis (*Odyssey* 5.243–61). At this point, it does not surprise us that the name of the "bright god" Lug perhaps finds its root in the name Ulysses.

To summarize the connection between Homer's works and Celtic myth, we note that in the *Odyssey*, the events set in Ithaca probably take place in the best month for sailing—that is, in July—so we can assume that Apollo's feast day, which virtually concludes the *Odyssey*, falls on a date corresponding to that of Lughnasa: the beginning of August, about forty days after the solstice. It would therefore be very appealing to suppose that "Apollo the Archer's feast day" (probably celebrated all over the Achaean world), when the archery contest, the massacre of the suitors, and Ulysses' triumph take place, falls right on the first day of the last month of summer—that is, on the day corresponding to the Celtic feast day of Lughnasa. The *Odyssey* itself confirms this idea with a prediction, destined to come true, regarding the day on which Ulysses is to return home, victorious: "At the end of this moon or at the beginning of the next one / he will return home and punish all they who / here fail to respect his wife and his son" (*Odyssey* 14.162–64).

That fateful day was marked by another prophecy referring to the cycle of time, one uttered by a miller woman who gives Ulysses a good omen on the morning of the massacre:

> *A miller-woman made a speech from the house,*
> *nearby, where the King's millstones lay.*
> *Twelve women in all worked with them,*
> *producing barley and wheat flour, food for men.*
> *The other women were sleeping, as they had ground their wheat,*
> *but one of them had not finished, she was the weakest.*
> *She stopped the millstone and uttered a sentence, an omen for the*
> *   King.* (*Odyssey* 20. 105–11)

This wonderful piece, with its arcane mythical flavor, can easily be interpreted as an allegory of the "Hours that grind Time": It was the last hour of the night (the wee hours) that prophesied the victory of the hero. This extraordinary poet never stops surprising us! As fascinating as Ulysses' adventures are, however, we cannot stay in his world any longer. After living for thousands of years in oblivion, Troy awaits us.

PART TWO
THE WORLD OF TROY

CHAPTER 6

IF "THIS IS NOT THE SITE OF THE ANCIENT ILIUM," WHERE WAS TROY?

Our exploration of the world of Troy follows a pattern of concentric circles, beginning with the congruence between Homeric Troy and the topography of the area around Toija, Finland—especially as it relates to the war itself—then comparing the Troad (the area surrounding the ancient city of Troy) with a larger area in southern Finland, and finally widening the picture to include neighboring islands. As these "circles" grow, we shall see that while a Mediterranean setting leaves us with contradictions and inconsistencies, the entire world of Troy as outlined by Homer squares with this area of the Baltic in exactly the same way as Ithaca and its archipelago does with the Danish islands.

THE CITY ON THE HILL OF HISARLIK

Strabo reports that the plain [of Troy] had been an inlet of the sea at the time of the Trojan War and that since then it had been filled in by silt brought down by the river. Schliemann was eager to disprove this statement, for it was one of the chief arguments against the Troy-Hisarlik theory. If the sea had come up to the walls of Troy, how could the Greeks and Trojans have ranged back and forth on the plain between the city and the sea, as Homer tells us? Schliemann, Burnouf, and Virchow sank shafts in different parts of the plain and the general conclusion reached was that there had once been an inland lake in the northern part of the plain and that the Menderes (Homer's Scamander) had flowed much closer to Hisarlik. Thanks to a series of core samples taken in 1977, we now know that in pre-historic times the plain was covered by an extensive arm of the sea, which reached up to Hisarlik in the Troy 6 period and considerably further upstream in Troy 2,* but which by Strabo's own time had been reduced to a very small bay at the river mouth. Strabo therefore was correct and the findings of Schliemann, Burnouf, and Virchow, based as they were on inadequate samples, were in error.[1]

This statement by David Traill, professor of classical studies at the University of California, in his *Schliemann of Troy,* casts a large shadow of doubt over Heinrich Schliemann's theory that Homer's Troy was the city brought to light on the Anatolian site of Hisarlik near the entrance to the Dardanelles in what is now western Turkey.

For his part, Moses Finley, in his famous essay "The World of Odysseus," claims:

Schliemann's achievements were epoch-making. Nevertheless, despite the claims, the unassailable fact is that nothing he or his successors have found, not a single scrap, links the destruction of Troy 7a with Mycenaean Greece, or with an invasion from any other source. Nor does anything known from the archaeology of Greece and Asia Minor or from the Linear B tablets fit with the Homeric tale of a great coalition sailing against Troy from Greece . . . nor is a Trojan War mentioned . . .

Not a scrap was uncovered at Troy to point to Agamemnon or any other conquering king or overlord, or to a Mycenaean coalition or even to a war. For that blunt assertion I have the highest, if reluctant, authority, that of Caskey, who wrote: "The physical remains of Troy 7a do not prove beyond question that the place was captured at all . . . Furthermore, if this citadel was not sacked—and indeed if it was not sacked by the Greeks under Agamemnon—we are left without a compelling reason even to go on calling it Troy.[2]

---

*Troy 6 and Troy 2 are two of the layers, numbered starting from the bottom, that archaeologists have unearthed at Hisarlik. Each layer corresponds to a city from a different "stage" or epoch of civilization. The lower the number, the more ancient the findings. Scholars usually identify the Homeric Troy with the seventh layer—Troy 7.

We should note that Finley is not the only one to have made such statements. Professor Fausto Codino, a specialist in Homeric poems, writes: "It is not sure that the burning of Troy 7 (the layer of Trojan excavations identified as being Homer's Troy) was caused by military action. If Troy had really been conquered and destroyed, it is not sure that the conquerors were Achaeans from the Greek peninsula."[3] In his turn, the German scholar Fritz Graf notes that "it is true that Troy 7 was actually destroyed by violent action, but it could have been the violence of an earthquake followed by a fire; there is no evidence to prove an enemy attack, let alone the origin of any possible enemy."[4]

Scholars' doubts accord with the fact that Strabo categorically denies that the Greek-Roman Troy, which roughly corresponds to Schliemann's site, is identifiable with the Homeric city: "This is not the site of the ancient Ilium *(d'ouk entaûtha hídrytai tó palaión Ílion),* if one considers the matter in accordance with Homer's account . . ."[5]

Another point to be considered in situating Troy is the location of the Trojans' allies. In the *Iliad* they seem to be located near the city, such as when Hector addresses them as "the crowd of my allies and neighbors"—*periktiónon,* which means literally "neighboring inhabitants" (*Iliad* 17.220). Homer's precise and consistent indications contradict the location of ancient Anatolian peoples such as the Lycians and Cilicians, whose historical settlements are extremely distant from the region of the Dardanelles. On this subject, Professor Martin P. Nilsson, a leading Swedish scholar, writes in *The Mycenaean Origin of Greek Mythology:*

> The astonishing fact is that none of the Trojan allies plays such a prominent part as the people hitherto not mentioned, the Lycians, who lived in the far-off south of Asia Minor. The passages where Lycia and the Lycians are mentioned are too numerous to be enumerated and I need only point to the prominent part played by the Lycian heroes Glaucus, Sarpedon, and Pandarus in various songs of the *Iliad.* However, in the fourth Book, it is said that Pandarus came from the town of Zeleia and the river Aesepus, which flows from Mount Ida to the sea, and these indications are reproduced in the Catalog of Ships. This contradicts the Lycian location of Pandarus . . . Moreover, the same thing seems to have happened in the case of the Cilicians. Andromache is said to be the daughter of Eëtion, ruler of the Cilicians and king of Thebes beneath Mount Plakos, a town which was taken by Achilles. Evidently this Thebes is not

far from Troy, but the existence of the Cilicians elsewhere than in southeastern Asia Minor is unknown.[6]

Although some tend to identify the Hittite city of Wilusa with Ilium, in *The Hittites* James G. Macqueen notices that it probably lay in the rich plain of Eskisehir, which is more than 180 miles east of the Dardanelles. In his turn, Professor Dieter Hertel, who worked an the site of Hisarlik, claims in his recent *Troy* that both Wilusa and the city found by Schliemann have nothing to do with the Homeric Troy.

A recent theory that places the Achaean camp on the headland that bounded the inlet at the foot of the hill at that time is absolutely inconsistent with the Homeric accounts. For instance, the *Iliad* mentions the point where the Scamander River meets the Simoïs, while the two Anatolian rivers traditionally identified with the Scamander and the Simoïs did not meet at that time.

To conclude, the connection between Homer's Troy and the city found on the hill of Hisarlik is far from proved. It seems very likely that Hisarlik was simply a well-fortified stronghold situated in a strategic position at the mouth of the Dardanelles, as recent archaeological excavations by Rose and Korfmann show. We also note that while this area has been subject to investigation for more than a century, remains of large walls have only recently been discovered, showing how difficult it is to uncover traces of lost civilizations. The Mycenaeans probably gave the Mediterranean Troy its name based on the fact that its positioning in relation to the landmarks around it corresponded to that of the original northern Troy, much like the case of the Peloponnese. As Strabo attests, however, the "Trojans" themselves were aware that their city was not the Homeric Troy.

A NEW SEARCH FOR TROY

Now that we have cleared the field of Schliemann's misleading Hisarlik—although he must be congratulated for having discovered the Mycenaean civilization and for having re-proposed the historicity of the Trojan War—we can begin our search anew for a more precise location of Troy, based on the places described in the *Iliad* and the rich geographical information Homer provides.

As we have noted, many passages from the *Iliad*, like this one recounting the dramatic meeting between Achilles and King Priam in the last book of the poem, state that the territory of Troy lay near a sea called Hellespont: "In the whole of the country that is bounded by Lesbos, Macar's home, / upper Phrygia and boundless Hellespont [*Hellespontos apeiron*], / people say that you, old man, stood out from all by your wealth and your children" (*Iliad* 24.544–46). The *Iliad* also uses the term *platýs,* meaning "broad" (*Iliad* 7.86, 17.432), to describe the sea. But the Mediterranean Hellespont—that is, the Dardanelles—is so far from being "broad" or "boundless" that, at a certain point "it becomes so narrow that it looks more like a river than a strait."[7]

However, the Homeric Hellespont does have a counterpart in the north of Europe, where, as we have seen, Saxo Grammaticus often refers to a people known as "the Hellespontians," enemies of the Danes: "After these events, Regner, who was preparing an expedition against the Hellespontians, convened a meeting of the Danes . . . After a series of repeated attacks, he defeated and subjected Hellespont and its King Dian. In the end he killed him."[8] According to other parts of the *Gesta,* this northern Hellespont seems to be located east of the Danish area.

If we consider that the name Hellespont means "the sea of Helle or Hellas," and that the sequence of the Catalog of Ships (as we shall see in chapter 10) locates Hellas on the Estonian coast facing the Gulf of Finland, it follows that the Gulf of Finland probably coincides with Homer's "broad Hellespont." This is corroborated by the fact that the Gulf of Finland—the geographic counterpart to the Dardanelles, given its location northeast of the basin to which it belongs—corresponds to the site of the "Hellespontians" as described by Saxo.

The next step is to fix the position of Troy in relation to the Hellespont. Here we ask for help from the goddess Hera herself, who says: "I am going to arouse [toward Troy] a violent storm of Zephyrus and bright Notus / from the sea [*ex halóthen*]" (*Iliad* 21.334–35). These are the west and the south winds, respectively; thus the sea—the "broad Hellespont"—lay *southwest* of the city of Troy. This definitively excludes Hisarlik as a possible site. Further, it suggests we should look for Homer's Troy in an area that faces the Gulf of Finland and, at the same time, is situated to the northeast of it. The only area that meets both requirements, apart from the Russian territory west of St. Petersburg, lies west of Helsinki, in southern Finland, where the Gulf of Finland begins. Given that nothing fitting can be found in the area near St. Petersburg, we turn our attention to this region of southern Finland.

In this area, situated between Helsinki and Turku, there is a veritable "mine" of toponyms, an amazing number of place-names that recall those around Troy and the Trojans' allies mentioned in the *Iliad* (especially in the list at the end of Book 2, after the Catalog of Ships). Here is Askainen, which recalls Ascania and Ascanius, the leader of a contingent allied to the Trojans (*Iliad* 2.862–63); Karjaa and Lyökki, which recall the Carians and the Lycians (Lýkioi), respectively; Raisio or Reso, which recalls both Rhesus, ally of the Trojans, and the river Rhesus in Troad; Åbo, the other name for Turku, the most ancient city in Finland, dating back to 1157 and built around the castle of Åbohus, which recalls the Abii, "the most law-abiding of men" (*Iliad* 13.6), and the city of Abydus; and Pargas, which recalls the town of Percotes, in the same area as Abydus (*Iliad* 2.835–36).

At the beginning of the *Iliad,* Tenedos and "holy Cilla" are mentioned together (*Iliad* 1.38, 452). Tenedos, which Homer never treats as an island, corresponds to today's Tenala or Tenhola, a municipality situated on a headland surrounded by islands. Cilla (Kílla in Greek), Apollo's shrine, is likened to Kiila, a coastal place in the same area. There are many other peculiar, often Greek-sounding place-names in the surrounding area that could be matched with allies and areas near Troy: Airisto can be likened to Arisbe; Mietoinen to Mydon (the charioteer of the king of the Paphlagonians, the Trojans' allies) and the Achaean town of Methone; Ampiala and Pesola to Amphius, Priam's ally, and his native town, called Paiso; Klaukkala to Glaucus, leader of the Lycians; Menonen to the Maeonians, other allies of the Trojans; Mestilä to Mesthles, head of the Maeonians; Paino to the Paeonians, "with their curved bows"; Friggesby to Phrygia; Tammela, which lies near a hilly region, to the "snowy Tmolus" (*Iliad* 20.385); Padasjoki to Pedasus; Rohdainen to the river Rhodius; Alavus to Alybe, "the birthplace of silver"; and Näst to Nastes, head of the Trojans' allies, known as the Carians.

Thus, southern Finland not only corresponds geographically to the Aegean region of the Dardanelles; it also reveals an amazing cluster of place-names that closely echo names in Homeric Troy. At this point, Priam's mythical city seems to be close at hand! And it is in the middle of this area, not far from Tenala and Kiila, where we find the Finnish village that lies, just as Homer says, in a hilly area near the intersection of two rivers, not very far from the sea. This small town has kept its ancient name virtually intact: Toija.

Interestingly, we can even explain the variation in the names Troy and Toija. In Finnish, words beginning with the consonant cluster *tr* are quite uncommon and usually betray a foreign origin. We can presume that when a Finno-Ugric people arrived in Finland, they mispronounced the pre-existing place-names due to a peculiar "phonetic sensitivity" that ignored the *tr* sound (a phenomenon that was more pronounced given the lack of a written language). Thus the name was altered from Troia to Toija.

TROY

The best method of verifying the congruence between the descriptions in the Homeric poems and the morphological features of the area we have just identified in southern Finland is to make our way to Toija, now situated about twelve miles from the coast, which in this area is full of islands, islets, and headlands. In ancient days Toija was much closer to the sea, but after the end of the ice age, the land of Finland began to rise;* over the thousands of years that have elapsed since Homer's time, the distance between Toija and the coastline has gradually increased. However, the location of the ancient "beach" where the Achaeans landed and camped, called *aigialós* by Homer (*Iliad* 14.34), is still marked by a place called Aijala, about four miles southwest of Toija, toward the sea.

From the village, a minor road leads to a hilly area that affords a view over the whole valley, which spreads in the direction of the sea. With our back to the north, we can see the river Kurkelanjoki (*joki* means "river") flowing from the left, which then broadens out onto the plain, forming a long, narrow lake called Lake Kirkkojärvi. About a mile farther downstream, another river, known as the Mammalanjoki, flows into this lake; and still farther two or three miles, near Aijala, the lake becomes narrower and reforms the riverbed. This "new" waterway, called the Kiskonjoki, continues to make its way down to the sea. This landscape corresponds to the one Homer describes in the *Iliad*: Here are the river Scamander, the river Simoïs, and the plain where Achaeans and Trojans bitterly fought so long ago. The only difference compared to the topography of the *Iliad* is the current partial flooding of the valley by the river (see fig. 6.1).But apparently this also happened at the time of the *Iliad*, as Homer writes regarding one day of the war: "The plain . . . was all full of flooded water" (*Iliad* 21.300). The fact that this flooding has gone from an occasional event to lasting reality is probably due to

---

*When warmer temperatures brought an end to the strong compression caused by the Quaternary glaciers, the land began a gradual uplift that will continue until it reaches its pre–ice age level.

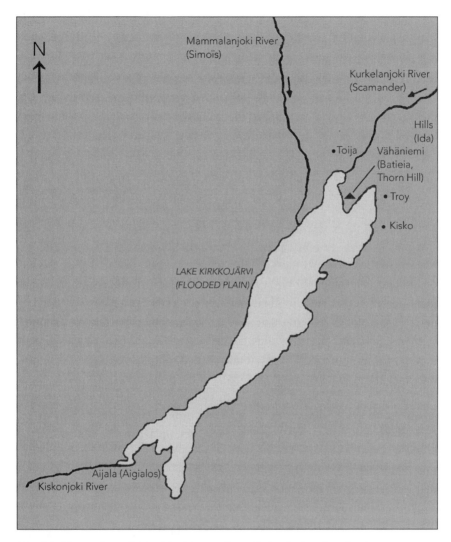

Fig. 6.1. The region of Toija (Troy) in southern Finland, showing the rivers Mammalanjoki (Simöis) and Kurkelanjoki (Scamander), Toija (Troy), Kisko, and Vähäniemi (Batieia, or Thorn Hill). Also indicated is the likely location of the Achaean camp, near present-day Aijala at the south end of the flooded plain that is now Lake Kirkkojärvi.

marked changes in climate as well as variations in ground level that have affected this area since the end of the Bronze Age.

In order to tour the plain below the village, we must follow the road around the lake. Starting from Toija and heading in a counterclockwise direction—that is, traveling along the west bank of the lake toward the south (fig. 6.1)—we come to some beautiful views of what must have been the ancient battlefield, "where many shields and helmets / fell on the dust" (*Iliad* 12.22–23). It is extremely exciting to think that it may have been in this place that the Trojan citizens witnessed the duels between Homer's heroes, and that Helen, on hearing Priam's and Hecabe's cries over her husband Hector's death,

> . . . rushed out of her room like a madwoman,
> having her heart in turmoil, her maids followed her;
> but when she reached the tower and the crowd of people,
> she stopped to watch from the wall and saw him
> trailed in front of the citadel: the fast horses
> pitilessly trailed him toward the Achaean ships. (*Iliad* 22.460–65)

From the battlefield we continue on our way for a couple of miles until we come to a crossroads, where we turn left for Aijala. The similarity of this name to the Greek term *aigialós*, meaning "beach" or "bank," suggests that the coastline existed here at a time when people in this region spoke a sort of Greek dialect (the Trojans spoke the same language as the Achaeans and had Greek names).

Passing Aijala, where the Achaeans built their camp near their ships, we cross over a bridge on the river Kiskonjoki, where the river reenters its bed after flooding the plain some miles upstream. We stop on the water's banks, perhaps standing in the very place where, almost four thousand years ago, a clear June night poured its faint light onto a dramatic scene. Here are

> . . . the banks of the Scamander, where many
> heads of men were falling and an incessant cry was rising,
> around great Nestor and warlike Idomeneus;
> Hector was fighting among them, performing fierce exploits
> with his spear and chariot. (*Iliad* 10.499–503)

After crossing the Aijala bridge, we follow a dirt track that takes us up along the east bank of the lake, toward the north. Here the ground is higher and its undulations are more marked. We take the road leading to Kisko, a mile east of Toija, and end up on the road for Salo, which in a few minutes leads us back to our starting point. We note that the land on the eastern side of Lake Kirkkojärvi around Kisko seems to be an ideal location for an ancient town: It lies near a river and is in a dominant position overlooking the valley.

While waiting for a definite answer on the subject from archaeology, we can propose a reasonable assumption regarding the exact location of ancient Troy after focusing especially on the salient features Homer mentions: the citadel, the mountains behind it, the plain with a hill alongside, the two rivers, and the coast overlooking the "Broad Hellespont."

According to Homer, Troy is located near the confluence of two rivers, "where the flows of Scamander and Simoïs meet" (*Iliad* 5.774). The former is probably the most important, as it is mentioned no less than twenty-four times in the *Iliad* (often by another name, Xanthos, meaning "blond" or "yellow") compared to seven references to the Simoïs. The city lay in front of "Scamander's plain" *(pedíon Skamándrion)* and the river (*Iliad* 2.465). It was a hilly area: The *Iliad* mentions a place called "the Fine Hill" (in Greek, Kallikolóne, *Iliad* 20.53, 51) and another hill in the environs known as Batieia—that is, Thorn Hill or Bramble Hill. Interestingly, Homer applies a very eloquent expression indicating the city's topography: "corrugated Ilium" *(ophryóessa)*, an adjective deriving from a term meaning "eyebrow," with clear reference to an uneven area.

From Troy the warriors pass through the Scaean Gates and continue down to the plain (*Iliad* 3.273, 6.393), toward the river (*Iliad* 21.1–3). These gates, the fabled entrance to Troy, are verbally "photographed" in the *Iliad*: "the high gates, with their solid leaves, / which are broad, smooth, well-joined . . ." (*Iliad* 18.275–76). We can infer from various passages that they directly face the plain—that is, the battlefield: "Priam got on and drew rein; / Antenor got on the splendid chariot beside him, / then the two, past the Scaean [*diá Skaiôn*], drove the fast horses toward the plain" (*Iliad* 3.261–63).

In another scene, almost like one in a film, the Trojan leader returns from the battle:

> *When Hector arrived at the Scaean Gates and the oak,*
> *the wives and daughters of the Trojans ran around him,*
> *asking after their sons, brothers, friends*
> *and husbands. He urged them all, one after the other, to pray to*
> *   the gods;*
> *a misfortune had hit many of them.* (Iliad 6.237–41)

The hero then returns to the same spot after calling at home: "He crossed the great city and reached the Scaean Gates, / through which he intended to go out onto the plain" (*Iliad* 6.392–93).

The Greek name of the gates—*skaiaí*—has a precise meaning that also indicates their placement. The term is the feminine plural of the adjective *skaiós*, "left" or "western." The Scaean Gates, then, were the western gates of Troy, situated on the side of the city that faced the plain and the river. Therefore, *Troy stood east of the river*, in a relatively high area, close to the east bank of the Scamander.

This location is quite rational: The ancients built their cities in strategic positions near rivers, often near points where crossing was easiest, for water supplies, of course, but also to foster trade. They also located cities on hills for security reasons: to defend themselves from floods and enemy attacks. The city of Rome is a good example of this siting: It lies in a hilly area next to the river Tiber, opposite the Tiberina island, which makes it easier to go from one bank of the river to the other.

As for siting the city at an easy crossing, the *Iliad* often refers to the "Scamander ford" that lies near Troy. When Hector is wounded by Ajax near the ships, "they carried him, heavily groaning, toward the citadel; / then they reached the ford of the fine river, / the whirling Xanthus" (*Iliad* 14.432–34). In another episode, the retreating Trojans, pursued by Achilles, split up at this ford, with some of them trying to cross the river and others continuing their flight toward the city (*Iliad* 21.1–9). Later, Priam passes by the same spot on his return from the Achaean camp, after ransoming Hector's body (*Iliad* 24.692). This ford thus lies somewhere between the city and the Achaean camp, which is situated along the coast.

At this point we can easily compare Troy's layout as it emerges from the *Iliad* to the morphology of the territory of Toija. Just beyond the lake, to the east of the village, there is a relatively high area where Kisko lies. This uneven region extends southward, covering more or less the whole eastern bank of Lake Kirkkojärvi, the body of water that has originated from the flooding of the plain by the river and its tributary (today's Kurkelanjoki and Mammalanjoki). The consistency of this topographical picture with Homeric Troy is stunning, while the layout of Schliemann's Anatolian Troy (Hisarlik) does not match at all, a fact that Strabo and his contemporaries knew perfectly well but which has perplexed many modern scholars such as Finley, Traill, and Hertel.

To sum up, Homer's Troy lay on one of the rises facing the east bank of Lake Kirkkojärvi. The most probable site is a hilly area covered by a thick wood, just north of Kisko (similar in name to Scaean Gates) and less than a mile east of today's Toija (fig. 6.1). This site dominates the plain (now covered by Lake Kirkkojärvi) where at that time the two rivers met and Scamander's ford lay.

Batieia (Thorn Hill)

We can now also locate Thorn Hill, which, according to Homer, lies "aside in the plain" (*Iliad* 2.811), facing the city. It must have been what is now the headland known as Vähäniemi (Cape Vähä), which stretches out from the northern bank onto the lake, directly in front of the hills surrounding Kisko.

The *Iliad* tells us that men called this hill Batieia, while the gods gave it another name: *sêma polyskárthmoio Myrínes* (*Iliad* 2.814), traditionally translated as "the tomb of dancing (or jumping) Myrine." But who is "Myrine" (she is mentioned nowhere else in Homer's works), and why does she "jump" (or rather "jump to and fro"—the prefix *poly*, also found in many modern words, means "many")? Is she perhaps a dancer or an acrobat? According to the speculations of certain mythographers, she is no less than the queen of the Amazons! But is this accurate?

We might ask at this point whether some kind of relationship exists between the names given by men and those granted by the gods. To reach an informed opinion on this question, we should look at one of the poems of the *Edda,* the *Alvissmal,* which is concerned with the different names that humans, gods, giants, and others give to the same object or place. For example, in the eighteenth stanza of the poem, we read that clouds are called *"Clouds* by men, *Storm Heralds* by the gods, / *Ships of the Wind* by the Vanir, *Hope for Rain* by the Giants and *Strength of Rainstorms* by the Alfis."* In the twenty-fourth stanza, we find that *"Sea* is the name used by men, *Eternal Depth* by the gods, / *Wavy Ocean* by the Vanir and *The Eels' Country* by the Giants." In other words, the Norse poet enjoys coining synonyms and metaphors.

Regarding our hill, then, it is quite reasonable to assume a semantic relationship between its two names, Batieia and "sêma polyskárthmoio Myrínes." The experts believe the name Batieia derives from the noun *bátos,* "thorn" or "bramble" (*Odyssey* 24.230). We can thus say that the hill in front of Toija/Troy is named Thorn Hill. The gods' name, Myríne, can be associated with the Greek root *myron,* meaning "perfume" or "scented essence" (*mýrtos* means "myrtle," which is a scented plant; and *myrríne* is the myrtle berry). *Moron,* the Greek name for the blackberry fruit that grows on brambles, also points to the root *myr*. Both myrtle and bramble belong to the Rosaceae family, prickly shrubs, like roses, that produce strongly scented flowers. As for the term *sêma*, it means not only "tomb" but also "sign" (*Iliad* 23.326, *Odyssey* 11.126). Thus the gods' name for Thorn Hill is definitely related to the human one: "The puzzling "sêma polyskárthmoio Myrínes" refers to the "sign" or "point" *(sêma)* where blackberry bushes or a scented member of the Rosaceae family *(myrínes)* sprouted here and there *(polyskárthmoio)* or perhaps stirred in the wind. In short, we have discovered yet another Homeric kenning. We can forget the queen of the Amazons and can now replace her with a beautiful "impressionist" image depicting the visible effect of the rustling bushes scattered on the hill in front of "windy Troy" during the flowering season.

The morphology of the hilly area surrounding Kisko, which lies northeast of the lake, fits very well with an episode of the *Odyssey* in which Ulysses recalls the exploratory mission of an Achaean platoon that travels as far as the Trojan walls: "When we approached the city and the high wall, / near the citadel, among thick bushes, / reeds and a marsh, under our arms / we lay low . . ." (*Odyssey* 14.472–75). There is still a reedy marsh there today, where the Kurkelanjoki widens and the flooded area begins, just below the rise north of Kisko, overlooking the valley.

Ulysses continues with his narrative: "The night was bad, after the north wind dropped, / and freezing; then the snow began to fall like icy frost / and ice congealed on our shields [*sakéessi peritrépheto krýstallos*]" (*Odyssey* 14.475–77). This kind of weather (not very common to a Mediterranean coastal area) fits with the fog, cold, and damp that are frequently mentioned in the *Iliad*. Thus we see that in the Trojan region, as everywhere else in the Homeric poems, northern climatic features are very apparent.

Ida

Now the time has come to look for one of the other essential mythical, poetic, and geographic elements of Homer's Troy: the mountainous area behind the city, which has traditionally been known as Mount Ida, though this familiar name is not found in either of Homer's epics. The *Iliad* describes this region quite specifically as a wild, uneven land, rich in waters and hills. It often mentions the "gorges of Ida" (*Iliad* 11.105), its "mountains" (*Iliad* 8.170), and its "heights" (*Iliad* 11.183). Moreover, the poet uses the descriptive and poetic expression "Ida with many springs [*polypîdax*]" (*Iliad* 13.307). Rather than being a single mountain, it is far more likely that Ida corresponds perfectly to the topography of the area behind Toija, where uneven ground stretches out to the northeast of Kisko, toward the lake Suomusjärvi, and is characterized by high spots, hills, and several lakes of different sizes. This real Ida of the *Iliad* can be reached by going up along the valley in which flows the river Kurkelanjoki, or the ancient Scamander.

In looking at the duel between Achilles and Agenor, we can see how perfectly the details of this area correspond to Homer's topography. Achilles, who has gone back to fighting to avenge Patroclus's death, has routed the entire Trojan army on the plain and the riverbanks, and is pursuing them threateningly close to the city wall. At this point, Agenor wonders whether he should confront Achilles or run away: "I could run away on foot from the wall elsewhere, / toward the Ileian Plain, until I reach / the gorges of Ida and hide in the bush" (*Iliad* 21.557–59). But the brave young Agenor eventually summons the courage to confront terrible Achilles. With his spear he even manages to hit the armor of his antagonist, though he fails to injure him. Agenor escapes Achilles' counterattack with the help of Apollo, who shrouds him in fog. Then the sun god leads Achilles along the same route Agenor has previously considered, in order to divert him and allow the Trojan soldiers to find shelter in the city: "[Apollo] paused before him on foot, and Achilles began to pursue him on foot; / he pursued him for a while along the wheat-producing plain, / following the whirling river Scamander" (*Iliad* 21.601–603). When Achilles eventually realizes he has been tricked, he heads back to Troy, where he finds Hector waiting for him at the Scaean Gates (*Iliad* 22.5–21). The decisive duel is about to start.

This passage confirms that the "gorges of Ida" are reached by going up the river Scamander and the "Ileian Plain." It becomes clear that the idea that the pursuit could have headed downstream toward the area occupied by the Achaean troops is totally out of the question. The correspondence between the highlands behind Troy and the Kurkelanjoki Valley is remarkable—so much so that we might assume that the poet actually visited these places.

Homer calls the two stretches of the Scamander Valley by two different names: Ileian and Scamandrian, for the parts above and below the city, respectively. This squares with the morphology of the area surrounding Toija, where the river Kurkelanjoki is rather narrow up to Vähäniemi (Thorn Hill), but from there widens to flood the plain (the ancient battlefield). Agenor, in fact, considers running away *on foot (posín)*, because the rough ground above Troy is not suitable for a chariot. Therefore, Troy must have stood near the northern edge of the present-day lake (where Toija and Kisko lie) and the beginning of the region Homer calls Ida, just beyond Troy. The city must have towered over the river and the plain, on a hill near present-day Kisko.

According to Homer, the Achaeans had raided the region of Ida in a preliminary phase of the war, before the events directly narrated in the *Iliad*. Aeneas, the Trojan hero, recalls that "Achilles . . . / with his spear drove me / from Ida, when he raided our cattle, / and plundered Lyrnessus and Pedasus" (*Iliad* 20.89–92). This is when Achilles abducts Briseis, the girl who was the cause of his quarrel with Agamemnon:

> *Achilles lay idle by his ships,*
> *angry at young, long-haired Briseis*
> *whom he had taken away from Lyrnessus after he toiled*
> *at destroying Lyrnessus and the walls of Thebes.* (*Iliad* 2.688–91)

Also nearby is Dardania, the ancient city of Dardanus, progenitor of the Trojan royal family:

> *Zeus, Gatherer of Clouds, fathered first Dardanus,*
> *who founded Dardania when sacred Ilium,*
> *city of mortal men, had not been founded in the plain yet,*
> *but they still lived in the slopes of Ida with many springs.*
> (*Iliad* 20.215–18)

Here Homer takes us into the dim and distant past of his own world. In fact, this territory inspired some of the most evocative tales in Greek mythology. Baby Paris was left here and grew up in the hut of a shepherd, unaware of his royal origins until he incautiously gave the golden apple to the goddess Aphrodite during the first "beauty contest" in history, which initiated the countdown to the destruction of Troy.

The tale of the prince brought up among the shepherds of Ida gives us another clue. During his youth on Ida (before getting into trouble with the wives of other men), Paris had been engaged to beautiful Oenone, the spring nymph who was the river Oeneus's daughter, as Robert Graves reminds us. The root of her name is also found in the name of one of the main lakes in this Finnish region, only twelve miles from Toija: Enäjärvi (lake Enä). In turn, the name Enäjärvi is rather similar to that of Aeneas, "whom divine Aphrodite begot for Anchises, / a goddess who made love to a mortal in the gorges of Ida" (*Iliad* 2.820–21). Aphrodite is frequently mentioned in relation to this region, perhaps indicating that she had a shrine here, but Homer mentions only the worship of Zeus, to whom Hector "burnt many ox thighs / on the tops of Ida with many gorges" (*Iliad* 22.170–71). The poet goes into more detail in another passage in which Zeus

> . . . *harnessed two bronze-hoofed horses to his chariot*
> . . . *then he mounted the chariot,*
> *whipped them to go and they flew with fervor between the earth*
>   *and the starry sky.*
> *He arrived at Ida of the many springs, mother of wild beasts,*
> *at Gargarus, where he has his shrine and fragrant altar.*
> *Here the Father of men and gods pulled up his horses,*
> *unharnessed them from the chariot, and cast much fog around.*
>   (*Iliad* 8.41, 44–50)

Given the presence of Zeus's shrine, we might suppose that Gargarus was the most important peak of Ida. It is also the place where Hera, with her amorous charms, manages to temporarily distract her husband, Zeus, from helping the Trojans, thus winning breathing space for her Achaeans, who are in dire straits. In order to execute her plan, she borrows an irresistible "embroidered, multicolored girdle" from Aphrodite, where "all charms lie: / here there is love, there is passion, there is the intimate / whisper, which even steals the minds of the wisest people" (*Iliad* 14.214–17). Significantly, this magic girdle has a counterpart in Norse mythology: Freyja, corresponding to Aphrodite, has a magic necklace or girdle called Brisingamen. The effect of Aphrodite's girdle is overwhelming: In the end, Zeus "slept peacefully on the top of Gargarus, / overcome by sleep and love, embracing his wife" (*Iliad* 352–53). Later, on waking up, he realizes the deception and becomes terribly angry with her.

Nowadays the Finns spend their winter weekends skiing on these slopes, unaware that they are trampling with their ski boots the same ground where lay the "fragrant altar" of the shrine of the king of the gods and where Paris awarded the golden apple to "divine Aphrodite."

ELOQUENT TOMBS

After this full immersion in the heart of Greek mythology, it is time to return to the present and point out that farmers often come across Bronze Age and Stone Age relics in the fields surrounding Toija and Kisko, demonstrating that there were indeed human settlements in this territory many thousands of years ago. Further, in the area surrounding Salo (just twelve miles from Toija), archaeologists have found splendid specimens of swords and spear points from the Bronze Age, which are now on display in the National Museum of Helsinki. These findings come from burial places including mounded stone tumuli found on hilltops that today rise from the plain, but which, thousands of years ago, when the coastline was farther inland, looked directly onto the sea. Many other tumuli, still intact, stand on the hills surrounding the valley between Lake Kirkkojärvi and Perniö, a village that lies a few miles west of Toija. These tumuli recall the description of Achilles' tomb in the last canto of the *Odyssey* and a passage in the *Iliad* in which Hector challenges an Achaean hero to a duel, with the plan to give back the corpse of his opponent in the case of his victory

> *. . . so that the long-haired Achaeans can bury him,*
> *and erect a mound for him on the broad Hellespont;*
> *and some day one of the men to come,*
> *sailing with a multioared ship on the wine-dark sea, will say:*
> *This is the mound of a man slain in ancient times:*
> *he excelled but renowned Hector killed him.* (Iliad 7.85–90)

The Homeric mounds "on the broad Hellespont" and the Bronze Age ones near Salo and Perniö are remarkably similar. The northern characteristics of the tombs described in the Homeric poems will not be unfamiliar to scholars. "Homer . . . describes Hector's and Patroclus's tombs as tumuli like those of our Thuringia culture."[9] Moreover, in *Beowulf* (the Anglo-Saxon epic about a Swedish hero, set in Denmark and dating back to the seventh century C.E.), the tomb of the protagonist is described by the hero himself as

> *a mound on the headland over the sea, which will rise over*
>   *Whale Cape*
> *to remind my people of me*
> *so that sailors will later call it*
> *"Beowulf's mound" when they drive*
> *their ships beyond sea's mist.*[10]

This is also reminiscent of Yngvarr's mound on the seashore where the breaking waves incessantly sing "Gymir's Song."

VIEW FROM ABOVE

Although all of these similarities between the region of the Finnish Toija and Homer's Troy—which can be verified by traveling the area—await more focused and in-depth archaeological investigation, an aerial survey of the territory of Toija and Kirkkojärvi gives us the best picture of where the ancient Trojan War may well have taken place.

Due to the unmistakable elongated shape of the now flooded plain, the territory of Troy, where Homer's fierce battle took place, can easily be spotted from a distance. As we approach from the air, we can see the slopes surrounding the village of Kisko, where Priam's city stood. Opposite them is the dark shape of Cape Vähäniemi, the ancient Batieia Hill, now covered by trees, protruding from the north bank of the lake where "the Trojans and their allies drew up" before the first battle (*Iliad* 2.815). This view from above shows the strategic importance of this rise in the defense of Troy against attacks from the coast. It is not by chance that the Trojan army chooses the area at the foot of this hill, in front of the Scaean (Western) Gates, to draw up its battle ranks and await the Achaeans, who are advancing up the valley along the eastern bank of the river: "The ground / rumbled terribly under their feet and their horses" (*Iliad* 2.465–66).

We can also see the Kurkelanjoki—that is, the Scamander—glittering in the sun. From above it looks like a thin, silver strip painted in the landscape, winding sinuously through the trees and flowing into the lake in a swampy area at the foot of Vähäniemi. On the east shore of the lake toward the south, we can see many creeks, and a little farther on, an islet that lies not far from the mouth of the Mammalanjoki (the ancient Simoïs) could be the Fine Hill mentioned in Book 20 of the *Iliad*. Approaching Aijala, the lake flows back into its riverbed and the Kiskonjoki begins. In ancient times, when this area formed coastline, this would have been a beach bounded by two headlands, where the Achaeans hauled their ships onto land, lining them up in many rows (*Iliad* 14.35–36). Here lay their fortified camp from which they launched their attacks on the city of Troy.

From above, everything in this broad region seems to tally wonderfully with Homer's descriptions of the world of Troy.

CHAPTER 7

WAR!

Homer's description of the Trojan War itself gives us many indications about not only its northern European location, but also its specific match to the Toija area. A visit to the coast on a calm summer evening enables us to enjoy the magical fascination of the never-ending northern dusk. A soft diffuse light spreads across the clear sky, little by little fading and turning the firs into dark silhouettes stretching as far as the shore, shrouded in profound silence. On the sea, whose color is more and more undefinable as the evening shadows sink lower, many small islands and islets appear to float dreamily on the horizon. Beyond them, our imagination can almost make out the black Achaean ships silently sliding across the sea.

THE ACHAEAN FLEET LANDS

What would a closer look reveal about the ships that carried the Achaeans from their lands to that fateful war with Troy? As we saw earlier, these boats presumably had a double prow, which gave them great maneuverability, as certified by the expression *amphiélissai* used so frequently by Homer. We can also deduce from the passage narrating Ulysses' arrival in Ithaca that the ship the Phaeacians use to take him has a flat keel and a minimum draft: The crew's impetus is so strong that the ship "mounted the beach by half the length [*hóson t'epí hémisy páses*]" (*Odyssey* 13.114).

Both poems mention ships having fifty oarsmen: Achilles' fleet (*Iliad* 16.170) and the Phaeachian ship with fifty-two oarsmen (*Odyssey* 8.35) that returned Ulysses to his home. Boeotian vessels, on the other hand, had no fewer than 120 men (*Iliad* 2.510). A detail from Ulysses' adventure on the island of Circe (*Odyssey* 10.203–208) allows us to calculate the number of men aboard his ship: forty-six, including the captain.

As mentioned earlier, Ulysses' ship had a removable mast, a feature typical of all Homeric vessels. Indeed, many passages in both the *Iliad* (1.434, 480) and the *Odyssey* (2.424–25, 8.52) confirm without a shadow of doubt that setting up and taking down the mast were customary at the beginning and the end of each mission, respectively. This type of mast indicates a rather advanced technology because it must ensure perfect stability of the sail in the presence of severe stresses and must also be easily and speedily erected and disassembled. The *Odyssey* expressly states that when Telemachus's ship returns to Ithaca, the crew takes down the mast "swiftly [*karpalímos*]" (*Odyssey* 15.497). The removable mast indicates that the Achaeans had a solid understanding of shipbuilding and reveals a seafaring tradition that likely far preceded Homer's time. Significantly, a sophisticated feature typical of Viking ships also was the removable mast,[1] which was lowered whenever there was the risk of ice formation, for ice on the mast could cause the ship to capsize. Thus, removable masts are a key indication that the shipbuilding technology that was already fully developed in Homer's time was eventually inherited by the Vikings.

All of the structural features of Achaean vessels were typical of Viking ships, which appeared thousands of years later, terrorizing the peoples of Europe's coasts. Therefore, it seems we cannot go too far wrong in using Viking ships as a guide to the shape and size of the vessels in Homer's world. Saxo Grammaticus speaks about "ships with one hundred men aboard."[2] As Rudolf Pörtner says, one of the five vessels (two warships and three merchant ships) found several years ago in the Roskilde Fjord not far from Copenhagen, "embarked about 50 to 60 warriors, had a mast and sail, and was undoubtedly one of the fearful long Viking ships Danish kings used for their attacks on England."[3] It measures ninety-two feet long and fifteen feet wide. We can assume that Homer's ships, having more or less the same number in their crew, were roughly the same size.

The second warship from Roskilde, which is smaller (fifty-nine feet long, eight and half feet wide), held twenty-four men. This type of ship could be used as a reference for the class of Achaean ships that seated twenty oarsmen and took young Chryseis to his father under Ulysses' command (*Iliad* 1.309), Telemachus to Pylos (*Odyssey* 2.212), and Antinous to try to intercept Telemachus (*Odyssey* 4.669). In fact, in another passage, the *Odyssey* explicitly mentions a kind of "merchant ship with twenty oarsmen" suitable for long crossings (*Odyssey* 9.322–23).

Tacitus also mentions the double prow, which allowed the Swedish sailors of his time to steer their ships in the narrow coastline fjords. The hulls of the famous Viking *drakkar* were periodically tarred so as to make them waterproof, and we can presume that the Achaean "black ships [*mélainai nêes*]" (*Iliad* 2.524) underwent a similar treatment. Further, after they were tarred, the sides of Viking ships were painted with bright colors, generally with red and white stripes, which corresponds to the red of Ulysses' ships (*Iliad* 2.637).

Homer also hints at shipbuilding activity when he recounts Helen's abduction: He mentions a Trojan named Tecton, "who was able to make any artifact, / since Pallas Athene outstandingly loved him. / He had built Paris' fine ships / which caused trouble for all Trojans" (*Iliad* 5.60–63). Troy's mooring may have been at the mouth of the Scamander, the place chosen by the Achaeans for their landing, which thus renders the port unusable for the Trojans, which is confirmed by the story of Iphidamas, who sets sail from Thrace, "then he left his fine ships in Percotes / and reached Ilium going on foot [*pezós eón*]" (*Iliad* 11.229–30). As usual, the poet of the *Iliad* is very precise in the details of Iphidamas's itinerary, which allows us to identify Percotes with today's Pargas, near Turku-Åbo, west of Toija. In short, after the Achaeans occupy the entire coastline, Percotes becomes an alternative port for Troy.

According to the *Iliad*, immediately when the Achaean ships land, the Trojans attack them and kill one of their leaders, Protesilaus: "A Dardanian warrior slew him / while he was leaping from his ship, first of the Achaeans" (*Iliad* 2.701–702). Then the Achaeans beach their ships in a number of rows along a long, broad shore bounded by two headlands:

> *The ships lay very far from the battlefield,*
> *on the shore of the grey sea. They had drawn*
> *the first ones as far as the plain and had built the wall facing the*
> *   sterns,*
> *since the beach [aigialós] could not hold all the ships,*
> *even though it was wide; the soldiers were crowded.*
> *So they arranged them in close rows and filled up the big mouth*
> *of the shore, bounded by the headlands.* (*Iliad* 14.30–36)

Thus the Achaean camp lay on the shore near the ancient mouth of the Scamander, rather far from the city of Troy. Besides revealing that the poet had a sound knowledge of the Toija region, these details enable us to locate precisely the area of the Achaean camp in the zone around Aijala: about four miles southwest of Toija, where the river reenters its bed at the end of the flooded area.

THE ACHAEAN CAMP

Today, due to the gradual uplift of the land that began thousands of years ago, Aijala lies a few miles from the sea. It is estimated that the land surrounding the Gulf of Finland is rising nearly sixteen inches each century. This means that the area around Toija and Aijala has risen by some fifty feet since Homeric times, leaving the sea far behind.*

Despite the fact that the site where the Achaean camp was located is no longer to be found by the sea, the main features of the coast facing Troy surely have not changed over thousands of years. The coastline is still low and very jagged, broken up into many irregularly shaped head-lands surrounded by several islands and islets that form a natural barrier against storms. In this area, the beaches bounded by headlands are low enough to allow mooring and beaching of craft. Therefore, the morphology of this coast corresponds exactly to the description in the *Iliad*.

After landing, the Achaeans build a great fortification in front of their ships: "They built a wall / and high towers to protect the ships and themselves. / They set up solid doors in them / so that there was a way for chariots through them" (*Iliad* 7.436–39). The poet provides us with various details of this wall around which a fierce battle is fought: It has towers and parapets (*Iliad* 12.373, 375) and stone and wooden foundations (*Iliad* 12.29), and is built of wood (*Iliad* 12.36) as well as stone (*Iliad* 12.178). During the Trojan attack, when "fight and noise were flaring up / around the well-built wall, the logs of the towers [*doúrata pýrgon*] creaked / when hit" (*Iliad* 12.35–37). In other words, it is rather like a sturdy fence of the kind that would be found in a northern environment where wood is

---

*It follows that the sites where present Finnish coastal cities now lie were under water four thousand years ago. Therefore, archaeologists should look for the remains of Achaean settlements farther inland, where the coastline was at the time of their creation. For example, if we follow the sequence of the Catalog of Ships, the Homeric city of Iolcus, from which an Achaean contingent left for Troy (*Iliad* 2.712), corresponds to present-day Jolkka, some twelve miles from the sea on the eastern coast of the Gulf of Bothnia.

plentiful. Constructed thus, it is therefore hardly surprising that the Trojans find it relatively "easy [*rheîa mála*]" (*Iliad* 15.362) to bring down the wall.

As for the landing situation, the crowding together of the Achaean ships along the shore at the mouth of the river obviously would prevent the vessels from setting sail simultaneously—a serious handicap if rapid flight was necessary. Thus Agamemnon (the commander in chief of the Achaean coalition) is understandably worried when the Trojans attack the Achaean camp (*Iliad* 14.75–79).

Homer gives us some information—scattered here and there, but very consistent—about the arrangement of the Achaean ships along the beach. Ulysses' ships are located in the middle while Achilles and Ajax have set up theirs at either end (*Iliad* 8.222–25). Nestor's ships are between those of Ajax and Ulysses. Ajax's ships are next to Protesilaus's, whose flagship, bravely defended by Ajax, is finally set on fire by the Trojans who attack the Achaean camp where the wall is "very low" (*Iliad* 8.683). The Trojans, however, suffer great losses on the left (*Iliad* 8.675), which is defended by Idomeneus's Cretans and Polypoetes' Lapithae (*Iliad* 12.117–30). Achilles' troops, led by Patroclus, are late in entering the battle because their location on the most strongly fortified side of the Achaean camp means they are unaware that the Trojans have broken through the Achaean lines on the other side. Because the "left" is to the west, it follows that Achilles' ships lie at the west end of the beach, at the river mouth, while Ajax's are on the opposite side, toward the east end of the shore, where the battle rages on long and fierce before Patroclus's counterattack.

Homer's relation of this successful counterattack includes the information that the camp lies by a river: "Among / the ships, the river [*potamoû*], and the high wall / he was pursuing and killing . . ." (*Iliad* 16.396–98)—the Scamander. This waterway flows into the sea at this point, as we learn from the description of the Achaean army gathering on the occasion of the first attack: "Many ranks poured into the Scamandrian Plain / from the ships and the tents" (*Iliad* 2.464–65).

After gathering, they move up the valley heading for Troy: "The earth loudly rumbled under their feet; / they were advancing very quickly across the plain" (*Iliad* 2.784–85). Because Homer never says that the Achaean army crosses the Scamander's ford, we deduce that its camp lies on the same side as Troy—that is, east of the river. They also do not cross the Simoïs (the Mammalanjoki), which makes sense because it flows into the Scamander (Kurkelanjoki) from the northwest (fig. 6.1). Homer also states that, at the beginning of the two-day battle, "an incessant cry broke out toward dawn [eôthi pró]" (Iliad 11.50). Here "dawn" means "east," which confirms the direction in which the Trojans, to whom the cry was directed, are lying. (To be precise, in the Northern Hemisphere the sun rises in the northeast during the month of June—exactly in the direction of Toija from the perspective of sailing up the river from the sea.) Here is another incongruity calling into question the traditional Anatolian location: If events were set there, the Achaean camp, located a certain distance to the west, would no longer lie on the banks of the Dardanelles, but instead lie directly in the Aegean Sea. Homer mentions together "the ships and the broad Hellespont" (Iliad 17.432) and repeatedly writes that the Achaeans "reached their ships and the Hellespont" (Iliad I15.233, 18.150, 23.2). This placement of the camp is confirmed by the episode in which some of the retreating Trojans, pursued by Achilles, try to cross the river at the ford of the Scamander, while others continue on toward the city (Iliad 21.1–9). It also squares with another of Homer's descriptive phrases: "On the left of the battle / near the Scamander's bank . . ." (Iliad 11.498–99). Since Homer specifies that the right corresponds to the east and the left to the west (Iliad 12.239–40), we can infer that the river runs along the western side of the valley. As we might expect, the territory of Toija fits perfectly with this layout.

As we can deduce from various references in the poem, it is a fair distance from the sea to the city. For example, during the fight over the body of Patroclus, "they were fighting under the Trojan wall, / very far away [pollón apáneuthe] from the ships" (Iliad 17.403–404). In addition, before Achilles' deadly attack, wise Polydamus in vain advises Hector to go back "to the city, rather than wait for daylight / here in the plain by the ships; we are too far from our walls" (Iliad 18.255–56). The presence of a Trojan spy in the area confirms that the Achaean camp is not within sight of the Trojan wall: "He was on the watch, relying on the speed of his feet, / at the top of old Aesyetes' tomb, / to inform [the Trojans] if the Achaeans moved from the ships" (Iliad 2.792–94).

To sum up, the Achaean camp stood where Aijala lies now, on a shore between two headlands near the ancient mouth of the river Scamander. Some miles upstream, on one of the hills surrounding today's Kisko,

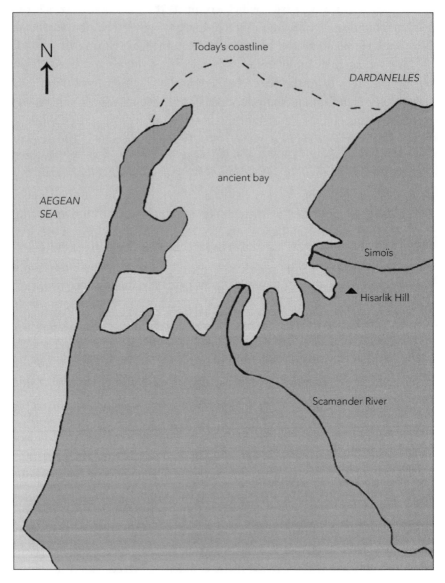

Fig. 7.1. The area around Hisarlik Hill as it appeared in the thirteenth century B.C.E.

Troy once stood. Both the city and the camp lay east of the river—that is, at the two ends of the Scamandrian plain, which extended from Batieia Hill, just in front of Troy, down to the sea (fig. 6.1). We have already noted that behind Troy, the Scamander's plain was called the Ileian plain. The battles described in the *Iliad* take place on this level area, now flooded, along the east bank of the river.

THE HISARLIK HEADLAND

At this point, we should examine the arguments against John Kraft's hypothesis, published in the journal *Geology*,[4] which suggests that the Achaean camp lies on the headland that bounds the inlet in front of Hisarlik toward the west (see fig. 7.1):

- The layout suggested by Kraft implies that the Achaean camp and Troy lie on opposite sides of the Scamander River. But we have just seen that they are on the same side of the river, which would be impossible on the Anatolian site (unless we imagine that the Achaeans beach their ships at the foot of the city, which contradicts the entire description in the *Iliad*).
- The Achaean wall is parallel to the beach where the Achaeans brought up their ships, not perpendicular to it, as Kraft's theory implies. This beach lies at the end of the plain and the ships are placed in rows parallel to the coast and to the wall (*Iliad* 14.30–32), which is built "before the sterns."
- When Patroclus chases the Trojans, he presses them against "the ships, the river and the wall" (*Iliad* 16.397), which corroborates the idea that the Achaean wall is close to the river and the ships, while according to Kraft's layout, the wall is at least a mile away from the river.
- Homer mentions the point where the Scamander and the Simoïs meet (*Iliad* 5.774), yet the Anatolian rivers corresponding to the Scamander and Simoïs do not meet but instead flow into the bay at two different points.

These discrepancies confirm that the site of Hisarlik does not represent Homeric Troy.

CHARIOTS, WARRIORS, AND WEAPONS

Chariots

The considerable distance between the two poles of the war—Troy and the Achaean camp—explains why Homeric heroes used their chariots to move across the battlefield. During duels, which were normally fought on foot, these chariots were left aside to protect the precious horses from becoming easy targets for enemy spears and arrows. The Trojan Asius, for example, used to fight "on foot in front of his puffing horses, which the charioteer / kept all the time behind him" (*Iliad* 13.385–86).

Many scholars say that the Trojan and Achaean use of chariots in this way is anomalous or absurd. According to Moses Finley, "there are the famous chariots, employed as taxis not only to transport the heroes to the battle but also to move them about within the mêlée . . . The fact of chariot-fighting had survived in the tradition and nothing else."[5] However, the "nonsense we read in the poems about military chariots" is not absurd at all when examined in light of other ancient wartime practices, such as those recorded in Julius Caesar's description of chariot fighting in ancient Britain:

> Their mode of fighting with their chariots is this: Firstly, they drive about in all directions and throw their weapons and generally break the ranks of the enemy with the very dread of their horses and the noise of their wheels; and when they have worked themselves in between the troops on horse, leap from their chariots and engage on foot *(ex essedis desiliunt et pedibus proeliantur)*. The charioteers in the meantime withdraw some little distance from the battle, and so place themselves with the chariots that, if their masters are over-powered by the number of the enemy, they may have a ready retreat to their own troops. Thus they display in battle the speed of horse, together with the firmness of infantry *(ita mobilitatem equitum, stabilitatem peditum in proeliis praestant)*.[6]

Julius Caesar underlines the effectiveness of this strategy in another passage:

> In the whole of this method of fighting since the engagement took place under the eyes of all and before the camp, it was perceived that our men, on account of the weight of their arms, in as much

as they could neither pursue the enemy when retreating, nor dare
quit their standards, were little suited to this kind of enemy; that
the horse also fought with great danger, because the Britons generally retreated even designedly, and, when they had drawn off our
men a short distance from the legions, leaped from their chariots
and fought on foot in unequal and to them advantageous battle *(ex
essedis desilirent et pedibus dispari proelio contenderent).*[7]

Therefore, the chariot fighting narrated by the *Iliad* is not "nonsense" resulting from the supposed ignorance of the poet (who has
proved himself very knowledgable on a number of subjects). On the
contrary, it is an extraordinary testimony of the uses of the chariot in
battle during the northern Bronze Age, methods that survived in the
civilization of the Britons in Caesar's age probably due in large part to
the Britons' isolation compared to the continental Celts.

The *Iliad* very realistically relates the difficulties caused by wounded
horses. For instance, in the duel between Patroclus and Sarpedon, the
latter "hit the horse Pedasus / with his spear on its right shoulder . . . /
the other two horses reared up, the yoke creaked, the reins / got entan-
gled as it fell into the dust" (*Iliad* 16.466–67, 470–71). Old Nestor also
runs into trouble when Paris hits one of his horses with an arrow:

> It reared up in pain, as the arrow lodged itself in its brain
> and, writhing because of the wound, upset the other horses.
> While the old man hurried to cut the harness
> with his dagger, Hector's quick horses
> arrived . . .
> and the old man would have certainly lost his life,
> if Diomedes had not perceived the danger. (Iliad 8.85–91)

We should note that the use of chariots was reserved strictly for
noblemen in their archaic society who could also afford charioteers (not
to mention bronze arms).

Some passages mentioning chariots also refer to military tactics
and the positioning of troops. For example, the Athenian Menestheus
is famous for "his art of marshalling cavalry and infantrymen" (*Iliad*
2.554). Nestor is also an expert at marshaling his soldiers (*Iliad* 2.555).
At the beginning of a battle

he ranged his charioteers with their horses and chariots in front,
and his best foot soldiers, backbone of his army, behind;
but he placed the worst in the middle,
so as to force them to fight even unwilling. (Iliad 4.297–300)

Warriors

Homer's warriors seem to follow the practice of honoring their leaders for the feats they as soldiers have accomplished, much like that described by Tacitus regarding the German infantrymen: "[T]heir most solemn pledge is to assign their feats to the glory of their leader" *(sua quoque fortia facta gloriae eius assignare praecipuum sacramentum est).*[8] This tradition allows us to interpret Nestor's boast when he recalls a battle he fought in his youth: He seized "fifty chariots, with two warriors / by each of them, who were tamed by my spear and bit the dust" (*Iliad* 11.748–49). It may also explain why Homer gives Paris credit for Achilles' death (*Iliad* 22.359–60): Because Paris is the son of Priam, he likely succeeds his brother Hector as commander in chief of the Trojan army, which we can deduce from the hierarchy of the Trojan army officers reported in detail in the poem (*Iliad* 12.88–102).

The Myrmidons specifically provide an interesting example of military strategy: They enter the battlefield drawn up in very compact and extremely effective ranks, "tightened together, shield to shield, helmet to helmet, man to man" (*Iliad* 16.215). This probably explains the decisive role the poet gives Achilles, leader of the Myrmidons, with regard to the outcome of the war; his contingent is what we might consider the counterpart to our armored divisions.

We should note that all of the warriors in the Trojan War are particularly strong, given the fighting they undertake wearing heavy bronze armor, which can be likened to a much heavier version of today's football protective gear. Interestingly and in keeping with his astute knowledge of detail, the poet seems very familiar with the repertoire of close combat, including the footwork, running, throwing, and dodging it involves. Accordingly, he does not forget to mention the champions who excel in each specialty. Ajax Oïleus "surpassed any other Hellene or Achaean in spearing" (*Iliad* 2.530) and was fast in pursuing the enemies (*Iliad* 14.521). The other Ajax—Telamonian Ajax—who is exceptionally tall and well built (*Iliad* 3.226–29), excels at close combat (*Iliad* 8.325). Achilles, who is called "swift-footed," excels at everything, but especially at sprinting and footwork (*Iliad* 8.325). Being quick on one's feet was an essential skill: Homer uses the expression "Ares' dance [mélpesthai Areï]" (Iliad 7.241) in reference to duels, and when Cretan Meriones manages to dodge the spear Aeneas throws at him, the latter ironically calls him "dancer [orchestén]" (Iliad 16.617).

This kind of fighting required young men of athletic build. It is no accident, then, that Hector has a newborn son and that other youthful warriors had been newly married shortly before the war. On the other end of the spectrum, we have old Idomeneus, king of Crete, who is turning "grey-haired" (mesaipólios; Iliad 8.361) and no longer has "firm legs to sprint / or throw himself after pitching or dodge a blow. / In close combat he averted his fatal day, / but his feet could not quickly take him any more away from the fight" (Iliad 8.512–15). It is not merely by sheer chance, therefore, that there seems to be only one father-son pair in the Achaean army: old Nestor and Antilochus.

Mystery Weapons

One of the weapons the Homeric warriors sometimes use—called chermádion in Greek—has been the source of a mystery that, when explained, could result in an interesting subject for archaeology. Chermádion is normally translated as "stone" or "flint," but it is not an ordinary stone, which is typically referred to by names such as pétre, lâas, and líthos. For example, Patroclus

> . . . jumped down from his chariot
> with his spear in his left hand; with the other he picked up
> a rough, sparkling stone [pétron] he wrapped up in his hand,
> and threw it with strength . . .
> The sharp stone [lâi] hit Hector's charioteer Cebriones . . . on the
> forehead,
> the stone [líthos] shattered his eyebrows. (Iliad 16.733–40)

Patroclus did not throw his spear to defend himself against Hector, who was approaching fast, but instead used a handy stone to knock out his enemy's charioteer. Homer uses all three above-mentioned synonyms for stone in the space of a few lines, but does not mention a chermadion. Whatever the chermadion is, it is certainly a lethal weapon. While Epeigeus tries to seize the corpse of Sarpedon, whom Patroclus has just killed, "Hector hit him / on the head with a chermadion, which split his skull in two / inside his strong helmet; he fell prone / over the corpse" (*Iliad* 16.577–80). Likewise, Diomedes, who lacked his spear when Aeneas attacked him,

> . . . *picked up a chermadion . . .*
> *and hit Aeneas on the hip . . .*
> *He broke his acetabulum and cut two tendons [*ámpho rhêxe
>   ténonte*];*
> *the jagged stone [*trechýs líthos*] ripped the skin. (Iliad 5.302–10)*

"Jagged stone" here obviously refers to the sharp end of the weapon. We find a similar description earlier on: Diores Amarincides "was hit on the heel by a chermadion, / . . . the cruel stone [*lâas anaidés*] shattered the two tendons / and bones" (*Iliad* 4.517–18, 521–22). As is obvious in these lines, chermadions usually wound by cutting: Patroclus "hit Sthenelaus / on the neck with a chermadion and cut his tendons [*rhêxen ténontas*]" (*Iliad* 16.586–87). In another example, Hector

> . . . *picked up a chermadion*
> *and headed straight for Teucer, intending to hit him.*
> *Teucer took a deadly arrow from his quiver*
> *and knocked it on the bowstring.*
> *While he was stretching, Hector struck him on his shoulder*
> *with the jagged stone in a very vulnerable point,*
> *where the clavicle divides the neck from the chest,*
> *and cut the bowstring [*rhêxe neurén*]. His wrist grew numb,*
> *he fell on his knees. (Iliad 8.321–29)*

There is further evidence that the chermadion is not merely a rock or stone, but rather an actual weapon. With reference to Ajax, the *Iliad* states that he could not yield to any man "vulnerable to bronze or big chermadions" (*Iliad* 13.323). In another passage, Agamemnon "tested ranks of soldiers / with his spear, sword, and big chermadions" (*Iliad* 11.264–65). This weapon, with its cutting stone that could be thrown or used in close combat, may be reasonably identified with an instrument commonly found in many archaic cultures: the stone ax. Other instances in which the chermadion is mentioned confirm this: When Achilles, armed with a

---

*The poet of the *Iliad*, unlike the poet of the *Odyssey*, is very precise in describing the human body and, in particular, every kind of wound. He surely moved on the battlefields; we might even suspect that he was a military doctor.

sword, attacks Aeneas, the latter "picked up a chermadion" (*Iliad* 20.285) to defend himself, each of them having already thrown his spear. Aeneas needed a weapon for quick defense, and in seizing an ax (which someone had probably lost on the battlefield), he finds one. Keeping the image of a stone ax in mind, we can visualize Ajax's deft, athletic movement:

> As Hector was retreating, great Ajax picked up
> one of the huge chermadions used as props of fast ships,
> which had rolled among the fighters' feet. He whirled it
> as a spinning top, which whizzed and hit Hector in the chest
> just above the rim of his shield, below his neck. (*Iliad* 14.409–13)

The effect of the blow is terrible:

> Hector fell down into the dust . . .
> All his comrades held
> their round shields over him, then they
> lifted him up and carried him away from the fray . . .
> When they reached the ford of the whirling River Xanthus . . .
> they lowered him down from the chariot onto the ground and poured
> water over him. Hector came to and reopened his eyes.
> He lifted himself up on his knees and vomited dark blood,
> then fell on his back again, and a black night
> fell on his eyes. (*Iliad* 14.418, 427–29, 433, 435–39)

At the beginning of this passage, Homer writes that the chermadions are "used as props [*échmata*] of the ships" (*Iliad* 14.410). We can compare this with the targets of the famous Ithacan archery contest: "the axes [Ulysses] used to knock in here at home, / twelve in a row, like keel props [*dryóchous*]" (*Odyssey* 19.573–74). The *Iliad* also narrates an episode linked with axes and seafaring: Axes are the prize in an archery competition in which the target is a pigeon fastened to the mast of a ship (*Iliad* 23.852). The relationship between ships and axes could have had a concrete and practical origin: In an emergency, ancient seafarers became woodcutters and carpenters in order to repair their ships or build rafts, as Ulysses does on the island of Ogygia. It seems likely that an ax was the most important tool for prehistoric sailors.

This is corroborated by the rupestrian engravings found in Scandinavia in which the coupling ship-ax is so common. Further, the identification

of Homeric chermadions with stone axes has been underlined by Scandinavian archaeology, for axes are very often found in burial sites dating back
to the epoch that preceded the time of the Achaean arrival in the Mediterranean. Archaeologists even talk about a "battle-axe people," referring to
stone axes that have been found that are very similar to the bronze ones of
the Mycenaean Age in Greece.

Today these ancient stone axes are known simply as stones or, to be
precise, thunderstones. According to Giorgio de Santillana and Hertha von
Dechend in *Hamlet's Mill,* Danish farmers who used to find them in their
fields called them "Zebedeus' stones," or similar names. In Finnish the term
stone seems still to be linked to the stone ax, for the word meaning "stone"—
that is, *kivi*—is similar to *kirves,* meaning "ax." In Greek, the word *chérma,*
which is practically a synonym of *chermádion,* could be linked to the word
cheír, "hand," obviously referring to the ax handle. Through the ages, the
meaning of this word probably shifted toward the jagged stone at the end
of the ax handle. It seems quite natural to link *chérma* and *chermádion* to
the Norse *hamar*—that is, "ax" or "hammer." What is more, in Old Norse
hamarr means "crag," and in Old Slavonic *kamy* means "stone."[9]

We can thus presume that while the leading warriors used chariots
and bronze weapons (except in emergencies), the privates—whom the
poet of the *Iliad* refers to as the "anonymous rank" ("I could neither mention them nor remember their name," *Iliad* 2.488)—were lightly armed
and fought on foot using the rather primitive chermadions, which were
commonly made to resemble their more precious metal counterparts. In
the Homeric world, the precious bronze weapons and armor—the one
Diomedes used was worth "nine oxen" (*Iliad* 6.236)—were sometimes
handed down from father to son. For example, the arms Achilles lent to
Patroclus for his nighttime counterattack were handed down to him by his
father (*Iliad* 17.196–97), while the less wealthy warriors were buried with
their poor stone axes, heritage of a previous epoch.

All of this corroborates the antiquity of the Homeric world. Archaism phenomena* are not, in fact, unusual to Scandinavian archaeology,
because obtaining metal objects was difficult in the region. On this sub-

---

*When one culture presents features or habits that are more archaic than those of coeval
cultures, this culture is said to present archaism pheonomena. In the case of Scandinavian
archaeology, archaism is evident in the discovery that stone axes were still used by the
culture when coeval cultures were using bronze axes. An example of an archaism phenomenon today can be seen in the use of certain models of cars in India that were driven
in Italy thirty or forty years ago.

ject Pia Laviosa Zambotti, professor of Scandinavian philology at the University of Milan, writes: "The passion for well-shaped stone tools goes back to the far-in-the-past Neolithic Age, while the lack of metal contributed to the growth of an industry founded on imitation, which used precious metal tools as a model."[10]

Perhaps some of those ancient chermadions still lie near Toija, in the muddy bed of Lake Kirkkojärvi, which covers the mythical plain where so many heroes fell "between the Rivers Simoïs and Xanthus." After four thousand years, they still wait for archaeologists to bring them back to light.

THE BATTLE WITH TWO NOONS

A significant consequence of changing the setting of Troy and the Trojan War from Anatolia to Finland is that it instantly clears up what has appeared to be a serious anomaly in the *Iliad* that greatly affects the intelligibility of the text: Homer's narration of the longest and fiercest battle, which consists of a series of front reversals and single episodes that stretches over a third of the whole poem, from Book 11 to Book 18.

In the course of this long battle, Homer mentions two noons (*Iliad* 11.86, 16.777), implying that the fight continues through the night, a time span he supports throughout the narrative, as in this passage referring to Sarpedon, king of Lycia, Zeus's son, who was slain by Patroclus: "Zeus spread a dreadful night [*nýkt'oloén*] out over the strenuous battle / so that the effort of the fight around his beloved son was dreadful" (*Iliad* 16.567–68). Most significant about this length of time is that the night *does not interrupt* the battle, which continues nonstop until the evening of the second day.

This lack of interruption during the night seems very odd for a battle fought in the traditional Anatolian context. In the Aegean world, even the shortest nights of the year around the summer solstice have at least five or six hours of darkness during which it would be impossible to fight without floodlights or infrared visors! In the past, the "dreadful night" was interpreted as a solar eclipse or a miraculous intervention by Zeus, and it was assumed that the entire battle must have taken place within one day—despite the fact that Homer tells us that Patroclus's repeated attacks against the Trojan walls alone take up "an entire day" (*Iliad* 18.453). Such compression, however, makes the course of the events and the episodes confusing and incomprehensible and conflicts with those puzzling "two noons."

Such a gross error on the part of the poet is quite out of the question.

Homer retains tight control over the action, never recording the events of the battle at random. That the narrative follows a strict plan is proved by the passages in which Zeus reveals his will, establishing what is ineluctably to follow: The course of events unfolds in accordance with what Zeus has announced in advance. This narrative artifice is used rather frequently in the *Iliad:* The poet first states Zeus's will—that is, a sort of plan of action—then he reports its actual development. Such references to "diagramming" the action and merging of past, present, and future are typical of epic poetry, where any surprises are left out. The poet, inspired by the Muse, places himself in a dimension outside time, relating events that he has witnessed whose sequences are obviously unchangeable. This could also be connected to the Homeric concept of Moira, or Fate, which suggests that as far as the poet is concerned, events that have already taken place are at the same time hidden in the ineluctable future of his characters. Simply put, the Homeric Fate seems to express the impossibility—not only for men, but also for the gods—of modifying past events.

In this case, the general plan of the battle is outlined as follows: Zeus

> . . . *wanted to give glory to Hector,*
> *Priam's son, so that he could set fire*
> *to the ships . . .*
> *Then he would have inflicted a counterattack*
> *on the Trojans from the ships and would have given glory to the*
>   *Danaans. (Iliad 15.596–97, 601–602)*

The narration of events then follows this outline, with Zeus even making an unequivocal reference to a definite hour for some of the action:

> *When Agamemnon, hit by a spear or wounded by an arrow,*
> *withdraws with his horses, I shall give Hector the strength*
> *to kill until he reaches the well-oared ships,*
> *the sun sets and darkness falls [knéphas élthei]. (Iliad 11.191–94)*

It is therefore clear that the Achaean counterattack starts in the evening and continues through the night. Yet it would be impossible to fight after dusk in the Mediterranean world! If, however, we place these events in the area of Toija, at about 60° north latitude, only six degrees from the Arctic Circle, the mystery begins to resolve. In this region in June the sun sets only slightly below the horizon and the nights are light enough to allow some visibility. Thus, as soon as we set it in its original context after these thousands of years, the great battle at last reveals its potent architecture: *The fighting indeed lasts nonstop for two consecutive days,* taking advantage of the residual night light due to the high latitude and the solstice season. With this fact in place, it becomes very easy to set all the single episodes (which hitherto appeared to occur almost haphazardly because of their compression into one day) into an extremely consistent overall picture:

First day. After the initial stage of the battle seems to favor no one, the Achaeans appear to prevail at about midday, even though Achilles abstains from fighting after a quarrel with Agamemnon, which is the *Iliad*'s starting point. Agamemnon, however, is wounded in the afternoon. Soon afterward, the Trojans launch a violent attack, break down the defensive wall, invade the Achaean camp, and, despite the desperate resistance of the enemy, even manage to set fire to Protesilaus's ship. At this point, as Zeus had announced, Patroclus launches his counterattack at the head of Achilles' fresh troops, and thereby reverses the situation: He drives away the Trojans from the ships and the camp, kills Sarpedon (the "dreadful night" falls while Achaeans and Trojans are fiercely fighting over his corpse), and pursues the enemy up to Troy.

Second day. Patroclus repeatedly attacks the walls of the city, which is about to fall, but on the fourth attack during the second afternoon of the battle, Hector manages to kill him. The situation is again reversed: The Trojans attack the Achaeans, who are dismayed at Patroclus's death, but the Achaeans succeed in retaking Patroclus's corpse after another furious fight. In spite of their tiredness, the Trojans gain ground and again press the Achaeans toward the ships, until "the sun set, then the noble Achaeans stopped / the violent fight and the battle" (*Iliad* 18.241–42) after two uninterrupted days of fierce fighting.

The *Iliad* itself corroborates this construction of events in the passage in which the goddess Thetis narrates to Hephaestus the main episodes of the battle that has just ended: "They fought an entire day [*pân êmar márnanto*] by the Scaean Gates" (*Iliad* 18.453). This obviously refers to the *second day* of battle.

The whole picture conjures up an enormous fresco filled with strong emotional elements: Here are warriors blinded by hate and eagerness for victory who, after some days of fighting (this not being the first battle in the poem), break all rules, ignoring any previous tradition for a nighttime pause in the fighting ("Night is falling now: it is good to comply with the night" [*Iliad* 7.282]). At the end of each day of fighting, the soldiers obviously are completely exhausted. Homer himself tells us that at a certain point well into the first afternoon, the defenders of the Achaean wall are "worn out" [*achnýmenoi*]" (*Iliad* 12.178) under Trojan pressure. The battle, however, is able to continue beyond sunset and into the next day because Patroclus's troops enter the fray in the evening, after they had rested, which is the course of action suggested by wise Nestor himself when he begs Patroclus to intervene as the Trojans are about to break through the Achaean lines: "Since you are fresh [*akmêtes*] you can easily drive / men worn-out with fight [*kekmeótas ándras aütêi*] back to the city, away from the ships and the tents" (*Iliad* 11.802–803). Soon afterward, Patroclus repeats the same concept to Achilles (*Iliad* 16.44–45) to hasten his assent to enter the field. Because he is furious with Agamemnon, Achilles himself does not want to fight; however, he is willing to send his Myrmidons into battle with his lieutenant to confront the emergency.

This reconstruction can even explain the strange death of Patroclus, who becomes vulnerable when all of a sudden he feels faint (the Trojan Euphorbus, who is the first to realize this, manages to wound him, but it is Hector who delivers the final blow): "He rolled his eyes / and Phoebus Apollo knocked off his helmet from his head" (*Iliad* 16.792–93); then "a malaise caused him to lose his senses [*tón d'áte phrénas heîle*], his strong limbs failed, / he stood dazed . . ." (*Iliad* 16.805–806). Interestingly, the *Iliad* poetically ascribes these symptoms to Apollo, the archer god who causes the sudden death of men with his "arrows" (*Odyssey* 15.410–11, 17.251). In the light of the above reconstruction of events, Patroclus's illness and death in this way make complete sense: This is the second afternoon of the battle and Patroclus, drunk with fight and eager to conquer Troy on his own (although Achilles had wisely warned him to limit himself to driving the enemies away from the camp; *Iliad* 16.87–96), has been fighting since the preceding evening. The sudden collapse that costs him his life occurs after almost twenty-four hours of uninterrupted, fierce battle.

With regard to this battle, then, the northern location in which dim light continues during the nights of the summer solstice season is essential to making sense of the rationale and consistency of the narration. More than just a clue to unlocking the *Iliad*, this setting is necessary to the story. But wouldn't residents of the Baltic area be so familiar with this "night light" phenomenon as to have a specific name for it? In answer to this, we can read the melancholy but beautiful account of the scene where the Trojans and Achaeans, during a truce, retrieve their dead scattered all over the battlefield:

The new sun lit up the fields
rising from the deep, quietly-flowing Ocean
into the sky. Then they met.
It was difficult to identify every man
but they washed away the clotted blood with water,
shedding scalding tears, and lifted them onto their wagons.
. . . The Achaeans
distressed in their hearts, piled up their dead on a pyre,
burnt them with the fire and returned to their ships.
When it was still dimly-lit night [amphilýke nýx], before dawn
*   broke,*
then a group of Achaeans gathered by the pyre,
and made a tumulus over. (Iliad 7.421–26, 430–35)

The adjective *amphilýke* (which is not commonly used in Greek) literally means "lighted around," from *amphí,* "around," and the root *lyk-,* which is close to the Greek word *leukós,* meaning "white," and the Latin noun *lux,* meaning "light."[11] Here is the "dimly-lit night" (*Iliad* 7.433) that precedes dawn, as Homer says. We can consider this term a linguistic fossil that has survived the end of the northern Bronze Age thanks to the fact that the Achaeans "ferried" it, along with the *Iliad,* to the Mediterranean, where the phenomenon connected with its real meaning never occurs. It is similar to the references to "the Dawn's dances" on Circe's island and to Zeus, who "spreads a colored arch [*porphyréen îrin*] in the sky for the mortals, / so as it is a portent of war / or freezing winter . . ." (*Iliad* 17.547–49). The only plausible answer to Homer's meaning in "a colored arch" leads us once more to a northern location: It seems to refer to the aurora borealis, which lights up the northern night skies with magical iridescence. This phenomenon must have fired the imagination of those ancient peoples so much that they ascribed it to Zeus himself, as Homer tells us.

The link Homer makes among the aurora borealis, freezing winter, and war raises some intriguing possibilities. We know that auroras are connected with solar wind—which is caused by the interaction between a flow of particles emanating from the sun and Earth's magnetic field—and that their intensity depends on solar activity. Is it not possible that solar winds alter the chemistry of the upper atmosphere and, consequently, influence the greenhouse effect, which regulates Earth's temperature? An increase in solar activity in turn increases the incidence of sunspots, which are "cold areas" on the solar surface—which could contribute to reducing, at least by a small degree, the temperature of our planet. In short, solar activity could be directly involved in producing glaciations. A rigorous winter can ruin a harvest and cause famine and migration. Moreover, the solar wind appears to affect the mood of many people. Here we arrive at the relationship stressed in the *Iliad* between auroras and wars.

STORMS AND FLOODS

Much as we have already verified in the other geographic environments through which the poet has led us, we can prove that the meteorological features of Troy are typical of a northern country. The *Iliad* repeats the expression "windy Troy" *(enemóessa)* no fewer than seven times. Further, the weather on the battlefield is usually inclement, as it is, for example, in the Achaean camp just before the "dreadful night" of battle: "All night wise Zeus planned trouble for them / frighteningly thundering" (*Iliad* 7.478–79). After the battle begins, Zeus "thundered powerfully and threw a fiery lightning / into the middle of the Achaean army" (*Iliad* 8.75–76), "then thundering he threw a terrible dazzling thunderbolt" (*Iliad* 8.133), and he "thundered three times from the mountains of Ida" (*Iliad* 8.170). Interestingly, afterward, "it lightened" (*Iliad* 9.237).

The next day, "Zeus the lightning thrower *(terpikéraunos)* / stirred up a windstorm from the mountains of Ida" (*Iliad* 12.252–53); later, during the fight over Patroclus's body, "he covered the Ida with clouds, / and lightning thundered very powerfully" (*Iliad* 17.594–95). Considering these weather conditions, it comes as no surprise that during the chariot race that takes place on the occasion of Patroclus's funeral, "there was a fissure of the ground, the collected rainwater / had broken the track and hollowed out all the ground" (*Iliad* 23.420–21).

Fog is also frequently present on the battlefield:

> *You were not able to say*
> *whether there was still the Sun or the Moon;*
> *in the battle fog had closed in upon the strongest men.*
>   (*Iliad* 17.366–68)

> *Around them*
> *and their shining helmets Zeus*
> *spread much fog.* (*Iliad* 17.268–70)

[Apollo] approached Patroclus, being shrouded in thick fog.
  (*Iliad* 16.790)

Sometimes the fog directly influences the course of events, such as when it hinders the retreat of the Trojans pursued by Achilles: "Hera / spread a thick fog in front of them to hold them" (*Iliad* 21.6–7), but on other occasions it protects endangered warriors:

Achilles hurled himself at godlike Agenor,
but Apollo did not allow him to gain glory;
he took Agenor away, hid him in thick fog,
and got him to safety away from the fight. (*Iliad* 21.595–98)

In another passage, Ajax calls out for the fog to dissolve and the sun to come out:

I am not able to see any of the Achaeans!
Men and horses are shrouded all and sundry in the fog.
Thou, Father Zeus, free the sons of the Achaeans from the fog,
make the sky clear [poiéson d'aíthren] and allow us to see!
  (*Iliad* 17.643–46)

All of this supports the idea that the *Iliad*'s action is set in June, when the short summer of the northern regions has not yet become stable, a picture that is further corroborated by the overflowing of the Trojan rivers two days after the battle fought during the "light night." In northern regions, the greatest floods happen in the late spring and at the beginning of summer, due to the melting of winter's ice. Achilles, who has taken the field again to avenge the slaying of his friend Patroclus by Hector the day before, risks drowning in the overflowing Scamander. The river (which the poet personifies) overflows its banks and floods the plain:

He swelled the wave of his current
raising it far up and shouted at Simoïs:
Dear brother, . . . help me as quick as you can, fill your course
with water from your springs, urge all your streams
and raise a great wave. (*Iliad* 21.306–308, 311, 313)

These descriptions are so vivid that they impart the feeling that their first bard was inspired by events that really happened.

WAR AND THE FABLED WALLS OF TROY

According to the tradition, the Trojan War lasted an enormous amount of time—ten years—because of the impregnable city walls, and ended with the stratagem of the wooden horse. This is the version given in the *Odyssey,* which is intended to enhance Ulysses' role in the war and, perhaps, to justify his lengthy absence from Ithaca.

Yet as far as the fabled wall of the city is concerned, the *Iliad* never describes it in much detail. In fact, the poem dwells more upon the wall of the Achaean camp, and Homer does give us some idea of the Trojan wall only in comparison to this structure, whose fame "will be as high as dawn extends, / and people will forget the one"—that is, the Trojan wall Apollo and Poseidon "built with hard work for the hero Laomedon" (*Iliad* 7.451–53). In essence, the poet considers the Trojan wall to be inferior to the "great Achaean wall" (*Iliad* 12.12), which itself is far from impregnable, given that its stone-and-wood structure is brought down by the first attack of the Trojans.

Other parts of the poem also describe the Trojan walls as being vulnerable, as here in a passage from the dialogue between Andromache and Hector:

> *Line up the army by the wild fig, where*
> *the city is more exposed and the wall proves to be accessible*
>   *[epídromon épleto teîchos].*
> *Their best men returned to attack there three times*
> *. . . either someone who is experienced in oracles told them,*
> *or their own mind inspires them and drives them.*
>   (*Iliad* 6.433–35, 438–39)

This vulnerability, it seems, is the principal reason why the Trojans and their allies do not barricade themselves inside the citadel when the Achaeans launch their first attack: "All gates opened and the army dashed out, / foot and horse" (*Iliad* 2.809–10).

The Trojan wall is no doubt similar to that of the Phaeacian city mentioned in the *Odyssey,* "assembled with pales [*skolópessin areróta*]" (*Odyssey* 7.45), which may sound rather primitive to us but is considered splendid by the poet: "It's wonderful to look at!" These archaic walls—comprising a kind of large fence with parapets and towers where the gates stood, such as the tower near the Scaean Gates (*Iliad* 3.153)—must have looked somewhat like the old forts in western films.

Should archaeologists take these considerations into account, they should expect to find not vestiges of cyclopean walls on the site of Toija, but only remains of a much lighter, simpler structure in accordance with the current thinking of scholars regarding the more archaic features of the Homeric world as compared to those of the refined Mycenaean civilization.

The vulnerability of the city walls is further confirmed by the fact that they nearly fall in the attack Patroclus carries out after the "dreadful night": "At this point the sons of the Achaeans would have captured Troy / under the leadership of Patroclus, who raged around with his spear. /. . . Three times he reached the elbow at the top of the wall" (*Iliad* 16.698–99, 702). Patroclus almost succeeds: "They fought the entire day by the Scaean Gates / and would have destroyed the city that day / if Apollo had not killed the gallant son of Menoetius, who was doing a lot of harm" (*Iliad* 18.453–55).*

The Trojan wall falls at last under another frontal attack after Hector's death, as Zeus had predicted in one of his prophetic speeches:

---

*Incidentally, the discovery (or rather, the rediscovery) of an important modern scientific concept was made possible by a reference to the death of Patroclus in the *Iliad*. In the seventeenth century, it was still believed that maggots were generated spontaneously during the process of putrefaction, until the Italian doctor and poet Francesco Redi published his work *Experiences on Insect Generation* in 1668, reporting experimental proof that flies' eggs produce putrefaction, not vice versa. Redi himself admitted that this idea came to him after he read the passage in the *Iliad* in which Achilles is worried that flies will cause Patroclus's corpse to decompose:

> I am very afraid
> that flies may penetrate Menoetius' strong son
> through the wounds the bronze opened
> and bear worms, which should deface his corpse,
> thus his flesh should rot, as his life was extinguished.
> Silver-footed Thetis replied:
> Son, do not worry about this;
> I will try to repel that wild race,
> the flies, which feed on the men killed in battle.
> Even if it lies a whole year
> his corpse will keep intact. (Iliad 19.24–33)

In other words, Homer was acquainted with a scientific truth humankind later forgot. This is yet another link to the *Iliad*'s northern location, where decomposition occurs only in summer, when flies appear, rather than throughout the year, as in the mild Mediterranean climate. This climatic factor explains how the ancient Achaeans could be aware of the cause of this phenomenon.

"Noble Achilles will kill Hector; / from then on I will provoke a nonstop / attack [*palíoxin diamperés*] / from the ships until the Achaeans / conquer Ilium" (*Iliad* 15.68–71).

The cities described in the *Iliad* are quite different from the mighty strongholds of Mycenaean settlements, and the remains of large walls recently found in the area of Hisarlik prove that Schliemann's city has nothing to do with Homer's Troy. Rather, Troy was like the other ancient cities of the north, where timber was plentiful. As Karl Schuchhardt writes: "Homer talks of the wooden walls surrounding the Phaeacian city and the Achaean camp as if they were a Germanic *Volksburg*."[12] Those cities may well have resembled Moscow of five or six hundred years ago, where the houses were made of wood. Even the Kremlin stronghold—situated on a hill 130 feet above the Moskva River in the heart of the city—was made of wood and surrounded by a fence until the fifteenth century.

In short, it is not necessary to use any particular stratagem to conquer Troy. As a matter of fact, the absurd wooden horse ploy is never actually mentioned in the *Iliad*. Homer discloses the fate of this prehistoric Fort Alamo in an almost cinematic scene: "Troy will blaze all being burnt by a violent fire, / the battle-fit sons of the Achaeans will burn it" (*Iliad* 21.375–76).

So how long did the war actually last? The *Iliad* contains many references that show that the Achaeans reached the Trojan territory just before the beginning of the events narrated in the poem. Although the *Odyssey* says the war took ten years, it also provides us with evidence that it was carried out in a much shorter time. It states that Aegisthus, after seducing Clytemnestra during Agamemnon's absence, places a spy in a watchtower in order to be forewarned of the return of his rival: "He kept watch for a year [*eis eniautón*]" (*Odyssey* 4.526). "A year" confirms the real duration of the war, which can be supported by a reconstruction of events using the information handed down to us in the Homeric poems (above all, the details in the *Iliad*, which is the more realistic of the two epics).

Here, then, is a synopsis of the chronology of the war:

After Paris abducts Helen, which most likely takes place during the summer seafaring season, Agamemnon and Menelaus set about rounding up allies from among the Achaean peoples and arrange a meeting point in Aulis, which is the most suitable place from which to sail for Troy. After their departure, which probably takes place in the beginning of the seafaring season of the following year, they stop at Lemnos, then reach the Troad, where they plunder several towns around Ida while awaiting the arrival of all the contingents. In the meantime, the Trojan allies are gathering. The Achaeans then decide to carry out a direct attack on Troy, despite internal conflict. A series of bloody pitched battles, the first ones narrated in the *Iliad,* take place in June, when the rivers overflow and the twilit nights make it possible for battles to rage continuously. Finally, after repeated attacks on the city walls, the Achaeans, although they have suffered heavy losses, conquer the city.

At this point, autumn is approaching and bad weather is making sailing increasingly dangerous. As Nestor narrates in Book 3 of the *Odyssey,* however, because the victors are eager to return home, they decide to leave. The poet spends a great deal of time describing rough seas, strong winds that cause Ulysses, Menelaus, and Agamemnon to sail off course, and the shipwrecks of Ajax Oïleus and part of Menelaus's fleet.

TROY AFTER THE WAR

One significant consequence of re-setting the war in this northern location is a confirmation of Troy's survival after the conflict. It is not deserted after the Achaeans plunder and burn it down, but instead is rebuilt, as the *Iliad* states: "At this point Zeus has come to hate Priam's stock, / so Aeneas' power will rule the Trojans now / and then his children's children and those who will come later on" (*Iliad* 20.306–308). Because the victors head for home immediately after the war, as both the *Iliad* (12.16) and the *Odyssey* (3.130–31) relate, rather than occupying the territory, the Trojans can rebuild their city unhindered.*

This version of the postwar facts is also found in other sources such as the *Homeric Hymn to Aphrodite,* when Aphrodite tells Anchises: "You'll have a son, who will reign over the Trojans; / his sons will have sons for good; / his name will be Aeneas."[13] Thus Troy was rebuilt and has survived more than three thousand years to reach our days, forgetful of its

---

*Virgil's quite tendentious and much more recent tale of Aeneas's flight by sea from the burning city of Troy was actually written in homage to the family of Emperor Augustus, who was considered Aeneas's descendant and, as we can see from Homer's words, is unrelated to the real destiny of the Trojan hero and his city after the war.

epic past until, in 1994, the Finnish press wrote of the theory presented in this book.

Given the survival of the northern Troy, we should look for signs of a "Finnish" Aeneas, who, according to Homer, was the first king of the dynasty that ruled Troy after the war. Knowing that we are dealing with a kingdom that, under Priam, dominated a vast area in southern Finland—"The whole of the country that is bounded by Lesbos . . . / upper Phrygia and boundless Hellespont"—it is very tempting to suppose a relationship between Aeneas's name and Aeningia—that is, Finland's name in Roman times.[14]

Although Homer is silent regarding Troy's history after Aeneas's succession, Norse mythology seems surprisingly able to tell us something more. As reported by Chiesa Isnardi, Odin, the Norse godhead and leader of the Aesir, was a king who came from Asia,* and more specifically from Troy. In particular, a passage from the *Younger Edda* states that the home of Norse gods "is known as Asgardh, but we call it Troy."[15] The *Iliad* hints at disagreements, based on dynastic reasons (*Iliad* 20.180–83), between Aeneas and Priam, who descended from two different branches of a very noble family that included all Trojan kings and whose progenitor was Zeus himself (*Iliad* 20.215–40). Thus we can imagine that dynastic conflicts broke out over Troy's sovereignty some generations after the war, which, according to Homer, resulted in the handing over of power from Priam and Hecabe's dynasty to Aeneas's. In fact, in the *Iliad,* Asius "was a maternal uncle of Hector / and a brother of Hecabe" (*Iliad* 16.717–18).

It could not be mere coincidence that the enemies of the Aesir, Odin's clan, were the Vanir, whose name can be connected with Aeneas, with the usual loss of the initial *v*. What is more, one of the Vanir was Freyja, the goddess of love, who corresponded in both function and name to Aphrodite, Aeneas's mother. Maybe in the end, Hecabe's descendants—that is, the Asians-Aesir, to whom Odin belonged—dethroned Aeneas

---

*Regarding the name Asia, which first indicated a region belonging to Lidia (Asia Minor) and later extended to the entire continent east of Europe, it is very likely that the Mycenaeans transplanted it from the Baltic. Homer mentions it in a line of verse: "In the Asian meadow, by the current of Cayster" (*Iliad* 2.461). Cayster was a river in Asia Minor whose northern prototype obviously lay in the Homeric world. We can infer that during the Early Bronze Age the name Asia indicated a region of southern Finland close to the Homeric Troy; after the Achaeans moved south, this name was attached to a region of Asia Minor.

(the Vanir), established their dynasty in Aeningia, and made Odin king of Troy. It is out of the question that Odin could predate the Trojan War because the *Iliad* lists all kings from the founding of the city, which dates from six generations before the war.

The Norse skalds' statements about the Trojan origin of Odin are supported by a statement in the *Volospá*, the first poem contained in the *Edda*, which gives the name of the Aesir's home as Idhavoll: "The Aesir gathered in Idhavoll / and built high temples and shrines."[16] Idhavoll means "the field of Idha," which once more recalls Ida, where Zeus had his shrine (*Iliad* 8.48). It is interesting to note that the Aesir returned there after the Ragnarok, a sudden collapse in temperature that gave rise to terrifying phenomena: "The Aesir meet again in Idhavoll / and talk about the mighty snake of the world."[17] The terrible Ragnarok could be a description of the same climatic changes that drove the Achaeans to leave Scandinavia and move toward the south, and perhaps points specifically to the catastrophic eruption of the Mediterranean volcano Thera (Santorini), which took place about 1630 B.C.E.

Over time, Odin—perhaps an outstanding king when the catastrophe happened—was deified and those distant events were assimilated and mixed with the myths of the former Indo-European legacy into one common memory. While Norse literature as we know it arose no less than twenty-five hundred years after the explosion of Thera, Odin's antiquity is confirmed by Sleipnir, his strange horse with eight legs, which very likely derives from an archaic Bronze Age depiction of the god on his chariot drawn by two horses, seen in profile.

To sum up, we have found many analogies between the world of Troy and a large area in southwest Finland. The region surrounding Toija fits very well with both Homer's descriptions of the topography and climate and the leitmotif of the war—that is, the incessant oscillation of the battles between two opposite poles: on one side, the fortified city, far from the sea hills rising behind it, and on the other, the Achaean camp, situated on the seashore between two headlands, near the mouth of the Scamander. The river, flowing in the valley below the hills, connected these two poles. The battlefield was the level strip along the river's eastern bank, forming a sort of "highway" for the chariots to go from Troy to the sea and back again.

A final image to consider is the splendid description of the Trojan camp set up in front of the Achaean ships and lit by fires blazing in the night:

> They stayed on the edge of the battlefield,
> brimming with pride the whole night; many fires were blazing . . .
> Between the ships and the running Scamander
> the fires the Trojans had lit in front of Ilium were shining.
> A thousand fires blazed on the plain; around each of them
> fifty men stood in the light of the burning fire;
> the horses, eating white barley and rye,
> were standing by their chariots waiting for dawn.
>   (Iliad 8.553–54, 560–65)

At last, we are able now to place this glorious scene in its real location.

CHAPTER 8

NEIGHBORING LANDS AND ISLANDS

TROY'S NEAR NEIGHBORS

The correspondence we have seen between Troy and Toija extends as well to the area surrounding the Finnish village. By widening our search to cover the entire region, we get a picture that turns out to be amazingly consistent with Homer's details regarding the overall setting, thus verifying the same kind of correspondence that we found in the case of Ithaca-Lyø and the islands surrounding it.

Phrygia

Traditional thought holds that the region adjoining Finnish Troad to the northwest was Phrygia, which marked the boundary of Priam's kingdom. The land in that direction is roughly similar to ancient Phrygia: vast and flat, stretching as far as the horizon, with wheat fields, vegetable fields, pastures, blooming meadows in the summer, and vast woods. If we proceed farther on, we come to Kiikoinen, which recalls the Ciconians, the name of whose leader, Mentes (*Iliad* 17.73), might be heard in the place-name Montola. Beyond Tampere is the village of Kapee, which recalls Capys, Assaracus's son and Anchises' father (*Iliad* 20.239), who were descended from Zeus, as Capys's grandson, Aeneas, proudly reminds Achilles before their duel.

According to well-established tradition, Phrygia was considered the original country of the Romans, a belief that is corroborated by the many place-names in southern Finland that recall those in Roman territory. Kullaa and Kaanaa lead us to Collatia and Caenina, two ancient towns in the region of Latium. The names Marttila, Juva, and Palus sound quite similar to Mars, Jupiter, and particularly Pale, a primitive goddess of agriculture to whom the Romans dedicated the feast called Paliliae. Likewise, Kurisjärvi, apart from the suffix, sounds very similar to Cures, an ancient town near Rome.

Although Virgil's story of Aeneas differs from Homer's account of the Trojan hero succeeding Priam after the end of the war, many place-names in the area sound remarkably like various characters from Virgil's *Aeneid*, such as Askainen, similar to the *Iliad*'s Ascanius, who fought with the Trojans against the Achaeans: "Phorcys and divine Ascanius led the Phrygians / from distant Ascania" (*Iliad* 2.862–63). Laitila recalls King Latinus and Latium, Lavia sounds like Lavinia, Larila recalls Laurentus, Eura is similar to Eurialus, Evajärvi recalls Evandrus, Turajärvi sounds like Turnus, Lauttijärvi is akin to Lausus, Kattelus recalls Catillus, Kaaro recalls Cora, and Kiikala is similar to Caecolus. These correspondences indicate that it is indeed possible that a primitive Indo-European people who had originally settled in Finland and Lithuania later moved into ancient Latium and retained in its historical memory the names Virgil handed down in his poem. Latin, which belongs to the same Indo-European family as Greek, Sanskrit, and the Germanic languages, could also have been imported into Latium by immigrants coming from the eastern Baltic area.

The Watery Torment of Tantalus

According to Greek mythology, which reminds us more and more of the northern Bronze Age, Tantalus (*Odyssey* 11.582) was king of Lydia, a region on the border of Phrygia—therefore, not far from Troad. In southern Finland, near Toija, we find Tanttala and the place-name Tammela, which sounds similar to the name Mount Tmolus (*Iliad* 2.866) and King Tmolus, Tantalus's father. In the same region is a hill known as Sipilänmäki—Sipilä Hill, with *mäki* meaning "hill" in Finnish—reminding us that Tantalus's tomb was on Mount Sipylus. His famous torment, requiring him to stand immersed in water that receded out of reach when he tried to drink from it, might well refer to the floods typical of those regions. Phenomena of this kind, which probably increased after the end of the climatic optimum, may have inspired this rather odd tale that was later enhanced by the detail of the fruits that moved away as he reached for them.

The passage in the *Iliad* that refers to Mount Tmolus also mentions a swamp: "Mesthles and Antiphus, / Talaemenes' two sons, who were born by the Gygaean Swamp, / led the Maeonians, who had been born under Tmolus" (*Iliad* 2.864–66). Lydia must have been a region abundant in water, for the *Iliad* later refers to "snowy Tmolus" (*Iliad* 20.385) and the "Gygaean Swamp . . . / near the Hyllus teeming with fish and the swirling Hermus" (*Iliad* 20.390–92). This all seems to point to a hydrographic background that is more Finnish than Anatolian. If we consider that the name Mesthles is very similar to Mestilä, a village near Lake Pyhäjärvi, we could assume that the latter corresponds to the Homeric Gygaean Swamp. In any case, the four mythical Greek names Tmolus, Tantalus, Sipylus, and Mesthles find their respective Greek counterpart in the place-names Tammela, Tanttala, Sipilä, and Mestilä in a region not far from the Finnish Troad. This can hardly be considered a coincidence.

Not very far from Sipilä lies Nivala, whose name is similar to Niobe, Tantalus's unlucky daughter. According to a heartrending passage in the *Iliad*, her legend is also linked to Sipylus after the death of her twelve children:

> *[N]ow among the rocks, on those lonely peaks,*
> *on Sipylus, where people say that the beds of the divine*
> *nymphs dancing around the Achelous lie,*
> *there she withdraws into her pain after the gods turned her into*
> *stone.* (*Iliad* 24.614–17)

As for the Achelous mentioned in this passage, there is a place called Ahola in central Finland.

Other Near Neighbors

The occurrence of matching place-names continues along the Trojan coast: The name of a river running twelve miles from Toija, in the area of Salo (where archaeologists have found several tumuli very similar to the ones described in the *Iliad*), is Halikonjoki—that is, the Haliko River. This is identical to Halikos, the ancient Greek name of the Platani River in southwestern Sicily, home in ancient times to the Elimi, who regarded themselves as descendants of the Trojans. At the mouth of the Platani (Halikos) are the remains of Eraclea Minoa, a Greek settlement connected to very ancient myths. The occurrence of the Greek name Haliko near Toija is not an isolated case: It is found in the middle of a rich vein of Greek-sounding place-names, which, in tandem with other kinds of evidence, makes it highly unlikely that these similarities are mere coincidence.

Padva, near Tenala, sounds very similar to today's Padua in Veneto, in northeastern Italy, which, according to Livy,[1] was founded by Antenor, who, after the city was destroyed, fled from Troy with his Eneti, or Veneti, allies of the Trojans (*Iliad* 2.852). Significantly, Tacitus locates the Veneti (an Indo-European population) in a northern area close to the Finns.[2] A Swedish legend, related by the novelist Selma Lagerlöf in her *Nils Holgersson* (quoted by Jean Markale), seems to lead us along a similar path:

> Once upon a time, there was here a seaside town called Vineta. It was so rich and happy that no other city could compete with its magnificence. Unfortunately, its inhabitants indulged in luxury and arrogance. As a punishment, the city of Vineta was submerged by a huge flood and was swallowed up by the sea.[3]

Going even further, it would be tempting to connect the location of Venice in the middle of the lagoon with its curved-prow gondolas to the ancestral memory of a far-off original homeland, immersed in the waters and swamps of far northern Europe.

Even the root of the name Helsinki, the city on the Gulf of Finland, seems to recall that of ancient Hellespont (meaning "Helle Sea" or "Hellas Sea"), which faced the Estonian coast where the Homeric Hellas lay.

THE ROUTE OF THE ACHAEAN FLEET: LEMNOS, SAMOTHRACE, CHIOS, AND CYPRUS

Along the Swedish coast facing southern Finland, where the two opposing banks are at their closest, lies a long bay known as Norrtälje. At first sight, the bay reminds us of Homer's Aulis, where the Achaean fleet gathered before setting sail for Troy. In the narrow stretch of sea between the two countries are the Åland Islands, forming a sort of natural bridge between the two lands. This is the route that present-day ferries follow, past the island of Lemland, whose name recalls ancient Lemnos, where the Achaeans stopped during their crossing. Neighboring islands recall Imber and Samothrace, the mythical site of the metalworking mysteries. Another island farther south, adjacent to the Estonian coast, is known as Hiiumaa, a name that recalls Chios, the island that Nestor's fleet passes on its return from Troy at the end of the war (see fig. 8.1, page 156). Taken together, these islands present a picture that matches Homer's description of the route the Achaean fleet traveled to and from Troy.

Aulis and Thebes

The Danaan ships gathered in Aulis
planning trouble for Priam and the Trojans. (Iliad 2.303–304)

Aulis is famous for Agamemnon's sacrifice of his daughter Iphigenia in order to be granted favorable winds for reaching Troy, as narrated in the tragedy *Iphigenia in Aulis,* by Euripides. On Greek territory, Aulis lies near today's Vathy. Its port is located on a rock that juts out into the Euboean Sea, forming two small coves in the Strait of Euripus, almost in front of Chalcis. Although the two references Euripides makes to Aulis's features—the one talking of the "strait of Aulis" and the other of its "narrow moorings"—probably refer to its Mediterranean location, they point to another of the absurdities that result when we try to superimpose Homeric geography onto the Greek world: The two small bays in the Strait of Euripus are woefully inadequate to harbor the nearly twelve hundred ships that set off on the expedition to Troy.

On the Baltic shores, however, the funnel-shaped bay known as Norrtälje that faces the Finnish coast where Troy stood (see fig. 8.1) is about ten miles long and relatively narrow. The name of the bay *(älje)* without its prefix seems to recall Homer's Aulis, and its geographic features are also consistent with its descriptions. Its shores are generally low and suitable for landing, and there are many sheltering islands and islets near its mouth. Given its size and shape, which can provide good shelter for many ships, as well as its excellent strategic position, it is the ideal gathering point for any fleet heading toward the opposite shore, which is less than one hundred sea miles away, with the opportunity to stop off at the Åland Islands lying in the middle of the waterway.

Nonetheless, for the ancient ships with their square sails and flat keels, setting sail from such a long bay with many reefs at its mouth would have been a very difficult task, especially if the wind was adverse. With regard to this fact, once again the details preserved in mythology fit the Baltic location like a glove. Iphigenia's tragedy is echoed in an episode in the *Gesta Danorum:* During a naval expedition, it happened that the seamen "reached a certain place, where they were pestered by an interminable windstorm, which prevented them from sailing. Therefore they were held up most of the year until they decided to propitiate the gods with human blood. They drew lots and destiny called for a regal victim."

Norrtälje is very accessible from Stockholm. At Gräddö, where the bay widens and flows into the open sea, the view is beautiful, with luxuriant

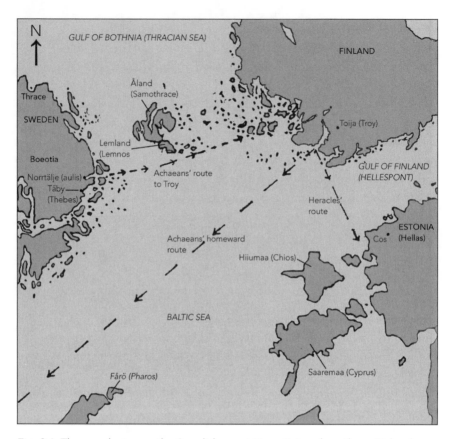

Fig. 8.1. The area between the Swedish coast (Boeotia) and southern Finland (Troas). Arrows indicate the Achaeans' journey to Troy and their homeward route. Also indicated is the route Heracles takes toward Cos when he is blown off course by the north wind after his departure from Troy.

woods of conifers along the shores that gradually widen. Our attraction to the area grows when we ponder that here the Achaean fleet gathered and Iphigenia's tragic destiny was fulfilled. From here the black ships of Agamemnon and his allies set sail for Troy, while today it is the departure point for the much less warlike ferries of the Kapellskär-Turku line, which follow virtually the same course, carrying passengers and cars toward Finland. Even if today's coastline does not coincide with that of those ancient days—in this area, too, the ground has been gradually and continually rising since the end of the ice age—its general appearance has nonetheless certainly remained the same: It is very jagged, with long bays and headlands that jut out into the sea among countless rocks and islets. The shape of this long, narrow Baltic bay, which is like that of a Norwegian fjord without the sheer cliffs, could also account for the similarity between the name Aulis and the Greek word *aulós*, which means "flute," "cane," or "tub" and indicates "a long, empty thing."[4] Interestingly, though, the shape of the Greek Aulis bears no resemblance to these terms.

According to Greek mythology, the city of Thebes "with seven gates" (*Iliad* 4.406) stood in Boeotia, which means that we should look for it in the same area as Aulis-Norrtälje—that is, in the region of Stockholm. Thebes was not an Achaean city and did not take part in the Trojan War; however, Homer mentions it on a few occasions with regard to the war. Both the described position of Aulis and the Catalog of Ships indicate that Boeotia stretched out into the region of present-day Stockholm, where a wealth of significant place-names can be found. First of all, about twenty-five miles south of Norrtälje, not very far from the motor-way toward Stockholm, is a town known as Täby, which could corre-spond to ancient Thebes. Other clues scattered throughout Stockholm's hinterland support the identification of Thebes with Täby. For example, Lyckeby could be linked to the name of the ancient Theban king Lycus or with Lyceum Apollo, whose presence in Thebes is mentioned in Greek tragedies. Aspen and Aspudden could refer to an ancient river mentioned in the *Iliad*: "Asopus with its thick canes and grassy bed" (*Iliad* 4.383).

In the same area, the name of a small town known as Tyresö sounds very similar to "Theban Tiresias" (*Odyssey* 10.492), the blind prophet of the *Odyssey*, who is held in such great esteem that he is referred to as *ánax*, "king" (*Odyssey* 11.151). The village of Duvnäs and the bay of the same name lying east of Stockholm toward Tyresö bring to mind Tiresias's daughter, Daphne. Other place-names in this area, such as the Island of Faringsö and the towns of Kynäs and Årsta, sound quite Greek. In particular, Kynäs recalls the Boeotian village of Cynoscephale, which lies near the Greek Thebes. Its name means "head of dog," and it is where the great poet Pindar was born.

A place called Bromma on the outskirts of Stockholm sounds very sim-ilar to the nickname of Dionysus, who was born in Thebes (*Iliad* 14.325): Brómios, meaning "the noise maker." But the most intriguing place-name is that of a hill south of Stockholm known as Nysättra, which reminds us of both "holy Nysa," a city the Catalog of Ships locates in Boeotia (*Iliad* 2.508), and one of the most mysterious places of Greek mythology, the legendary Mount Nysa, where young Dionysus (whose name means "god of Nysa") was raised. This mountain does not exist in Greece, though ancient scholars put forward the most fanciful hypotheses in order to find its location, going so far as to search for it in Arabia and India. Next to Nysättra in Sweden there is a site called Vidja (the letter *v* in its name certifies the presence of the ancient digamma—a letter transliterated as *v* or *w*, appearing in certain early forms of Greek and not found in either Homer's language or classical Greek), whose name recalls the nymphs known as the Hyads. According to Greek mythology, the Hyads nursed the baby Dionysus on Mount Nysa: "Nurses of raving Dionysus / . . . on holy Nyséion" (*Iliad* 6.132–33). All that remains of Vidja now besides its name are some houses scattered here and there. Near Nysättra there is a small rise that serves as a pasture reached by following a dirt road often blocked by flocks of sheep. It is easy to see that this rustic country evokes an archaic pastoral world dating back four thousand years.

Traces of cults linked to the metalworking mysteries* found in the area of Stockholm fit with the Kabiric tradition of ancient Boeotian Thebes, where there was a mystery shrine dedicated to the Kabirs, the metalworking gods for whom blacksmiths were "priests." Names such as Hammarby—there are two "hammer" villages, one lying north of Täby, the other near Stockholm—Karby, and Kairo seem to bridge the millennia, providing the ideal link between the Bronze Age metalworkers and the steel industry of modern Sweden. But not only place-names suggest the tradition of metalworking mysteries. Certain passages in an essay by Karl Kerényi about the metalworking mysteries clearly refer to a northern archaic world with marshy landscapes and arctic fen birds:

> In Eleusis the primordial scenery of the mystery event, with its fenbirds, was lost, but its memory still lived on in Boeotia. People said that Persephone played with a goose in a grotto near Lebadeia, where her abduction took place. This version of the myth corresponds with a vase which was found near Kabirion (the Kabiric shrine near Thebes). It depicts the goddess Demeter and winged Hekate Angelos, looking for the abducted girl, who were both assigned an aquatic bird.[5]

---

*The metalworking mysteries refer to ancient metallurgical works that were surrounded by a halo of religious enigma: Blacksmiths were considered guardians of the secrets of their art, to which they gained access only after initiation ceremonies. Incidentally, the custom of the ancient corporations of arts and crafts to jealously guard their secrets was quite widespread in the ancient world until the Middle Ages. We need think only of alchemy (which likely originated with ancient metalworking secrets) and the art of the cathedral builders, whose tradition gave rise to modern speculative Freemasonry, with its rituals, legends, initiation ceremonies, and so forth.

After noting other fascinating parallels between swans and the cult of Eleusis, Kerényi goes on to dwell "on discoveries made in the Kabiric sanctuary near Thebes," especially "vases having characteristic pictures . . . The most characteristic group dates back to at least the second half of the fifth century B.C., but the depicted patterns are much more ancient. The fen-birds, with long or short legs, continue an archaic tradition." Moreover, the initiates said that "a primordial female entity, incarnated in the goddess called 'Stork,' had founded the secret cult." These references clearly demonstrate the persistent presence of an extremely ancient northern tradition that could not be wiped out even from many centuries in the warm, dry Mediterranean world. What is more, Kerényi underlines the similarities and shared themes between some legends of the "Finno-Ugric peoples from Russia" and the myth of the birth of Helen from a fen-bird egg.

Lemnos

Many ships laden with wine arrived from Lemnos;
Jasonides Euneus had sent them. . . .
He separately presented the Atreids, Agamemnon and Menelaus,
with one thousand measures of wine.
The other long-haired Achaeans bought wine,
some for bronze, some for shining iron,
some for hides, some for cattle,
and others for slaves; then they had a sumptuous feast.
     (Iliad 7.467–75)

From this colorful passage indicating the close relationship King Euneus, son of Jason, the mythical leader of the Argonauts, could maintain with the Achaean chiefs at war, we infer that Lemnos was not very far from the Troad. Agamemnon later refers to this stay in Lemnos when he reproaches his men who are yielding ground to the Trojan attack at a critical moment in a battle near the Achaean ships:

Shame on you, Argives, handsome but cowardly men!
Where have your boasting and claiming to be the best got to,
as you used to trumpet abroad in Lemnos,
gobbling down beef,
and gulping down brimming tankards of wine? (Iliad 8.228–32)

The *Iliad* mentions Lemnos, Samos, and Imbers together (*Iliad* 24.753) and in pairs (*Iliad* 14.281, 24.78), making it clear that they all belong to the same area. In the passage where all three are mentioned, Queen Hecabe is mourning her son Hector, slain by Achilles: "Swift-footed Achilles caught other sons of mine / and sold them beyond the tireless sea, / in Samos, Imbers, and smoking Lemnos" (*Iliad* 24.751–53). This mention of the slave trade using prisoners of war reveals the true reason why shrewd King Euneus is so interested in cultivating his friendship with the Achaean chiefs: He is counting on doing a roaring trade as a result of the nearby conflict. In fact, when Achilles takes Priam's son Lycaon prisoner, he "sent him to well-built, fine Lemnos / by ship and sold him. Jason's son bought him, / then a guest ransomed him, paying a tidy sum" (*Iliad* 21.40–42). The slave trade was widespread in the Viking world as well: Pörtner underlines that northern traders excelled in this very profitable business.

Lemnos is mentioned in no fewer than seven books of the *Iliad,* generally in connection with metallurgy. The tale of Hephaestus, the smith god hurled down from Olympus, is set there: "[Zeus] seized my foot and hurled me from the heavenly threshold: / I plummeted for a whole day, and at sunset / crashed half dead onto Lemnos. / Here the Sintians helped me after falling" (*Iliad* 1.591–94). This passage likely refers to the meteoritic origin of iron and could also be related to a solar myth: The god who traverses the sky "for a whole day" and reaches the earth "at sunset" is the sun, which is linked with metallurgy. (Smiths produce a casting of incandescent metal—that is, a sort of mini sun.) The *Odyssey* also refers to the close relationship between the smith god and Lemnos, which was "by far the dearest of all lands to him" (*Odyssey* 8.284). This line is taken from the episode in which Hephaestus sets the classic trap for his wife, Aphrodite, and her lover Ares: When he pretends to leave, Ares rises to the bait and rushes to his beloved, announcing: "Hephaestus is no longer here, / but maybe he is in Lemnos now, with the rough-speaking Sintians" (*Odyssey* 8.293–94).

In the sequel to this episode, the two lovers are trapped in a net "as fine as a spider's web" (*Odyssey* 8.280) rigged by the clever husband to fall over the bed at just the right moment. As to this net, Robert Graves says: "It seems that Aphrodite's priestesses used to wear it during Spring Festivals, and so did the Scandinavian priestesses of the goddess Holle, or Gode, on May Day."[6] This tale could be connected to the ancient metallurgic activity on the island, for it seems to be an elaborate metaphor for the metal-melting process, particularly when the blacksmith, represented by Hephaestus, finds copper (Aphrodite) and iron (Ares) "trapped" together on the bottom of the melting pot.

Both poems mention Hephaestus in connection with the Sintians, mythical inhabitants of Lemnos (*Iliad* 1.594, *Odyssey* 8.294). It is noteworthy that their name is exactly the same as today's Sintians, a tribe of Gypsies (Roma) whose members are traditionally metalworkers and coppersmiths. Furthermore, Homer refers to Lemnos as "smoking [*amichthalóessan*]" (*Iliad* 24.753), which might well have something to do with metalworking activity. Actually, Greek Lemnos was also called Aithále by Polybius, from the verb *aíthein*, which expresses the concept "to smoke" or "to burn." Corroborating this, in the *Iliad* we find the word *aithalóen*, meaning "burned" (*Iliad* 2.415). Interestingly, the ancient Greeks used the same name for the island of Elba in the Tyrrhenian Sea, near Tuscany, where the Etruscans established many furnaces for producing iron: Aitháleia or Aithalía—that is, "smoking." Perhaps the name Italia (Italy) originates in this name, referring to the large number of volcanoes (Etna, Vesuvius, Stromboli, and so forth) in the south of the country, where this name originated. Considering that in continental Greece there are no volcanoes, these natural phenomena would have made a strong impression on the early Greek colonizers who settled along the Italian coasts. Thus southern Italy (also called Magna Graecia) was justifiably considered "the smoking land" by its ancient Greek neighbors.

SAMOTHRACE AND THE THRACIAN SEA

Homer's Samothrace, lying near Lemnos, could be identified with the largest island of the archipelago known as Åland, near Lemland. Here the place-name Sålis reminds us of the ancient city of Sale in Greek Samothrace, mythical home of the Kabirs and the metalworking mysteries. References to metalworking can also be found in Åland's place-names such as: Hammerland and Hammarudda (*hammare* means "hammer" in Swedish); Kasberg, which sounds similar to *koes*, the name of the Samothracian priest-followers of Kabiric cults; and Emkarby and Ödkarby whose root *kar* could be linked to the Greek term *káeira*, a variant of *kabeira*, meaning "kabiric." In the Baltic area, Åland-Samothrace and Täby-Thebes lie in close proximity, which explains the common Kabiric tradition, but their Greek counterparts are quite far away from each other. As usual, Baltic rather than Mediterranean geography accords much better with Greek mythology.

The most important passage that the *Iliad* dedicates to Samothrace is in Book 13. The Trojans are raging through the Achaean camp after breaking down the wall in the afternoon before the "dreadful night." The god Poseidon is very worried, because his Achaeans are forced to retreat as far as the ships: "He was sitting down following the war and the battle / on the highest peak of wooded Samothrace" (*Iliad* 13.11–13). This reference to "the highest peak of . . . Samothrace" fits perfectly with the topography of the archipelago, where significant rises are found only on Åland itself. The highest peak is the Orrdalsklint, lying on the eastern side, toward Finland. At 423 feet, it is considered high for the Baltic area, making it readily identifiable with the "stand" of the sea god from which he watches the dramatic match between the Achaeans and the Trojans. Judging by what the *Iliad* tells us, we can assume that in the Early Bronze Age a shrine dedicated to the god of the sea stood on the top of the peak, an ideal position for this purpose.

Leading to the top of the Orrdalsklint is a very pleasant path, made easier by iron stairs in the steepest spot. The wonderful view at the peak includes on one side the entire surface of the island and on the other, toward the east, countless little islands spread across the sea (the Broad Hellespont) and stretching toward the Finnish coast. It is thrilling to think that thousands of years ago, the poet of the *Iliad* himself might have come up here, to "the highest peak of . . . Samothrace," to admire this wonderful view, and was so struck by it that he mentioned it in his poem.

Extremely ancient traces of human settlement dating as far back as 6000 B.C.E. have been found in the area surrounding Orrdalsklint (and have been accurately rebuilt on-site). There are other traces of this same epoch on the island: On a hill in the north lies the ancient fortified site of Fornborgen, dating back to the Bronze Age. The remains of the wall, made of large stones laid one on top of the other, are still visible.

Having identified the Homeric Samothrace with Åland, it is natural to identify the Gulf of Bothnia, which begins beyond the Åland Islands, with the Thracian Sea, whose Mediterranean counterpart lies in the northernmost part of the Aegean Sea. (This is a logical correspondence to the one between the Gulf of Finland and the Dardanelles.) A passage in the *Iliad* corroborates it, stating that Boreas and Zephyrus—that is, the north and the west winds—cross the Thracian Sea by blowing toward the Troad to stir up fire on Patroclus's pyre (*Iliad* 23.208–30). This sea, therefore, lay northwest of Troy, corresponding to the position of the Gulf of Bothnia in relation to the area of Toija.

THRACE

We can now identify the position of Thrace, from which a contingent of allies of the Trojans came (*Iliad* 2.844). By considering that Iphidamas crosses the sea when he leaves from Thrace on his way to Troy (*Iliad* 11.221–30), and that Homer refers to "the wine the Achaean ships / carry across the wide sea [*ep'euréa pontoon*] from Thrace" (*Iliad* 9.71–72) to supply the Achaean camp, it follows that Homer's Thrace lay on the western side of the Gulf of Bothnia, along today's Swedish coast, opposite Finland. According to the *Iliad*, which mentions "the snowy mountains of the Thracians" (*Iliad* 14.227), this region also stretched to the hinterland. A Swedish village, Trekilen, twenty-five miles north of Östersund, seems to retain in the root of its name the memory of the proud Thracian warriors.

Interestingly, Homer establishes a precise connection between Ares, the god of war, and Thrace, from where he probably came and where he likely had a particular cult: "Ares, the destroyer of men, leaves for the war / and his strong, fearless son Terror, / who terrifies the firmest warriors, follows him. / They advance in arms from Thrace toward the Ephyrs . . ." (*Iliad* 13.298–301). In another episode, in the middle of the *Iliad*'s first battle, "Dreadful Ares went to incite the Trojan ranks / disguised as Acamas, the swift Thracian captain" (*Iliad* 5.461–62). What is more, the sole passage where the *Odyssey* mentions this region refers specifically to Ares, who "leapt up and went straight to Thrace" (*Odyssey* 8.361) as soon as he was set free from the bed to which Hephaestus had chained him along with beautiful Aphrodite.

AEGAE AND IMBERS

In watching the battle proceedings, the god Poseidon grows very angry at the development of the war and is unwilling to passively accept the defeat of his Achaeans at the hands of the Trojans. He decides to intervene in spite of Zeus's prohibition:

> *He came down from the steep mountain.*
> *. . . The big mountain and the forest shook*
> *under the immortal feet of advancing Poseidon.*
> *On his way he leapt three times* [trís oréxato]; *in the fourth he*
> *   reached his destination,*
> *Aegae, where his famous, shining, golden dwelling*
> *stands in the depths of the sea, undying forever.* (Iliad 13.17–22)

Aegae (Aigá), where the Danaans used to bring Poseidon "many beautiful gifts" (*Iliad* 8.203), could be linked to today's Angö, located on a small island east of Åland. The only way to reach it is by crossing some sea straits between the islands, starting from Åland—a journey that makes it easy to decipher the meaning of the above passage: The three leaps could refer to the god jumping from one island to the other. Interestingly, we can compare this potent image of the god who comes down from the mountain to a passage from the Rig Veda in which Vishnu is represented as "the bull who resides on the mountain and, being one, measured this seat *with three steps.*"[7] If we consider that Vishnu is strictly linked with water and the sea itself—in Indian mythology he is called Narayana, "he that moves the waters," and is the fish who help Manu, Noah's counterpart to survive the Flood—we might assume that Homer drew Poseidon's three leaps from a common Indo-European legacy. In any event, Poseidon reaches Aegae, but he does not stop there. The account of his trip continues with a superb description in which Homer mentions the island of Imbers:

> He arrived there and harnessed his two swift, bronze-hoofed horses
>   to his chariot with long golden manes.
> He dressed in gold as well, picked up his beautiful,
> golden whip, mounted his chariot
> and drove off over the waves. The sea animals jumped below him
> everywhere, leaving their caves, and paid homage to their King.
> The sea joyfully opened up for him, and his horses flew
> quickly, without wetting the bronze axle below;
> in great leaps they took the god to the Achaean ships.
> There is a large cave down under the sea depth,
> halfway between Tenedos and steep Imbers.
> Here Poseidon the Enosichthon stopped his horses
> and unharnessed them from the chariot . . .
> Then he made his way to the Achaean camp. (Iliad 13.23–35, 38)

Poseidon's journey from the mountain of Samothrace to the Achaean camp takes place in two stages: one in Aegae and the other in an unidentifiable place somewhere "halfway between Tenedos and steep Imber," which may well refer to another shrine to the sea god on one of the many islands that act as a bridge between Åland's archipelago and the Finnish coast. Thus, Imbers faced the Trojan shore. Perhaps it is the island known today as Lumparland, lying east of and adjacent to Lemland, Åland, and Angö itself. The suffix *land* is commonly used in the names of the larger islands of the archipelago, but the root Lumpar seems to sound rather similar to Imber, the ancient name of the island.

THE SEA GODS' ARCHIPELAGO

The Åland archipelago—which lies in a strategic position in the northern Baltic region, where it forms a kind of natural bridge—was clearly a site for worship and shrines dedicated to the sea gods, while today it is a sort of prescribed route for people who, just as their ancestors did in the Bronze Age, sail between the opposite banks, which are quite close together near the mouth of the Gulf of Bothnia. In the same area, deep down under the sea "halfway between Samothrace and steep Imbers" (*Iliad* 24.78), the *Iliad* locates the cavern where Thetis lives with the other sea goddesses known as the Nereids (*Iliad* 18.38), the daughters of the Old Man of the Sea. The bard who was the first to sing of brave deeds of Thetis's son Achilles was surely familiar with these sites. (On the other hand, the author of the *Odyssey*, who glorifies Ulysses, the hero who was born in the southern Baltic region, locates the Old Man of the Sea—no longer the *Iliad*'s Nereus, but his alter ego Proteus—on an island known as Pharos, corresponding to the modern Fårö lying in the middle of the Baltic Sea.)

Some of the tiny islands and their waters forming a sort of belt between the Åland Islands and the Finnish coast have names that correpond remarkably to those in Homer's text. The Kihti Islands and Applö remind us, respectively, of the Cyclades Islands and Apollo, protector of the nearby Trojans. Emphasizing this connection is a stretch of isleted sea called Delet (or Teili) between the Kihtis and the Ålands, recalling the little island of Delos in the Cyclades archipelago where Apollo was born. From here, the great god made his way to the far-off land of the Hyperboreans on a chariot driven by white swans. This tale, like many other stories in Greek mythology, fits more naturally in a northern or, even better, Arctic setting than in a Mediterranean one, and evokes certain themes from other mythologies. In the Homeric poems, Delos is mentioned only once, in the passage in the *Odyssey* (6.162) in which Ulysses begs Nausicaa to help him. Delos lay along the "route where it was my lot to have a rough time" (*Odyssey* 6.165). Delet is found east of Lemland, facing Finland, making it plausible that the Achaean ships visited the local shrine of the mighty god after they had stopped off in Lemnos on their way to Troy.

One corresponding name among these islands is Korppoo, which recalls Corfu. Another intriguing analogy can be heard in the name of an archipelago that is part of a national park along the "Trojan" coast in southern Finland: Saaristomeren in Finnish and Skärgaardshavets in Swedish. *Saari* and *skär* mean "island" in Finnish and Swedish, respectively, and *skär* is close to the name of the island of Scyros, from which, according to a non-Homeric legend, Achilles tries to "dodge the draft," disguising himself as a woman to avoid taking part in the Trojan War. Here he also finds time to marry Deidamia and to have a son. This could be compared to an episode in Rune 29 of the *Kalevala,* which tells us that one of the saga's main characters, Lemminkäinen, hides on a far-off island named Saari to avoid getting involved in a war and, in the meantime, enjoys some fun with the local girls. Another episode, this one in Rune 12, also recalls part of Achilles' history: In it Lemminkäinen manages to thwart the attack of a ferocious dog because "my mother washed me, plunged me into the water when I was a baby." This is certainly similar to the Greek myth in which the goddess Thetis makes her son Achilles invulnerable by plunging him into the water of the Styx. If we also consider that in Norse literature the *verpa vatni* is a magic ritual, a kind of "baptism" of warriors, which makes them invulnerable, we gain support for the idea that these tales about Achilles—who, according to the Catalog of Ships in the *Iliad,* came from southeastern Estonia—date back to an epoch before the Achaean migration to the Mediterranean.

CHIOS AND CYPRUS

Having earlier verified the congruence between Baltic geography and the route of the Achaean fleet to Troy, with the departure from Aulis-Norrtälje and the stop-off at Lemnos-Lemland, we must now examine the return Achaean voyage after the war. Nestor says this of the journey:

> *Fair-haired Menelaus*
> *joined us in Lesbos where we were pondering on the long voyage,*
> *whether to sail over steep Chios,*
> *toward the island of Psyria, keeping it on our left,*
> *or down Chios, past windy Mimas.*
> *We asked the god for a sign: he actually*
> *showed it and led us to cross the sea in the middle,*
> *toward Euboea. (Odyssey 3.168–75)*

NEIGHBORING LANDS AND ISLANDS   167

This passage fits very well with Baltic geography. Chios is identifiable, in both name and position, with Hiiumaa (or Chiuma; the suffix -*maa* meaning "land"), which faces Estonia. Thus, the Achaeans, coming from the Gulf of Finland, passed by Hiiumaa (see fig. 8.1, page 156) and headed straight for the island of Öland, parallel to the Swedish coast. (As we shall soon see, the sequence in the Catalog of Ships confirms Öland's identification with the Homeric Euboea.) From there they continued their voyage toward southern Sweden and Denmark.

In support of this correspondence are the analogies between some place-names found in Hiiumaa and present-day Chios in the Mediterranean world. For example, the name of the city of Kärdla resembles Kardamyla on the Aegean island, and Männamaa could correspond to Marmaron. In other words, Mediterranean Chios appears almost to be a kind of replica of Baltic Hiiumaa.

Another fairly large island, Saaremaa, lies not very far from Hiiumaa. The southeasternmost of the large islands in the Baltic Sea, it can be identified with Homeric Cyprus, site of the cult of Aphrodite, protectress of the Trojans: "She has a sanctuary and a fragrant altar in Paphos"—namely, a city in Cyprus (*Odyssey* 8.363). Besides its location, Saaremaa's shape is vaguely similar to that of Cyprus: Both islands have a rather oblong main section from which projects a sort of handle.

While the Cypriots do not take part in the Trojan War, the *Iliad* mentions their king Cinyras when describing Agamemnon's armor:

> He put across his chest the cuirass
> Cinyras had given him
> when he heard the sensational news in Cyprus, that the Achaeans
> were ready to sail against Troy;
> he gave it to him to ingratiate himself with him. (*Iliad* 11.19–23)

According to Homer's description, the cuirass is very valuable* and therefore fit for the expedition's supreme leader: "There were ten strips of blue enamel, / twelve of gold and twenty of tin. / Toward the opening

---

*In the northern Bronze Age, tin was a precious metal noted for its shine (the *Kalevala* often mentions the "tin buckle" that adorned girls' breasts), but also because it was so rare and had strategic value as an essential element in the production of bronze. In Homer's work, it is often associated with gold in ornamental couplings, such as in Agamemnon's cuirass, the decoration of Diomedes' chariot (*Iliad* 23.503), and the shield Hephaestus makes for Achilles (*Iliad* 18.574).

of the neck there were three enamel snakes / rising up from every side" (*Iliad* 11.24–27). Perhaps shrewd Cinyras had sent Agamemnon this gift as a way of avoiding taking part in the war. A certain Echepolus, from Sicyon, gives Agamemnon a valuable horse for the same reason, "so that he did not have to follow him to windy Ilium, / and went on enjoying himself at home" (*Iliad* 23.297–98).

There is a likely correlation between the names of the cities of Kuressaare and Kyrenia, found in Saaremaa and Mediterranean Cyprus, respectively. As we have said, this widespread phenomenon of corresponding place-names supports the idea that a common cultural and ethnic substratum dating back to the Early Bronze Age links the whole of Europe, from north to south. In addition to the pairs we have mentioned—Lyø and Ithaca, Lemland and Lemnos, Hiiumaa and Chios, Öland and Euboea, Zealand and the Peloponnese—we may include other geographic "pairings," such as Bornholm and Naxos, Karlskrona and Athens, and so on. To indicate these corresponding places we might use a Greek term employed in geometry: *homotopes*, deriving from *homos*, "same," and *topos*, "place."

It is extremely important that the first sign of the unity of Europe is found in its most ancient and venerable cultural reference—that is, Homer's poems, which we are rediscovering now as an unexpected but fascinating bridge between the Baltic and Mediterranean Seas, the northern and southern points of the continent.

As we have seen in parts 1 and 2, the respective congruities of Troy and Ithaca corroborate and strengthen each other. What is more, these contexts about which we have an enormous quantity of information available (for they form the main settings of the *Iliad* and the *Odyssey*) are only the tip of a Homeric Achaean world that can be entirely and accurately reconstructed in the Baltic, as we shall see in part 3.

PART THREE

THE WORLD OF THE ACHAEANS

CHAPTER 9

CLIMATE AND CHRONOLOGY: THE NORTHERN ORIGIN OF THE MYCENAEANS

The textual indications in the *Odyssey* and *Iliad* that have led us to a Baltic location for both Ithaca and Troy, as well as for Ulysses' adventures after the war, similarly guide a broader reconstruction of the original home of the Achaeans. The poems provide precise geographical detail about the wider Achaean world, along with many cultural details that tally with archaeological discoveries relating to the northern European Bronze Age. Key to envisioning that world and the reasons for its movement to the south is an understanding of the climatic conditions that made the entire European continent look and feel much different from how it does today.

THE POSTGLACIAL CLIMATIC OPTIMUM

In the Bronze Age, until the second millennium B.C.E., the climate in northern Europe—including Scandinavia and the Baltic region—was significantly milder than it is today. As we have mentioned, this period of warmth is known as the *postglacial climatic optimum*. As the *Treccani Italian Encyclopedia* explains under "Olocenico, periodo" (Holocenic period), after the end of the last glacial age, several climatic phases occurred in succession in northern Europe, each of them having distinctive features with regard to vegetation:[1]

- **Recent Pre-Boreal** (8000–7000 B.C.E.). The climate is still cold, continental (characterized by a significant temperature variance between summer and winter; winter is quite cold, as at middle latitudes and at the center of the continents). Red fir, alder, and hazel trees begin to spread.
- **Boreal** (7000–5500 B.C.E.). Summers are warm and winters are relatively mild.
- **Atlantic** (5500–2000 B.C.E.). The climate is warmer than that of the Boreal phase; winters are mild and humid. Oak trees spread.
- **Sub-Boreal** (2000–500 B.C.E.). The climate cools. Beech and fir trees prevail.

We are most interested here in the Atlantic phase, the time of the climatic optimum, and the Sub-Boreal stage, the time, as we shall see, during which Homer's works may well have their setting.

The climatic optimum of the Atlantic period peaked around 2500 B.C.E. and lasted until 2000 B.C.E. According to Pia Laviosa Zambotti, it was "the best climatic period Scandinavian countries have ever known, which justifies the high cultural level achieved in Scandinavia around 2500 B.C. . . . This long, favorable climatic period saw the development of Northern cultures, including the Maglemose and Ertebölle civilizations and Bronze Age culture, and saw the construction of dolmens and 'passage grave' tombs."[2]

As Mario Pinna, professor of earth sciences at the University of Turin, explains in his treatise on climatology, a great deal of evidence—in particular, research on pollens—proves beyond doubt that the climatic optimum actually occurred. During it, continental glaciers became smaller than they are today, leading to a rise in sea level of six to ten feet and the subsequent submersion of lower coastal areas. The melting of Arctic ice and the consequent rise in sea levels led in turn to the expansion of internal bodies of water, including the Baltic Sea and the Mediterranean Sea.

With the earth's warmer temperatures (the average temperature was about seven degrees warmer than it is today), temperate climates moved toward the poles, greatly altering the distribution of vegetation. Throughout Eurasia the conifer and hardwood forests were pushed far to the north and the trees associated with more temperate climates—oaks and hazels—took their place, spreading into Scandinavia. In eastern Europe, the transition from arid steppes to hardwood forests occurred at the latitude of St. Petersburg and the Upper Volga, while the tundra completely disappeared from the European continent. Conditions were ideal for the spread of forest vegetation across central and northern Europe, aided by an increase in rainfall toward the end of the climatic optimum, when the average temperature was still relatively high.

As we may expect, this movement in vegetation in terms of both latitude and altitude (in Eurasia, tree lines were roughly one thousand feet higher than today, and snow lines followed suit) resulted in a great change in landscape.

In order to get a good picture of the effects of such a mild climate in the north, we can look at a similar climate phenomenon that occurred a bit closer to our own time: the so-called medieval warm period, which occurred from about 800 to 1200 C.E. During this time, the polar ice pack in the Arctic Ocean decreased considerably and icebergs became rare around Iceland and Greenland, which were blooming landscapes. This explains why Norwegians named the land they discovered Greenland: On their arrival there they encountered vast, green meadows—a very different landscape is found there today.

During the medieval warm period, the increase in temperature by about four degrees in northern countries was accompanied by a decrease in strong winds and storms due to a slowing of atmospheric circulation. Taking into consideration the favorable sea conditions that resulted from the reduction of storms and icebergs in the North Atlantic Ocean, it comes as no surprise that the Vikings found it much easier to sail between Norway, Iceland, and Greenland, which facilitated their settling of these lands so far from the European continent. A mild climate and an abundance of fish in the sea were likely the determining factors that made it possible for Scandinavian peoples to colonize those Arctic lands that were prosperous for a few centuries.

With the rather dramatic changes of the medieval warm period—including the spread of vineyards over England and even Norway, according to Franco Ortolani, professor of earth sciences at the University of Naples (Italy)—resulting from an average increase in temperature of about four degrees, we can certainly imagine the effects of the seven-degree increase during the climatic optimum. By taking into account the fact that the medieval warm period lasted only four or five centuries, while the prehistoric optimum lasted millennia, we can see that the effects of the optimum's climate change on northern Europe must have been culturally significant indeed, which seems to have been the case, for it is at the height of the climatic optimum that northern cultures flourished.

MYCENAEANS IN THE NORTH

Our contention here that the people of Homer's works were among those who lived and flourished in northern Europe during the climatic optimum is supported by evidence in the northern world suggesting a Mycenaean presence there in a very distant past, *preceding* that in the south. One such sign is a graffito of a Mycenaean dagger engraved on a monolith found by archaeologists in 1953 in the megalithic complex of Stonehenge, in southern England. Other remains found in the same area and revealing a Mycenaean presence date from the beginning of the second millennium B.C.E., *before* the Mycenaeans settled in Greek territory, around 1600 B.C.E. On this subject, we may turn to the words of Stuart Piggott, quoted by A. R. Burn in his *Penguin History of Greece:*

> On Salisbury Plain, a chief's grave contained an inlaid sceptre "paralleled only," says Professor Piggott, "to one of the early shaft graves" of Mycenae. "In Britain too," he adds, "the final monument of Stonehenge, with its architectural competence and sophistication, is best explained in terms of the momentary introduction of superior skills from an area of higher culture, which in the circumstances can hardly be other than Mycenae."[3]

In *Before Civilization*, Colin Renfrew claims:

> In Wiltshire and Dorset, the ancient Wessex, a good number of burials had been found, beneath circular burial mounds, with very rich grave goods. Most of these graves contained bronze daggers, the hilts occasionally decorated with little gold studs. There was other goldwork too, and at Rillaton in Cornwall a burial had been found accompanied by a very beautiful little cup of gold, often compared with Mycenaean examples . . . [T]he chief early bronze age culture for Czechoslovakia and Germany, the Unetice culture, displayed a number of forms resembling Aegean ones, and some of the bone metal types in the Hungarian bronze age were decorated with spirals and other motifs similar to some on the goldwork of the Mycenaean shaft graves. Calibration sets all these dates between 2400 and 1900 B.C., and it seems likely that the Unetice culture had begun well before 2000 B.C. These dates fit very well into the emerging pattern for the chronology of central Europe. . . . They do

suggest, however, that the Wessex culture, which has many evident links with late Unetice, may also be much earlier than had been thought. In 1968 I wrote an article suggesting a duration for the Wessex culture between 2100 and 1700 B.C. This was supported by the radiocarbon dates for Stonehenge, which suggested that the sarsen structure with its trilithons was constructed before 1800 B.C. and probably before 2000 B.C.[4]

How do we account for these seeming Mycenaean traces in southern England? Homer offers us the clue: In the *Odyssey*, a seafaring trader (the Taphian ruler Mentes), who has just landed in Ithaca, says: "I am sailing on the wine-dark sea for foreign populations, / to Temesa for bronze [*es Temésen metá chalkón*]; I am carrying shining iron" (*Odyssey* 1.183–84). Scholars have never been able to locate Temesa in the Mediterranean region. However—keeping in mind that bronze is an alloy of copper and tin, and that Cornwall, in southern England, is one of the few places in the north where tin is found—it makes sense to look near there for Temesa, the overseas center for metal trade. It then becomes easy to see the correspondence between Temesa and the river Thames, which was called Tamesis in Latin and Tamis, Tamisa, or Tamensim by the first English chroniclers.[5] This squares with the fact that the Bronze Age marked a great millennium of open-sea navigation. Geoffrey Bibby notes that the location of the raw materials tin and copper necessitated new navigational routes.

If we follow Homer's lead, then, it seems likely that during the climatic optimum, the ancient Achaeans would have sailed overseas to "foreign populations" in Temesa-Thames (which faces the North Sea and Scandinavia) to exchange bronze produced with tin and copper from Cornwall for iron from the north of Sweden. This would have taken them on a sea route that would naturally have passed by the South Fyn Islands, quite close to where the Baltic Sea meets the North Sea, thus explaining Mentes' stop at Lyø (Ithaca) on his way to Temesa.

Tacitus makes an interesting remark concerning the chief city on the Thames, London, which figures in our puzzle here: "Londinium is very famous for its sizeable trade of goods."[6] It is reasonable to believe that the commercial development of the area, a result of its geographic position, had started long before the time of Tacitus. In fact, the remains of a wood bridge dating back to 1500 B.C.E. were recently found near London's Houses of Parliament, testifying to an important settlement there one thousand years earlier than scholars have supposed until now.

It could not be mere chance, then, that Temesa is the only market for bronze mentioned in the Homeric poems.

The theory that the Achaeans came from the Baltic area is further supported by the strict correlations archaeology has revealed between the Scandinavian Bronze Age and the coeval Aegean civilizations. A note-worthy example is the extraordinary tomb found near Kivik, in southern Sweden, consisting of a large circular stone tumulus called Bredarör that is 250 feet in diameter. It contains a sarcophagus that is roughly twelve feet long and built of square stone slabs engraved with stylized figures of human beings, animals, and objects such as axes and wheels. Archaeologists recognize the similarity between these figures and the Bronze Age finds in both Aegean and Near East areas. Klavs Randsborg analyzed the figures on the slabs and, in his *Kivik Archaeology and Iconography*, compares them to the pictures on a sarcophagus from Hagia Triada in Crete and the stelae of the shaft graves from Mycenae. These puzzling similarities have bewildered scholars in the past—so much so that in the nineteenth century, one of them even attributed the construction of the Kivik tomb to the Phoenicians! Randsborg deals with these parallels with due caution, suggesting that the reader come to his or her own conclusions. This prudence is quite understandable given that such similarities are inexplicable *unless* we allow for the possibility that the Mycenaeans did indeed come from northern Europe.

Rupestrian engravings like those found on Kivik's tomb are typical of the northern Bronze Age. As Bibby notes, northern carvings focus "on three main topics, i.e., ships and shipping, agriculture and livestock, and weapons and duels"[7]—all of which existed at the center of the Homeric world.

The Mycenaean traces in the northern world that predate by some centuries their appearance in Greece fit perfectly with our theory of a Baltic origin of the Mycenaean culture, especially considering that there has been close contact between the Scandinavian-Baltic world and the British Isles since ancient times. In fact, the ancient Jutes from Jutland are among the ancestors of the English. Similarly, at the beginning of the *Gesta Danorum*, Saxo recalls the Danish origin of the mythical progenitor of the Angles, and Pia Laviosa Zambotti claims that

> . . . uninterrupted relations among Scandinavia, Jutland, and the British Isles took place from the Mesolithic Age on. They must have been fruitful and particularly active during the Neolithic Age, not only regarding the Baltic-Arctic, Sub-Megalithic, and Northern

Megalithic cultural cycles, but even later on, when the British Isles played an important role in the diffusion of the Iberian bell-shaped vase culture and when Ireland, with its gold production, became a source of constant contact with the north.[8]

The northern Bronze Age civilization of the British Isles and the Baltic-Scandinavia area "took advantage of increasing trade, and reached a remarkable level of development (superior to that of the corresponding Bronze Age civilization of southern and western Germany) especially as far as the fashioning and taste in decoration of bronze objects are concerned, which attest to a very high standard of living."[9] During this time in Scandinavia "the art of founding . . . reached a level of perfection that could be compared only to the best works of the Aegean-Mycenaean civilization."[10]

As Siegfried Fischer-Fabian writes, extraordinary objects were fashioned from bronze by these peoples:

[T]he variety of Germanic bronze objects was amazing. There were precious swords; valued ornaments; gold-plated cult discs; clips; buckles; helmets; shields; chokers; and even shaving, ear and manicure sets . . . Fifteen-hundred years before the arrival of the Romans in the northern territories, there were already such very high standards of living and civilization that they can only be compared to the Greek civilization of the same period.[11]

A visit to the Bronze Age rooms in the National Museum of Copenhagen allows any of us to come to the same conclusion.

All of the connections we have established thus far between Mycenaean culture and northern Bronze Age culture tally with a recent, extraordinary archaeological discovery: a bronze disk, about one foot in diameter, portraying the sun, moon, and stars (the cluster of the Pleiades is recognizable) found in Germany near the village of Nebra, about thirty miles west of Leipzig. Amazingly, the disk, which dates back to the Early Bronze Age (1600 B.C.E) depicts a subject very similar to that portrayed on Achilles' shield in the *Iliad:* the sky with the sun, moon, and stars—specifically, the Pleiades (*Iliad* 18.483–87). Coupled with bronze swords found at the same site, which were fashioned in a technique unique to Mycenaean swords, this archaeological find contributes to the amazing correspondence among the northern world, the Homeric world, and the Mycenaean world.[12]

NORTHERN CULTURAL CORRESPONDENCES

Further evidence of the Baltic origins of Homer's people can be found in similarities between various aspects of the culture he describes and what is known of the northern European Bronze Age.

Homeric and Viking Societies

Despite the years separating the two cultures, the social relations, interests, and lifestyles of the Homeric world and Viking society are surprisingly similar. Here is Pörtner's portrait of the Vikings:

> They were a bit of everything, that is, farmers, explorers, colonizers, the most daring sailors, the most feared warriors of the time, pirates, traders, heroes, merchants, rascals, skilful artisans, intelligent organizers, murderers, artists of genius, rash warriors and cold opportunists, gross individualists and desparagers of institutions, but also sons devoted to the family stock.[13]

Pörtner also quotes Edith Ennan: "The Germanic civilization . . . undoubtedly includes a warlike aristocracy as a dynamic factor. However, the nobles were landowners, and therefore maintained country features."[14] All of these characteristics—especially the double vocation of seafaring and agriculture—are also typical of the Homeric world.

Another significant similarity between the two worlds is the *agorá*, the public assembly in the Homeric world, and its Viking correspondent, the *thing*. These two exemplified the most important political institutions in the running of the community for both peoples. Tacitus also informs us that in his time (the first century C.E.) as well, the northern peoples held public assemblies[15] that appeared to be very similar to the *thing*, and thus to the *agorá*.

There are certain linguistic supports for this correspondence as well: In the *Odyssey* we find the expression *agorén thémenos* (*Odyssey* 10.188, 12.319), meaning "convening the assembly." The word *thémenos*, deriving from the verb *títhemi*, "to establish," or "to institute," is directly connected with the name of Themis, the goddess of assemblies. Homer says: "In the name of Themis / who breaks up and convenes the assemblies [*agorás*]" (*Odyssey* 2.68–69). Thus, the *agorá* is strictly linked with Themis-thémenos and with, we are tempted to suggest, with the name of the Norse *thing*, the counterpart of the *agorá*, which may well derive from *thémenos* and Themis, the Homeric patroness of assemblies.

Another point is the distinction—typical of the prefeudal Germanic society—between the king's public assets and his personal possessions, a differentiation mentioned in both the *Odyssey* (1.392, 2.335) and *Beowulf*.[16] Another, somewhat peculiar, parallel between *Beowulf* and the *Odyssey* can be seen in the squabble between Unferdh and Beowulf at king Hrodhgar's court[17] and the one that arises between Euryalus and Ulysses at Alcinous's court (*Odyssey* 8.158–85). Interestingly, the conclusion of the squabble is the same in the two epics: The instigators (Unferdh and Euryalus) are reconciled with their respective antagonists,[18] each of whom is given a sword by his provoker (*Odyssey* 8.403).

As with the the free men in the two epics, we can find similarities among the slaves. The conditions of the slave Mesaulius, "whom the swineherd [Eumaeus] / bought on his behalf during the King's absence" (*Odyssey* 14.449–50), are very similar to those of Germanic slaves as recorded by Tacitus: "Each one rules his home; the owner calls for a given amount of wheat or animals or clothes, like a tenant farmer, and the slave is obliged to obey up to this point; his wife and children do the rest of housework."[19] These same conditions found in Viking Sweden eight hundred years after Tacitus—when slaves "could possess a hut and livestock" and "were permitted to sell the surplus of their mini-farms at market"[20]—can also be found in the *Odyssey:* "A kind boss gives his servant / a house, a piece of land and a good-looking wife, / if he has worked hard for him and a god has made his work fruitful" (*Odyssey* 14.63–65). In a word, the parallels in slave conditions among the Homeric Achaeans of the Bronze Age, the Germans of the Roman period, and the medieval Vikings testify to the continuity of the northern world throughout the ages.

Evidence of this continuity can also be seen in the very names of Bronze Age peoples and those of medieval times, such as in the remarkable relationship between the Argives (Argeioi, or Vargeioi, one of Homer's names for the Achaeans) and the Varangians (Swedish Vikings). Keeping in mind both the digamma and the fact that the vowels *a* and *i* are often interchangeable (for example, *ambush* corresponds to the Italian term *imboscata*), Achaeans (Achaioi) thus can be readily seen in the term "Vikings." The connection between Dane and Danaan (Danaioi) is still more obvious. Thus, the three main names that Homer gives the protagonists of his poems—Danaioi, Argeioi, and Achaioi, which were never found in the Mediterranean area—probably came down to modern times as the Danes, Varangians, and Vikings.

We also note that "Dudon [Dudone di San Quintino, medieval historian], who wrote a story about Aquitania, believes that the Danes owe their origins and name to the Danaans."[21] Dudon's opinion on the relationship between the Danes and the Homeric Danaans is shared by other medieval historians such as William of Jumièges. These comparisons have hitherto been interpreted as a means of artificially exalting the origin of the Danes, but now, owing to the information collected here, we could start to see them in a new light.

Clothing, Tableware, Food, and Drink

We can find further evidence of a connection between the culture of Bronze Age northern Europe and that of Homer's world if we look closely at some of the descriptive text in Homer's works. For example, the "tunics and thick, heavy cloaks" that Homer often cites as the garb of his characters can be compared to the clothes of a man found in a Danish Bronze Age tomb: According to Geoffrey Bibby, who describes this man, "the woolen tunic comes down to the knees and a belt ties it at the waist. He also wears a cloak, which a bronze buckle pins on his shoulder."[22] Interestingly, Ulysses also wears "a golden buckle [*peróne chrysoîo*]" (*Odyssey* 19.226) on his cloak. Both of these descriptions fit with what Tacitus says of Germanic clothing: "The suit for everyone is a cape with a buckle [*sagum fibula consertum*]."[23] He continues: "The richest are distinguished by a suit that does not flutter, as do those of the Sarmatians and Parthians, but which is close-fitting and tight around each limb." Homer tells us that Ulysses wore a remarkably similar close-fitting garment, "a shining tunic around his body / like the peel on a dry onion" (*Odyssey* 19.232–33). The remains found in Danish tombs also allow us to visualize the clothes of Homeric women. Following Bibby's account, we can imagine that Penelope wears "a short-sleeved blouse with a cut-work skirt, a knitted hairnet, a belt with a round bronze plate (eight inches in diameter) in front."[24]

Likewise, as we shall see in more detail later in this chapter, the clothing described in the two poems reveals evidence of a colder, northern climate. In the episode of the *Iliad* in which Telemachus and Peisistratus are guests at Menelaus's house in Sparta, the two ready themselves for a meal after a bath: "They wore thick cloaks and tunics . . ." (*Odyssey* 4.50). The same is said of Ulysses when he is a guest at Alcinous's

house: "(The maids) dressed him in a fine woolen cloak and tunic; /
he left the bath and joined the lords / who were drinking" (*Odyssey*
8.455–57)—and this is during the sailing season, not the harsher winter!
Similarly, Nestor's cloak is "double and large; a thick fur stuck out"
(*Iliad* 10.134); and when Achilles leaves for Troy, his mother thought-
fully prepares him a trunk "filled with tunics, / wind-proof thick cloaks
and blankets" (*Iliad* 16.223–24).

There are also distinct similarities between Bronze Age northern
European customs and culture related to food and eating and those
described in Homer's works. While pottery tableware was prevalent in
Greece, the northern world was marked by "a stable and highly advanced
bronze founding industry,"[25] which accords perfectly with the details in
Homer's poems. He never mentions pottery but instead speaks of vessels
made of metal, often of gold or silver. In Ulysses' palace in Ithaca, "a
maid came to pour water from a beautiful / golden jug [*prochóoi chrys-
eíei*] into a silver basin [*argyréoio lébetos*]" (*Odyssey* 1.136–37). People
pour wine "into gold goblets [*ení chryséois depáessin*]" (*Odyssey* 3.472)
and "gold glasses [*chrýseia kýpella*]" (*Odyssey* 1.142). Lamps (*Odyssey*
19.34), cruets (*Odyssey* 6.79), and urns (*Iliad* 23.253) are made of gold.
As interesting proof that vessels are made of metal, when one falls to the
ground, instead of breaking it "booms [*bómbese*]" (*Odyssey* 18.397).

And what of the poor in Homer's work, who surely cannot use
tableware of gold and silver? Nor do they seem to use the pottery so
common in the south. If we peep into Eumaeus's hut, we find the faithful
herdsman pouring wine for his guests "into a wooden jug [*en kissybíoi*]"
(*Odyssey* 16.52), which is very similar to the one Ulysses uses for the
strong liquor he offers Polyphemus (*Odyssey* 9.346). Wood, of course, is
the cheapest and easiest material to procure in the north, considering its
abundance there. (Estonia and Latvia, in fact, have a very ancient tradition of using wooden beer tankards.)

The subject of tableware segues to that of food. Characters in Homer's poems frequently enjoy a large meal *(deîpnon)* first thing in the morning (often after a bath): "In the hut Ulysses and his faithful swineherd /
lit the fire and prepared a meal at sunrise" (*Odyssey* 16.1–2). Menelaus
got up and "told his wife and servants / to prepare breakfast in the hall"
(*Odyssey* 15.93–94). Telemachus tells his men: "At sunrise, in return for
the journey, I will give you / a great banquet of meat and sweet wine"
(*Odyssey* 15.506–507). This can be likened to the tradition of generous
breakfasts among today's Nordic people, which is likewise connected to

both ancient customs and climate. Once again, we turn to Tacitus for testimony on the Germans: "As soon as they wake up . . . they wash with hot water . . . then they eat."[26]

Tacitus also informs us that among the Germanic peoples of his day, "everyone has his own chair and table." This individual table (*trápeza* in Greek) is typical of the Homeric world, too (*Odyssey* 1.138), where it is used for both breakfast and the second meal of the day at sunset (*Iliad* 19.207–208). This second meal, called *dórpon* in Homer's works, corresponds to today's dinner.

The wine in Homer's epic is often described as "sweet," no doubt from the common practice of mixing it with honey—something altogether usual in the north, where wines were sour and unpleasant without sweetening, due to the low sugar content of the grapes. (We have only to think of the sophisticated work involved in producing champagne!) In support of this practice, we can point to one of Circe's recipes as given in the *Odyssey*: "She blended cheese, meal and honey / with Pramnian wine" (*Odyssey* 234–35). And the *Iliad* informs us (11.639) that this undoubtedly energizing "Pramnian cocktail" is also in vogue during the Trojan War, when Nestor drinks it from "a magnificent goblet / adorned with golden studs" (*Iliad* 11.632–33).

Throughout the *Iliad* the tendency of the Achaeans to drink to excess emerges. Achilles rather untactfully refers to Agamemnon as a "drunkard" (*Iliad* 1.225) on the occasion of their squabble at the beginning of the *Iliad*—and the latter's acceptance (with pleasure) of the gift of "one thousand measures of wine" sent to him by Euneus from Lemnos seems to confirm this suspicion. In his distinctive, concise style, Tacitus comments similarly on the drinking habits of northern peoples: "Simple food . . . but not the same moderation in drinking; if you comply with their wish to get drunk by giving them as much as they desire, vice will defeat them more easily than weapons."[27]

The food of the Achaeans in Homer's work is as simple as the German roasted meat and bread described by Tacitus. The *Odyssey* mentions *gastéres,* the roasted guts of goat stuffed with blood (*Odyssey* 18.44), which is rather similar to the traditional Finnish *musta makkara*. Both poems reveal that the diet of those in the noble class is based on meat (beef, pork, goat, and game), much like that of the Vikings, who, as Pörtner tells us, apart from being heavy drinkers, "ate meat in large quantities, so much so that they seemed to regard the pleasure of eating meat as one of the joys of life."[28] Confirming the northern, rather than

Mediterranean, nature of their diet, Homer's heroes virtually ignore fruit, vegetables, olives, and olive oil. Similarly, the Germans generally did without fruit until they came into contact with the Romans.

Fauna and Flora

Homer's descriptions of animals and trees among whom his people live are also much more suited to a northern European environment, such as the delightful "flock / of winged birds, which are feeding by the river, / geese, cranes or long-necked swans" (*Iliad* 15.690–92). In fact, geese and swans are depicted in rock carvings found in Alta, northern Norway, dating back to the fourth millennium B.C.E. Likewise, the "poplar / which has grown in the sward of a large marsh" (*Iliad* 4.482–83) evokes more a Finnish landscape than a dry, rugged Grecian one.

A very particular case of northern fauna represented in Greek works is that of the Cerynean hind captured by Hercules in one of his labors. Pindar mentions her "golden horns."[29] Intriguingly, the sole European doe that has horns is the female reindeer. If we also consider that in the myth four companions of the hind are yoked to Artemis's wagon, and that of all European deer, only reindeer are strong enough to be able to pull a wagon or sled, we can conclude that the Cerynean hind likely refers to a reindeer, which further supports the notion that Greek mythology originated in the north. Another indication of this is the similarity between the term Cerynean, a Greek descriptive related to a particular place, and *hreinn*, the Old Norse word for "reindeer."

Similarly, Homer's habit of giving objects and slaves a value in terms of "oxen" fits very well with a northern setting, whereas in the Greek world, other kinds of livestock were more important. According to Homer, a new vase decorated with flowers was worth "the price of an ox" (*Iliad* 23.885); a big tripod was worth twelve oxen (*Iliad* 23.703); a woman slave who "was able to do many jobs" was valued at four oxen (*Iliad* 23.705); and Ulysses' nurse, Eurycleia, had cost Laertes twenty oxen, perhaps because she was "still very young" (*Odyssey* 1.431). Eurymachus proposes the same sum—twenty oxen each—as compensation from the suitors, "for what people had drunk and eaten at Ulysses' palace" (*Odyssey* 22.56). A prince of the blood, such as Priam's son Lycaon, whom Achilles takes prisoner, is bought for no fewer than a hundred oxen in Lemnos (*Iliad* 21.79)—that is, the same price as one of the golden fringes of Athena's aegis (*Iliad* 2.449) or of Glaucus's golden armor (*Iliad* 6.326). Diomedes' bronze armor is said to be worth only nine oxen (*Iliad* 6.236), which is nevertheless still a considerable sum. The highest price cited in the two poems concerns the cost of a bride: Trojan Iphidamas paid "one hundred oxen and promised one thousand other" (*Iliad* 11.244) for the hand of Cisses' daughter. Unfortunately, the poor man—if we could call him that—does not have time to settle the debt with his father-in-law because Agamemnon slays him.

The poet describes the dancing girls portrayed on Achilles' shield as *alphesíboiai* (*Iliad* 18.593), a term that could be translated as "much desired" or "courted," but which literally means "capable of giving oxen"—that is, the girls were a source of wealth for their parents at their weddings. Pörtner writes that during the first Viking Age, cows were still used "as the current monetary unit."[30] As we can see here, from the Early Bronze Age to the first millennium of our era, certain practices remained untouched. A statement from Tacitus bridges these two distant epochs: "Cattle and oxen . . . are the Germans' only and highly valued wealth" *(solae et gratissimae opes sunt)*.[31]

Language

Although scholars generally accept that Mycenaeans were not autochthonous of Greece, traces of their migration from "somewhere" have so far never been identified. However, both the Mycenaeans and the Dorians (who reached Greece in the twelfth century B.C.E., coming from the north) certainly spoke a form of Greek in their original homeland, wherever that was, where their language is no longer spoken today. Homeric geography allows us to locate this homeland in the Scandinavian-Baltic area, which is supported by the prevalence of Achaean-like place-names and particularly by the genuinely Greek name of the Hellespontians, who, according to Saxo, were located in the east Baltic.

Although this fits with archaeological evidence of the northern origin of the Mycenaeans, the question can be raised regarding why we do not find other traces of the proto-Greek language—which was spoken during the Early Bronze Age—in the northern world. While awaiting corroboration of a Greek substratum in the Finnish language, we note that the survival of place-names after the extinction of the original language is a common phenomenon. For example, the Etruscan language and literature died out two thousand years ago in what is now Tuscany, where it was supplanted by Latin. Yet many Etruscan place-names exist today. The same happened to the Greek language, which was widely spoken in southern Italy at around the same period. Many place-names there still recall their Greek origin, including the charming Melicuccà (literally, "swan song"), a village in the region of Calabria. Analogously, the archaic Greek spoken in the Baltic area during the Bronze Age must have been replaced by invaders speaking German and Finno-Ugric languages. In the meantime, the Achaeans had transplanted their language to Greece, when, thirty six hundred years ago, they relocated there and founded the Mycenaean civilization.

This idea is also supported by the survival in the eastern Baltic area of a peculiar language quite similar to Greek and Latin (whose roots are frequently close), Lithuanian, which has retained some very archaic features: "The Baltic languages, especially Lithuanian, preserve an archaic quality that enables them to be compared to the most ancient linguistic forms of the Indo-European family . . . The original vocalization is more faithfully conserved in these languages than in any other living Indo-European language."[32]

In concert with this, we can note a peculiar Lithuanian agrarian rite concerning the wheat harvest, reported by James Frazer in *The Golden Bough*: "Near Ragnit, Lithuania, reapers leave the last tuft of wheat standing and say: 'Old Boba is sitting there.' Then a young mower sharpens his sickle and cuts the tuft with a stroke. People say that he cut Boba's head."[33] It is astonishing that we find here a piece of Greek mythology: The Lithuanian old Boba is Baubo, an Orphic goddess connected with the myth of Demeter, the Greek goddess of crops. According to Kerényi, Baubo was Trittolemus's mother, "he who, after getting the gift of wheat, went round to spread worldwide Demeter's gift . . . In the vase paintings he is sitting holding the spikes in his hands."[34] In short, the Lithuanian farmers still remember Boba-Baubo, "wheat's mother" in Greek mythology.

THE DECLINE OF THE CLIMATIC OPTIMUM

The theory that Homer's world is actually a northern one depends on the eventual movement of this northern Bronze Age culture to the south— to the Mediterranean, where it became the great Mycenaean culture of Greece. The explanation for why and how it is that these northern peoples moved south can be found in one great change affecting the region they had lived in for so long: the decline of the postglacial climatic optimum.

After the peak of the warmer temperatures of the climatic optimum, between 2500 B.C.E. and 2000 B.C.E., Europe entered the Sub-Boreal stage, during which the climate cooled gradually, as Pia Laviosa Zambotti reports:

> [T]he temperature dropped . . . Beech trees spread and leafy flora migrated from northern Sweden to more southern areas. . . . This cold climate, the peak of which coincides with the Iron Age, blocked the northern culture's most promising energies. The legendary Fimbul-Winter spread poverty and death with its chill, thus forcing the peoples [of northern Europe] to migrate.[35]

In the first half of the second millennium B.C.E., then, the Northern Hemisphere underwent a radical change in climate, with a general lowering of temperature, an advance of the glaciers both in northern Europe and in mountainous areas, and an increase in rainfall in the Mediterranean and Near East regions. This cooling process reached its climax around the middle of the second millennium B.C.E.

Evidence of Climate Decline

In the depiction of weather in both the *Odyssey* and the *Iliad,* we see the beginnings of what may well be the instability and change associated with the decline of the climatic optimum. Throughout both texts there are numerous references to rain, wind, and cold that suggest a world growing climatically harsher. One important clue in Homer's work that indicates a climate in decline is the bad weather that makes the homeward journey of the Trojan War veterans so difficult. Here is Nestor's dramatic account of his departure, along with his foreboding of impending disasters: "I ran away with all my ships / because I realized that a god was plotting disaster. / Warlike Tydeus's son [Diomedes] also ran away, urging his companions" (*Odyssey* 3.165–67). We could also hold the climatic decline responsible for the difficulties the Achaean ships encounter at the beginning of the war, when they set sail from Aulis.

At the same time, Homer presents details congruent with a northern Europe that had been experiencing effects of the optimum up to this time. Thus, amid references to "the never ending heavy rains [*athéspha-ton ómbron*]" (*Iliad* 3.4), we find mention of plants such as grapevines and animals such as big cats (lions or leopards), though these are spoken of only in similes or in relation to their skins. In addition, these animals are never described in their typical savanna-like setting, but are instead depicted as, for instance, "a lion grown in the mountains [*oresítrophos*], confident of his strength," who "comes out in the rain and the wind" (*Odyssey* 6.130–31)—a portrayal that conjures an image more akin to a northern mountain lion.

As we have seen, one of the most important features of the climate described by Homer is the frequent presence of fog, which is found more or less everywhere: over both sea—which is usually described as "wine-dark," "gloomy," and "misty"—and land, including Scheria, Ithaca, the Cyclopes' land, Troy, and the Peloponnese. Fog at times appears in conjunction with wind for an especially inhospitable mix: "Notus [the south wind] sheds the fog on mountain tops, / unwelcome by shepherds but better than night for thieves, / and one can see no farther than he can throw a stone . . ." (*Iliad* 3.10–12). This refers to what is known as *advection fog*,[36] which occurs when the south wind blows across a colder landmass.

The poem also often dwells upon violent, windy storms:

> *A goatherd from his position watches a cloud*
> *coming from the sea under the howl of Zephyrus [the west wind];*
> *from afar it appears as black as pitch,*
> *getting closer from the sea; it brings a great storm . . .*
>   (*Iliad* 4.275–78)

> *Zephyrus collides with the clouds*
> *of white Notus, upsetting them with a deep storm;*
> *swollen billows unceasingly break, and foam*
> *squirts upwards under howling gushes . . .* (*Iliad* 11.305–308)

> *A gale with terrible winds*
> *under Zeus's thunder breaks out onto the plain;*
> *with appalling roar it hurls itself upon the sea, where many*
> *billows churn on the howling sea,*
> *rolling with their white foam one after the other.* (*Iliad* 13.795–99)

Those who populate Homer's work seem used to meeting the challenge of this frequent wind: "The rafters a good builder connects / to a high house to withstand the strength of the wind [*bías anémon*]" (*Iliad* 23.712–13), or the man who "with closely joined stones connects the wall / of a high house to withstand strong winds" (*Iliad* 16.212–13).

Nor is wind a stranger to the world of the *Odyssey*. The following relates a significant detail concerning the climate of Crete:

The noble Achaeans [as they were waiting to sail for Troy] stayed
*   there for twelve days;*
a violent wind of Boreas [the north wind] was blowing, so much
*   so that in the land*
it prevented men from standing [oud'epí gaíei eía hístasthai]; some
*   adverse god roused it.*
On the thirteenth day the wind fell and they left.
*   (Odyssey 19.199–202)*

Along with fog and wind, rain is omnipresent in Homer's world.
The *Iliad* often mentions torrential rain and disastrous floods:

A swollen river
in flood runs quickly and overflows the banks;
neither the raised banks
nor the fences of the gardens in bloom can stop the swell,
which floods suddenly when Zeus's rain falls . . . (Iliad 5.87–91)

A swollen river runs down to the plain
in flood from the mountains, following Zeus's rain;
it drags many dry oaks and many pines
and discharges much mud into the sea . . . (Iliad 11.492–95)

A boulder falls from a crag;
a swollen river has pushed it down from the hilltop
breaking the props of the hard rock;
it plunges from above bouncing and rumbling
in the wood. (Iliad 13.37–41)

In the end,

the storm lashes the whole black land
on a late summer day, when Zeus pours his heaviest rain,
as he is indignant and gets angry with the men
who arrogantly pass twisted sentences in the assembly
and trample on justice. (Iliad 16.384–88)

Incidentally, here we find one of the themes common to many civilizations: that of a flood provoked by God to punish men for their sins.

Of course, wind, fog, and rain obviously occur in the Mediterranean, but they are not as prevalent as they are in Homer's text, especially during summertime. What is more, along with fog and wind and rain, snow—certainly not a typical element in the climate of the Mediterranean coast!—is frequently mentioned as falling on the Homeric landscape, where it appears in large quantities even on lowlands, as in this wonderful passage from the *Iliad*:

> *Snowflakes fall heavily*
> *on a winter day, when wise Zeus sets about snowing . . .*
> *He soothes the winds and pours out unceasingly until he covers*
> *the top of the mountains, the high rises,*
> *the grasslands and the tilled fields of the men.*
> *He even pours out on the seashore and the headlands;*
> *the lapping waves halt the flakes, but everything else*
> *is covered and hidden when Zeus's snowstorm falls.*
> (*Iliad* 12.278–86)

The epic is full of similes involving the frozen precipitation of the north:

> *The snowflakes fall*
> *that the strong wind, stirring the dark clouds,*
> *pours heavily on the land . . .* (*Iliad* 12.156–58)

> *Icy snow or hail is blown from the clouds*
> *under Boreas's push . . .* (*Iliad* 15.170–71)

> *Zeus's icy, thick snowflakes swirl*
> *under Boreas's push . . .* (*Iliad* 19.357–58)

> *Fine-haired Hera's husband throws the thunderbolt*
> *preparing an endless heavy shower, hail storm*
> *or snowfall, when the snow covers the fields.* (*Iliad* 10.6–8)

In this last passage, we note that once again snow is found on the fields—the lowlands.

Finally, we recall the beautiful expression describing Ulysses' fluent speech: "His words were like snowflakes in winter" (*Iliad* 3.222). This is metaphorical language in currency that would be most familiar to northerners, consistent with the scene of "a freezing winter which stops / farm work and torments livestock" (*Iliad* 17.549–50).

Regarding the seasons themselves, we may find a parallel between the ancient Germans—that is, the northern peoples contemporary with Tacitus for whom "winter, spring and summer have meaning and names, but they are unaware of the name and produce of autumn"[37]—and those people in Homer's works, who experience "only three seasons, winter, spring, and summer; the latter being divided into *théros* and *opóre*."[38] Interestingly, *opóre*, late summer, has a specific name in today's Finnish language: The *ruska* is the transition between summer and winter and is a far shorter period than what is known as autumn in the temperate belts. It is that time when woods blaze with a riot of reds, browns, and yellows before snow and frost take away the last leaves and remove any trace of fine weather.

In speaking of weather we must ask, What of the sun, that element seemingly most present in the Mediterranean? The *Iliad* hardly ever refers to its heat or rays. Nor does the *Odyssey* mention the sun shining in Ithaca. Ajax even goes so far as to ask of Zeus: "Free the sons of the Achaean from the fog, / make the sky clear and allow us to see!" (*Iliad* 17.645–46). This truly conflicts with the traditional location of the war in Asia Minor, where the relentless Mediterranean sun would certainly shine down on the bronze-clad warriors. In their depiction of an overcast northern world, the poems suggest that their original versions could not have been much altered during their long stay in the warm Aegean climate.

As for warmth, those instances when the warriors of the *Iliad* do sweat seem to be brought about not by the heat of the sun but from nerves or terror or the efforts of battle: Ajax, left alone to defend his ship, is wet with sweat not from heat, but from stress as he desperately fights off the furious Trojan attack: "Round his forehead the shining helmet / was beaten and boomed terribly . . . / He was panting heavily and sweating profusely / from his whole body; he couldn't manage to get / his breath back" (*Iliad* 16.104–105, 109–11). Likewise, terror and exhaustion are at work when Achilles catches Priam's son, Lycaon: "He had neither his helmet nor shield nor spear, / but he had thrown everything to the ground; sweat had exhausted him / as he fled from the river, and fatigue tired him out" (*Iliad* 21.50–52). The same condition applies to Nestor and Machaon as they run from battle, pressed by the Trojans, and "dried the sweat from their tunics / standing in the breeze on the seashore" (*Iliad* 11.621–22).

Similarly, the shock due to wounds causes Diomedes to sweat: He "was easing the wound Pandarus had inflicted on him with an arrow. / The sweat under the wide belt of his buckle exhausted him . . . / he was wiping away the blood by lifting the belt" (*Iliad* 5.795–98). And Eurypylus "was wounded by an arrow in his thigh / and was returning limping back from the battlefield. He was damp with sweat / from his shoulders and head, and from his grave wound / blood was dripping" (*Iliad* 11.810–13). Likewise, after being stunned by a blow from Ajax, Hector "recovered consciousness, / and recognized his companions around him; breathlessness and sweat / stopped" (*Iliad* 15.240–42). The sheer physical exertion of fear, fleeing, boxing (*Iliad* 23.688), or wrestling (*Iliad* 23.715)—but never the heat of the sun beating upon their battle attire—causes Homer's characters to sweat.

Specific Causes of Migration

Some scholars and writers have connected instances of famine and epidemics with the worsening of the climate after an optimal period. But they most often make this analogy in reference to the period between the thirteenth and eighteenth centuries, following the medieval warm period. Colder weather causes the failure of crops, which was likely one of the major factors that drove the ancient Baltic peoples to search for better living areas to the south. According to Saxo, the Longobards migrated from the Baltic to the Mediterranean area because "the extremely harsh climate ruined crops and there was a serious shortage of food."[39]

Regarding disease, a terrible plague hit Europe in the fourteenth century, after the warm period began to decline, at about the same time that the so-called St. Vitus's dance also wreaked havoc. Similarly, we may recall the plague—*noûson kakén, Iliad* 1.10—that rages in the Achaean camp at the beginning of the *Iliad*. The poet says that "Apollo's arrows" caused it (*Iliad* 24.603–606). This fits with the splendid description of Sirius, the shiniest star of the firmament, which heralds the winter and its burden of sickness and suffering:

> *The late summer star rises; its bright rays*
> *twinkle among many stars in the dead of the night.*
> *People call it by the name of Orion's Dog*
> *and it is the brightest, but it is of ill omen,*
> *and brings much fever to the unhappy mortals.* (*Iliad* 22.27–31)

Beyond these portents of doom, we know that an actual catastrophic event did occur in about 1630 B.C.E.: the eruption of the Mediterranean volcano Thera (Santorini), which presumably extinguished the Minoan civilization in Crete and certainly had severe climatic consequences all over the world (evidence of the eruption has been found even in the annual rings of very ancient American bristlecone pine trees), giving rise to atmospheric phenomena that must have terrorized the Bronze Age civilizations of northern Europe.

If we consider that the climatic optimum had begun to decline some centuries before, this event probably quickened the final collapse of the more benevolent climate. The intensely frigid cold that followed the eruption was likely a key factor that caused some peoples such as the Achaeans to leave their original homeland and look for more hospitable lands to which they could transplant their proto-Greek language and continue the cults of their traditional gods. Those who remained in the north gradually gave up their language and their old gods, which were in decline even in the *Iliad,* as can be seen in the ridicule accorded them in the grotesque battle narrated in Book 21. Thus, the large-scale migrations of Indo-European peoples (including the Achaeans/Mycenaeans) that took place in the first half of the second millennium B.C.E. were the result of a worsening climate whose decline was hastened by natural disaster.

Homer's world represents the last of the Achaeans' Bronze Age greatness and the beginning of a new time in a northern region that was in great flux. We may now head south to Greece, where, first of all, we must listen to the poet Hesiod.

A CULTURE ON THE MOVE

The great Greek poet Hesiod sets "those who died at Thebes and Troy" in an intermediate period between the Bronze and Iron Ages,[40] as if he were aware of the gap between the two epochs or, rather, the break marked by migration from the Baltic to the Aegean world after the Trojan War.

This significant move can be dated to around the beginning of the sixteenth century B.C.E. As the French scholar Pierre Lévêque reports, "towards 1600–1580 B.C. there was a dramatic change in Greek civilization. Archaeologists define it as the passage from the middle Helladic to the recent Helladic."[41] The latter period, which lasted until about 1100 B.C.E., is also known as the Mycenaean period, from the name of the most important site in Argolis. It coincides with the Achaeans' (Mycenaeans') arrival in Greek territory and the concurrent appearance of "northern" tendencies, such as a preference for amber, which came only from the Baltic area, and helmets decorated with boar tusks, such as the one Ulysses wears (*Iliad* 10.261–65) during his night raid with Diomedes in Trojan territory. These two "fashions" appeared at the beginning of the recent Helladic period but disappeared soon after.

The prevalence of amber in Greece with the arrival of the Achaeans and its subsequent rapid disappearance is actually quite significant. Colin Renfrew claims that "amber from the Baltic first makes its appearance in the Aegean around the time of the shaft graves of Mycenae."[42] On this subject, Martin Nilsson writes:

[A]mber is found frequently and in great quantities in many Mycenaean tombs of the mainland, e.g., in the earliest shaft graves at Mycenae, in the bee-hive tombs at Kakovatos-Pylos, which belong to a transitional stage between the Early and Middle Mycenaean periods, and in many other tombs; it is found in almost every new excavation of Mycenaean cemeteries. The curious fact is that it is especially found in earlier Mycenaean tombs, while it is scarce or altogether absent in later tombs. The extreme scarceness of amber in Crete is in striking contrast to the abundant finds on the mainland . . . There is only one explanation of the difference, *viz.*, that a people immigrating from the north brought the taste for and the use of amber with it . . . [43]

Also: "[A]nalysis has shown that this amber is of northern, probably Baltic origin, and the amber must certainly have come overland from the north."[44]

As to the boar tusks on Ulysses' helmet, Scandinavians and Germans often reproduced boars on their helmets as symbols of a warrior's force. Moreover, Tacitus informs us that the Nordic warriors "wear amulets in the shape of a boar [*formas aprorum gestant*] as a protection from all dangers."[45]

Mycenaean archaeology provides us with a good deal of further evidence of the migration of Mycenaeans from north to south. Nilsson writes:

A very important discovery was made in a chamber tomb at Dendra. It seems to have been a cenotaph. In the tomb there was a hearth, and a sacrificial table, and two stone slabs were found there; these slabs were rectangular with a projection of the same form on one small side and covered with small, shallow cavities. Their similarity with the menhirs, known from the Bronze Age of Central Europe, is striking, and their identity with these sacred stones seems hardly possible to deny. If this is so, it is a very striking corroboration of the northern origin of the Mycenaeans.[46]

Regarding Nilsson's reputation, Giorgio Pasquali claims that this renowned scholar has been praised for the "amplitude and, we could almost say, completeness of his knowledge of sources, without any tendentiousness, and a repugnance for too-audacious hypotheses."[47] It is perplexing that his well-documented research on the Mycenaeans' northern origin, supported by incontestable archaeological proof, has not been given due recognition, particularly considering that his conclusions fit perfectly with the traces left by the predecessors of the Mycenaeans in England.

The southern migration is also apparent in various distinctive characteristics of Mycenaean architecture. On this subject Lévêque claims:

Owing to many of these characteristics (gable roofs, closed buildings, fixed fireplaces) the Mycenaean palaces recall the cold and damp northern countries from which they undoubtedly came. . . . They are very different from the typically Mediterranean architectural conception of the buildings of Crete.[48]

What is more, as Nilsson tells us, the structure of the *megaron*, the main hall of the Mycenaean buildings, "was also very well suited for a chief surrounded by retainers and table companions, and is identical with the hall of the old Scandinavian kings."[49]

The migration of Mycenaeans from the north is further corroborated by the physical features of these Mycenaeans themselves, which we may discern from a variety of sources: As mentioned earlier, the great Greek poet Pindar describes the Danaans as "fair-haired."[50] According to Giulio Giannelli, professor in Greek literature at the University of Florence, "The Indo-Europeans who settled in Greece must have been tall and blond, just like Homer's well-built blond heroes."[51] And as we read in the *History of the Ancient World,* published by Cambridge University, the remains found in Mycenaean graves suggest men who had the "physiques of champions."[52] The features of the so-called golden mask of Agamemnon, which is one of the most famous Mycenaean archaeological finds, might also suggest a northern cultural origin. They bear a resemblance to elements found at certain northern archaeological sites, such as a figure carved on a stone in Snaptun's Furnace in Jutland, which likely dates back to the Viking era, and a Swedish mask found in Valsgärde in Uppland.

Further, anthropological studies of human remains found in Kalkani's Mycenaean necropolis make it clear, according to Nilsson,

> that it would be possible to refer the skulls of the women to the Mediterranean race, but that the skulls of the men have a larger capacity than is usual in this race, and that no objection can be made if they are thought to belong to men of a Nordic race. The same difference is observed between the king and queen from Dendra . . . Consequently, anthropology does not oppose but seems to corroborate the opinion that the Mycenaeans were immigrants from the north. They may often have taken indigenous wives . . . In the Mycenaean Age, the dominating people had northern connections.[53]

As for the probable language of the Mycenaeans, the famous philosopher Bertrand Russell writes in the first chapter of his famous *History of Western Philosophy:* "There are traces which most probably confirm that they were Greek-speaking conquerors, and that at least the aristocracy was made up of blond Nordic invaders who brought the Greek language with them."[54] As if to underscore this, in *Four Thousand Years Ago,* Bibby underlines the common origin of the Achaean princes of Greece and Asia Minor in the fifteenth century B.C.E. and the sun-worshipping farmers of Scandinavia.

DATING THE HOMERIC WORLD

Radiocarbon dating adjusted with dendrochronology—that is, tree-ring calibration—has recently corrected the theory of an Eastern origin of European civilization. In *Before Civilization,* Colin Renfrew describes the consequences of this discovery:

These changes bring with them a whole series of alarming reversals in chronological relationships. The megalithic tombs of Western Europe now become older than the Pyramids or the round tombs of Crete, their supposed predecessors. The early metal-using cultures of the Balkans antedate Troy and the early Bronze Age Aegean, from which they were supposedly derived. And in Britain, the final structure of Stonehenge, once thought to be the inspiration of Mycenaean architectural expertise, was complete well before the Mycenaean civilization began. . . . The whole carefully constructed edifice comes crashing down, and the story-line of the standard textbooks must be discarded.[55]

The Linear B Tablets

In order to examine in further depth the relationship between the Homeric world and the Mycenaeans who settled in Greece, we turn to the writing of the Mycenaeans, the so-called Linear B, which was found on tablets dating from the fifteenth century B.C.E. in the archives of Cnossus Palace, as well as on others discovered in Pylos and Mycenae and dating back to the thirteenth century B.C.E. The English architect Michael Ventris deciphered the inscriptions on the tablets in 1952 and learned that the Mycenaeans spoke a Greek dialect that was quite similar to Homer's Ionian.

The tablets carry the names of Zeus, Hera, Athena, Poseidon, Hermes, Artemis, Ares, and Hephaestus. Thus, the gods of the religion described by Homer must date back to a former age rather than to the few centuries preceding the Mycenaean arrival in the Mediterranean region.

Other names on the tablets include some of those contained in the Homeric poems, such as Achilles (A-ki-re-u in the syllabic Linear B writing) and Hector. As Fritz Graf notes, however, these names often belonged to common people—smiths, shepherds, and even slaves—in the Mycenaean world. This could mean that the heroic times were regarded as part of the distant past even in that period, which preceded the classical Greek era. (We have only to think of names commonly used nowadays that are linked to the origins of Christianity: Joseph, John, Mark, Mary, Ann, and so forth.) Interestingly, the word *oka,* meaning "ship," followed by captains' names, is found on a series of tablets in Pylos, recalling, of course, the *Iliad*'s Catalog of Ships.

That there is a relationship between Homer's world and Mycenaean civilization is doubtless, but scholars deny that the former reflects the reality of the latter, noting that the two worlds do not coincide at all. On this subject, Moses Finley claims:

> Today it is no longer seriously maintained, though it is still said often enough, that the *Iliad* and the *Odyssey* reflect Mycenaean society . . . The world of Odysseus was not the Mycenaean Age of five or six hundred years earlier, but neither was it the world of the eighth or seventh centuries B.C. . . . The decipherment of the Linear B tablets and archaeology together have destroyed the old orthodoxy.[56]

Furthermore, Fausto Codino states:

> If we try to reconstruct a historical-political evolution by arranging the scattered clues contained in the two poems in a plausible chronological order, we have to admit that once again, the few reliable conclusions philologists reached to this end are of some help which can be problematic.[57]

Actually, the parts of the poems that are considered to be of later composition seem to better reflect what we know of the Mycenaean world, which fits very well with our theory in this book.

In his turn, Fritz Graf claims: "Mythical epic tales in Greece have deep roots that date back to the third millennium B.C.—that is, a long time before the Mycenaean civilization began to flourish."[58] Therefore, they most likely originated *outside* the Greek world. Besides,

> . . . there are important places, according to mythology, which don't have a great Mycenaean past (for example, the cities of Argos and Sparta, or Ithaca, where Schliemann searched in vain for Odysseus' palace). There are also Mycenaean settlements or buildings that have no identifiable mythical counterparts, for example, Gla in Boeotia, Asine in Argolis or Miletus. There is no mention of myths in the Mycenaean colonization of Ionia, nor in the Mycenaean conquest of Minoan Crete . . . Myth and epos do not provide any reliable picture of the Mycenaean world.[59]

Thus, Greek mythology reflects not the Greek context, which is much too recent, but rather the original Mycenaean (Achaean) one, which was certainly coastal (the Mycenaeans were expert seafarers, and such sea-manship takes a long time to develop) and situated in the north.

Most scholars now agree with what Finley has maintained since the 1950s: The Homeric world predates and is more primitive than the Mycenaean culture. King Priam's sons pasture their flocks in the gorges of Ida (*Iliad* 11.106); near the royal palace in Ithaca a manure heap stands (*Odyssey* 17.297) and swine graze (*Odyssey* 20.164): Here we are far from the sumptuous palaces of Aegean civilizations. Stuart Piggott corroborates this view when he stresses the close relationship between the world Homer describes and prehistoric Europe of the second millennium B.C.E., which was very distant from the refined Asian civilizations.

That Homer's world predates Mycenaean civilization in the south clarifies why it is decidedly more archaic than the Mycenaean civilization that emerges from the Linear B tablets (which represent a time some centuries later than when the Mycenaeans settled in Greece). Evidently, the contact of the rough, barbaric Achaean civilization with the refined Mediterranean and Eastern cultures—namely, those of Crete, Egypt, Syria, and so forth—favored the rapid evolution of the former, thanks to seafaring and trade. In fact, archaeologists have found Mycenaean trade stations scattered all along the Mediterranean coast.

Homer's archaism also sheds light on certain questions that have puzzled historians of religion, such as why Dionysus—a very important god in the Greek world, both in Mycenaean civilization and in classical Greece—is almost entirely neglected by Homer. By admitting that Homer precedes the Mycenaean age, everything becomes clear, for after the Achaeans settled in Greece, the features of their gods gradually changed as they came under the influence of the great Near Eastern civilizations. This is could also explain the significant differences between Homer's and Hesiod's pantheons, which are inexplicable if these two poets are seen as being almost contemporaries.

Although our task here is mainly geographical rather than chronological, what we have expounded so far enables us to place the events narrated by Homer in the interval between two significant occurrences: the beginning of the decline of the climatic optimum (in about the twentieth century B.C.E.)—for the two poems clearly describe an unsettled climate—and the rise of the sixteenth-century Mycenaean civilization in Greece, which took place at about the time of the disastrous explosion of Thera, an event that must have dealt the final blow to the northern climate. The Trojan War took place within this interval, presumably around the eighteenth century B.C.E.—that is, five hundred years before the traditional date of its occurrence, at about the beginning of the Sub-Boreal phase (or Early Holocene 3), which followed the optimum. Of course, archaeology will have the last word on this matter.

THE MIGRATION OF ORAL AND WRITTEN MYTH

At this point we may well wonder how the material of Homer's poems, with all of its references to a northern culture, was preserved from such a distant past until the eighth century B.C.E., the time of Homer's writing (as most scholars agree), long after the Achaean migration to southern Europe.

Here we can consider two possible means of transmission: written and oral. The persistence of such clear northern references over such a long period might lead us to believe there exists some written record that was handed down through time. The Linear B tablets prove that the Mycenaeans knew how to write, even if just syllabically, which, though functional, is less refined than an alphabetical system. Though the tablets found so far hold texts dealing only with trade and administration, this does not mean that the poems could not have been transmitted through writing.

But would those who would know the most intimate details of a battle like that fought in the *Iliad* choose writing as their method of transmission? The warriors who fought in Troy seem to have been no more cultured than Charlemagne (a famous example of an illiterate king). A passage from Book 6 of the *Iliad* hints at the existence of writing, however, referring to King Proetus, who plots Bellerophon's* death: "He sent him to Lycia and gave him wicked signs, / plotting many deadly [instructions] on a folded tablet, / and told him to show it to his father-in-law, so that he died" (*Iliad* 6.168–70). Thus, we cannot exclude the possibility that the primitive cores of the two poems were passed on through the Mycenaean age in part by means of a form of writing, with limited adjustment over time to make them more suitable to the evolution of the language. For example, there exist many different versions of the Indian epic poem known as the *Ramayana*, each accommodated to one of the countless languages of that subcontinent.

---

*It is also noteworthy that when the poet of the *Iliad* relates the most significant events in Bellerophon's life in Book 6, he totally ignores the winged horse Pegasus, whereas the subsequent Greek mythographers have abundantly "embroidered" on this subject. This omission would be incomprehensible if Homer had lived around the eighth century B.C.E., but can be easily explained by the antiquity of the original nuclei of the two poems, which reach back much further than the beginning of Greek literature.

Yet no trace of writing dating back to the second millennium B.C.E. has yet been found in the northern world. We could presume, then, that the Achaeans started writing after their settlement in the Mediterranean, when they came into contact with the highly civilized local peoples.

More likely, judging by the strong cultural references in the two poems, is the possibility of oral transmission from generation to generation, which would have enabled the works to "sail" without excessive loss through a period of almost one thousand years, from the Achaean migration in the sixteenth century B.C.E. to the eighth century, which produced the versions we know today.

In his *Prehistoric India to 1000 B.C.*, Stuart Piggott makes some interesting observations on this subject: "Not so long ago, an Indian priest appeared in Benares who dictated a long religious work in verse, which was unknown and not transcribed until then. Judging by its style and language, it could at least belong to medieval times, when it began to be handed down orally."[60] We can also take into account the extraordinary story concerning the French ethnologist Alexandra David-Néel (1868–1969). She had the opportunity to listen to a Tibetan bard who, over a period of several weeks, acted out the whole epic poem of Gesar of Ling, the mythical hero of Tibet. In her introduction to the French version of the poem, she writes:

It is very likely that originally the songs celebrating Gesar were handed down only orally. This custom still exists, for many bards are illiterate. Afterward, in an uncertain time, the stories were collected, put down in writing, and grouped according to their subject. It is possible to find such manuscripts devoted to Gesar that people lent to one another in order to copy . . . Each manuscript reports a specific part of the adventures of this hero, but nobody has ever collected the whole epic . . . Not many bards know the whole of Gesar's story in detail, but they know a certain number of cantos, which they act at the meetings to which they are invited . . . These bards would feel deeply offended if anyone ventured to tell them that they have *learned* the cantos of the poem; instead they claim that Gesar or another divine being directly inspires them and tells them the words they utter.[61]

This passage may provide the best answer to some unanswered questions regarding the way the ancient bards handed down the Homeric poems, which, in their opening lines, actually claim to be inspired by a divine being, the Muse. Moreover, Homer's epics have quite a few parallels with Gesar's saga, the roots of which date back to the old Indo-European tradition, as Gianfranco de Turris shows in his preface to the Italian edition of the saga. Further, given the consistent nature of the culture of the northern world from the Bronze Age to the Viking era, we may discover other pieces of information regarding oral transmission by delving deeper into the lifestyles and working systems of the Norse skalds as well as by analyzing their works in the light of what has emerged so far.

Concerning the antiquity of the Homeric poems, Professor Geoffrey Kirk writes in his essay on early Greek poetry in *The Cambridge History of Classical Literature:*

> A recent linguistic argument suggests that the Homeric modes of separating adverbial and prepositional elements that were later combined into compound verbs belong to a stage of language anterior to that represented in the Linear B tablets. If so, that would take elements of Homer's language back more than 500 years before his time.[62]

He also notes that the version handed down to us is contemporary with the introduction of the alphabet to the Greek world:

> Yet one of the curious things about Homer is his appearance on the scene just at the end of the oral period—at the exact epoch in which writing, through the introduction from the Levant of a practicable alphabetic system in the ninth or early eighth century B.C., began to spread through Greece.[63]

At this point, this "curious" thing could be easily explained by the thesis we are outlining and supporting in this book. Given that the two poems preceded the introduction of the alphabet, the version handed down to us basically consists of their *transcription* into the new writing system (which involved some accommodations of the text to the language of that time). This mixed method of transmission, both oral and written, explains the countless number of geographic and non-geographic incongruities. For example, there is no trace of the Phaeacians in the Mediterranean (although Homer calls them "famous seafarers"), nor is there any evidence of Scheria. And why would a poet of the eighth century have made up the significant island of Dulichium? As we have seen, this island is mentioned repeatedly in both the *Odyssey* and the *Iliad* and is given a definite geographic location, but has never been discovered in the Greek world. The presence of Dulichium in the Homeric poems and its seeming counterpart, Langeland, in the Baltic Sea is as much a fact as is the absence of Dulichium in the Mediterranean. *Contra factum non valet argumentum,* "concrete facts count more than any reasoning."

Of course, there are many "long islands" scattered in the seas—in the Mediterranean as well as the Baltic. Yet what unequivocally links Langeland with the Homeric Dulichium is that the Danish South Fyn archipelago is the only one in the world that squares with the features of the group of islands near Ithaca as they are described in both the *Iliad* and the *Odyssey.*

Linguistic Puzzles

Given the extreme antiquity of the two poems and their inevitable vicissitudes through the ages, we should not be surprised by variations in meaning of certain terms used by Homer, which, having been moved from a totally different setting to the Greek one, could have undergone a sort of semantic drift. This linguistic phenomenon often makes it difficult to determine the original sense of words. It could have at times misled even the ancient Greek scholars, who were unaware that they were dealing with such ancient texts essentially extraneous to their culture, being both temporally and geographically very distant.

Besides the case of the *lotós,* the "clover" the Lotus-eaters used to crop as animals, we have already come across the *antolaí*—that is, the "staying" of the sun over the horizon on the island of Circe—and the *amphilýke nýx,* the "dimly-lit night" at summer solstice. Another example is the adjective *hierós,* which primarily means "sacred" in classical Greek but in Homeric language usually means "eminent," "important," "remarkable," "great," "large," or "broad," without any specific religious connotation. Therefore, some seemingly curious expressions in the *Iliad,* such as "the *sacred* wall," "the *sacred* farmyards," "the *sacred* platoon," "the *sacred* fish," "the *sacred* chariot," "the *sacred* ring," "*sacred* Ilium," "*sacred* Alpheus," and "*sacred* Cythera," regain sense and perspective.

Sometimes the passing of time and changes in context have acted in a different way, such as in the case of the adjective *amphiélissos,* which refers to the double prow of the Achaean ships, similar to that of the Viking ships, but which took on the more abstract meaning of "uncertain" or "unsteady" in classical Greek. Another significant example of these misunderstandings can be seen in the term *hecatomb.* It has traditionally been understood to mean a "sacrifice of one hundred oxen," from *hekaton*, "hundred," and *bous*, "oxen." However, the *Iliad* narrates that a *hecatomb* was loaded on a ship with only twenty oarsmen (*Iliad* 1.309–10); then, when the ship reached its destination, it was sacrificed, roasted, and eaten at a banquet (*Iliad* 2.458–68). Here is a very tough job! In fact, from the context, it is clear that this hecatomb was in reality only one cow. Similar sacrifices of a cow or an ox, made in an identical manner, are found elsewhere in the *Iliad* (3.421–31, 7.316–20) and in the *Odyssey* (3.454–63). What is more, Homer also uses this term in the plural: *teleéssas hekatómbas*—that is, "perfect hecatombs" (*Iliad* 2.306)—making it very unlikely that we are dealing with hundreds of oxen. On the other hand, he often quotes other animals as being hecatombs, such as goats (*Iliad* 1.315) and lambs (*Iliad* 4.120), and even mentions a "fifty rams' hecatomb" (*Iliad* 23.146–47).

Perhaps the hecatomb originated from some archaic practice, such as the sacrifice of one out of every hundred newborn animals, making its meaning something akin to "the hundredth." We also note that, considering the digamma or usual loss of the initial *v* in Greek words, *hecatomb* is very similar to the Latin word *victima*, which has the identical meaning of an "animal sacrificed in a religious rite." This has nothing to do with those imaginary one hundred oxen, but is perfectly consistent with the use Homer makes of the term *hecatomb*.

The fact that the ancient Greeks misunderstood its meaning is further evidence of the time lag and the discontinuity between their later culture and that of Homer's world. For example, the Athenian general Conon offered a one-hundred-oxen hecatomb as a sacrifice to the gods after the battle of Cnidus (394 B.C.E.).

Another peculiar expression, *nýmphe neís*, which occasionally occurs in the *Iliad* (6.22, 14.444, 20.384), is traditionally interpreted as "water nymph" or "Naiad nymph." If we examine the passages in which it appears, however, this traditional translation seems puzzling, for in these passages the poet is always referring to normal women, mothers of soldiers fallen in battle. We can see this in more detail in a passage that refers to the fierce battle under the Achaean wall:

> *Swift Ajax Oïleus*
> *sprang with his sharp spear and hit Satnius*
> *Enopides, whom a beautiful* nýmphe neís *had borne*
> *to Enops the cowherd on the banks of the Satnioïs River.*
>   (*Iliad* 14.442–45)

The key to the answer is that the word *nýmphe* in the Homeric poems means not only "nymph," but also "wife," "lady," and "bride" (as in modern Greek). Penelope is referred to in this way in the *Odyssey* (4.743), and *nýmphe* usually has this meaning in the *Iliad* as well (3.130, 9.560, 18.492). This term also appears in the masculine form, *nýmphios,* meaning "bridegroom" (*Iliad* 23.223, *Odyssey* 7.65). We find the same root in the Latin verb *nubere,* "to marry." At first glance, this meaning of the Greek term *nýmphe* appears to be much more suitable than the traditional "nymph"for Satnius's mother. We still have to understand the meaning of *neís,* however, which accompanies the "bride." Homer comes to our aid yet again, for the word *nêis* in the *Odyssey* means "fledging," "inexperienced" (*Odyssey* 8.179) and therefore fits very well in this instance. The clue to the puzzle is the expression *nýmphen néen,* "young bride," used to refer to Penelope with her newborn Telemachus: "We left her a young bride [*nýmphen néen*] / when we went away on war. She was nursing her babbling baby, / who is counted among the men now" (*Odyssey* 11.447–49). Thus Penelope was in exactly the same situation as Satnius's mother and all the other *nýmphe neí* in the *Iliad:* They were all "young brides" and "new mothers" of soldiers, like poor Satnius, who were killed in battle. These unlucky women have nothing to do with imaginary water nymphs!

Such instances attest to the archaic nature of the original core of the Homeric poems, so distant from the Mycenaeans that the ancient Greeks themselves had forgotten the real meaning of the expressions we try to reconstruct. Another example of this disconnect is found in the work of Hesiod, the earliest poet of Greek literature (the seventh century B.C.E.), who claims that Hyperion is a Titan, father of the sun, the moon, and the dawn,[64] whereas in Homer, the Hyperion sun is the midnight sun, a phenomenon unknown to the Greek world.

Swan Song of a Lost Civilization

As we have seen, many details in the two Homeric poems reveal the northern matrix of the texts. The sheer number of these details alone— geographical, climatological, morphological, and cultural—indicates that the texts themselves likely changed little over their long stay in such a different, southern world.

The Homeric poems, or at least their original nuclei, may well be considered as cultural "fossils" dating back to the northern European Bronze Age that survived its collapse thanks to the Achaean migration to southern Europe.

Because of the likely oral origin of these two poems, we are able to realize, perhaps, why we know so little about Homer himself—even where he was born, where he lived, and where he died. Fausto Codino says: "If it were possible, we should follow the preliminary scheme typical of each literary work: historical setting, sources, author's biography and personality. In this case, all these aspects are unknown to us."[65] In fact, it is possible that in speaking of Homer, we are actually dealing with two different poets from two different locales: The origin of the *Iliad*, the poem of Achilles, seems to be the region around the Gulf of Finland, while the nucleus of the *Odyssey*, the poem glorifying Ulysses, likely originated in what is now Denmark. As is true of all epics and sagas handed down orally through time, whoever "authored" the *Odyssey* and the *Iliad* is as lost in myth as those characters he presents.

The *Iliad* and the *Odyssey* are, in a sense, the "swan song" of the lost civilization of the northern Bronze Age as well as a sort of spiritual testament to a most glorious common exploit. The words Homer ascribes to Helen seem to have a clairvoyance peculiar to the greatest poets: "Even in the future, we shall be sung / by men to come . . ." (*Iliad* 6.357–58). This makes the devotion of the descendants of the Achaeans to Homer's works even more touching, for his poems represent the memory of their forefathers and the heritage of their lost world, which they bravely and admirably rebuilt in the world of the Mediterranean from the Mycenaean Age on.

THE PATH OF MIGRATION AND THE SEED OF WESTERN CIVILIZATION

How exactly might the Achaeans have traveled from the Baltic to the Mediterranean? Presumably they would have followed some of the large Russian rivers from north to south, as the Swedish Vikings known as the Varangians did twenty-five hundred years later. Pouring onto the Sarmatian Plain around the beginning of the ninth century C.E., the Varangians followed the Dnieper River, called the Boristenes in ancient times, and conquered the city of Kiev, where they founded the kingdom of Rus, the first nucleus of the Russian empire. From Kiev, they continued downriver until they reached the Black Sea. In the year 886 they arrived at and besieged Constantinople. "All Russian historians agree with the idea that there is a 'tendency toward Byzantium' fostered by the courses of the southern Russian rivers."[66]

These waterways were extremely significant in providing migration routes for peoples and civilizations from north to south (see fig. 9.1). It is easy, then, to assume that the Achaeans also chose one of these most natural routes connecting the Baltic and Mediterranean worlds for their journey south when the climatic collapse forced them to migrate from their home territory (though they likely did not completely exclude the land routes that other northern peoples, such as the Cimbrians, Burgundians, Goths, and Longobards, followed much later in their migrations from the Baltic area to southern Europe). We can posit that, using the rivers, the Achaeans would have reached the Dnieper after sailing up the western Dvina and then followed its course to the Black Sea. Then they probably crossed the Dardanelles heading for the Aegean Sea, to finally settle in the Peloponnese, where they founded the Mycenaean civilization. In *Ancient Europe,* Stuart Piggott offers an interesting detail that may support the theory of this route: Mycenaean shaft graves are similar to the coeval wood-hut graves of southern Russia, where archaeologists have found remains in a peculiar burial position, bent with knees jutting out, just as are found in Mycenaean burial sites.

In medieval times, the Dnieper route was an important waterway to and from the Mediterranean Sea for Scandinavian merchants. The Volga River was just as important, for it joined the northern world with the Caspian Sea and was thus the main route between Scandinavia, Iran, and India. (As we discuss in chapter 14, this may well have been the route followed by the Aryans, who spoke a language similar to that of the Mycenaeans and settled in India in the same period as the latter did in Greece.)

When the Mycenaeans, who were expert seafarers, reached the Aegean, they likely began to explore their new world and soon realized that it was geographically rather similar to the one they had left, leading them to rename many corresponding places and their peoples with those from their original homeland. Thus, the large, flat island on the southwestern side of the Baltic Sea was identified with a mountainous peninsula found in a corresponding position in the Aegean world: the Peloponnese. Homer's "Broad Hellespont," facing northeast, found its *homotope*—its geographic counterpart—in the Dardanelles, which are comparably situated.

We could assume that the *Odyssey* and the *Iliad* helped the Achaeans to keep alive their memory of the Baltic—its geography, peoples, history, and mythology. Transplanted to the Mediterranean, this heritage was destined to be the first seed of Western civilization, for the evolution of Mycenaean culture in the Aegean, stimulated by contact with the

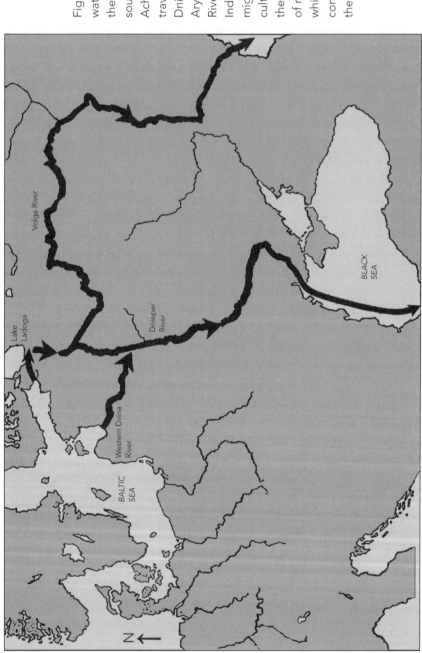

Fig. 9.1. The main waterways connecting the Baltic region to southern Eurasia. Achaeans presumably traveled south on the Dnieper River and Aryans on the Volga River during the Indo-European migration. Steppe cultures flourished in these areas as a result of migration and trade, which developed considerably during the Viking age.

advanced Mediterranean and Near Eastern peoples, led to the birth and development of Greek culture. Subsequently, Greek culture spread across the world, eventually by means of the Roman Empire, until this grand circle, which had begun many years before with the Achaean migration from the north, finally closed when the Romans came into contact with the Germans, eventually giving rise to modern European civilization.

Interestingly, the most important value that Europe has given the world, the idea of democracy, is found in both the Greek *agorá* and the Viking *thing*, the public meetings held in Athens and Iceland, respectively. Rather than being mere coincidence, it seems this concurrence is the result of a common origin. Europe, then, may well have a fundamentally unitary cultural and political substratum going back to the Bronze Age, evidence of which has been left us in the Homeric poems. These are the true "threads of Ariadne" that lead us back to the most ancient roots of our civilization, allowing us to find our origins again. It was a time worthy of the great epics that preserved it, as reflected by Geoffrey Bibby:

> The long period of universal peace known as the European Bronze Age, when art and handicrafts almost reached a level of perfection, which was illustrated in the graffiti drawings, has represented one of the first peaks in the graph of human progress. Even today, it is not excessive to consider it, as the Greeks did, a sort of Golden Age.[67]

In this chapter we have established the nature and chronology of the Bronze Age culture that existed in northern Europe at the time of the climatic optimum, evidence of this culture in Homer's work, and the striking archaeological similarities between it and the Mycenaean culture of Greece that postdated it. Now we shall devote some time to the reconstruction of the original world of the Achaeans by means of a real geographical summary that has been miraculously handed down to us from Homeric times: the *Iliad*'s Catalog of Ships, an extremely precious "photograph," dating back to the early Bronze Age, of the peoples settled along the Baltic coasts at the beginning of the second millennium B.C.E., before the migration of the Achaeans to the Mediterranean.

CHAPTER 10

THE CATALOG OF SHIPS: THE NORTHERN ACHAEAN WORLD

In Book 2 of the *Iliad* there are 266 lines of verse, known collectively as the Catalog of Ships, that present a list of the twenty-nine Achaean fleets that take part in the Trojan War, together with the names of their forty-six captains and their places of origin. Interestingly, the sequence is not hierarchical; for example, the commander in chief Agamemnon, who "was the most eminent, he led a great many troops" (*Iliad* 2.580), is listed ninth. Instead, it seems to be organized geographically. Amazingly, whereas superimposing this verbal "map" on the Mediterranean results in a number of puzzling inconsistencies, when it is grafted onto the Baltic coastline, Homer's descriptions of places and peoples fit perfectly.

There are clues within Homer's text that aid us in superimposing the Catalog of Ships on the Baltic world, as we can see, for instance, in the directions Nestor, an old chariot driver, gives to his son Antilochus prior to the chariot race held on the occasion of Patroclus's funeral:

> Direct your chariot and horses close to it [the turning post] until
>   you nearly graze it,
> and in your nice cabin bend
> a little to the left. Cheer on
> your right-hand horse, and loosen the reins;
> the left horse must graze the turning post
> until the wheel-hub seems to touch it . . . (*Iliad* 23.334–39)

Significantly, in these directions we note that the vehicles turn in a counterclockwise direction. Likewise, the suitors sitting in Ulysses' hall stand up in turn in counterclockwise order to take part in the archery competition—"Stand up friends, all in turn from the right, / beginning from the side where one pours wine" (*Odyssey* 21.141–42)—and Hephaestus pours wine to the other gods in Olympus in the same counterclockwise direction (*Iliad* 1.597).

The verbal map of the Baltic drawn by the text of the Catalog of Ships follows this same movement. As we shall see in this chapter, starting from what is now central Sweden and moving in a counterclockwise direction around the coast of the Baltic Sea to finish in Finland (see fig. 10.1), the Catalog of Ships paints a remarkably accurate picture of this northern world. In the course of our journey, we will attempt, with all due caution, to find interesting corroboration of this northern location of Homer's world in place-names that recall their Mediterranean counterparts. Though these similar-sounding names do not provide proof of the theory presented in this chapter, they do make for more food for thought.

THE BOEOTIAN AREA

Peneleos and Leitus led the Boeotians
with Archesilaus, Prothoenor and Clonius.
Some lived in Hyrie and stony Aulis,
in Schoenus, Scolus and mountainous Eteonus; . . .
others had Arne rich in grapevines, others Mideia,
divine Nisa and farthest Anthedon;
fifty ships of them left,
on each of them a hundred and twenty Boeotian youths
embarked. (*Iliad* 2.494–97, 507–10)

The Catalog of Ships begins in Boeotia, with the reference to "stony Aulis" in the text above confirming the location of Homeric Boeotia in central Sweden, close to the Bay of Norrtälje, a little north of Stockholm. This area—which we have previously identified with Aulis (see chapter 8), the place from which the Achaean fleet set sail for Lemnos and Troy—faces the isles of Åland and the Finnish Troad. With the beginning of the sequence in the catalog geographically fixed at this spot, we might speculate that Hyrie, mentioned above, could be today's Herräng,

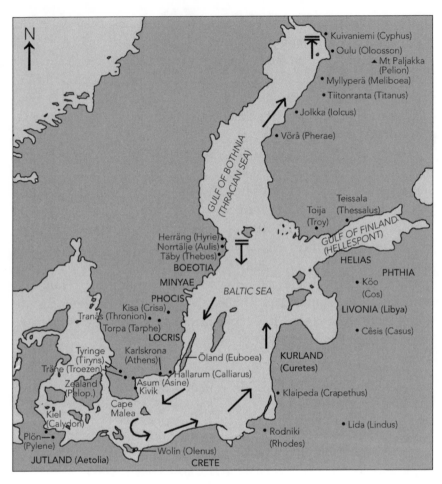

Fig. 10.1. A map of the Baltic showing the counterclockwise progression of places and peoples as listed in the Catalog of Ships

which lies about thirty miles northeast of Uppsala. As we have seen, this region incorporates the Boeotian city of Thebes, famous in Greek mythology, which may well correspond to present-day Täby, lying near Stockholm not far from Norrtälje (Aulis).

By following the coast in a counterclockwise direction—that is, going south along the western side of the Baltic, after Boeotia and Minyae ("the people that dwelt in Aspledon and Minyaean Orchomenus / were led by Ascalaphus and Ialmenus, sons of Mars . . ."; *Iliad* 2.511–12), Homer comes to Phocis.

The Phoceans were led by Schedius and Epistrophus,
sons of mighty Iphitus the son of Naubolus.
These were they that held Cyparissus, rocky Pytho,
holy Crisa, Daulis, and Panopeus;
they also that dwelt in Anemorea and Hyampolis,
and about the waters of the river Cephissus,
and Lilaea by the springs of the Cephissus . . . (Iliad 2.517–23)

Following a map of the Baltic region, we can see that Crisa and
Lilaea suggest the present-day Swedish town of Kisa and the Lillan
River. Among the cities of Phocis, the catalog mentions Pytho, where
Apollo's shrine stood, with its "stone threshold" (*Iliad* 9.404, *Odyssey*
8.80). The geography of the catalog as we've established it locates Pytho
in southern Sweden, and facts related to Pytho support this northern
location: Pytho is another name for Delphi, site of the most famous
oracle of Apollo in classical Greece. Greek mythology closely links
Apollo with the Hyperboreans, the mythical inhabitants of the extreme
north. In fact, Pindar calls them "Apollo's people, the Hyperboreans."[1]
Further, the first-century Greek historian Diodorus Siculus, in a passage
on Apollo's cult, states that the Delphians and the Hyperboreans were
"on very friendly terms," and that "they have inherited this tradition of
friendship from ancient times."[2]

Interestingly, the *omphalos,* the sacred egg-shaped stone representing
the navel of Gaia, the Earth goddess, was kept in Apollo's temple in Delphi.
As Professor Vittorio Di Cesare, of Bologna, informs us, there is a striking
similarity between Delphi's omphalos, whose surface was decorated with
a net design, and certain ancient spherical stones with similar net decoration found on women's tombs in southern Sweden. Taking the analogy still
further is the fact that people used these stones for oath-taking between
the fifth and twelfth centuries C.E. It seems, then, that Diodorus's statement
regarding the links between Delphians and Hyperboreans can be corroborated both archaeologically and geographically.

After Phocis, Homer mentions the cities of the Locrians, "who live
in front of holy [eminent, great] Euboea" (*Iliad* 2.535). In this area
lay "Tarphe and Thronion, on the banks of the River Boagrius" (*Iliad*
2.533), which could be today's Torpa and Tranås, lying inland near each
other in an area with plentiful water. As to "Calliarus . . . and lovely
Augeiae" (*Iliad* 2.531–32), they could correspond to present-day Hallarum and Augerum, respectively. More important than the similarity

in the sound of the place-names, which cannot provide proof positive, is the fact that mentioned next in line after the land of the Locrians is Euboea, the perfect counterpart of which is, as we have determined, the island of Öland, facing the Swedish coast (fig. 10.1). The Greek Euboea and the Swedish Öland are both roughly oblong and follow the contour of their respective mainlands, from which they are separated by narrow inlets. Öland (where today's Kalkstad recalls Homer's Euboean Chalcis) can be reached by a bridge near Kalmar.

Now let us review these first regions in the catalog with regard to their spatial relation to each other in the north versus their distance from each other in the Mediterranean world. After Boeotia, Homer places the lands of the Minyaeans, Phoceians, and Locrians facing Euboea (*Iliad* 2.535). Directly following these he lists Athens ("And they that held the strong city of Athens, the people of great / Erechtheus . . ."). From this organization we can infer that Boeotia, the first land mentioned, was located some distance from Euboea and even farther from Athens. It turns out that not only this sequence of regions in the catalog but also the distances between them fit perfectly along the Swedish coast: The "Boeotian" area, including Norrtälje (Aulis) and Täby (Thebes), is more than 120 miles from the northernmost point of Öland (Euboea).

This spatial orientation does not, however, correspond to the Mediterranean world, where Boeotia lies right in front of Euboea, which faces the Bay of Aulis (today's Vathy) and is situated next to Attica, while Locris and Phocis lie on the opposite side of Boeotia. What's more, besides being unfit for a large fleet, the position of the Greek Aulis behind Euboea does not appear to be very well chosen for a campaign bound for Asia Minor.

ATHENS TO CAPE MALEA

The position of Homer's Athens is linked to Cape Sunium, "the cape of Athens" (*Odyssey* 3.278). Therefore, traveling down along the Swedish coast, guided by the sequence in the catalog, we must look for a geographic point corresponding to Sunium, keeping in mind as well the map of Greece. With the help of the locations of Greek Euboea and Swedish Öland in their respective contexts, it is easy to identify the homotope of the Mediterranean Sunium as lying east of the city of Karlskrona, where the Swedish coast suddenly bends westward, opposite Öland's southernmost point (see fig. 10.2). The identification of Athens with the Swedish city of Karlskrona is congruent not only with the Catalog of Ships' sequence, but also with a tale told by Nestor in the *Odyssey* regarding the return from Troy to the Peloponnese, in which he states that Athens is situated before Cape Malea—which, as we shall see shortly, is identifiable with the cape at the southwestern end of Scania, near Malmö (*Odyssey* 3.278–87).

Karlskrona, which was founded about three hundred years ago, is the most important seaside town in this area. It lies in an enviable position, facing south on a small peninsula that is ringed by a series of islands, some of which are connected by bridges to the mainland. It is not surprising, therefore, that Karlskrona can boast not only of its naval museum, but also of its highly developed merchant and military seafaring activity. In short, Karlskrona has the same seafaring vocation as did its distant Bronze Age predecessor. It is easy to see from this that geography and climate often determine the destinies of cities and peoples.

The name of Athens is plural—Athênai—a form that probably refers to the primitive location of the city, which was fragmented among various islands and peninsulas. We can find an indirect corroboration of this in another example from the classical world: the plural form of the name Syracuse (Syracusae) in Sicily, deriving from the peculiar topography of this city, which spans the mainland and the facing island, as Cicero authoritatively attests to in his *Verrinae*. This also explains why the name of Boeotian Thebes occurs in the plural, a detail that cannot be accounted for in Greek geography: Its Baltic precursor lay not too far from the islands where Stockholm stands today. (The name of another very important Homeric city, Mycenae, is also in the plural form, an important factor in locating it in the area of Copenhagen.)

Interestingly, we can compare some place-names in this area, in particular the small islands near Karlskrona, to those in the Greek world: Aspö could call to mind the Athenian place-name Asopus; Säljö could be Salamis, the island facing Athens, Ajax's homeland; and Fäjö recalls the exploits of the Athenian hero Theseus (Faia being the name of the wild sow he slays). Coming back onto dry land, Kylinge and Kallinge sound somewhat Greek and Lyckeby, with its river Lyckebyån, is similar in sound to the Athenian Mount Lycabettus. A particularly interesting place-name is Hallarum, a small town lying near Karlskrona, which could correspond to Homeric Calliarus (Kallíaron), a city of the

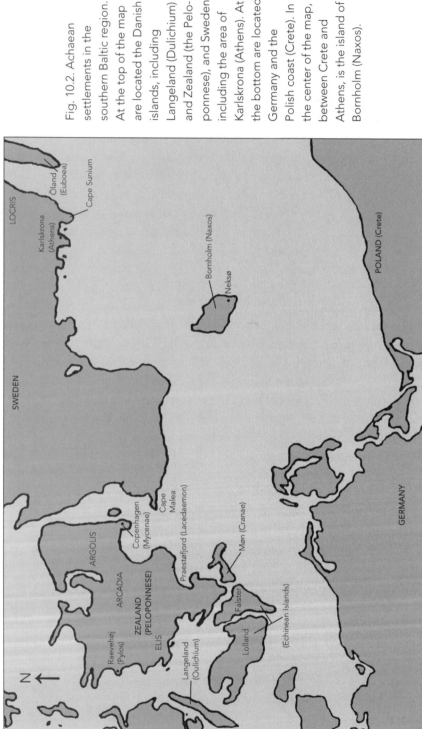

Fig. 10.2. Achaean settlements in the southern Baltic region. At the top of the map are located the Danish islands, including Langeland (Dulichium) and Zealand (the Peloponnese), and Sweden, including the area of Karlskrona (Athens). At the bottom are located Germany and the Polish coast (Crete). In the center of the map, between Crete and Athens, is the island of Bornholm (Naxos).

Locrians, "who live in front of holy Euboea" (*Iliad* 2.535). Ancient Calliarus was thus next to Athens, which the catalog mentions directly after Euboea, confirming that Hallarum is probably its present continuation.

This setting on Swedish territory of the mythological Athens of Erechtheus, Aegeus, and Theseus is corroborated by a long digression in the dialogue *Critias*,[3] in which Plato pauses to describe ancient Athens as it was in extremely remote times after Athena and Hephaestus had founded it. The city lay in a totally different region from the one we know today: "In those times it had rolling hills for mountains; the plains, which are known today as the Phelleus fields, were covered in fertile soil; there were vast forests on the mountains. . . . There were abundant waters and springs everywhere." And the city itself was quite different: "In those times, the area of the Acropolis was not like it is today. . . . It was so vast that it stretched as far as Eridanus and Ilissus, including Picnus, and Mount Lycabettus bordered it on the opposite side."[4] The vastness of this distant prehistoric city, as described in the *Critias*, is consistent with the adjective "broad" *(euryáguia)*, which Homer applies to his Athens.

These unique images of primordial Athens fit with a geographic context that is entirely different from that of Greece today. Plato himself underlines the dissimilarity and tries to explain that the cause of this difference is the action of atmospheric agents. Yet the geography of this Athens fits perfectly in Sweden's vast, undulating land, replete with its rivers and other waters. This passage of the *Critias*—a sort of "message in a bottle" adrift in the sea of time through thousands of years to somehow reach Plato twenty-four hundred years ago and then us today—is, then, an extraordinary testimony to the real appearance of the ancient northern Athens, which emerges distinct from the depths of prehistory, with its "houses, gardens, gymnasiums" and, above all, its inhabitants, "the most famous of all men at that time."[5]

At this point, we should note that while we have a certain conception of the importance of Athens in the Greek world, in the *Iliad* the Athenian contingent plays an extremely limited role in the Trojan War. It is quite likely that if the *Iliad* had been set in the Greek arena, where Athens was a prominent city from the Mycenaean Age on, Homer would have given its role much greater emphasis.

Listed next in the catalog are the cities under the rule of Diomedes: Tiryns, Troezen, and Asine, which could be identified with the present-day cities of Tyringe, Träne, and Asum in the southernmost region of Sweden, known as Scania. This is the location of the imposing tomb of Kivik known as Bredarör, mentioned earlier as showing interesting similarities to corresponding Aegean remains. The large circular pile of stones that stands near the sea is, without doubt, impressive; however, it is the inner chamber that is even more noteworthy. We enter it through a portal reminiscent of the Mycenaean style. In its dark interior, we are barely able to make out a wall behind which lies a room dimly lit by lamps. In the center of this room lies an ancient sarcophagus of engraved stone slabs.

As we come closer, we find ourselves gazing at those silent, enigmatic, almost alien markings on the ancient stone. Here are human silhouettes, a chariot with its charioteer, wheels, yoke, and two horses, crescent-shaped axes, animals, and waves. It is easy to see why many visitors here have been struck with a subtle sense of *déjà vu* and an understanding of why a nineteenth-century scholar ascribed Kivik's tumulus and the sarcophagus engravings to the Mediterranean culture of the Phoenicians.

There are other archaeological remains near Kivik's monument that date to the Bronze Age. This could mean that one of the most important cities of the area once existed on this spot. If we take the *Iliad* as our guide, we could suppose that it was Homer's Argos, Diomedes' city. Maybe this ancient king or one of his successors was buried in Kivik's tumulus.

Following the geography as presented in the *Iliad,* this area is where we can locate the infamous Cape Malea, the spot where the fleets of Ulysses, Agamemnon, and Menelaus ran into gales and stormy seas on their return from Troy (*Odyssey* 3.278). The geographic position of cape immediately south of Malmö—that is, the headland of Falsterbo—fits very well with their return course. Conversely, the location of Cape Malea in the southern Greek world, in front of the island of Kythera (see fig. 2.1, page 26), reveals yet another glaring southern inconsistency with Homeric geography: It lies south of Argolis, where Agamemnon is heading. Scholars have wondered why his fleet coming from Troy would pass that way (we could liken it to a ship that was sailing from San Francisco to San Diego being caught in a storm near Cape San Lucas). Once again, we can see that the Aegean world does not match the world that Homer describes.

THE PELOPONNESE AND ITHACA'S ARCHIPELAGO

Our journey around the Baltic takes us next across the strait between southern Sweden and Denmark to the large island of Zealand, where Copenhagen lies. Details in the *Odyssey* have already guided us to identify this island as the Peloponnese, which, in the Catalog of Ships, corresponds to the territories under the rule of the Atreids—Agamemnon and Menelaus, sons of Atreus, who reigned over Argolis and Lacedaemon, respectively—as well as Nestor's Pylos, Arcadia, and Elis.

The Peloponnese is the geographic entity that, along with Athens, people consider the heart of the Greek world. However, as we have explored earlier, there are two glaring incongruities between the Greek Peloponnese and Homer's description: The Greek version is not an island and it is mountainous. Homer's description of it as a flat island makes much more sense in reference to the Danish island of Zealand than to the Greek peninsula. Atreus's father, Pelops, for whom the island is named, is mentioned twice in the *Iliad*. The meaning of what Greek mythology says about him is enhanced from the Baltic context: He is torn to shreds and the sea goddess Tethys eats one of his shoulders. Considering that the Baltic coastline underwent considerable shifting during the postglacial period, these tales could be a metaphor for ancient floods that had lasting effects: The sea, personified by the sea goddess, erodes, or "eats," a portion of the land, the Peloponnese, or Pelops's Island.

A visit to Helsingborg, a Swedish city that faces the island of Zealand on the Öresund Sound, makes it easier to visualize the immense Achaean fleet heading for Aulis and Troy four thousand years ago. Homer himself does not paint this picture for us, but we can find a similar one in the *Gesta Danorum*, in which Saxo describes the Danish and Swedish fleets facing each other before the naval battle of Brávellir: "You could have seen the bows of the ships ploughing the waves everywhere, while the unfurled sails on the ships' masts covered the surface of the sea."[6]

We reach Zealand (and Helsingør, Hamlet's city) after crossing the sound. Starting from Helsingør, the catalog pauses first in Agamemnon's territory, which Homer refers to as Argos. This region thus must have been situated along Zealand's northeastern coast, facing the sound, corresponding to the position of the Greek Argolis (see figs. 10.2 and 2.1, page 26).

The *Odyssey* tells us that on Agamemnon's return after the war, the storm he encounters near Cape Malea blows him toward "the borders of the land where Thyestes had had his house / and his son Aegisthus lived then" (*Odyssey* 4.517–18). From there he manages to return home, where his tragic destiny awaits him. This passage seems to suggest that his "well built"(*Iliad* 2.569) city of Mycenae was located on Zealand's northeastern side. It was by the sea, as we can infer from Diomedes' words to Agamemnon, when he mentions "the ships / that followed you from Mycenae" (*Iliad* 9.43–44).

Another detail suggesting this location as the original for the city of Mycenae is that Homer describes it as "broad [*euryáguia*]" (*Iliad* 4.52), unlike its Greek counterpart, which is perched on a narrow rock buttress a few miles from the sea. Agamemnon also rules the city of Sicyon, often mentioned in Greek mythology. According to the *Iliad*, it stretched over a "vast area" *(eurýchoros)*, which again fits with Agamemnon's "broad Mycenae," presumably located in a neighboring area.

Interesting, too, is that the name of Mycenae appears in the plural (Mykênai), just as Athens and Thebes do, indicating that its territory likely straddled the mainland and one or more islands. On the eastern side of Zealand there is only one island near the coast—Amager—and Copenhagen lies astride both it and the mainland. It is probable, therefore, that Homer's Mycenae was located on the same site as Copenhagen itself (which was founded in the twelfth century). It certainly must have been one of the most important cities of northern Bronze Age civilization. The status and bearing of Agamemnon, the commander in chief of the Achaean expedition, "golden Mycenae's king" (*Iliad* 7.180), reveal this: "He was coated with gleaming bronze, / he stood out proudly from all heroes / as he was the most eminent" (*Iliad* 2.578–80). Throughout the history of humankind, some places have always been the seat of large cities, such as Thebes (now Stockholm) and the ancient capitals of two pre-Columbian empires, Aztecan Tenochtitlán (now Mexico City) and Incan Quito, present-day capitals of Mexico and Ecuador, respectively.

According to logic and the catalog's sequence, the kingdom of Menelaus (Homeric Lacedaemon—that is, Laconia) is next to the kingdom of his brother Agamemnon. The analogy between Zealand and the Greek Peloponnese, with the Gulf of Fakse being a counterpart of the Gulf of Laconia, suggests that Lacedaemon lay on the southeastern side of Zealand. By looking at figure 10.3, we can realize why Homer calls it "the concave [*koîlen*] Lacedaemon" (*Iliad* 2.58, *Odyssey* 4.1): It stretches along the coast, "curving" dramatically around the Gulf of Fakse and its hinterland (where we find some Greek-sounding place-names, such as Nysø and Karise). Here a village known as Fårup recalls the Homeric city of Pharis. The Catalog of Ships mentions Pharis and Sparta together, Phârín te Spárten (*Iliad* 2.582), indicating their proximity. Thus Homeric Sparta, from which Paris abducts beautiful Helen, probably stood in the environs of today's Fårup. Although the place-name Sparresholm, six miles from Fårup, seems to have a more recent origin, dating back to just the seventeenth century, further investigation could be helpful in identifying whether it refers to an older place-name.

The name Lacedaemon appears to be a compound word, probably deriving from *lakís* (in Latin *lacer*), meaning "laceration, tear," and from the verb *daíomai*, meaning "to divide." In other words, Lacedaemon could mean roughly "the torn piece," which fits the morphology of the innermost part of the Gulf of Fakse, where a strip of land stretches out into the sea like a sort of natural dam to form the border of an inlet known as Praestøfjord. We can deduce from this that the long, narrow prominence was originally called Lacedaemon because it looks like a "torn piece" jutting from the coast, and that this name was later extended to the neighboring region.

Before leaving Laconia, we should note that the *Odyssey* locates the city of Messene here (21.13–15), which does not at all have a correspondence in Greek geography. It could correspond to today's Mosebølle, near Praestøfjord. In its turn, the *Iliad* mentions the city known as Messe, "with many doves [*polytrérona*]" (*Iliad* 2.582).

In chapter 11 we shall look more closely at the particular locations of the Achaean peoples who lived on the Peloponnese and confirm that we can easily identify not only Agamemnon's and Menelaus's kingdoms, but also Arcadia, the river Alpheus, Elis, and King Nestor's Pylos—whose location was held to be a mystery even by the ancient Greeks. In fact, by setting Homer's poems in the Baltic, the age-old puzzle regarding Pylos is solved at once, along with the problem of the border between Argolis and Pylos, a geographic feature mentioned in the *Iliad* but impossible to locate in the Greek world (*Iliad* 9.153).

The key to this puzzle—the location of Elis southwest of Zealand—is confirmed by its placement in the catalog, which mentions "those from Dulichium and sacred Echinean / Islands, lying beyond the sea opposite Elis" (*Iliad* 2.625–26). As we have seen, these islands of the South Fyn archipelago match Homer's descriptions of Ithaca's archipelago: Dulichium is Langeland, close to Lolland and Falster, the Homeric Echinean Islands that look to the southern coast of Zealand (see fig. 10.3). After Dulichium, the catalog cites the islands of Zacynthus

(Tåsinge); Same (Aerø); other smaller islands; Ithaca (Lyø), the westernmost island; and Epirus (Fyn). This placement of Ithaca's archipelago after Elis on the one hand can be verified in the clues given in the *Odyssey*, and on the other confirms the counterclockwise direction of the catalog's sequence.

FROM AETOLIA TO PHTHIA

Past the archipelago of Ithaca, the catalog tells us, "Thoas, Andraemon's son, headed the Aetolians / who lived in Pleuron, Olenus, Pylene, and Calydon" (*Iliad* 2.638–40). In the area of the Baltic where this description leads lived the ancient Jutes, who gave their name to Jutland. It would be tempting to match the Jutes with the Aetolians, given the location of their territories, and to assume that the Jutes in fact descended from these "brave" men (*Iliad* 9.529).

The Aetolian cities of Olenus, Pylene, and Calydon may be identified as today's Wolin, Plön, and Kiel, respectively. The name of Wolin, an island near the Polish coast that housed the Viking fortress of Jomsborg during the Middle Ages, is very similar to Olenus (with the usual absence of the digamma). As for Calydon, "blond-haired Meleager's" town (*Iliad* 2.642), it is regarded as a "pleasant city [*eranné*]" (*Iliad* 9.531), but its description in the *Iliad* as lying in a flat country—"Where pleasant Calydon's plain [*pedíon*] is richer" (*Iliad* 9.577)—clashes with its mountain position in the Greek world.[7] It accords perfectly, however, with the topography of its location in the Baltic world.

According to the *Iliad*, Calydon is besieged by the Curetes (*Iliad* 9.529), whose name could recall two small towns between Berlin and Hamburg known as Kyritz and Köritz. A further connection might be gleaned from the fact that the name of a town lying just outside Hamburg—Altona—sounds a bit like Meleager's mother's name, Althaea (*Iliad* 9.555). Significantly, Greek mythology links Meleager's life to that of an ember kept by his mother, while as Fritz Graf reports, many tales from Lithuania and Iceland feature a similar life-giving ember.

Just after Aetolia in the catalog comes Crete. As we shall see in chapter 12, this large island kingdom corresponds roughly to the Baltic coasts of Germany and Poland together with their hinterland and probably also includes a portion of German territory west of the river Oder. The towns of Kyritz and Köritz are found nearby.

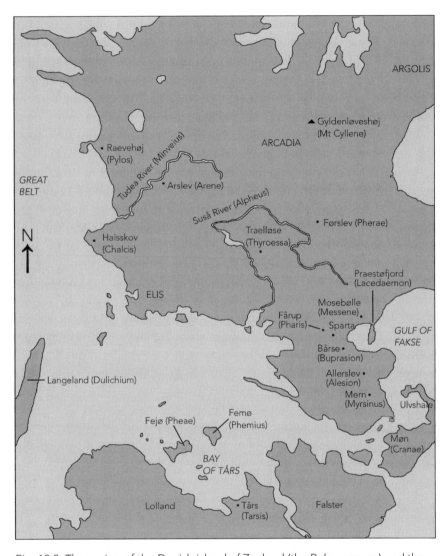

Fig. 10.3. The region of the Danish island of Zealand (the Peloponnese) and the Achaean kingdoms. This area is the scene of Telemachus's journey from Pylos (Raevehøj) to Sparta, near Pharis (Fårup), with a stopover in Pherae. Here we also locate the Pylians' expedition against the Epeans, as narrated by Nestor in Book 11 of the *Iliad*. At the southernmost point of the island lies Myrsinus (present-day Mern), and just off the coast of Zealand we find rocky Møn (Cranae), where Paris and Helen enjoyed their tryst after fleeing Sparta.

In contrast, the location of Crete in the Greek arena runs into inconsistencies with regard to Homer's geography and Greek mythology. For example, in the myth telling of Zeus's birth on Mount Ida, the Curetes reside in Crete, but in the Mediterranean world, the "Cretan" Curetes and those who fought in Calydon are quite far from each other geographically: They are, in fact, separated by the sea—the Mediterranean Crete is an island and Calydon lies in Greece. According to our northern reconstruction, however, the Homeric Calydon and Crete lie on the same side of the Baltic, thus making it credible that Crete's and Calydon's Curetes were one and the same.

Saxo, however, indicates that the name of the Curetes has a counterpart in the Baltic arena: On the western side of Latvia, toward Lithuania, lies Kurland, whose name derives from an ancient people of Finnish origin known as the Curians. As Giacomo Prampolini, professor of the history of religions, writes: Remarkably, scholars have found in the area near Kurland "the figure of a supreme god called Dievas in Lithuania and Dievs in Latvia. In local folklore he curiously shows features typical of both Hellenic Zeus and the Christian God."[8] Interestingly, in Greek, the genitive case of Zeus—the god whose birth Greek mythology connects to the Curetes—is Diós. If we consider the usual loss of the digamma *(v)* between two vowels, the word *diós* is originally *di(v)os*—quite similar to Dievas and Dievs.

After Crete, the catalog mentions the Rhodians, "the ones from Lindus, Ielysus, and white Cameirus" (*Iliad* 2.656). Homer never describes Rhodes as an island, making it possible that it was sited on the peninsula east of Poland, where Kaliningrad stands today. By comparing maps of the Baltic and the Mediterranean, the correspondence between this Baltic peninsula and the Aegean Rhodes is evident. In fact, not far from this Baltic location we come across place-names such as Rodniki and Rodnikovo, and Lindus, one of the three Rhodian cities cited by Homer, finds a counterpart in the city of Lida in Belarus.

Trying to follow the catalog's sequence in the Mediterranean world produces increasing difficulties at this point, yet with Crapethus and Casus (*Iliad* 2.676) corresponding to today's Lithuanian city of Klaipeda and the Latvian city of Cêsis (not far from Riga), we can see that its sequence grafts easily onto the eastern side of the Baltic.

Next in the catalog we come to Nisyrus and Cos—"And those that held Nisyrus, Crapethus, and Casus, with Cos, the / city of Eurypylus, and the Calydnian islands, these were / commanded by Pheidippus and Antiphus" (*Iliad* 2.677). Traveling along the eastern side of the Baltic, we reach Estonia, where we find the small town of Kõo, about sixty miles from Tallinn.

Heracles' failed expedition against Troy decades before the Trojan War—"when Zeus's bold son / set sail from Ilium after he destroyed the city of the Trojans" (*Iliad* 14.250–51) —corroborates the correspondence of Kõo to Cos. In his angry reproachment of his wife, Hera, with regard to Heracles' attempt, Zeus provides a valuable geographic reference:

> *You, with the North Wind, having won the storms over,*
> *pushed him [Heracles] across the unfruitful sea, plotting his ruin,*
> *and you drove him to well-inhabited Cos,*
> *but I rescued him from there and guided him back*
> *to Argos. (Iliad 15.26–30)*

In the Mediterranean world, however, the distance between the Dardanelles and the Aegean island of Cos, located southwest of the Anatolian peninsula, is quite far (see fig. 2.1, page 26). Given that there are a number of islands in the area—Tenedos, Lesbos, Chios, Samos, Ikaria, Leros, and Kalinos, for example—some of which are quite large and thus a hindrance to ships, it seems unlikely that Heracles' path lay there.

Yet in the Baltic world, it is possible that a ship heading from Troy (on the Gulf of Finland's northwest coast) to Argos (in the southwestern Baltic region) could be diverted by a gale from the north toward Cos in Estonia on the gulf's southern coast (see fig. 8.1, page 156). Moreover, Homer informs us that Heracles' two grandsons, sons of King Thessalus, rule over Cos and take part in the Trojan War (*Iliad* 2.679). Interestingly, we find the place-names Teissala and Tessjö—similar to Thessalus—on Finland's southern shore, across from the Estonian coast.

Following Nisyrus and Cos, the catalog takes us to Hellas and Phthia. Looking at our map of the Baltic, Hellas can be placed on the Estonian coast facing the Gulf of Finland, opposite Troad. The name Hellespont (Hellas Sea) is also related to this area: As we have seen, Saxo seems to locate a "Hellespontian" people in this eastern Baltic region, and in the last chapter of the *Germania,* Tacitus mentions a people known as the Hellusians (Hellusii),[9] who are not given a precise place of origin but presumably lived in the far northern regions, where they may well have been linked with Saxo's Hellespontians.

Neighboring Phthia—where Achilles' Myrmidons and Protesilaus's Phthians lived—can be located in an area near the border between Estonia,

Latvia, and Russia, which includes the fertile hills of southeastern Estonia as far as the Russian river Velikaja and the Lake Pskov, as we shall see in the next chapter.

FROM PHERAE TO THE MAGNETES

The list of the Achaean fleets in the catalog proceeds along the Finnish side of the Gulf of Bothnia, beyond the "enemy" territories of Troad and Phrygia. Here the text mentions

> . . . those who inhabited Pherae, near the Boebeian marsh,
> Boibe, Glaphyrae, and fine Iolcus.
> Admetus's dear son led eleven ships of them,
> Eumelus, whom a divine woman bore to Admetus,
> Alcestis, Pelias' most beautiful daughter. (Iliad 2.711–15)

In the Baltic we find Iolcus, its name almost intact, in the Finnish village of Jolkka on the coast between Vaasa and Oulu. In Greek mythology, Iolcus is linked with Jason and his Argonauts. Pherae could be identified with the modern city of Vörå, situated near the river called Kyrönjoki not far from Lake Lappajärvi, which is perhaps analogous to the Boebeian Swamp. Perhaps the name of Pherae can be found in the name of today's Pehro River (Perhonjoki), which flows near Jolkka. Pherae's king, Eumelus, to whom we could link the place called Jumaliskylä, which lies east of this area, is Penelope's brother-in-law through marriage to her sister Iphthime (Odyssey 4.798). The two sisters thus lived in opposite areas of the Baltic: one in Ithaca (Lyø), in the southwest, and the other on the distant shores of the Gulf of Bothnia—and, in fact, the Odyssey states that they lived "very far apart [apóprothi]" (Odyssey 4.811).

The name of the river Kyrönjoki seems to lead us to Cheiron, "the wisest of the Centaurs" (Iliad 11.832). Sworn enemies of the Lapithae, the Centaurs were in actuality normal men without the traditional horselike features that were the result of Greek mythographers' embellishments.

The Centaurs are also called Pherians in the Iliad. It may not be sheer coincidence that in his History of the Goths, Jordanes (a Goth historian who lived in the sixth century C.E.) mentions the Fervir people near the Finnaith—that is, the Finns—in his list of Scandinavian peoples. Homer calls the Pherians lachnéentas (Iliad 2.743), which is usually translated as "shaggy" in reference to their supposed feral appearance. This term, however, can also mean "wrapped in a fur coat" (*láchne* in Greek), which would make sense, given the latitude of their country. We should note that before mentioning the Finnaith and the Fervir, Jordanes includes the Suethans (probably ancestors of the Swedes), "who supply the Romans with marten furs, by a trade across many other peoples; they are famous for the wonderful black of their furs" *(famosi pellium decora nigredine).*[10] Here may be the cause of the misunderstanding regarding their appearance.

The Centaur Cheiron offers more clues to the Baltic location of Homer's work. The *Iliad* connects him with Peleus and his mighty son, "swift-footed" Achilles, through Achilles' famous spear: "an ash from Mount Pelion, whom Cheiron had given to his father / from the top of Pelion, to kill heroes" (*Iliad* 16.141–44). This weapon, often found at Bronze Age archaeological sites and in rupestrian engravings, was widely used in Scandinavia. Saxo states that "no other population is as expert as the Finns in javelin throwing,"[11] leading us to the conclusion that the tradition of javelin throwing (an Olympic sport) in this part of the world dates back to ancient times. As for Mount Pelion, it could correspond to the Paljakka, mountains located in central and northern Finland.

The friendship between Achilles' father, Peleus, and Cheiron also offers a clue to the original homeland of the Myrmidons, who, by the time of the events of the *Iliad,* were settled in Phthia. Another hint of this comes in the invocation offered by Achilles: "King Zeus, Dodonean, Pelasgian, you who live far away [*telóthi naíon*] / and rule over stormy Dodona" (*Iliad* 16.233–34). This ritual wording of the worship of Dodonean Zeus suggests that the Myrmidons and the Pelasgians came from the area of Dodona, situated "far away" from Estonia. According to the catalog, Dodona lay near the northernmost point of the Gulf of Bothnia. It is very likely that the climatic decline at the beginning of the Sub-Boreal phase after the climatic optimum had forced the southward migration of many peoples, such as the Phaeacians, who were compelled to move from the north to the south of Norway. The adjective *stormy* is eloquent as used here to define Dodona, for it allows us to visualize the Myrmidons and their successors, the Peraebians (*Iliad* 2.749–50), with the former being driven out by the unforgiving weather.

So Peleus was maintaining contacts that dated back to the time when his ancestors still lived in the Centaurs' land. The catalog mentions Dodona immediately after mentioning the Lapithae and the war in which they defeated the Centaurs and drove them away from Mount Pelion (*Iliad* 2.744). That the wood of the spear Cheiron gave Peleus came from Pelion (*Iliad* 16.143) points to the amazing consistency of the events, details, and geographic locations narrated by Homer.

Cheiron was also a famous doctor who knew which herbs to use in the treatment of wounds. He taught both Achilles (*Iliad* 11.832) and Asclepius, father of Machaon (*Iliad* 4.219), the use of these medicines. Machaon, of course, was the "great doctor" (*Iliad* 11.518) of the Achaean army who came from one of the last places listed in the catalog, Tricce (*Iliad* 2.732)—which confirms his Finnish origin and explains his familiarity with Cheiron.

Lake Lappajärvi, near the river Kyrönjoki, seems to recall the mythical Lapithae, the Centaurs' neighbors and enemies, who took part in the Trojan War under the rule of Polypoetes. From the catalog's sequence, we can infer that the Lapithae lived in Finland, although far from Troy (Toija). It would be tempting to regard them as the ancestors of today's Lapps (Sami), who, over the thousands of years from the Trojan War to the present, have kept both their ancestors' name and their willingness to fight (as evidenced by their heroic resistance against the Russian army during World War II). As far as the Lapp (Sami) language is concerned, we discover that "anthropologically speaking, they are a completely isolated people. Therefore, it is necessary to admit that they originally spoke a different language, then took their present language from a Finno-Ugric people."[12]

Other details work to suggest a northern origin for the Centaurs. The war between the Centaurs and the Lapithae mentioned in both the *Odyssey* and the *Iliad* ("The wine also drove Eurytion mad, the famous Centaur, / in bold Peirithous' palace / when he called on the Lapithae . . . / this caused the war to break out between the Centaurs and the heroes"—*Odyssey* 21.295–97, 303) easily recalls for us a passage from Tacitus referring to the brawls among drunken Germans at banquets "that often end in killings and woundings."[13] Likewise, we might recall Archbishop Elphegus, whom drunken Vikings slew during a banquet. The fact is that the Viking world was as barbaric as the Achaean, and there is a substantial continuity between them down through the centuries, as evidenced by Tacitus's *Germania*.

As we approach the end of the Catalog of Ships, there are a number of names in the final lines that could be compared to those of places in present-day Finland. Tricce sounds similar to Tyykiluoto (taking into account, as elsewhere, the unique pronunciation of the consonant cluster *tr* in the Finno-Ugric language); Methone is similar to Mietoinen;

Meliboea to Myllyperä; and Olizon to Oulunsalo. The name of Mount Titanus with its "white peaks" (*Iliad* 2.735) is similar to the root of Tiitonranta, and the city of Oloosson, ruled by Polypoetes, sounds almost like Oulu. (Its counterpart in both geographic and lexical senses is the Greek city Volos, in Thessaly.)

The penultimate fleet mentioned in the Catalog of Ships is that of Gouneus, who

> . . . *led twenty-two ships from Cyphus.*
> *The Enienes and the hard Peraebians followed him;*
> *they built their houses around stormy Dodona*
> *and tilled the soil along the pleasant Titaresius River.*
>   (*Iliad* 2.748–51)

On our journey around the Baltic, we have reached the northernmost point of the Gulf of Bothnia, where the name of a coastal village called Kuivaniemi (*niemi* means "cape," or "point" in Finnish) could be compared to Homer's Cyphus (Kýphos). Dodona was probably called "stormy" (*dyscheímeron*) because of its high latitude as well as the complex hydrographical system in that area, where floods were frequent. The name of the Peraebians (Peraiboí) is similar to Pieria (Pereíe). Perämeri is the Finnish name of the sea facing the Gulf of Bothnia in this region that stretches toward Lapland and the Arctic Circle.

Finally, we reach the last people mentioned in the Catalog of Ships:

> *Prothous, Tenthredon's son, led the Magnetes,*
> *who lived around the River Peneus and leafy Mount Pelion.*
> *Quick Prothous ruled them;*
> *forty black ships followed him.* (*Iliad* 2.756–59)

Near a mountainous region, the river Iijoki (which corresponds to the Peneus) flows into the Baltic Sea between Oulu and Kuivaniemi, which likely correspond to Oloosson (*Iliad* 2.739) and Cyphus (*Iliad* 2.748), respectively. Near the lower course of the river we find Mannisenranta (*ranta* means "bank"), which could recall the Magnetes, a people whose name has always been connected with magnetite, the iron mineral (Fe_3O_4) well known for its magnetic properties. In fact, the Swedish region adjacent to the north of this area in the Gulf of Bothnia contains immense iron mines.

Thus we finish our journey around the Baltic, guided by the Catalog of Ships. In the process, as we have all along, we have discovered notable inconsistencies between Homer's world and the Mediterranean and have come upon still more cultural and morphological similarities between the world of these texts and this northern European region. In the next chapters we shall explore a few significant areas of the Baltic to more vividly experience some of the most important locales and dramatic events of Homer's two poems.

CHAPTER 11

THE REGIONS OF THE PELOPONNESE

In this chapter we shall reconstruct the Homeric Peloponnese, a task that cannot be accomplished for the Greek arena, where there are marked incongruities between Homer's descriptions and the land itself, but one that is easily carried out on the Danish island of Zealand (see fig. 10.2, page 214). Here, using the geographic data found in the two poems against the topography of this part of the world, we can easily resolve many ancient conundrums regarding Homeric geography, such as the location of Dulichium and Cranae, Pylos's incomprehensible position, Telemachus's odd (in terms of both setting and chronology) journey from Pylos to Sparta, Agamemnon's absurd course near Cape Malea, and the seemingly impossible border between Argolis and Pylos.

As we have seen, the Catalog of Ships names in geographic order the various Achaean settlements on the Peloponnese: Agamemnon's Argos; Menelaus's Lacedaemon; Nestor's Pylos; Arcadia; and Elis, "where Epeans rule" (*Odyssey* 13.275). If we consider that the Catalog of Ships' counterclockwise sequence from east to west on the Baltic mentions Ithaca *after* the five regions of the Peloponnese and Dulichium, we can then deduce that the first two of these regions—Argos and Lacedaemon—lay to the east and Pylos was situated to the west. As to Elis, the *Iliad* reports that it faces Dulichium (*Iliad* 2.626). This sequence, paired with the geographical details in the account of Telemachus's visit to Nestor and Menelaus, enables us to reconstruct the entire map of these regions on the island of Zealand (see figs. 10.2 and 10.3).

PYLOS

According to Homer, we find in the land of Nestor "the ones who lived in Pylos, lovely Arene / and Thryoessa, Alpheus' ford" (*Iliad* 2.591–92). From ancient times, the location of the Homeric Pylos has been a mystery. In ancient Greece, its name was even synonymous with "nonexistent place" or "impossible to be found," as Aristophanes says in his comedy *The Knights*. Strabo, for his part, proposes a rather complicated theory on this topic, but as yet nobody has managed to link Homer's data with a plausible place. As usual, Homer's details are consistent but turn out to be incongruent when applied to Greek terrain. In his *Mycenaeans and Minoans*, Leonard Palmer honestly admits that "modern researchers, although they were provided with the powerful equipment of organized science, did little more than specify Strabo's theory,"[1] and Fritz Graf frankly states, "Mycenaean Pylos's geography is not the one Homer suggests."[2]

By moving the poem's setting from the Mediterranean to the Baltic, however, and identifying the Homeric Peloponnese with the Danish island of Zealand, old confusions are readily solved. Like the catalog's sequence, the details of Telemachus's journey show that Homer's Pylos lay on Zealand's western side. The goddess Athena sends the west wind to drive Telemachus's ship toward Nestor's city (yet, as we have already noted, in the Mediterranean world the north wind would be much more suitable for a voyage from Ithaca to the area of Pylos, situated on the western side of today's Peloponnese). After stopping off in Pylos, Ulysses' bold son continues on to Sparta, Menelaus's city, which thus lay farther east.

Pylos was quite vast, bordering Agamemnon's territory (*Iliad* 9.153), Arcadia (*Iliad* 7.134), and Elis (*Iliad* 11.671), which helps to explain why Nestor led no fewer than ninety ships (*Iliad* 2.602) in the Achaean armada, a fleet second in size only to that of Agamemnon. His vast lands also explain why other chiefs had such great respect for the old king—even haughty Agamemnon, who "honored him very much" (*Iliad* 2.21).

As to the border between Nestor's and Agamemnon's kingdoms, the *Iliad* lists under Agamemnon's rule seven cities that lay "near the sea, at the end of sandy Pylos" (*Iliad* 9.153). Yet on the Greek Peloponnese, Argolis and Pylos are not neighbors but rather lie opposite one another, with the former on the northeast and the latter on the southwest. In the Greek world, then, a border near the sea is an impossibility, while in a Danish setting this discrepancy does not exist, as we shall soon see.

Cowboys of the Bronze Age

The river Alpheus, which, in Nestor's kingdom, "flows broad over the Pylian country" (*Iliad* 5.545), can best be identified with Zealand's most important river, the Suså. To corroborate this somewhat, a place on the river known as Lynge recalls the name of Olympia, which lies near the Greek Alpheus.

This identification of the Alpheus provides the key to solving another problem: the inconsistencies between the harsh Greek morphology and the setting of events connected with the military expedition of a young Nestor to defend the city of Thryoessa, "a steep hill / far off on the Alpheus, at the end of sandy Pylos" (*Iliad* 11.711–12), against the Epeans, who are besieging it. From Homer's reference we can deduce that the Alpheus marked the border between Pylos and Elis, where the Epeans lived. According to the old king's detailed account, after his army spends the night in Arene near the mouth of the river Minyeius, "toward midday we reached the River Alpheus" (*Iliad* 11.726). Here the Pylians attack the Epeans and defeat them:

> We chased them through the vast plain [diá spidéos pedíoio],
> killing them and seizing their fine arms.
> We went with our horses as far as Buprasion rich in wheat,
> Olenian Stone and Alesion Hill. (*Iliad* 11.754–57)

This reference to the "vast plain" is perfectly consistent with what Nestor has previously described—"From the plain [ek pedíou] we took very rich spoils, / fifty herds of cattle, as many of sheep" (*Iliad* 11.677–78)—as well as with the description of the Alpheus, "which flows broad." It is easy to see that we are very far from Greece's mountainous soil, where we could not find such a level landscape.

Yet the landscape described by the old king fits perfectly with Zealand's flat territory (fig. 10.3, page 221): Young Nestor moved southward with his soldiers, from Pylos toward Arene (Arslev), which lay near the river Minyeius, present-day Tudeå (a name that recalls Diomedes' warlike father, Tydeus, who played a leading role during the first war between the Achaeans and the Thebans). From here, the Pylians reach Thryoessa, "the Alpheus' ford [Alpheioîo póron]" (*Iliad* 2.592), which was perhaps present-day Traelløse, lying about twenty miles southeast of the river Suså. A rise here that is roughly 120 feet high could be Thryoessa's Hill. After the Pylians win the battle, they chase the Epeans into their territory as far as Buprasion (Bårse), which is twenty miles southeast. As for Alesion Hill, it could correspond to another rise near Allerslev, which is three miles farther on in the same direction. Incidentally, Saxo tells of a military expedition that closely follows this campaign of the Pylians: the pirate Hacon's expedition, which left from the site where Kalundborg now lies for the river Suså, where Hacon joined in battle with the Danes.[3]

Interestingly, we should note that from eventful episodes such as Nestor's early campaign, what emerges is an extremely vivid and realistic image of the life of those archaic herdsmen and warriors. We might even go so far as to define these ancient men as the "cowboys" of the Early Bronze Age, engaged in continuous skirmishes, ambushes, cattle rustling, and wild chases across plains, hills, and rivers in a vast, flat, northern European landscape. Instead of Winchester rifles and Colts, their arms were arrows and spears, yet the events and their atmosphere and the cast of characters involved do recall our tales of the American West.

TELEMACHUS'S JOURNEY TO SPARTA AND BACK

As we can deduce from the arrival of Telemachus's ship at the beginning of Book 3 of the *Odyssey*, Nestor's city of Pylos is located near the sea. Furthermore, when Telemachus and Nestor's son Peisistratus leave Nestor's palace on their way to Sparta, Peisistratus "whipped the horses and they eagerly flew / to the plain leaving the high stronghold of Pylos" (*Odyssey* 3.484–85). On their return from Sparta, Peisistratus takes Telemachus to the beach, where his companions, ready to depart, are waiting for him. Nestor's son then "drove his horses / back to the city of Pylos, and soon [*thoôs*] reached his palace" (*Odyssey* 15.215–16).

Pylos, then, lay on the western side of Zealand, between Kalundborg and the mouth of the river Tudeå, beyond which the Pylians had marched in their campaign in Thryoessa. On this coast, which is mostly sandy (confirming the description "sandy Pylos"), there are not many suitable locations for the ancient city. A clue comes from Dr. Preben Hansson, of Korsør, who informs us that a Megalithic and Bronze Age tomb with geometrical engravings lies on the archaeological site of Raevehøj near Dalby, almost opposite the small peninsula of Reersø, and that other tumuli stand in the environs. Though the morphology of this area, slightly above sea level, matches Homer's description of Pylos, definitive proof is in the hands of archaeologists.

Lacedaemon's position dictates that Telemachus cross the whole of Zealand from northwest to southeast on his journey from Pylos to Sparta, where he meets Menelaus. This is why wise Nestor advised him to travel by land instead of by sea, which saved him from sailing around half the island and considerably shortened his journey. The *Odyssey* supplies us with enlightening details concerning Telemachus's journey:

> *Telemachus got on the beautiful chariot.*
> *Next to him Nestor's son Peisistratus, leader of men*
> *mounted the chariot and took the reins in his hands . . . The*
>   *[horses] shook the yoke they carried together all day long.*
> *The sun sank and all the ways became dark.*
> *They reached Pherae and Diocles' house,*
> *Ortilochus' son, whom Alpheus begot.*
> *They spent the night there as he gave them hospitality.*
> *When the rose-fingered Dawn broke,*
> *they yoked the horses and mounted the decorated chariot;*
> *they passed through the forecourt and the echoing porch.*
> *He whipped the horses to go and they eagerly flew.*
> *They reached the wheat-producing plain [pedíon pyrephóron],*
>   *where then*
> *they ended their journey, so quickly their horses carried them*
>   *indeed.* (Odyssey 3.481–96)

In this passage the discrepancy between Homeric geography and the morphology of the Greek world is glaring. The chariot of Nestor's son—which reminds us of the chariot engraved on Kivik's sarcophagus—rapidly crosses a "wheat-producing plain" that is wholly unlike Greece's rugged territory. What is more, if the *Odyssey* had been set in Greece, there would have been no sense in carrying out this journey by land across the mountains; Telemachus would have used his ship. What justifies the choice of land travel is the flatness and relatively small size of Zealand compared to its Greek homotope.

But the illogical land journey of Telemachus as set in the Greek world is not limited to morphology. There is a marked discrepancy in chronology—perhaps the result of an awkward attempt to extend the time of his trip, given that his journey to Sparta appears far too short relative to a Greek context.

In examining in detail the timing and stages of Telemachus's journey from Pylos to Sparta, we find significant evidence in support of a Danish setting:

- **First stage (from Pylos to Pherae):** Telemachus is a guest at Nestor's house in Pylos. After a solemn sacrifice and a parting morning banquet—it was commonplace for these peoples to have a generous and very early lunch and then dinner in the evening—he and Peisistratus leave by chariot for Pherae, a midway stopping place. They arrive in Pherae at around sunset: "The sun sank and all the ways became dark" (*Odyssey* 3.487).
- **Second stage (from Pherae to Sparta):** The following morning, the two young men set out from Pherae to Sparta:

> *[Peisistratus] whipped the horses to go and they eagerly flew.*
> *They reached the wheat-producing plain, where then*
> *they ended their journey, so quickly their horses carried them*
> *   indeed.*
> *The sun sank and all the ways became dark.*
> *They reached the concave sunken Lacedaemon*
> *and drove their chariot up to Menelaus's palace.*
>   (*Odyssey* 3.494–97, 4.1–2)

The repetition of the line "The sun sank and all the ways became dark" emphasizes that the two arrive in Sparta at sunset or just after. This, however, conflicts with the rest of the episode in Book 4, which clearly depicts the arrival in Sparta as occurring in the morning, not the evening. Once Telemachus and Peisistratus arrive at Menelaus's palace, they enjoy a sumptuous "lunch [*deîpnon*]" (*Odyssey* 4.61). After a series of greetings and pleasant conversation with their host and his wife, Helen, they have "dinner [*dórpon*]" (*Odyssey* 4.213) and retire for the night (*Odyssey* 4.294–303).

To verify all of this, let us look closely at the words *lunch (deîpnon)* and *dinner (dórpon)*. Their different meanings are clear throughout the poems; moreover, in one particular passage from the *Odyssey*, referring to the day of the slaughter of the suitors, they are intentionally opposed: "They ended the lunch [*deîpnon*] having fun, . . . but the dinner [*dórpon*] would have been very bitter" (*Odyssey* 20.390–92).

There are two possibilities to explain this inconsistency: Either the travelers sleep a second night at the end of the second stage of their journey in a place that Homer forgets to mention (an unlikely hypothesis, given that the poet is very precise in his descriptions and reckonings) or the second occurrence of the line "The sun sank and all the ways became dark" (*Odyssey* 3.497) is simply a later interpolation. If it is removed, everything falls back into place: "They ended their journey, so quickly their horses carried them indeed. / They reached the concave sunken Lacedaemon / and drove their chariot up to Menelaus's palace"—which indicates they have arrived on the same morning, just in time to participate in the wedding banquet in progress at the palace. This hypothesis, which supports the line "so quickly their horses carried them indeed," seems by far the more reliable.

To sum up, it takes less than one day for the two to travel from Pylos to Sparta: The first stage, from Pylos to Pherae, takes about half a day, from late morning to sunset, and the second stage, from Pherae to Sparta, is even shorter. From this we can gather that Pherae was closer to Pylos than to Sparta—which gives rise to the question of why Telemachus decides to stop over at Pherae instead of going straight on to Sparta. We may answer this by assuming that, aside from the risks of a night journey, it may have been considered uncouth to arrive at someone's house late at night (just as it is nowadays), especially when the host was a powerful king like Menelaus.

An examination of Greek geography makes it seem unlikely that a journey from Pylos to Sparta in that setting could take the short time it would in the Danish world. The route passing through Messene and Kalamata is much more than sixty miles long, with a rough topography very different from the plain described in the *Odyssey*. It is likely, then, that some ancient Greek bard tried to extend the second stage of the journey for logic's sake by interpolating the line "The sun sank and all the ways became dark."

If Telemachus's journey gives rise to problems in the Greek context, it tallies perfectly with a Danish setting. On the island of Zealand (fig. 10.3), a journey corresponding to the first stage—that is, between Raevehøj's site (most likely corresponding to Homeric Pylos) and Førslev-Pherae—traverses about thirty miles of flat land, just as Homer narrates. This can easily be covered in one afternoon. As for the second stage, the even shorter distance of about twelve miles between Førslev and the area of Fårup and Praestøfjord—that is, Lacedaemon—squares with the description of the speedy morning journey, which allows the two young men to arrive in Sparta in time for lunch: "They reached the wheat-producing plain, where then / they ended their journey, so quickly their horses carried them indeed" (*Odyssey* 3.495–96).

Another consideration arises from this: Because Pherae lies near Sparta, Telemachus has no reason to make another stop there on his return journey to Pylos, as Book 15 of the *Odyssey* narrates. The morning of Telemachus's departure from Sparta is very likely his third day there, if we consider that on the day after his arrival, Menelaus privately supplies him with information about Ulysses (*Odyssey* 4.316–31, 555–60). Having no more reason to stay on, Telemachus wakes up very early—"before dawn" (*Odyssey* 15.50)—very anxious to return home (*Odyssey* 15.66), which is a natural response to the situation pending there. Soon after awakening, he meets Menelaus, who immediately gives orders for the preparation of breakfast [*deîpnon*] (*Odyssey* 15.94), after which Ulysses' son leaves with his friend Peisistratus. He is so anxious to return that he does not stop at Nestor's palace in Pylos again, saying, "I must go home as soon as possible [*thâsson*] (*Odyssey* 15.201), although he is aware that Nestor "would have been incensed" (*Odyssey* 15.214) by this disrespect. Nevertheless, he heads directly for Pylos's beach, where his ship is anchored, and immediately sets sail for Ithaca (*Odyssey* 15.209–10).

We can therefore presume from this chronology that the original version of the *Odyssey* did not provide for any midway stopover at Pherae on the return journey: The two young men leave Sparta in a great hurry right after an early breakfast and reach the beach at Pylos on the evening of the same day. Intriguingly, the eight lines concerning the return stopover in Pherae (*Odyssey* 15.185–92) are copied verbatim from those relating to their journey out (*Odyssey* 3.487–94), supporting the conjecture that they are an interpolation. The rationale of the story's "editor" might have been that if the journey from Pylos to Sparta seemed too short to fit Greek geography—so much so as to require the journey's extension to the evening of the second day—the completion of the return journey in one nonstop day would have appeared absurd. It would be most logical, then, to add another stop at Pherae on the journey back to the ship, even though such a stop on a hasty trip and given the close proximity of Pherae and Sparta made no sense at all. Yet this added text serves as an example of a later bard's loss of historical memory regarding the pre-Greek setting of the *Odyssey*. We could go on to deduce from this that these bits of text were added after the twelfth-century B.C.E. fall of the Mycenaean civilization, assuming that the last Mycenaeans, despite the fact that four or five centuries had passed after their migration from the north, were still aware that these tales referred not to their new home but to their ancestors' ancient homeland. The collapse of the Mycenaean world and the onset of the Hellenic dark age did not prevent the poems from being transmitted, but they did efface any remaining memory of the original setting of the two poems.

This attempt to "tidy" the Homeric text in order to make it conform to Greek geography must have been because this part of the narrative is related to the heart of the Peloponnese, an area much more familiar to the bards and their listeners than those places on the outskirts of the Greek world, such as Ithaca's archipelago, Troy, Pharos, and other locales that have presented their own geographic anomolies.

An attempt to specifically place Telemachus's midway stopover point of Pherae points up a similarity between this place-name and that of a little village, Førslev, about halfway between Zealand's western and eastern sides. Besides the fact that the root of this name recalls Pherae, the village lies very close to the island's major river, the Suså, identifiable with the river Alpheus, which the *Odyssey* directly relates to Diocles, the ruler of Pherae.

A Danish setting for Telemachus's journey also squares with the words he addresses to Menelaus after reaching Sparta: "You reign over the wide plain [*pedíoio euréos*] / where there is a lot of clover and galingale" (*Odyssey* 4.602–603). Indeed, Homer sometimes uses the adjective *wide*—"In wide Sparta [*ení Spártei eureíei*]" (*Odyssey* 11.460)—to describe the city itself.*

---

*We can reflect on the name Sparta in the context of its location in an area that looks like a "torn piece" jutting from the coast of Zealand. In the ancient Norse language, *spar(r)i* meant "beam, plank." Also, according to Robert Graves, Spartans represented their Dioscuri (the twins Castor and Pollux, whom Helen recalls in Book 3 of the *Iliad*) with "two parallel wood planks joined together by two other cross planks" (which still serve today as the symbol of the constellation Gemini, the Twins). Thus, the root of Sparta's name, if compared to the Norse, seems to conceal a meaning closely linked to the symbol of the city, the "two beams" of its mythical protectors. Actually, in many languages it is not at all uncommon to find words that derive from place-names. (For example, *faïence* in French indicates a kind of majolica that comes from the city of Faenza in Italy; in turn, *majolica* derives from Late Latin *maiorica*, Majorca. Other words derived from place-names include the game known as Shanghai and the wool known as cashmere.) Thus, the glorious name of Sparta perhaps still resounds in the Swedish word *spår*, which means "binary" or "double beam or rail."

Helen of Sparta

Now that we have reached Lacedaemon and Sparta with Telemachus, it is time to go with him into Menelaus's palace and admire, through his eyes, the regal bearing of beautiful Helen, "looking like Artemis with her golden distaff" (*Odyssey* 4.122). Three maids follow the queen. One of them, Phylo, whom the poet pictures while she is handing her mistress "a golden spindle and a wheeled silver basket / with golded rims" (*Odyssey* 4.131–32), reminds us of Fulla, the Norse goddess, Frigg's faithful maid and keeper of her jewel case.[4]

Like Penelope, Helen is described as weaving and spinning wool, common tasks for women in the Homeric world. In the *Iliad* she works on "a large web" *(mégan histón)* upon which she embroiders the events of the war the Trojans and Achaeans are waging over her (*Iliad* 3.125–28). We can imagine Helen's weaving as comparable to the eleventh-century Norman Bayeux tapestry, which (according to tradition) William the Conqueror's wife, Mathilda, personally fashioned, depicting scenes from her husband's war on English soil. The huge dimensions of Mathilda's tapestry (230 feet long by 20 inches high) indirectly lead us to realize why, according to the *Odyssey,* the suitors find it "normal [*épeithon Achaioús*]" (*Odyssey* 19.151) that Penelope work three whole years on her famous web, also defined as "large" *(mégan)* or "oversized [*perímetron*]" (*Odyssey* 19.140).

Helen and Penelope on the one hand and Mathilda on the other show us that it was common for high-ranking women in the north to spend their time weaving depictions of important stories, a custom that could have been prevalent for almost three thousand years. Among those ancient peoples, the memories of the past were preserved not only by bards' cantos, but also by noblewomen's weaving, suggesting a relationship between the Homeric term *histós*, meaning "tapestry," and our word *history (historíe* in Greek).

Honeymoon Island

In the sequel to an earlier episode in the *Iliad* in which Helen is working on her web, Paris approaches her, seductively reminding her of their first love encounter, "when at first, from lovely Lacedaemon / I abducted you and sailed on the sea-crossing ships; / then we mixed in love and bed on the island of Cranae" (*Iliad* 3.443–45). In Paris's speech we not only hear of "lovely" *(erateinês)* Lacedaemon, so different from Greek

Laconia's dry, uneven morphology, but we also learn that not far from Lacedaemon there was an island named Cranae, where, after their elopement, the two lovers landed and spent their first time together. (To stay in Sparta would have been too risky for them; Menelaus could have returned at any moment.)

Today, a few miles from Homeric Lacedaemon, there is an island called Møn, which, on first sight, appears to be very suited for such a pleasant interlude. Møn is currently a popular tourist spot, famous for its sheer white cliffs (over four hundred feet high), which make its eastern side stand out among the generally flat Baltic shores. Its identification with Homer's Cranae is corroborated by the fact that the name Cranae means "the rocky" (*Iliad* 3.445) in Greek, and by the fact that Cranae has never been identified in the Mediterranean region. Møn's high cliffs are a geological singularity in the flat Baltic world, whereas in the mountainous Greek world it wouldn't make sense to single out any one of the many rocky islands by describing it as such.

Møn's most beautiful beaches lie on the little peninsula of Ulvshale, which faces the gulf of Fakse and Praestøfjord—that is, Homeric Lacedaemon. Therefore, Paris's ship, after setting sail from Sparta with its charming abductee, probably dropped anchor on Møn's northern coast, on the flat area to the west of the cliffs, and there began one of history's most romantic and fatal honeymoons.

On Møn there are many Neolithic tombs and a village called Kraneled, which is almost the only place-name in Denmark with the prefix *krane* (as Finn Madsen first noted when he passed along this bit of information). As to the suffix *-led,* it is a root that means "lead" or "leader" in Danish. Given that Kraneled is only about half a mile from the coast, toward the southeasternmost point of the island, we could suppose that in the Bronze Age—or at least when the island still went by its old name—it had a harbor, probably the first place encountered by sailors coming from the southeast Baltic, directly after the cliffs, where, of course, it is difficult to dock. Thus, its new name, Kraneled—"lead" or "beginning of Cranae"—may survive today as the last vestige of the ancient Achaean name for this "rocky" island.

At this point, we can try to imagine the mood of that young, beautiful queen after her departure from this island as she gazed from Paris's ship at those white cliffs that were fading away, her last image of the world she was leaving behind. Though Homer is silent on this part of

Helen's portrayal, we can turn to the words of Laura Orvieto and her unforgettable *Stories of the History of the World*:

> A sweet magic sent by Aphrodite got her [to] believe all the words of the Trojan prince, long to be with him for ever, dream a wonderful world of love and joy in the far-off city where the ship was carrying them. . . . And the ship was speeding along as fast as the wind, carrying Helen far, farther and farther away.[5]

The Ten Days of Telemachus and the Return of Ulysses

After our reconstruction here, we can now note that Telemachus's adventures in the *Odyssey* take place over a period of ten days, divided as follows:

- **First day:** Telemachus meets in Ithaca with Mentes, who urges him to stir himself.
- **Second day:** The Ithacan assembly meets and Telemachus departs in the evening for Pylos.
- **Third day:** Telemachus arrives in Pylos and meets with Nestor.
- **Fourth day:** Telemachus and Peisistratus depart from Pylos and journey by chariot to Pherae.
- **Fifth day:** The two arrive at Menelaus's palace, have lunch, converse with Helen, and then share dinner with their hosts.
- **Sixth day:** Telemachus talks privately with Menelaus about Ulysses' fate.
- **Seventh day:** Telemachus and Peisistratus depart from Sparta, return to Pylos, and board their ship for Ithaca.
- **Eighth day:** Telemachus arrives in Ithaca, meets with Eumaeus and Ulysses, and acknowledges Ulysses.
- **Ninth day:** Telemachus returns to the palace to prepare for the massacre of Penelope's suitors.
- **Tenth day:** The massacre of the suitors takes place.

It may be said that these ten days form the narrative backbone of the *Odyssey*. The other great narrative vein of the poem is the one that gives it its name and protagonist—that is, the return of Ulysses to Ithaca, which covers about one third of the poem and which is divided into the story of Ulysses' voyage from Ogygia to Ithaca, including the stop in Scheria, and Ulysses' first-person narrative at the Phaeacian court of his wanderings from the time of his departure from Troy after the war to his arrival in Ogygia.

There is a considerable difference between the tale that takes place over ten days and the story of Ulysses' return. The former is characterized by such remarkable realism that we cannot completely discount the possibility that it arises from real events, although this is very difficult to prove. In the latter part of the overall poem, however, the poet, perhaps inspired by a repertoire of myths and folktales, tends to flights of fancy that at times seem to refer to an original Indo-European heritage and are also redolent of extremely archaic "shamanistic" themes. Nevertheless, as we have seen, even this "make believe" part of the story has many links to reality.

ARCADIA AND ELIS

Having located Pylos, Pherae, and Sparta and delineated Telemachus's journey among these places, we now we must add Arcadia to the picture of the Homeric Peloponnese. It was located next to Pylos, as stated in an episode where Nestor narrates one of the skirmishes between neighboring peoples (*Iliad* 7.134). Besides this, Homer gives us some rather specific information about the Arcadians: "Atreides Agamemnon, king of men / gave them good ships to cross the wine-dark sea, / . . . as they were not interested in seafaring" (*Iliad* 2.612–14). This leads us to suppose that Arcadia had no outlets to the sea and lay next to Agamemnon's territory—that is, toward the center of Zealand.

Travelers leaving Copenhagen and heading for the interior of Zealand will soon feel themselves immersed in a very particular "Arcadian" atmosphere: The soft, undulating landscape, its streams, herds of cattle, even vegetation, all lend something to this sensation. Here in Arcadia stood the mythical Mount Cyllene, "near Aepytus' tomb" (*Iliad* 2.603). What a great triumph it would be if archaeologists managed to find its remains! Beyond their similarity in names, which in this case is fortuitous, we can link this mount and beautiful Gyldenløveshøj, the highest point on Zealand. According to Greek mythology, on Mount Cyllene "covered with a wood" *(kataeiménon hýlei)* the god Hermes was born.[6] A pleasant path through the thick wood that blankets the slopes allows us easily to reach the top of this peak. At the end of the trail stands a war memorial, a sign that in a certain sense this place has remained a sacred site over the years.

Finally, in order to completely reconstruct the layout of the Achaean settlements on Zealand, we must locate "beautiful Elis, where Epeans rule" (*Odyssey* 13.275). We have already learned that Elis bordered Pylos. The Catalog of Ships also mentions "those from Dulichium and the sacred

Echinean / Islands, lying beyond the sea opposite Elis" (*Iliad* 2.625–26). From these clues, we can determine that Homeric Elis stretched along Zealand's southwestern coast, facing Dulichium (Langeland) and the Echinean Islands (Falster and nearby Lolland).

It is now possible to see why Argolis and Pylos are presented as adjacent in the text of the *Iliad* while in Greek geography Elis is situated between these two regions: Homer places Elis opposite *(Élidos anta)* Dulichium (*Iliad* 2.626)— that is, facing Ithaca's archipelago. In the Baltic (Danish) context, the archipelago lies southwest of Zealand. Thus Pylos lies north of Elis, bordering on Argolis along the sea, just as Homer indicates (fig. 10.2, page 214). In the Greek world, the Ionian islands lie northwest of the Peloponnese, which explains why the opposite region, the area facing northwest, was called Elis (see fig. 2.1, page 26). As a result, Greek Elis was wedged between Pylos—which was necessarily placed farther south—and Argolis, creating a separation that contradicts the description in the *Iliad*.

It is easy to see the key role Dulichium (Langeland) plays in this reconstruction of the Homeric world: It serves as a sort of "joint" between the regions of the Peloponnese (Zealand) and the archipelago of Ithaca (Lyø), and thus fits perfectly with all of Homer's details.

The course Telemachus follows to return from Pylos to Ithaca squares with this setting: His ship "passed beautiful Elis, where the Epeans rule; / he then steered it toward the steep islands, / being troubled as to [whether] he could succeed in escaping death or capture" (*Odyssey* 15.298–99).* This confirms that Pylos lay along Zealand's western side, north of Elis and the northernmost point of Dulichium (Langeland). We have already verified the consistency between Homer's data and the layout of the area facing Ithaca's archipelago (see chapter 2), but we can further verify this

---

*The translation "steep islands"—an attempt to translate *nésoisin thoêisin*—has puzzled scholars. In Homeric epos, the adjective *thoós* means "fast" or "quick"; thus it does not make sense to ascribe it to an island. This problem may have originated from an ancient corruption of the text. In both the *Odyssey* (7.34) and the *Iliad* (15.391), the adjective is usually connected to ships and, in particular, to the ship used by Antinous to try to intercept Telemachus (*Odyssey* 4.669). If we consider, therefore, that the term *nêsos*, "island," is quite similar to *neûs*, "ship" (related to *navis* in Latin, "to navigate"), we can infer that in the original version of the *Odyssey*, Telemachus heads not for those absurd "fast islands," but toward the "fast ships" of his enemies, for he was aware that they were lying in wait for him. This clearly emerges from the following: "being troubled as to [whether] he could succeed in escaping death or capture." (In fact, the night before, the goddess Athena had acquainted him with their criminal plan.) Homer himself corrobo-

layout from the geographic details of the war between the Pylians and the Epeans, which, as in real life, indicate that this territory is flat.

According to the Catalog of Ships, Elis's territory stretches as far south as Myrsinus, which is defined as "the last" (*eschatóosa*, "extreme," "the farthest"; *Iliad* 2.616). It would be tempting to identify Myrsinus with the present-day city of Mern, lying only six miles from Zealand's southernmost point. The catalog describes it as being next to Buprasion and Alesion Hill, which are also mentioned on the occasion of the Epean rout after the battle of Thryoessa. Mern does in fact lie very near Bårse and Allerslev (fig. 10.3, page 221).

As a final indication of his tale's northern context, Homer does not fail to mention the fog once. As Nestor says, witnessing the battle of Thryoessa: "I was about to kill the two young Moliones, Actor's sons, / but their father Poseidon, the powerful Enosichthon, / saved them from the battle by hiding them in thick fog" (*Iliad* 11.750–52). As we have seen in connection with the "heavy clothes" (*Odyssey* 4.50) Telemachus wears for the banquet held at Menelaus's palace in Sparta, the climate of the Homeric Peloponnese is quite rigorous. Why should we be surprised? We are actually in Denmark, on the island of Zealand, which is not only the heart of the *Gesta Danorum*, but also—many years before melancholic Prince Hamlet—the center of Homer's world and characters.

THE STRUCTURAL UNITY OF HOMER'S WORLD

In order to verify the consistency of Homer's genealogies and the structural unity of the *Iliad*, we can look closely at the unfinished duel

---

rates this interpretation in the story of the suitors, who, after returning from their failed ambush, by turns tell their stories of the events of that dramatic night:

> . . . *At sunset*
> *we did not pass the night on land,*
> *but we were waiting for the dawn on the sea,*
> *by sailing with the fast ship [neí thoêi],*
> *spying on Telemachus, to catch him*
> *and kill him* . . . (*Odyssey* 16.366–70)

This is the perfect parallel to the passage that suffers from the translation "fast islands" (an error likely originating in oral transmission or transcription), text in which Telemachus claims both his fear of and his desire to run the blockade of his enemies through a daring night navigation against their "fast ship." Interestingly, Eumaeus also calls Antinous's vessel a "fast ship" (*Odyssey* 16.472).

between Nestor and "the two young Moliones, Actor's sons." In this passage, the old king recalls an episode that has taken place at least forty years before, when he himself was young (*Iliad* 11.670, 684) and on his first campaign (*Iliad* 11.719), and his opponents shared his youth. He met them face-to-face later, in less dramatic circumstances, "when the Epeans buried mighty Amarynceus / in Buprasion, and his sons held contests for the king" (*Iliad* 23.630–31). Then "Actor's sons beat me in the chariot race; / . . . they were twins: one reined, reined / all the time, the other spurred with the whip" (*Iliad* 23.637, 641–42).

The catalog states that these twins, Actor's sons and Nestor's peers, are named Cteatus and Eurytus and mentions them as the respective fathers of the leaders of the Epeans in the Trojan War: "Amphimachus and Thalpius led the ones, / they were respective sons of Cteatus and Eurytus, Actor's sons" (*Iliad* 2.620–22). Therefore, the scions of Actor's twin sons took part in the Trojan War. Other grandchildren of old Actor (who belonged to Nestor's father's generation) also took part in the Trojan War: Eudorus, "fast runner and strong warrior" (*Iliad* 16.186); a son of Hermes and Echeclus's wife (*Iliad* 16.190); and Patroclus, the son of Menoetius, Actor's son.

In another adventure of his youth, Nestor took part in the Lapithae's expedition against the Centaurs:

> *I never saw nor shall see men*
> *such as Peirithous and Dryas, shepherds of peoples,*
> *Caineus, Exadius, godlike Polyphemus*
> *and Theseus, son of Aegeus, equal to the Immortals.*
> *They grew the strongest of the men on the earth:*
> *they were the strongest and fought against the strongest,*
> *the mountain Centaurs, and horribly massacred them.*
> *I had to deal with these men after I left Pylos,*
> *down there in a far off land.* (*Iliad* 1.262–70)

The consistency in timing between these two Early Bronze Age events and the details of the complex genealogy of their participants is significant, speaking to the historicity of Homer's work: Restless Nestor, who in his youth had fought alongside Peirithous and Caineus in the war against the Centaurs, meets Polypoetes and Leonteus, their son and grandson, respectively, in the Trojan War as an old man some thirty years later:

Polypoetes, the strong warrior . . .
was born of noble Hippodameia and Peirithous
on the day the latter took revenge on the Centaurs,
he chased them away from Pelion and pursued them up to
        Aethices . . . (Iliad 2.740–744)

And Leonteus was "son of bold Coronus, son of Caineus" (*Iliad* 2.746) or the grandson of Caineus, another comrade of Nestor in that first campaign (*Iliad* 1.264). Intriguingly, the name Caineus recalls the region Kainuu in northern Finland, not far from Mount Paljakka, which corresponds to Pelion, the Centaurs' mountain.

Similar genealogies arise regarding the royal Trojan ancestry as reported in detail in Book 20 of the *Iliad* (16.132), and connections to these are found throughout the poem: Priam's three brothers, Clytius, Lampus, and Hicetaon, are mentioned at the beginning of the poem, sitting among the "Elders" near the Scaean Gates (*Iliad* 3.147–49). Their sons take part in the battles together with Priam's sons—that is, their cousins and peers. Caletor, Clytius's son, falls during the attack on the Achaean ships (*Iliad* 15.419), and directly after this, Dolops, Lampus's son, falls at the hands of Menelaus (*Iliad* 15.541). At this point, Hector urges Melanippus, Hicetaon's son, to avenge "his slain cousin" (*Iliad* 15.554), and Melanippus in turn is killed by Antilochus, Nestor's son.

Clearly there are strong links between these complex events and genealogies, pointing once again to the fact that the core of the *Iliad*, inclusive of the Catalog of Ships, is tied together by genealogical, chronological, geographical, and narrative threads. These same threads are in evidence in the *Odyssey*: Iphiclus, king of Phylace, whom the catalog mentions as the father of Protesilaus (who falls on landing), is also mentioned in the *Odyssey*. There he is caught up in a complex affair involving cattle rustling and marriages, Nestor's father and sister, and the soothsayer Melampus, great-grandfather of a guest of Telemachus (*Odyssey* 15.225–56). In this case as well, all the interrelations among the different generations are chronologically exact, further corroborating the reliability of the information in the two poems.

In the next chapter, we shall conclude our reconstruction of the northern world of the Achaeans, starting with the "vast land" of Crete.

CRETE, THE RIVER EGYPT, PHAROS, AND PHTHIA

CRETE

In all the passages where Homer mentions Crete (four times in the *Iliad* and fifteen in the *Odyssey*), he never refers to it as an island. On the contrary, he defines it as a rich, beautiful, vast "land" *(gaîe)*, full of streams and "innumerable [*apeirésioi*]" (*Odyssey* 19.174) inhabitants. In fact, the adjective *eureîa*, "vast," is used no fewer than seven times in reference to Crete. Many different peoples lived in this land: "All languages are mixed: there are the Achaeans, / the magnanimous Eteocretans, the Cydonians, / the Dorians with their three clans and the noble Pelasgians" (*Odyssey* 19.175–77). According to the *Odyssey,* there were ninety cities in Crete (*Odyssey* 19.174), while the Catalog of Ships in the *Iliad* speaks of a hundred cities (*Iliad* 2.649). From this persistent reference, not found in connection with any other area in Homer's world, we can deduce that Crete was one of the largest and most densely populated regions the Achaeans inhabited in their Baltic homeland.

In looking for a site in the Baltic area that accords with Homer's references to Crete, we have to take into consideration the location of Athens. Greek mythology has established such close contacts between Athens and Crete that we cannot help but assume that they were quite close to each other physically, despite the sea between them. Thus, in locating Crete in the Baltic context, it must be near the corresponding Baltic Athens.

The Catalog of Ships, mentioning Crete soon after Ithaca and Aetolia, steers us to the southern Baltic coast, which is today split between

Germany and Poland. In comparing the Aegean Sea to the Baltic, the first thing that catches our eye is the similarity between Mediterranean Crete's position in relation to the Aegean and Poland's position (or, rather, that of the peninsula-like area between the cities of Stettin and Danzika) in relation to the Baltic. Crete and the Polish coast are rather similar in their oblong shape, roughly 150 miles long, oriented from west to east. What is more, each marks the southern boundary of its respective sea.

It is clear that long, narrow, dry Mediterranean Crete is not large enough to provide a home to the many different peoples cited as belonging to Homer's "vast land," let alone house them in ninety or a hundred cities. It does not have any rivers worth mentioning, and its beautiful sea is far different from the "foggy" or "dark" waters described by the poet. The hinterland of the Baltic's southern coast, however (not limited to present-day Poland, but extending into Germany), stretches over a large expanse of land, including the well-irrigated Pomeranian area. In short, it has all the characteristics of the "vast land" of Crete, where "King Minos, / intimate of great Zeus, reigned for nine years" (*Odyssey* 19.178–79).

This location of the Homeric Crete on the southern Baltic shores also complies with the condition of proximity to Athens. The Polish coast faces the area of Karlskrona, where Athens lay, and nearby Torhamn— that is, the ancient Attic city of Toricus, which, according to classical mythology, faced Crete. In the Greek world, although the Aegean Sea is much narrower than the Baltic, the distance between Athens and Crete is much greater, meaning they are by no means in close proximity.

Theseus and the Minotaur

While investigating the relationship between Athens and Crete, we can also look closely at the famous myth of Theseus and the Minotaur, which may have some analogies in the Baltic world. The name of a headland near Karlskrona, known as Knösö (quite similar to Cnossus), could be a remnant of the age when Theseus's Athens was subject to the Cretans and was thus compelled to send seven boys and seven girls every year to be sacrificed to the Minotaur in the labyrinth. In more realistic terms, a Cretan post could have been placed on Knösö in order to control navigation at a strategic point.

The myth also mentions the island of Naxos, on the route between Athens and Crete, where the Athenian hero abandoned Ariadne on his way back to Athens after killing the Minotaur. Significantly, halfway between the Swedish city of Karlskrona (Athens) and the Polish coast

(Crete), we come across the island of Bornholm, which lies in the position where we might expect to find Naxos (see fig. 10.2, page 214). In Bornholm there can be found megalithic tombs and a town called Neksø, which seems to corroborate the island's identification with ancient Naxos. (Bornholm's chief town, Rønne, recalls the name Ariadne.) The identification of Homeric Naxos corroborates the soundness of the argument that led us to locate Athens and Crete independently.

Cold and Stormy Crete

The *Odyssey* provides further confirmation of the Baltic location of Crete in the dramatic account of the shipwreck of Menelaus's fleet:

> But when, by sailing the wine-dark sea
> with his hollow ships, he reached steep Cape Malea
> in a hurry, then Zeus the Thunderer prepared him
> an evil way, he roused the blow of howling winds
> and huge waves as high as mountains,
> then he divided the ships and pushed some toward Crete
> where the Cydonians live near Iardanus' stream.
> There is a naked, steep cliff on the sea
> at the end of Gortyn, in the misty sea. (Odyssey 3.286–94)

Ulysses' ships run into similar trouble: "The violence of the wind pushed him to Crete / when heading for Troy, diverting him from Cape Malea" (*Odyssey* 19.186–87). Bearing in mind Cape Malea's position at the southwesternmost end of Scania (the southernmost region of Sweden, facing Zealand), it seems plausible that a strong northwest wind blows the ships off course toward the area we have just identified with the Homeric Crete.

The reference in the *Odyssey* to "twelve days" during which the north wind lashes the Cretan coast proves most enlightening: "A violent wind of Boreas was blowing, so strong that in the land / it prevented men from standing" (*Odyssey* 19.200–201). This harsh climate explains why in Crete Ulysses wore "a purple cloak, thick / and double" (*Odyssey* 19.225–26) and is given another, similar "double" *(diplaka)* cloak (*Odyssey* 19.241) by a friend. Homer also mentions Crete's "snowy mountains [*órea niphóenta*] (*Odyssey* 19.338), probably a reference to the so-called Pomeranian Switzerland—that is, the area of morainal highlands of glacial origin that lies east of the river Oder.

In this geographic context, we can locate some of the places mentioned in the episode of Menelaus's shipwreck: Gortyn could survive in present-day Gostyn, which lies not far from the sea, east of the mouth of the Oder; the Oder itself could be identified with the river Iardanus, "where the Cydonians (Kýdones) live" (*Odyssey* 3.292), as the names of the villages of Gardno (near the right bank, toward the river mouth) and Cedynia (lying farther upstream) indicate. We also find traces of the Cydonians farther east, in the city of Gdynia. The Homeric Iardanus can also be discerned in the names of the cities of Gardna and Jezioro (lake) Gardno. As to the name Crete, it perhaps still resounds in the Polish town of Krotoszyn.

As far as Cnossus (Knosós in Greek) is concerned, we have already found some place-names that could correspond to it, not in Poland, but rather in some "strategic" places located in the Baltic: Knösen, corresponding to the Homeric Cape Malea, and Knösö, not far from the ancient Cape Sunium, near Athens (Karlskrona). This could confirm the Cretans' prowess in seafaring: They perhaps had ports and stations in strategic points in the Baltic.

Minos, king of Crete, is often mentioned in the two poems, even though he lived two generations before the Trojan War began. As a matter of fact, he was the grandfather of Idomeneus (*Iliad* 2.451), one of the oldest Achaean captains. We may find the root of his name in a small Polish town—Mniszek—lying south of Danzika, and in the name Mannus, who, according to Tacitus,[1] was the mythical founder of the Germanic people.

We find the name of Daedalus, the builder of the labyrinth, in the place-name Dedelow, in Germany near the Polish border. Scholars link Daedalus with a character known as Wayland Smith (son of the king of the Finns) in the *Edda*. According to the *Volundarkvidha*, Wayland manages to take flight with artificial wings to escape from a king who has imprisoned him. According to Carlo Mastrelli, scholar in Scandinavian philology, in his introduction to *L'Edda, carmi norreni* (The Edda, Norse poems), this legend has Germanic origins. Thus, along with the link to Dedelow, the myth fits this geographic setting. Another mythic correspondence can be seen in an episode from the Finnish *Kalevala* in which Lemminkäinen manages to escape from enemy territory by flying home like an eagle, even though here, as in the Daedalus myth, the sun, which "burnt his cheeks," became a problem.[2]

Finding Lost Peoples

The identification of Homer's Crete with northern Poland leads us to a tempting hypothesis regarding the origin of the name given to the present inhabitants of this Baltic country. The *Odyssey* mentions among those who lived in Crete at that time the "noble Pelasgians [*dîoi Pelasgoí*]" (*Odyssey* 19.177), a name that sounds remarkably like Polska, leading us to guess that today's Poles inherited their name from these distant ancestors. Additionally, Homer mentions the Pelasgians in conjunction with the Dorians (*Odyssey* 19.177), a name that recalls the ancient German region of Thuringia. These can be added to the list of Homeric peoples—the Danaans, Pelasgians, Curetes, and Lapithae—whose traces are found not in the Mediterranean but rather in the Baltic world, in today's Danes, Poles, Kurlandians, and Lapps.

Yet another example of this type of correspondence can be seen in the Baltic region of Livonia, divided today between Estonia and Latvia. We could assume that Livonia is related to the Homeric Libya, which the *Odyssey* mentions in two episodes, one telling of a ship heading for Libya, sailing "in the open sea off Crete" (*Odyssey* 14.300). Although vague, this description squares with Livonia's position in relation to the Polish coast, which we have established as the Baltic Crete. This line may in fact be referring to one of the shipping routes in the southern Baltic during the Early Bronze Age.

The name Livonia derives from the Livonians, an ancient Baltic people nearly extinct today. They have long been farmers and breeders who attach special importance to livestock: In their culture, newlyweds traditionally receive domestic animals as wedding presents, and animals "play a leading role in funerals."[3] These details remind us of a passage in which Homer describes Libya as a land of stockbreeders, where "flocks lamb three times in the course of a year. / Neither the owner or the shepherd ever lack / cheese, meat or sweet milk, / but sheep provide plentiful milk all the time" (*Odyssey* 4.86–89). Interestingly, the mild, humid climate along the Latvian coast allows Mediterranean plants to thrive there in certain areas. Germans even refer to the area as Gottesländchen (God's Land) because of its climate.[4]

If today's Livonians truly are the descendants of the Homeric Libyans, then they would be an extraordinary example of cultural persistence over the course of four thousand years, from the Early Bronze Age to the modern era. The name of ancient Libya still echoes in the city of Liepāja, in western Latvia, which is called Libava in Russian and Libau in German.

Mediterranean Crete

There are some significant indications that, apart from the name the Achaeans gave it after they came down from the north, Mediterranean Crete has nothing to do with the "vast land" described in the *Iliad* and the *Odyssey*. First of all, while the Minoan civilization of Aegean Crete in the Mediterranean is rich in figurative arts, the representation of ships is scant and, when present, of poor quality for what is supposedly a seafaring culture. And though Crete plays a significant role in Greek mythology, "there is nothing in Minoan-Crete art which seems to illustrate any type of known legend," as Professor Pierre Vidal-Naquet writes in his preface to the *Iliad*.

As we have learned, the *Odyssey* tells of the coexistence of many different peoples on Cretan territory and of the warlike nature of these groups. This, however, seems contradicted by the lack of defensive structures found in the Mediterranean Crete's Minoan settlements. At this point, we turn to Martin Nilsson's words on the relationship between Minoan and Mycenaean civilizations:

> So many differences exist between the Mycenaean and Minoan civilizations which cannot be explained by an organic development of the Minoan culture under different conditions, and which very definitely point northward, that we may state confidently that they were brought in by a people with Northern connections who overtook the Minoan culture but mixed it up with elements of their own.[5]

The deciphering of the Linear B tablets in the fifties revealed an archaic Greek language that was probably imported by Mycenaean invaders, who—according to our theory—zealously renamed every place based on names from the Baltic Crete: Cnossus, Amnisus, and so on. Only after we decipher the other form of writing found in Aegean Crete, Linear A, will we discover the original names of these cities and the peoples who lived in them before the Mycenaean invasion. At present, we have one linguistic clue unrelated to Greek civilization: Crete's Egyptian name, Keftiw.

As we have noted all along, the Greeks themselves, who were descended from the Achaeans, continued the tradition of naming their new settlements according to their places of origin. They also, it seems, considered geographic analogies: The Aegean island of Tinos, for example, shaped roughly like Sicily but on a smaller scale, has located on it the port of Panormos, which lies in a position identical to that of Palermo in relation to the island of Sicily. This naming phenomenon occurred in later periods as well, and was prevalent in the European colonization of the New World. A recent example is that of the Pontine Marshes fifty miles southeast of Rome, which were drained by farmers from Veneto in the 1930s. These people transferred the names of their mountains from the eastern Alps—Sabotino, Montello, Mount Grappa, Monte Nero, and so on, where Italians and Austrians fought during World War I—to those lowlands of southern Latium, although the latter lacked any resemblance to their original northern highland home. If the historians of a distant future, misled by these namesakes, attempt to place the events of World War I on the plains of lower Latium, they will be just as puzzled as Strabo was when he tried to fit the Homeric poems onto the Mediterranean world. The old adage "Homer is a poet, but not a geographer" originates from this misunderstanding, although, as we are discovering here, his knowledge of geography was quite sound.

THE RIVER EGYPT

The *Odyssey* mentions the river Egypt (Aígyptos) on several occasions, and its location is linked in the poem with that of Baltic Crete. As we have already seen, Menelaus is caught in a storm off Cape Malea and is blown toward Crete, where "the waves wrecked the ships against the rocks. / However, wind and water pushed and carried / five ships to Egypt" (*Odyssey* 3.298–300). As we shall see, this and several other indications in Homer suggest that the river Egypt is not the Nile at all and that the land of Egypt referred to is not the land we think of as Egypt today.

Nevertheless, the river Egypt must have been very important. First, it was navigable—in fact, Ulysses tells us that he anchored his ships there (*Odyssey* 14.258) after sailing from Crete. After a while, he even met the country's king: "I ran up in front of the king's horses / and hugged and kissed his knees. He was merciful and spared me. / He let me sit beside him on his chariot and drove me to his palace" (*Odyssey* 14.278–80). Besides the fact that the gesture of putting one's head on the knees of a person as a plea, apology, or act of submission was typical of the Vikings, the surprisingly informal attitude of this king, who drives himself through his city to his palace, confirms that we are indeed far from the Nile Valley.

Ancient Egyptians called their country Kem—not Egypt—while the original name of the Egyptian Thebes was Wó'se. By considering that the names Egypt and Thebes are of Greek origin, we can suspect that both of these were place-names originally referring to a northern territory and its capital city, which were later transposed by the Achaeans into the corresponding Mediterranean sites after their migration south. Thus we can search for a river having Nile-like characteristics in an area of the southern Baltic, with the southern Baltic corresponding to the southesastern Mediterranean, near the delta of the Nile River. There is a river in this area that corresponds quite well to the Nile: the Vistula, whose wide delta, stretching for several miles, opens out onto the eastern Polish coast (see fig. I.2, page 5). Its resemblance to the Nile Delta and its analogous position in relation to the sea are evident. Moreover, the Nile and the Vistula have the same south-to-north orientation.

Interestingly, until the third century C.E., a barbaric people lived near the mouth of the Vistula: The Gepids "lived on an island, called Gepidos in the language of their fathers, surrounded by the Vistula's fords" *(Commanebant in insula Visclae amnis vadis circumacta, quam pro patrio sermone dicebant Gepidos).*[6] The name Gepidos clearly recalls Aígyptos, corroborating the idea that the Homeric Egypt was situated around the Vistula delta.

It is easy to see why the Achaean invaders called the Nile Valley, or, rather, the original land of Kem, the same name—Egypt—they had previously used for the great northern river in their lost homeland. But there is more: While the Achaeans were settling down on Greek soil, nurturing the early Mycenaean civilization, the city of Wó'se (not yet called Thebes) gave rise to the royal dynasty that drove the Hyksos from the Nile Valley and restored Wó'se as the capital of the whole nation. Thus, when the Mycenaeans came in contact with the ancient Egyptians, Egypt's principal city was Wó'se—which explains why it was renamed "Thebes": Perhaps the Mycenaeans were keeping alive the memory of this city of northern Egypt, which was left along the southern Baltic shores. Wó'se's change to Thebes is an example of how the Achaeans altered the preexisting Mediterranean toponymy in order to reconstruct their original world.

What about the Egyptian Thebes referred to by Homer? It would be tempting to place it by the Vistula delta, where today the Polish city of Tczew is located. Homer emphasizes the extraordinary affluence of this city's inhabitants—"In Egyptian Thebes / . . . there is enormous wealth [*pleîsta ktémata*] in the houses" (*Odyssey* 4.126–27)—probably due to the city's position near the river Vistula. Pia Laviosa Zambotti writes: "The trade of Baltic amber, which made use of renowned 'shopping centers' in Eastern Prussia, must also have strongly appealed to Pontus and Mesopotamian peoples. Zlota civilization developed on the river Vistula's upper course, which was the most direct way leading to this Eldorado of antiquity."[7]

This, then, was the secret of the "enormous wealth" of Thebes's lucky citizens: amber! In their dealings with this product, they exploited their city's enviable position by the "River Egypt" and, above all, the navigability of this waterway, which is explicitly reported in the *Odyssey*. The flat keels of the Homeric ships, as well as their maneuverability from their double-prow design—which Homer actually recalls in this episode (*Odyssey* 14.258)—were well suited to this purpose.

At this point, we realize why Homer never mentions the Nile River. It managed to escape the wholesale change of names that was undertaken through the cultural and commercial supremacy gradually imposed by the Greek-speaking peoples in the Mediterranean area after their migration (or rather, *migrations*—the Mycenaeans were followed in four or five centuries by the Dorians from the north). Who would have thought that the well-known Egyptian Thebes, ancient Wó'se in the Land of Kem, has nothing to do with the Homeric "Thebes on the River Egypt," but instead lies thousands of miles away from its Baltic homotope? We might here reinterpret the meaning of Hermes Trismegistus's famous expression "As above, so below" from a geographic perspective: "As in the northern world, so in the southern world." The new understanding of the name Egypt also allows us to explain a rather curious tale from Herodotus: "As Heracles reached Egypt, the Egyptians after crowning him led him in a procession to offer him as a sacrifice to Zeus. At the beginning he kept quiet, but when the preparation of the sacrifice started by the altar, he resorted to force and carried out a massacre of all of them."[8] What is strange in this tale (which seems to recall the biblical myth of Samson) is the fact that the Egyptians did not make human sacrifices. Thus we can deduce that these strange Egyptians were not the extremely civilized inhabitants of the Nile Valley, but instead the ones who, in ancient times, lived close to the Homeric Egypt River.

PHAROS, HOME OF THE OLD MAN OF THE SEA

A passage from the *Odyssey* in which Egypt is mentioned has particularly puzzled ancient and modern scholars: "There is an island in the boundless sea / in front of Egypt; people call it Pharos, / as far-away as a hollow ship in a whole day [*panemeríe*] / sails, which a howling wind pushes from behind" (*Odyssey* 4.354–57). Menelaus stopped there on his return journey from Troy: "The gods kept me there for twenty days and the sea winds / never rose to blow" (*Odyssey* 360–61).

In the Mediterranean, the Homeric Pharos was identified with the little island on which, in the Hellenistic period, the famous "lighthouse" (*faro* in Italian) signaled to sailors the entrance to the port of Alexandria. The fact that it stands only a half mile from the Egyptian coast has given rise to one of the most famous incongruities of Homeric geography: Homer stresses that the course between Pharos and Egypt is "long and difficult [*dolichén argaléen te*]" (*Odyssey* 4.483). Scholars—Strabo in particular—have performed sophisticated lucubrations to solve this puzzle, but, as Strabo said, giving up, "These things are really full of enigmas!"[9]

In short, the reason why Homer locates Pharos a long way from Egypt has always been incomprehensible in the Mediterranean setting. Can Baltic geography and the position of its "Egypt" solve this mystery? In the center of the Baltic, two hundred sea miles from the Polish coast and exactly north of the mouth of the river Vistula—"in front of Egypt"—there is an island called Fårö. If we consider Pörtner's statement that in favorable conditions, Viking ships, similar to the Achaean ones, were able to sail at an average speed of almost ten knots, it follows that they would be able to cover this distance in one day when helped by a strong wind, especially because there are at least eighteen to twenty hours of daylight available for sailing at these latitudes in summer.

Interestingly, the island of Fårö lies exactly on the Achaeans' return course from Troy—that is, it would be met in a course that cuts across the middle of the Baltic from Troad in southern Finland to Öland (Euboea). This explains why Menelaus stopped there. In a word, Fårö (Pharos) can be included with Lemland (Lemnos), Tåsinge (Zacynthus), Neksø (Naxos), and Høgoyggj (Ogygia) on the list of the islands of Greek mythology whose names and geographic positions have both northern origins and southern counterparts.

Nevertheless, we could wonder if the poet really means to refer to the north when he says "in front of Egypt" (Aigýptou propároithe). We have already noted that in the Homeric world "left" is equivalent to the west and "right" to the east (*Iliad* 12.239–40). This implies that at that time, the bearings related to the cardinal points—basic knowledge in any seafaring civilization—were exactly the same as ours. In other words, the north was in front, as it still is today. A passage from the *Odyssey* corroborates this: Nestor informs Telemachus of the two alternative return courses after the war—that is, "to sail over [*kathýperthe*] steep Chios, / . . . or down [*hypénerthe*] Chios" (*Odyssey* 3.170–72). Here, north is up and south is down. This indicates that the Achaeans oriented their maps as we do now, which confirms that the poet's intention when he writes that Pharos (Fårö) lies "in front of Egypt"—that is, the Vistula River—is as we have interpreted it.

The identification of Pharos with Fårö fits very well with the portrayal of the northern atmosphere of this island. It is the scene of the ambush that Menelaus, eager to find his way home, lays for Proteus, the Old Man of the Sea. The poet introduces Proteus as a shepherd of seals that come up from the depths of the sea to sunbathe on the rocks:

> *When the Sun reaches the middle of the sky,*
> *then the truthful Old Man of the Sea surfaces from the sea,*
> *under Zephyrus' blow, hidden in a dark shiver,*
> *and once out, he rests in the hollow caves;*
> *around him the flipper-footed seals of the nice sea daughter*
> *sleep close together as they come out from the foamy sea,*
> *giving off the strong smell of the sea depths.* (*Odyssey* 4.400–406)

Proteus's daughter provides Menelaus with this tip, which allows him to take her father by surprise and—after a long fight in which Proteus uses all the transformative powers that have made his name proverbial—to immobilize him, thus forcing him to disclose the path to Menelaus's home.

Menelaus's adventure in Pharos is one of the most evocative episodes in the *Odyssey*: In it Homer not only blends reality and fable with masterly skill, but also paints a vivid picture of a northern world much more than a Mediterranean one. Whoever has had the opportunity to photograph seals in northern seas—on the Orkney Islands, for instance—can appreciate both the realism of this wonderful description and its exquisite poetry.

We should note how important this island, lying halfway between opposite shores of the Baltic, must have been for ancient seafarers. Homer says of this place: "There is a good port, from where / they set afloat their ships after they draw water" (*Odyssey* 4.358–59). And we can infer from the tale of Proteus that besides stopping for water and a refreshing pause in their trips, Bronze Age sailors visited a kind of oracle shrine there, which provided them with predictions for their future, giving hope and encouragement to those who risked their lives in Baltic storms: "(Proteus) will tell you the course, the length of your voyage, / and your return, how you'll sail across the teeming sea" (*Odyssey* 4.389–90). The mythical aura that we feel in Menelaus's adventure, much like that in a fairy tale, leads us to believe that here we can find traces of an even more ancient age than the one in which the Homeric poems are set. As we have already noted, the author of the *Odyssey* often uses folklore or legendary material dating back to a period that his contemporaries must have considered part of a dim and distant past. These set pieces in the poems are often imbued, as they are in this case, with extremely archaic magical and shamanistic motifs.

We can detect a similar atmosphere and note similar details in certain Celtic legends, as Ananda Coomaraswamy says in his preface to *Sir Gawain and the Green Knight*: "In the Gaelic tradition, the seal women get rid of their fur and appear as beautiful young girls; marriage to a human being makes this interruption of the spell permanent."[10] Thetis —who is a sea goddess and daughter of Nereus, another Old Man of the Sea (*Iliad* 1.538)—has the power to transform herself much like these Celtic seal women. In fact, as Kerényi tells us, she uses this power when she marries Peleus: "The reluctant bride used all the transformation arts of the ancient sea goddesses. She changed into fire and water, bared her teeth like a lion and tried to prevent being embraced by taking the form of a snake."[11]

This brings us to looking more closely at the motif of the sea gods' predilection for transformation: "The truthful Old Man of the Sea, / immortal Egyptian Proteus, who knows / all the depths of the sea" (*Odyssey* 4.384–86) could be a metaphor, or rather a sort of kenning, for the "spirit of the sea" in its perpetually changing aspect. One moment it is calm and kind, the next, angry and threatening. In a cruel game of chance in which the stakes are the ship's safety and the sailor's life, seafarers need intuition, skill, experience, and luck. The sea gives the omen of a safe return to those seafarers who know how to scan it, interpret its signs, wait patiently, and seize the right time to successfully conclude their voyage.

As for the theme of telling the future, we can find in Norse mythology a remarkable counterpart to the Old Man of the Sea: Marmendill (or marmennill) is a very odd creature who, as Chiesa Isnardi reports, resembles a man with a seal-shaped body below the waist who lives in the sea depths and is capable of telling the future. What is more, like Proteus, he talks only when he feels like it. The *Hálfs Saga ok Hálfs-rekka* narrates his eventful encounter with the Viking king Hjörleif. On this occasion, there is a wrestling contest (a *glíma,* which is a traditional Icelandic form of wrestling) before the prophecy that could be compared to the struggle between Proteus and Menelaus, in which the revelation of the hero's destiny is at stake.

There is another remarkable similarity between Proteus and the Norse seal man. As Chiesa Isnardi writes, a Viking text (the *Land-námabók,* or *The Book of Settlement*) tells that "one of these creatures (marmendill) told Selthorir where he had to settle. The first part of his name, that is, *Sel,* means 'seal,' since at the moment of the prophecy he was lying in the boat and was covered with a sealskin."[12] This episode, which also has a peculiar "shamanistic" atmosphere, finds a precise analogy in the *Odyssey*—that moment when Menelaus and his companions, aided by the Old Man's daughter, are waiting for the Old Man to arrive in order to seize him and extort his predictions: "She plunged into the sea's vast womb / and returned carrying four sealskins from the bottom, / all of them just skinned, and so she was setting the trap against her father. / . . . She had us lay down in line and threw a skin on each of us" (*Odyssey* 4.435–37, 440). By comparing these lines to the Norse story of Selthorir, who is covered with a sealskin while he awaits the marmendill's prophecy, the common roots of the two tales are immediately apparent, despite the fact that they belong to two cultures separated by thousands of years.

It is also significant that Homer repeatedly calls Proteus "the truthful [*nemertés*] Old Man of the Sea" (*Odyssey* 4.384, 401, 542). This adjective—*nemertés*—which seems to be an integral part of his name, is formed by the negative prefix *ne-* and the root of a verb meaning "to fail" or "to mistake." It therefore literally means "infallible," with obvious reference to the prophetic gift of the Old Man. Bearing in mind the interchange between *m* and *n* that is found, for example, in the Latin conjunction *cum* (with) in relation to Greek *sýn,* and in the Lithuanian name of the river Nemunas, which turns into the Memel in German, we could conjecture that the word *marmendill* derives from an extreme corruption of the Homeric *nemertés*.

Finally, what could have suggested the odd equation of the seal and prophetic skill? Perhaps it originates from some noted behavior of these animals to divine weather or sea forecasts—that is, to glean a sort of "weather report." We can think of the saying, which has survived until the present day, that seagulls flying low herald an impending storm.

As we see here, the correspondences between Greek and Norse myths often concern typical marine topics, supporting our theory that the Achaeans and the ancient Scandinavians had a common origin and that their original common home most likely lay near the sea. Homer uses no fewer than four terms to indicate the sea—*háls*, *thálassa*, *póntos*, and *pélagos*—which both corroborates the idea that the Achaeans' familiarity with the sea reached back to a very distant past and helps us to understand the seafaring skill of their Mycenaean descendants.

PHTHIA

The Homeric Phthia, Achilles' homeland, lay near Hellas, as the Catalog of Ships tells us:

> *Those who inhabited Pelasgian Argos,*
> *some lived in Alus, Alope, and Trachis,*
> *some had Phthia and Hellas with its beautiful women;*
> *they were called Myrmidons, Hellenes, and Achaeans;*
> *Achilles was the leader of fifty ships of them. (Iliad 2.681–85)*

By following the catalog's sequence, we have learned that Hellas lay along the Estonian coast. At this point, it is easy to locate neighboring Phthia. Homer says that between Phthia and Troy "there are many shady mountains and the echoing sea" (*Iliad* 1.156–57). From this we can infer that Phthia lay in the hilly Estonian hinterland. This is confirmed when Homer mentions Phthia "with its fertile clods, mother of flocks" (*Iliad* 9.479), for the most fertile part of Estonia is not along the coast, where the ice-age glaciers eroded the soil, but on its southeastern side, toward the border with Russia and Latvia, where we find morainic hills rich in sediments deposited by the retreating glaciers.[13]

Phthian Politics

Achilles did not rule the whole region of Phthia. As a matter of fact, immediately after him the catalog mentions

> . . . the ones who had Phylace and Pyrasus full of flowers,
> Demeter's shrine . . .
> Protesilaus had ruled them
> when he was living, but then he was dead.
> He left his wife with scratched cheeks in Phylace
> and a half-built house. A Dardan warrior killed him
> when he was jumping down from his ship, the very first of the
>   Achaeans. (Iliad 2.695–703)

Protesilaus's younger brother, Podarces, succeeds him in the command of the forty Phthian ships. While translating the emotional impact of the young wife in despair and alone with her unfinished house, this passage omits the names of both this people and the region where they live. Although another passage calls them Phthians (Iliad 13.686–99), the catalog states that Achilles' followers, coming from Phthia and Hellas, were "Myrmidons, Hellenes, and Achaeans," without mentioning the Phthians. We can infer from this that in former times the Myrmidons—whose original homeland was father north, as we have seen—had come to occupy a part of Phthia. Thus the Phthians were obliged to share their territory with invaders who were stronger (as the course of the Trojan War shows) but not strong enough to drive out or overwhelm the Phthians. The size of their respective fleets corroborates this, the Myrmidons having fifty ships against forty, certainly a lead, but not enough to establish clear supremacy.

In the catalog, Homer omits the names of other peoples whose cities and captains he includes, but in this case it is likely that the omission is intentional, taking into consideration that the poet of the Iliad, who exalts Achilles' character, was perhaps linked with Achilles' entourage. As we have noted earlier, the Phthian ships landed in the aigialos, near those of Ajax (Iliad 13.681), at the opposite end from Achilles' ships. This suggests that there were old grudges between these two peoples. This is not unusual; in fact, Homer often includes as part of his narrative the history of skirmishes between neighbors, such as that of the Pylians against the Epeians (Iliad 11.671)—both of whom took part in the Achaean coalition against Troy—and the Phaeacians against the Cyclopes (Odyssey 6.5).

The Phthians are unlucky in the Trojan War; their leader, Protesi-laus, is the first to fall and his ship is the only one the Trojans succeed in burning. It could not be sheer coincidence that Patroclus's success-ful counterattack, leading the Myrmidons, occurs immediately after the Phthian ship is set on fire. He and his men easily drive away the Trojans from the half-burned ship (*Iliad* 16.284–95). In this the poet seems to underline the differences in the behavior of the Myrmidons and that of the Phthians, whose ships are rescued thanks to the intervention of their neighbors. What is more, at one point Ajax stands in heroic defense of the ships against the overwhelming Trojan forces, while Protesi-laus's brother Podarces, head of the Phthians, is mentioned only once, although his ships are nearby. All of this is consistent with an unusually critical comment from Homer about the chief of a contingent: When Podarces takes the place of Protesilaus in command of the Phthians, his army "missed the other, who was better" (*Iliad* 2.709). It is very likely that this was quite significant—from a "political" point of view—for the Achaean audience of the original version of the poem, and gives an additional touch of realism to Homer's narrative.

Estonian Place-names

As we have seen regarding other places in the northern world, the names of places in southeastern Estonia, the country where the Homeric Phthia lay, also find correspondences in Homer's narratives. Here the villages of Ahja and Pölva (or Pölwe), both lying near the river Ahja, remind us of Achilles and his father, Peleus, respectively; present-day Vôru, nearly fif-teen miles south of Pölva, echoes the name of Borus [Bôros] (*Iliad* 16.175–78), Achilles' brother-in-law; the name of the Latvian village of Alûksne, twelve miles from the Estonian border, is similar to Alus (*Iliad* 2.682); and in nearby Russia, the root *palk-* of today's Palkino, twenty-five miles east of the point where the borders of Estonia, Russia, and Latvia meet, recalls Phylake, unlucky Protesilaus's city. From this we can deduce that Phthia probably extended east into Russian territory as far as the Velikaja River flowing into Lake Pskov, which is contiguous with Lake Peipsi, once joined to the Baltic Sea in prehistoric times. Another similarity is found in the words of Phoenix, Achilles' old preceptor: "I lived at the end of Phthia ruling the Dolopes" (*Iliad* 9.484). In fact, the name of Dulovka, lying twelve miles east of Palkino and six miles east of the Velikaja, could con-tain the last vestiges of the Homeric Dolopes. It is likely that the Velikaja River was the border between Phthia and the Dolopes' land.

A few miles north, the Velikaja meets the city of Pskov and flows into the lake of the same name. Pskov, previously Pleskov, is one of the most ancient Russian cities.[14] It is very tempting to suppose that its name derives from that of Pelasgian Argos [Pelasgikón Argos] (*Iliad* 2.681), ruled by Achilles (the Pelasgians were scattered through many countries of the Homeric world). We should not forget, however, that considerations based on geography and climate are far more reliable than are similarities in place-names.

The Borderland

As for the name Phthia, it is quite likely connected to the Greek verb *phthío* or *phthíno* (meaning "to finish"), which, in turn, recalls the Latin word *finis*, meaning "end" or "border." Phthia, therefore, was the borderland of the Achaean world, which squares with its peripheral location in the Baltic region. This is of use in clearing up another ancient question: Why was Phthia the land of refugees in the Homeric world? In the Myrmidon army, in fact, there were no fewer than three—Phoenix, Epigeus, and Patroclus—while another exile, Medon, was enlisted with the Phthians. In Phthia, it seems, far from the Baltic, and behind the "many shady mountains" that Homer describes as lying between this land and the sea, many people with accounts to settle (usually murders) took refuge to escape the revenge of the relatives of their victims. (We should note that in the Greek world, Phthia's location is not peripheral, which leaves both its name and its function unexplainable.)

To sum up, the Homeric Phthia extended over a vast territory, from southeastern Estonia to the border with present-day Latvia and Russia and farther, to the Velikaja and Lake Pskov. This country, shared by Phthians and Myrmidons, was fertile and suitable for breeding stock (*Iliad* 11.289–29 mentions the coveted herds of Protesilaus's father). The proximity of these two peoples in the catalog's sequence, corresponding to a real geographic proximity discernible only from a passage in Book 13, points to the striking accuracy of the *Iliad*.

ACHILLES' SHIELD

Before leaving the homeland of Achilles, we must look more closely at this warrior's famous shield made by Hephaestus, the smith god. Homer dwells upon its decorations for some 125 lines of verse (*Iliad* 18.483–607), inaugurating a genre that was later typical of the Viking skalds and providing a wonderful snapshot of everyday Achaean life. Before looking specifically at these decorations, however, we should understand their layout on the surface of the shield. To this end, we turn to a passage telling of the duel between Achilles and Aeneas, during which Aeneas's spear hits Achilles' shield:

> Proud Aeneas's strong spear did not pierce
> the shield. The gold, god's gift, stopped it;
> it passed through two layers, but there were three others,
> since the lame god has assembled five layers [pénte ptýchas],
> two of bronze, two of tin inside,
> and one of gold; this stopped the ashen spear. (Iliad 20.267–72)

At first, it seems absurd that the golden layer is enclosed between the others, like a slice of cheese in a sandwich: In this it would be invisible, sacrificing all of its ornamental purpose. Since the time of ancient Aristarchus (220–150 B.C.E.), however, this is how scholars have envisioned the shield. Yet this arrangement cannot be correct. Here is the comment of Codino in a footnote on this passage: "The last four lines of verse were already considered to be spurious by the Alexandrian philologist Aristarchus. Line 268 states that the shield was not pierced, but the following lines absurdly state that the golden layer was contained between two of bronze and two of tin."[15]

So is there an interpretation that restores sense to these lines and their depiction of the shield? Another passage from the Iliad explains how Hephaestus made the shield:

> He manufactured a large, heavy shield,
> decorating it everywhere; around he set a shiny, triple [tríplaka],
>   gleaming
> border, and a silver belt.
> There were five layers [pénte ptýches] in the shield;
> he made many decorations with his wise mind. (Iliad 18.478–82)

We especially note the "five layers" mentioned in this passage. The word layer (in Greek ptýche) also appears in a reference to Ajax's shield, made of layers of cowhide. Of it the Iliad says that Hector succeeds at piercing "six layers, / but it stopped at the seventh hide" (7.247–48). Whether metal or hide, the Homeric shields clearly consisted of several layers laid one upon the other to ensure the greatest resistance coupled with handiness and lighter weight.

Here, then, is the solution to the problem that induced Aristarchus—and many other scholars—to consider the four lines of the *Iliad* concerning Achilles' shield to be spurious: The shield is made up of five layers—five metal plates laid one upon the other, having five different gradually decreasing diameters. The layers appear, then, like a target of five concentric rings. This structure is very functional: In the center are the two bronze layers, which are the strongest and, of course, have the main purpose of warding off blows. The other three—the golden layer and the two of tin—are wider and their external edges are mainly decorative, forming the "triple gleaming border." They are also useful, however, as an auxiliary defense, for their borders increase the protected area available to the warrior and they strengthen the bronze layers. (The golden layer, after all, stops Aeneas's spear after the two of bronze had reduced its thrust.) The decorations, of course, cover the whole first layer of bronze (which could be considered as a sort of bull's-eye in the center of the shield) as well as the external rings of the other four layers.

This kind of structure meets the requirement of limiting the weight—gold and tin, the metals used for the larger layers, are very malleable, and thus can be hammered very thin. The shield is, nonetheless, "large and heavy" (*Iliad* 18.478). To get a rough estimate of its weight, we can assume that the five layers have diameters of 16, 24, 32, 40, and 48 inches, respectively, and that the bronze plates are .08 inch thick and the other layers .02 inch thick. Given that this sort of calculation is based on inevitably arbitrary data, the resulting weight is about forty-five pounds—heavy, but surely bearable for a champion in top form.

We should also consider that Homer's heroes do not carry their shields with their forearms, as Mediterranean and Near East warriors did, but rather with a belt (*Iliad* 18.480) on their left shoulder (*Iliad* 16.106). This is the so-called archer shield, which allows the bearer free hands to use the bow. It is found in some primitive African and Indonesian cultures, which tallies with the antiquity of the Homeric world. That the ancient Greeks could be so perplexed regarding the structure of Achilles' shield is surely another sign that their culture had lost continuity with Homer's.

If the narration of the *Iliad* was inspired by real events, it is possible that Achilles took the field with his "parade shield" to exhibit wealth and power (he had given his battle shield to Patroclus, whose arms were seized by Hector when he fell). By following the sequence of the decorations on the shield, it is simple to reconstruct their layout on the surface and to see that they are more suitable for review than for battle. The central bronze layer is decorated with the earth, the heavens, and the stars (a configuration that is amazingly similar to the bronze disk portraying the starry sky found at the German site of Nebra). The second layer (or ring around the bull's-eye), also of bronze, depicts two cities, one at peace, the other at war. The third layer of gold—whose inner portion, covered by the bronze layers, blocks Aeneas's spear—contains farming and breeding scenes. The plowed soil is "of gold" (*Iliad* 18.599), which corroborates the placement of this decoration on the golden ring. (It could not be sheer coincidence that the productive assets of farming and breeding, which give wealth to humans, are found in the golden layer, the most precious of all.) The fourth layer, made of tin, shows dancing "youths and much-courted girls" (*Iliad* 18.593). Finally, Hephaestus "set the great strength of the River Ocean, / along the outermost border of the solid shield" (*Iliad* 18.606–607)—that is, on the fifth layer, also made of tin. Regarding the depiction on this last layer, it is interesting that the idea of the ocean surrounding the whole earth is found in Norse literature as well.

Thus we can read this grand image of the world following a "vertical" sequence, starting from the "upper" (central) layer and "descending" toward the edge: the sky, the cities (which usually stand on hills), the fields, and the sea (perhaps the dance on the fourth layer is set on the seashore?). This arrangement recalls the decorations on ancient Finnic and Lappish shamanistic drums, which are divided into zones reflecting the division of the universe (typical of shamanism) into heaven, earth, and hell. On these round drums there are some celestial symbols, symbols related to the human world, and others regarding the Underworld (analogous to the River Ocean, considering that in shamanistic conception hell is connected with rivers and other waters).

The shields' connections with these shamanistic drums suggest that their depictions invoked a magical protection to be added to the conventional one. This might explain why Agamemnon's shield displayed "a terrifying Gorgon" (*Iliad* 11.36), and, according to Chiesa Isnardi, "the Viking shields decorated with terrifying pictures had apotropaic properties"[16]—that is, they offered protection from evil souls and bad luck. (The disk of Nebra might also have had a "magic" value; perhaps it belonged to a priest-shaman-astrologer of the German Early Bronze Age.)

The five topics depicted on Achilles' shield—the world, cities, labor, dancing (we might say leisure today), the River Ocean that encircles all—are arranged with supreme art and intelligence by the poet (or still better, by the "wise mind" of the god Hephaestus, as the *Iliad* says). With the description of this shield, Homer has left us an extraordinary document of Early Bronze Age civilization in the north and its *Weltanschauung*, its "worldview"—a most worthy closure to our reconstruction of the lost world of the Achaeans.

PART FOUR
THE MIGRATION OF MYTH FROM THE HYPERBOREAN PARADISE

CHAPTER 13

FINDING THE HOME OF
THE GODS

In this chapter we attempt to locate some of the mythical geographic places that Homer himself relegates to legendary, or at least foreign, settings such as Olympus and Ethiopia. Apart from fitting in very well with the previously outlined picture of a northern Achaean world, these subjects will provide us with some very interesting information on the history of the Baltic Achaeans and their origin, taking us back to the most ancient roots of the Indo-European world.

TO THE ENDS OF THE EARTH

As we have seen, the outer border of Achilles' shield depicts the River Ocean encircling all. While an all-encompassing ocean is easy to imagine, Homer's designation of it as a river—particularly a river that flows through the sea, but is separate from it—is mysterious: "When the ship left the River Ocean's [Potamós Okeanós] stream, / it reached the waves of the wide sea / and the island of Aeaea" (*Odyssey* 12.1–3). Homer speaks of its "great strength" *(méga sthénos)* and "deep stream [*bathyrreítao*]" (Iliad 21.195), and defines it using the rather curious adjective *ápsorros,* which means roughly "the one which flows away" (*Iliad* 18.399, *Odyssey* 20.65). (The use of this term to refer to the River Ocean is also found in Hesiod.)[1] Another singular aspect of this rather strange river is that it "flows without any noise [*analarreítao*]" (*Iliad* 7.422, *Odyssey* 19.434).

Consulting the map of the North Sea, which is bounded on the north by the Orkney and Shetland Islands, we come across the great "sea river" known as the Gulf Stream, whose warm waters move silently from southwest to northeast without mixing with the freezing waters of the Atlantic. If we identify the Gulf Stream with the River Ocean, whose "deep stream" in the sea relentlessly "flows away" "without any noise," in the opposite direction to that of the human settlements and carries Ulysses to the "home of Hades," all of Homer's information makes sense. In particular, it reveals the meaning of *Odyssey* 12.1–3, which, as usual, poor old Strabo labored over in vain. At this point, it may be possible to explain the name Okeanós by tracing it back to the adjective *kýanos*, meaning "blue." In certain circumstances, the Gulf Stream's waters are actually blue, which distinguishes them from the surrounding gray sea. Therefore, the Potamós Okeanós could be the Blue River, or Gulf Stream, which Benjamin Franklin represented, on a map dating to 1770, as an immense river flowing between liquid walls.

One of the Gulf Stream's branches follows the Norwegian coastline up to the far north, where it enters the Arctic Ocean, thereby explaining why the ancients believed that the River Ocean surrounded the entire earth. Accordingly, in the *Iliad* the sun rises from the River Ocean (*Iliad* 7.422) and sets there (*Iliad* 8.485). The association of the River Ocean with the "ends of the earth" occurs in both the *Odyssey* and the *Iliad*:

> *Menelaus, Zeus's pupil, you are not fated*
> *to die in Argos where horses graze,*
> *but the Immortals will lead you to the Elysian plain,*
> *at the ends of the earth [peírata gaíes], where blond*
> >   *Rhadamanthus lives*
> *and life for mortals is most wonderful:*
> *there is neither snow nor cold nor rain,*
> *but the Ocean always gives off the breath*
> *of noisy blowing Zephyrus to comfort those men.*
> >   (*Odyssey* 4.561–68)

> *I am going to see the ends of the fruitful earth,*
> *the Ocean, origin of the gods, and Mother Tethys,*
> *who fed and brought me up in their home.*
> *I shall see them and settle their endless dispute,*
> *as they have been abstaining from love and bed*
> *for a long time, since their hearts have been filled with bile.*
> >   (*Iliad* 14.301–306)

Could there be a more poetic and, at the same time, precise way of saying that the waters of the Gulf Stream and the Atlantic never mix?

Strabo would be delighted that the mythical Potamós Okeanós, with its beauty and strength, reflects a geographic reality that the Achaeans probably forgot over time after their migration to the Mediterranean region, where the Gulf Stream could be neither seen nor accessed. In this way the word *ocean* in the Homeric poems came to indicate the immense sea stretching beyond the Pillars of Hercules. This might cause us to ask: Did the Greeks coin the name Pillars of Hercules or simply give the Strait of Gibraltar an appellation previously used by their northern ancestors to indicate the limits of the River Ocean?

THE PILLARS OF HERCULES AND THE GIANT WITH A HUNDRED HANDS

According to Aristotle,[2] the Pillars of Hercules were also known as the Pillars of Briareus. This leads us to a passage of "De facie" in which Plutarch terms Briareus "the guardian of the islands and the sea known as Cronious [the North Atlantic Ocean],"[3] and locates him near the island where the ancient god Cronos resided. Considering this with the fact that Plutarch also stresses the relationship among Cronos, Briareus, and the northern seas in "De Defectu Oraculorum" (chapter 18) and places Briareus near Ogygia, we can deduce that the Pillars of Hercules lay in the area surrounding Ogygia. The circle with Ogygia begun by Homer finally closes with these words: "A goddess lives there, / terrible Atlas's daughter, he who knows / all depths of the sea. He himself supports the great pillars [*kíonas makrás*] / that hold up the earth and the sky" (*Odyssey* 1.51–54).

As we have seen, the morphology of the Faeroes, the group of islands that includes Ogygia, lends itself perfectly to being envisioned as pillars. Moreover, in the above-mentioned passage, the Homeric term for pillars is *kíonas*, and one of these towering islands is known as Kunoy. We can assume that owing both to their strategic position in the North Atlantic Ocean near the Gulf Stream and their particular shapes, the Faeroe Islands were an important reference point for Bronze Age seafarers. A passage from Tacitus seems to confirm their significance: He writes that northern European coastal peoples "tried to sail the Ocean from that side; and rumor had it that the pillars of Hercules still existed . . . Drusus Germanicus did not lack audacity, but the Ocean stopped him from exploring both its waters and the traces of Hercules."[4] (Drusus Germanicus was a Roman captain who ventured out to explore the North Sea in the year 12 B.C.E. but was forced to give up by terrible weather conditions.)

It is natural enough that the Achaeans, having migrated to the Aegean Sea, identified the Strait of Gibraltar and the sea beyond as the counterpart of their lost pillars and River Ocean. Because the reference to pillars was meaningless in a Mediterranean context, however, the Greeks made up the story of the pillars Hercules erected in the strait. According to another famous tale, Hercules alternated with Atlas in supporting the world on his shoulders. Regarding Atlas, Hesiod hands down a vivid description: "Atlas supports the vast heavens, under an ineluctable destiny, / at the ends of the earth [peírasin en gaíes], / in front of the Hesperides who sing harmoniously."[5] We can imagine that to the Greeks' distant ancestors in Scandinavia, these islands, under the joint warming influence of the Gulf Stream and the climatic optimum, appeared as a sort of earthly paradise, the memory of which faintly glimmers in the Hesperides. We hear an echo of this in the lines Homer devotes to the fabulous home of Calypso, Atlas's daughter (its paradisal features seeming to refer, on one hand, to the the Celtic tradition of the island of everlasting youth in the remote western ocean and, on the other, to Genesis):

Clear water gushed out from four aligned springs,
close together but turning toward opposite sides;
all around there were soft meadows of violets and celery
in bloom. Even an Immortal coming here
would be enchanted in admiring this and be delighted in his heart.
    (Odyssey 5.70–74)

When the climatic optimum began its decline, these islands gradually became increasingly difficult to reach, which is what perhaps gave rise to the legend of fearful Briareus, also known as Aegaeon, mystifyingly described as a giant "with a hundred hands [hecatóncheiros]" (Iliad 1.402). As the name Aegaeon (Aigaíon) implies—it has the same root as Aegae [Aigás] (Iliad 13.21, Odyssey 5.381), a shrine dedicated to Poseidon—this character is definitely linked to the sea and, in fact, is mentioned together with the sea goddess Thetis. Interestingly, a sea giant mentioned in various Norse sagas and who has virtually the same name—Aegir—parallels Aegaeon in his northern home. It is remarkable that the name Aegir, by way of the Homeric Aegaeon, has managed to survive to the present day in the name of the Greek Aegean Sea. Chiesa Isnardi says of Aegir: "[H]e is the husband of Ran 'the plunderer,' who welcomes drowned people into her kingdom . . . Aegir and Ran's children are the sea waves."[6] One saga from the *Edda* relates: "The King's ship managed to struggle out of Ran's hand / with great difficulty."[7] Isnardi notes: "This is an allusion to the hand of Ran, wife of the giant-god of sea Aegir, which seizes all who are drowned, dragging them into her kingdom." In short, Ran's "hand" is a deadly danger to sailors.

This comparison between Aegir and Aegaeon reveals at last the real meaning of Briareus's "hundred hands": They represent another Homeric kenning, a transparent metaphor for the terrifying features of the stormy sea that sinks ships and mercilessly seizes their crews, dragging unfortunate sailors to their watery death. At this point, it seems natural to liken the name Briareus to the root of Brimir, another Norse giant, whose name, Isnardi underlines, is linked to *brim*, meaning "wave, sea."

Homer tells us that Aegaeon-Aegir-Briareus's neighbor Cronos lives on "hellish" Tartarus, "at the farthest limits / of earth and sea" (*Iliad* 8.478–79). Perhaps this island is Iceland, whose spectacular volcanic phenomena, glaciers, and dark winters are so evocative of Dantean images. To this geographic picture we can add another detail: Tartarus "is as far away from Hades as the earth is from the sky" (*Iliad* 8.16). Perhaps the distance between Iceland and the White Sea (where we have located the home of Hades; see chapter 4) was the longest longitudinal distance known at that time. There is evidence, however, that Achaean seafarers in the very distant past made oceanic voyages to other distant locations.

BEYOND THE OCEAN

In his dialogue *Timaeus*, Plato makes a precise reference to a continent situated beyond the Atlantic Ocean: "In past times the seafarers used to pass by other islands to reach the continent that surrounds the opposite side of the sea."[8] This hearkens to Plutarch's observations in "De facie quae in orbe lunae apparet," which served as a starting point for our research: "There are other islands beyond Ogygia that are at the same distance from one another," and beyond these we reach "the great continent which surrounds the ocean." Then Plutarch adds a surprising statement: "The coast of that continent is inhabited by Greeks along the shores of a gulf having at least the size of Meotis [the present-day Sea of Azov, a shallow arm of the Black Sea] which flows into the sea at about the same latitude as the mouth of the Caspian Sea. They call themselves the Continentals."⁹

These words might seem absurd if we assume that the "Greeks" Plutarch mentions are those from the Mediterranean. But the possibilities change entirely if we consider that he is referring to a primitive Achaean settlement in Scandinavia.

Plutarch also tells us of successive waves of colonization on this "great continent." Following in the footsteps of the mythical "Cronos people" (whose name is heard in Cronious, the northern sea), the last to arrive were "Heracles' companions" who "lit again the Greek spark with a strong, bright flame, which had almost been put out by the language, customs, and style of life of the barbarians."¹⁰ This vivid picture emerges from the mists of a remote prehistoric time, but even by the time the Achaeans were fighting at Troy, Plutarch's overseas "continental Greeks" had presumably lost all contact with their place of origin.

In assessing these statements, we must consider the fact that the Viking seafarers, whom we have linked with the Homeric Achaeans, managed to cross the Atlantic Ocean. Leaving from the Norwegian coasts, using stop-over points such as the Shetlands, the Faeroes, Iceland, and Greenland, and taking advantage of the climate and weather conditions of the warm medieval period during which the polar ices had retreated and icebergs had virtually disappeared, they reached the American continent around the year 1000 C.E. During this time, Leif Eriksson landed in Vinland, the name they gave to the land over the sea. After this period, the climate became harsh again and the route they traveled became blocked or too hazardous to allow further journeying.

The Vikings' transoceanic travel indicates that the North Atlantic route was surely within the reach of expert seafarers as long as there were favorable climatic conditions. Given the possibility of stopping at various points along the way, it was much shorter and easier than the long, nonstop crossing Columbus and his small crew undertook from the Canary Islands to the Bahamas. What is more, Columbus's flagship, *Santa Maria,* had a crew of only thirty-nine men, less than that of any Achaean ship. We can assume, then, that starting from Scandinavia, the advanced seafaring civilization described in the Homeric poems was able to reach and colonize the American coasts, stopping along the way at intermediary islands mentioned by Plato and Plutarch. Skilled and resourceful seafarers that the Achaeans were, and able to avail themselves of climate conditions that were even milder and more lasting than those the Vikings experienced thousands of years later, they were sooner or later bound to cross the Atlantic Ocean from the Scandinavian coasts. Thus Plutarch's mention of the "continental" Greeks, although it at first seems far-fetched, probably refers to North American prehistoric settlements of peoples from the north of Europe during the climatic optimum. This is confirmed by the specificity of Plutarch's description of a world that was virtually unknown to him and his contemporaries.

In the name of the Faeroes' westernmost island, Mykines, so similar to the name Mycenae, we might find another trace of the Achaeans who perhaps were able to sail there from the Scandinavian coasts. Might Mykines have been a prehistoric Achaean settlement along the North Atlantic course? The *Odyssey* provides other hints of travel on the vast ocean, referring to ships that used to cross "the immense abyss [*méga laîtma*] of the sea" in connection with the crossing from Ogygia to Scheria (*Odyssey* 5.174). Moreover, Ulysses addresses Polyphemus: "We are Achaeans who, after leaving Troy, were sent off course / by all the winds on the immense abyss of the sea [*méga laîtma thalásses*]" (*Odyssey* 9.259–60). He also speaks to "the mast of a black, large merchant ship / with twenty oarsmen, which crosses the immense abyss" (*Odyssey* 9.322–23). Interestingly, many years later the Vikings crossed the Atlantic with their *knorr*, wide ships suitable for sailing the ocean.

Actually, Plutarch's information on the geography of the Atlantic Ocean and the continent beyond the sea turns out to be exact. It follows that the author drew from well-informed sources, unknown to us now, that referred to what must have been an extremely ancient tradition, for when the Homeric poems were composed, the decline of the climatic optimum had made it virtually impossible to make the voyage to Ogygia—"the fearful immense / abyss of the sea, not even well balanced ships / go through it" (*Odyssey* 5.174–76). By the time Plutarch wrote, the North Atlantic route had been abandoned. Its memory, however, remains in Heracles' mythical feats, which are often set in the far west, and in an enigmatic passage from Seneca's *Medea*:

In the future a time will come
when the Ocean will unfasten its seals;
an immense continent will appear;
Tethys will uncover new worlds,
and Thule* will not be any longer the last land.

In addition to alluding to a continent overseas, Plutarch's "De facie quae in orbe lunae apparet" "inspired both Copernicus and Isaac Newton," according to Giorgio de Santillana in *The Origins of Scientific Thought*. "There Copernicus found the mention of Aristarchus's heliocentric system, and Newton, who had read this dialogue in his adolescence, found the first allusion to the gravity force."[11] If the theory expounded here is finally verified, the revolutions in thought inspired by the "De facie" will number three.

Mysterious Guidance

A puzzling claim made by Alcinous, king of the Phaeacians, to Ulysses may contain a clue regarding a tool that made such long ocean journeys possible:

Tell me who your country, your people, your city are,
so that our ships guided by a mind [tityskómenai phresí] take you
    there.
. . . Our ships know the thoughts and minds of men,
they know the cities and rich fields of all
people, and sail across the abyss of the sea very fast,
shrouded in fog and cloud [eéri kaí nephélei kekalymménai]. They
    never
are afraid of suffering damage or getting lost. (Odyssey 8.555–63)

Initially, we might think that the poet is dealing with a fairy tale or myth—one that vaguely recalls the fabulous ships found in Celtic legends. Yet if we prune the poetic amplifications from these lines, they seem to hint at a "mind" that points out the way and pilots Phaeacian ships in the fog. The word *phresí*—that is, the "mind" that guides the ships—has a complex meaning, including "diaphragm" and "heart" (its

---

*Thule was a name used by ancient Greek and Roman writers to refer to a land (probably Iceland) in the northernmost part of the habitable ancient world.

root is linked with the Sanskrit word *bhurati,* meaning "to move" or "to stir").[12] It seems very possible that what the poet is actually referring to is a sort of compass, a secret of the Phaeacians. Only ships equipped with this object—which the archaic mentality would have considered magic or, better still, animate, due to the pendular movement of the magnetic needle that invariably returns to pointing north—would sail under conditions of very poor visibility, as the words "shrouded in fog and cloud" suggest.

In an even more vague and elliptical way, the poet seems to refer to this "mind" again when he describes how the Phaeacians "relying on their quick, fast ships / cross the immense abyss . . . / Their ships are as fast as the wing and thought [*nóema*]" (*Odyssey* 7.34–36). Recalling that the Chinese used the compass in very ancient times, we can envision those "famous seafarers," the Phaeacians, venturing across the "immense abyss" *(méga laîtma)* of the Atlantic Ocean, guided by a primitive compass.

ATLANTIS

In the *Timaeus,* Plato refers not only to a continent beyond the Atlantic but also to mythical Atlantis. The existence and whereabouts of this island—which was supposed to have sunk into the Atlantic ages ago—can now be addressed in the context of the Baltic location of the primitive Achaean world. This may help to explain a problematic passage in which Plato refers to Atlantis as an "island" *(nêsos)* rather than a continent, yet states that it is "larger than Libya and Asia put together."[13]

Misunderstanding this latter statement creates uncertainty about the island's real size and the credibility of its existence as a whole, especially considering modern knowledge regarding geophysics, the origin of the continents, and continental drift.

It is important here to understand how the ancient Greeks typically indicated the size of islands. We are aided in this by a passage by Diodorus Siculus that indicates the "size" of what today is Great Britain: "The shortest side is 7,500 stadia long, facing Europe; the second side goes from the Channel to the top of a triangle and is 15,000 stadia long; the last is 20,000 stadia long. Therefore, the island's perimeter is 42,500 stadia."[14] (A stadium is equivalent to roughly 600 feet.) For ancient seafaring peoples, the "size" of an island was the *length* of its coastal perimeter, which is roughly assessable by circumnavigating it. This was the method adopted by Christopher Columbus in his journeys, as we can see, for example, in his letter to Luis de Santangel. On this subject, Luigi de Anna, professor of Italian literature at the University of Turku, in Finland, says: "When Columbus states that the island of Juana is 'wider' he is referring to the coast perimeter, not to the area. We find this practice, that is normal for Columbus, also in other passages of his texts."[15] For us, however, the concept of any territorial area concerns its *surface* area (the measurement of which requires much more sophisticated survey methods). This difference has often misled people to think that Atlantis was not an island, as Plato clearly states, but a continent. In short, Plato (or rather his source), expressing the breadth of Atlantis, compares its *perimeter* (not its *area*) to Asia Minor and Libya's coastal length—the latter presumably constituting part of the North African coast, unless Plato's source was referring to their northern counterparts—which, put together, must have formed a route that was very familiar to the ancient Greeks.

Following Plato's very coherent indications, then, we discover that Atlantis was definitely not a continent, but instead a broad island that lay "in front of the Pillars of Hercules," which we have now situated in the North Atlantic Ocean. This could be the key to its location and to its link to primordial Athens, which, as we have seen, lay on the southern coast of Sweden.

Pia Laviosa Zambotti reports that an island probably existed in the North Sea between the British Isles and Denmark during the megalithic period,[16]and that in even more distant times, during the Joldia Period, there was a large island in the Baltic that included present-day Bornholm, the Danish Islands, and Scania.[17] (Incidentally, some scholars compare the Atlantean civilization to the megalithic civilizations of northwestern Europe.) In any case, it is clear that due to several floods and geophysical events during the last ice age, vast northern lands were submerged, including this island in the North Sea.

The idea of a lost northern island fits with another precise piece of information given by Plato, that the Atlanteans ruled a region known as Gadiric (Gadeiriké, from the name Gadirus—that is, brother of Atlas)[18] on Europe's continent, facing Atlantis. It is interesting to compare this name with the present-day territory of Agder, in southern Norway on the North Sea. (Gadiric may also correspond to the Homeric Cythera, whose southern counterpart can be found in the area of Cadiz, at the tip of the Iberian Peninsula.) Recall that southern Norway is also where we have located Phaeacia, whose characteristics, described in the *Odyssey*, are reminiscent of those that Plato ascribes to Atlantis: the Phaeacian people's call to seafaring, along with their lineage from Poseidon; the features of Alcinous's palace (walls covered with metal and two springs in the garden); Alcinous's relationship with his wife (who was his brother's daughter);* and so on. It follows that the myth of the sunken island in the Atlantic could be less fantastic than many people have believed.

It is also significant that both Plato and the *Iliad* mention the sacrifice of a bull dedicated to Helikonian Poseidon (*Iliad* 20.403–404), a practice not at all characteristic of the Homeric Achaeans, who usually sacrificed cows or heifers, but quite typical of the Phaeacians, who "sacrificed twelve choice bulls to Poseidon" (*Odyssey* 13.181). There is a significant parallel to this in the passage from Plato's *Critias* in which the sacrifice of a bull takes place in Poseidon's shrine in Atlantis,[19] and interestingly, the *Iliad* mentions a shrine dedicated to Poseidon in a place called Helike (8.203), which is probably identifiable with today's Heligoland, a Frisian island. This squares with Jurgen Spanuth's locating of Atlantis in the North Sea, which he explains in his *Atlantis of the North*. It is amazing that Spanuth comes to the conclusion that Atlantis lay in the area of Heligoland without taking into account its resemblance to Helike or the sacrifice of the bull described in the *Iliad*.†

The puzzling "elephants" that, according to Plato's *Critias*, lived in Atlantis could have represented the last memory of the woolly mammoths that lived in an Arctic land in a very distant past. According to recent reports, remains of mammoths that date back to 1700 B.C.E. were found on the Siberian island of Wrangel. From this finding we might assume that the end of the climatic optimum also caused the extinction of the last mammoths.

The myth of Atlantis probably conceals an even more ancient substratum: the memory of yet another former homeland perhaps located on an Arctic island (one of the Spitsbergen?), where mammoths may still

---

* We have already seen that incest was practiced in the family of Aeolus, the king of an island likely belonging to the Shetlands and thus lying near Norway.

† It is worth noting that, apart from the Phaeacians, the Celts also practiced a sacrifice of bulls, which was an important element of their rituals. We might surmise that the traditional Spanish bullfight, the *corrida*, originated from the practices of the Celtiberians, a Celtic population that settled on the Iberian Peninsula during the Iron Age.

have lived—and this may have been the original country of the Atlanteans before they settled in Heligoland's area. The overlapping of these two layers of myth and location could explain many of the puzzles in Plato's tale.

ETHIOPIA

The identification of the River Ocean as the Gulf Stream gives us a clue regarding another mystery of Homeric geography that caused Strabo and other scholars to labor in vain: the location of the Ethiopians, who are mentioned in both the *Iliad* and the *Odyssey*. According to Homer, the route to Ethiopia is always via the Ocean. Considering this and the fact that the Suez Canal was not in existence then, we must conclude that he is not referring to present-day Ethiopia.

In the *Iliad,* the gods' messenger, Iris, flies "to Ocean's stream / and Ethiopians' land, where they are making a hecatomb / to the gods" (*Iliad* 23.205–207). The beginning of the *Odyssey* at first seems to give more precise information, but it turns out to be just as cryptic: "[Poseidon]went to the Ethiopians living far off, / the Ethiopians divided into two, most distant of men [*éschatoi andrôn*], / the ones of the setting Hyperion and the ones of the rising" (*Odyssey* 1.22–24). While the god Poseidon is on his way back from the land of the Ethiopians, he spots Ulysses from the Solymi Mountains, as the hero sails toward the Phaeacian land. Here is a piece of information we may use, for the identification of Phaeacia with Norway's coastline considerably narrows our focus to the area of northern Scandinavia.

After noting that the expression "most distant of men" fits in very well with the Ethiopians' relationship with the Ocean "at the ends of the earth," let us follow the Gulf Stream's (River Ocean's) northernmost branch: It flows along the Norwegian coastline until it enters the Barents Sea. After North Cape, it reaches the farthest cape of the Nordkyn peninsula. Farther on, Tanafjorden opens out, after which the coast begins to turn southward. It seems, then, that the *Odyssey* locates the home of the Homeric Ethiopians, "most distant of men," in this area, at the ends of Europe (in the Mediterranean context, they were located beyond Egypt, once again at the "ends of the earth").

The Nordkyn peninsula is almost a polygon-shaped island. Only a very thin isthmus at the midpoint of its southern side links it to the mainland. Two fjords begin at this isthmus, going in opposite directions. Both the northern position and the peculiar shape of this peninsula seem to reflect Homer's lines. During the height of the climatic optimum, forty-five hundred years ago, these extreme parts of the European continent were habitable. If people were therefore living around this isthmus—on the border of the two fjords, facing west and east, respectively—they might conceivably have been described as "divided into two [*dichthá dedaíatai*], most distant of men, / the ones of the setting Hyperion and the ones of the rising" (*Odyssey* 1.23–24). We have already noted that in the *Iliad* the Hyperion is mentioned in connection with "the farthest borders / of the earth and the sea" (*Iliad* 8.478–79). Thus we can imagine that during the unending arctic summer days, the two groups of people watched the shining of the Hyperion, the midnight sun, from opposite sides of the isthmus.

The name of the Ethiopians seems to lead back to the root of the verb *aíthein*, "to burn," "to blaze." The name Ethiopian, then, could mean "those of the flame." An explicit reference to a fire cult is contained in this definition, which fits with their connection to the sun and the northern location of the forge of Hephaestus, god of fire par excellence.

The Arctic location of Ethiopia is corroborated by references in Greek mythology, such as the myth of Perseus: Immediately after beheading the Gorgon Medusa in the land of the Hyperboreans (mythical people of the north), Perseus reaches Ethiopia, where he rescues Andromeda by killing the monster that threatens her with death. Considering that this episode directly follows his Hyperborean adventure, an Arctic location for Ethiopia makes much more sense than an African one.

Interestingly, there are parallels between Perseus's myth and stories found in the *Kalevala* (Finland's national epos), such as the adventure, in Rune 31, of the royal baby Kullervus: His uncle shuts him up in a barrel and throws him overboard in the vain attempt to get rid of him, much like the infant Perseus is cast into the sea in a wooden ark. Additionally, the name Perseus is similar to that of Perse, Circe's mother, who lives on an Arctic island. In short, the whole picture—including the many typically shamanistic motifs in the Perseus myth: Medusa's hair of snakes, the mirror Perseus uses in beheading her, and Perseus's winged horse—seem to suggest a remote Arctic world, steeped in shamanistic and solar motifs, that most likely preceded that of the Homeric poems.

As usual, there are place-name parallels that support this conclusion: The names Perseus and Perse seem to recall the Porsangerfjord, a fjord that lies directly after North Cape. And the name Tana, as in Lake Tana, the source of the Blue Nile situated in present-day Ethiopia, is found in the

Tanafjorden, almost contiguous with the Porsangerfjord, which hints even more at the possibility of a relationship existing between Homer's Arctic Ethiopia and the African Ethiopia. This certainly suggests some theories with regard to the search for the Indo-Europeans' primordial home, a subject we shall soon address. Both the *Iliad* and the *Odyssey* also ascribe to the Ethiopians a particularly close relationship with the gods: "Zeus left for the Ocean yesterday / for a banquet with the noble Ethiopians. All the gods followed him" (*Iliad* 1.423–24). This leads us next to look nearby for Olympus, the famous "home of the gods."

OLYMPUS AND PIERIA

Blue-eyed Athena headed
for Olympus, where people say that the Gods' everlasting home
   stands.
Winds never shake it, and there is never rain,
nor is it ever touched by snow, but the sky
opens cloudless, the light spreads white;
the blessed gods enjoy themselves uninterruptedly.
   (*Odyssey* 6.41–46)

From this passage of the *Odyssey* we can clearly sense that Olympus, completely idealized here, lies somewhere "out of this world." The *Odyssey* mentions Olympus only twenty times, though the *Iliad* refers to it much more often, almost ninety times, indicating perhaps that it lay closer to the setting of the latter poem, toward the north of the Baltic area.

From the various passages of Homer mentioning this home of the gods, we can deduce that it was not a single mountain. In the *Iliad,* in which Olympus is described as "great," "shining," "snowy," and "with many valleys," there is a recurring line that corroborates this notion of the place as multiple mountains: "On the highest top of Olympus with many peaks [*polydeirádos*] (*Iliad* 1.499, 5.754, 8.3). In other words, the name Olympus, like Ida, indicates a mountainous *region* rather than a single mountain.

We find more information about the Homeric Olympus in certain passages referring to what seems like a specific route leading from the gods' home to the world of mortals. The *Iliad* narrates that Hera leaves Olympus and goes down to Pieria and "lovely Emathia." From there she heads for Thrace and then "traveled across the foamy sea from Athos / and reached Lemnos" (*Iliad* 14.229–30). Similarly, the *Odyssey* states that Hermes leaves Olympus and makes his way to the island of Ogygia, "flying down to Pieria he jumped from the sky above the sea" (*Odyssey* 5.50). Both passages, then, refer to Pieria (Pieríe or Pereíe) as the first stop on a journey starting from Olympus.

This is the key to the location of Olympus, given that Pieria is linked with the Peraebians, the Achaean people mentioned penultimately in the Catalog of Ships (*Iliad* 2.749). They live on the Finnish side of the Gulf of Bothnia, near its northernmost point, which fits with the passage of the *Iliad* in which Pieria is linked to Pherae, the city of King Eumelus: "The best horses belonged to Pheretides, / and Eumelus drove them; . . . / Apollo of the Silver Arrow had bred them in Pieria" (*Iliad* 2.763–64, 766). The presence of Apollo in Pieria is another sign of its proximity to the Olympian home of the gods.

Bearing in mind that the catalog locates Pherae near Iolcus, the modern-day Finnish Jolkka (*Iliad* 2.711–12), and that the Centaurs, who lived in the same area, were also called Pherians, we can deduce that the Homeric Pieria probably lay in the hinterland of the Finnish side of the Gulf of Bothnia, toward Lapland. (Interestingly, in Finnish the Gulf of Bothnia is known as Perämeri.) Therefore, we might look for the region of Olympus in this area.

According to Homer, the Peraebians lived near the river Titaresius (*Iliad* 2.751), which was "an effluent of the waters of the Styx" (*Iliad* 2.755), the river the gods swear upon in the most solemn oaths. In chapter 4 we discovered that in Ulysses' voyage to Hades, the "waters of the Styx" correspond to northern Finland's Lake Kitka and Lake Livojärvi, which are found roughly midway between the northern end of the Gulf of Bothnia and the coast of the White Sea. We also verified that the Homeric Titaresius coincides with today's Livojoki River. To this we add that, according to the *Iliad*, Zeus's priests, known as the Selli (*Iliad* 16.234), live near the Peraebian city of Dodona (*Iliad* 2.750). It seems reasonable, then, to link the name Selli to the modern town called Salla, which is found only a little farther north of Lake Kitka. Similarly, the name of the town of Perälä in the same area could be compared to the Peraebians as well as to Pieria.

To this collage we can add a passage from the *Odyssey* that narrates a presumably very ancient myth concerning the attack launched by two giants, Otus and Ephialtes, against the home of the gods: "They threatened the Immortals / to start a terrible battle on Olympus. / They planned to place Ossa on Olympus, then on Ossa / leafy Pelion, and climb the sky" (*Odyssey* 11.313–16). In this passage, Olympus is described as a single peak, which might mean that it was the highest in the group. As we have seen, Mount Pelion, the mountain of the Centaurs, can be likened to present-day Mount Paljakka in northern Finland. Robert Graves compares this tale of Otus and Ephialtes with a Hurrite one in which two godlike brothers attack Mount Hazzy (virtually identical to Ossa). Significantly, in the area we have identified with Pieria, close to the Russian border, there is a place-name Hossa, which sounds similar to the name of both Homeric Ossa and Hurrite Hazzy.

In short, a collection of congruent data enables us to locate the area of Olympus "with many peaks" in a mountainous region between Lapland and Karelia, near the border between Russia and Finland (see fig. 4.3, page 72). The place-names Pyhätunturi (Sacred Mountain) and Pyhäjoki (Sacred River), found a little farther northwest, seem to confirm the sacral nature of this territory. Here the name Pallastunturi (so like Mount Pallas) has preserved the most important appellative of Athena, the preeminent Achaean goddess. In this region we come across the Greek name for the gods' mythical home, Oúlympos,* almost entirely unchanged. Here the Oulankajoki (Oulanka River) flows toward the Russian border, almost at the latitude of the Arctic Circle, in a mountainous area where we also find the town of Oulanka and the large Finnish national park known as Oulangan Kansallispuisto.

Having established all of this evidence, it is easy now to reconstruct Hera's route from Olympus to Lemnos, passing through Pieria, Emathia, and Thrace. She leaves from the Oulankajoki area, goes down through Lapland (Pieria), then travels along the Gulf of Bothnia's western side from north to south (Emathia and Thracia), and finally cuts across the sea toward Lemland. This serves to confirm the Swedish location of the Homeric Thrace, where, according to the *Younger Edda*, the god Thor lived. It is exactly where we previously located it: along the Gulf of Bothnia's southwestern coast and its hinterland. This also enables us to locate Emathia (*Iliad* 14.226)—which has been identified with a part of Macedonia in the Mediterranean context—in the coastal plain that borders the northwestern side of the Gulf of Bothnia. There is a river known as the Ume in this area of Sweden, which could bring to mind the name of "lovely Emathia."

---

* As to the relationship between Oúlympos and Oulanka, interchanges between *p* and *k* are very common in Greek dialects: There is, for instance, *poû* and *koû* (where) or *póte* and *kóte* (when).

Olympus thus stood far from the Achaean settlements around the Baltic, somewhat remote from the human world, with the region of the Peraebians being the point of the gods' contact.

In this Finnish area, a geographic picture has emerged that, with its rich details, is consistent with what Greek mythology has handed down to us. At this point, we can presume that the Baltic peoples of the Early Bronze Age still had memories of a civilization that flourished in northern Scandinavia in a former epoch, when the climatic optimum was at its peak. This presumption is supported by traces of extremely ancient human settlements found in Finnmark (the northernmost region of Norway). These include specifically the rock carvings of Alta, dating back to the Stone Age. The traditions of many Indo-European peoples seem to testify to a similar memory of a previous Arctic civilization, a topic that we shall explore in detail in chapter 14.

This theory of the cultural memory of a still more ancient civilization could explain why Homer often uses two different names—one given by men and the other by the gods—for the same object or place. The most famous case is the river that "the gods call Xanthus and men Scamander" (*Iliad* 20.74), but we can also note "the giant with a hundred hands / whom the gods call Briareus, but men Aegaeon" (*Iliad* 1.404–405) and "the songbird on the mountains which / the gods call Chalkis, but men Cymindis" (*Iliad* 14.290–91). This suggests that the "language of the gods" referred to an extremely ancient traditional formulary that may have included even magic and religious hymns.

This points to an broader consideration: It is difficult to believe that elaborate and complex works like those of Homer appeared out of nowhere, from a poetic and cultural desert. If both poems originated in the Greek world around the eighth century B.C.E., it is extremely unlikely that they emerged from an absence of any literary background. To the contrary, they seem to be the highest achievement of a poetic tradition that developed over a long period of time but which may well have been lost after the migration from the north. Remains of this tradition are perhaps found in some passages of the *Homeric Hymns*—a collection of poems of different origins ascribed to Homer—and in ancient Indian literature, but most of it is hidden behind the immense mythological corpus from which all Greek writers, from Hesiod onward, drew their inspiration.

This hypothetical primordial northern civilization reached a significant level of development, as we can deduce from the description of Hephaestus's extraordinary "automated" smithy on Mount Olympus:

He went back to the bellows,
turned them to the fire and set them in action.
All twenty bellows blew on the furnaces
emitting a modulated kindling puff [pantoíen eúpreston aütmén],
now fit for quickening, now for the opposite,
according to Hephaestus's purpose and the progress of the work.
     (*Iliad* 18.468–73)

The astounding sophistication of this process is also marked in the products Hephaestus is working on:

He was making twenty tripods
to place around the walls of the fine hall:
he was fitting golden wheels under their bases,
so that they by themselves could enter [autómatoi dysaíato] the
          gods' meetings,
then return home. It's wonderful to look at! (*Iliad* 18.373–77)

And the description of the two "robots" working in his laboratory is even more astonishing: "Two golden maids . . . , / looking like living girls, / had a mind in their breasts [nóos metá phresín], they had voice / and strength" (*Iliad* 18.417–20).

All of this seems more remarkable still when we compare it to the almost cinematic, vivid realism in the description of Hephaestus as he prepares to meet Thetis, Achilles' mother, who has come to his workshop to ask for new armor for her son:

He moved the bellows away from the fire,
and collected all tools he had worked with into a silver case;
then with a sponge he dried his face, his hands,
his sturdy neck and hairy chest,
he put on his tunic, took his big stick, and limped out
of the door. (*Iliad* 18.412–17)

We should also note Hephaestus's similarity to Ilmarinen, the mythical smith from the Finnish *Kalevala*. He lives in Karelia,[20] where he forges a wife of gold and silver[21] who is similar to the creations of his Homeric counterpart.

Mountain Copper

Another link between Homer's world and a far northern civilization can be found in a mysterious metal known as *orichalcum,* upon which Plato dwells in his *Critias* when he describes the wealth of the sunken island of Atlantis. As a matter of fact, he writes that among its resources, there were

> . . . all kinds of hard and malleable metals that can be mined. First of all, there was the metal of which we know only the name today, "Orichalcum," but which in those days really existed; it was mined in several parts of the island and was the most precious of all metals at that time, after gold.[22]

This passage tells us that orichalcum was not an alloy, as some scholars have supposed, but rather a precious metal, which is evident from examples of Greek literature other than the *Critias:* In the *Second Homeric Hymn to Aphrodite,* the earrings on the goddess's statue are of "precious orichalcum and gold flowers,"[23] which corroborates the idea that this was a noble metal, comparable in value to gold. Furthermore, Hesiod's *Shield of Hercules* mentions "orichalcum greaves." Incidentally, the use of precious metals for greaves (leg armor) is also found in the *Iliad:* Before the two-day battle, Agamemnon dons his armor: "First he put on his beautiful greaves / fitted with silver ankle bands" (11.17–18). Achilles and Patroclus have similar armor (16.132), and those Hephaestus fashions for Achilles are made of tin (18.612), which, in those days, was considered a precious metal.

In identifying orichalcum, we should bear in mind that in the ancient classical world, gold and silver were the only precious metals known. Platinum—the main deposits of which are found in the Ural Mountains, Alaska, and South America—was unknown in Europe until Antonio De Ulloa discovered it in 1735 in Colombian drifts, although some pre-Columbian peoples knew of the metal and worked it. Because orichalcum was not an alloy but a real metal, and all the existing metals are included in Mendeleev's Periodic Table of Elements, it follows that it may be one and the same with today's platinum, which, along with gold, is still the most precious metal. We note that the word *orichalcum (oreíchalchos)* means "mountain copper," which further corroborates its nature and origin. Used in these ancient times, it must have been extracted in the Ural Mountains, the first mountainous region beyond the immense Russian plain and within traveling distance from the flat Baltic region.

The primitive location of the Achaeans in the Baltic explains why the Greek world had a hazy memory of this metal. Although the distance from the Baltic area to the nearest deposits in the Urals was not exactly short, almost a thousand miles, this probably did not prevent the trade of orichalcum until the decline of the climatic optimum made such trade impossible. (Even in the days of the Trojan War, contacts with the Urals had probably been cut off.) This would explain both Homer's silence on this subject and the persistence of its memory, however feeble, in the Greek world.

THE MOON OF HERMES

In one of the *Homeric Hymns,* we find another indication that the Homeric Pieria lay in what is now Lapland and that the original Achaean homeland was situated at very northern latitudes. The *Homeric Hymn to Hermes* tells of the birth of the god Hermes in a dark cave and of his first nocturnal feat. On the fourth day of the lunar month, toward the end of night, the newborn baby goes to Pieria and, in the moonlight, steals fifty cattle from Apollo's herd.

Scholars have deemed this tale impossible from an astronomical point of view. For instance, Carl Robert (quoted by Jean Humbert in the preface to a French edition of the *Homeric Hymns*) remarks that "on the fourth day of the lunar month, the divine Selene* certainly does not shine when the end of the night approaches. Her crescent, which is still very slight, disappears very quickly beneath the horizon and only casts a very dim light."[24]

Beyond the Arctic Circle, however, the phases of the moon have a very different appearance from those in more southern regions. Were we exactly at the North Pole during the winter solstice, we would be able to watch the moon shine uninterrupted for fourteen days. The moon rises when it is at the end of its first quarter—that is, when it is a half circle—and starts to trace a trajectory above the horizon without setting, waxing and rising up in the solstice night along a spiral path

---

* The moon, known as Selene, is the daughter of a mysterious "king" *(ánax)* called Pallas (*Hercules' Shield* 122), whose name corresponds to that of the mountain known as Pallastunturi, Mount Pallas, located in Finnish Lapland.

until it reaches its maximum height and complete fullness a week later. After this, it starts to wane and descend toward the horizon, describing again a spiral trajectory, until it sets at the end of the following week. (To simplify, we have ignored Earth's motion around the sun and the angle of the plane of the moon orbit with the ecliptic.)

This phenomenon is verified at other points within the Arctic Circle, although it becomes less marked as we move farther away from the North Pole. At this point, if we consider that the myth of Hermes stealing from Apollo's herd is set in Pieria—that is, in northern Finland, where we find the name of the Lapp god Tiermes, which sounds quite similar to Hermes*—the astronomical anomaly of the *Hymn to Hermes* is easily explained. The new moon in the fourth day of its cycle actually shines in the darkness of the solstice night, lighting up with its arcane radiance the plain from which Hermes steals the cows and creating an unreal arctic landscape: "(Hermes) . . . put out the embers and covered the black cinders with sand / in the last hours of the night; Selene's beautiful light was shining up above [*kalón dé phóos epélampe Selénes*]."[25]

This extraordinary literary fossil that preserves the image of the moon shining through the Arctic night certifies the Achaean presence in

---

*The comparison with Tiermes gives us a clue to understanding the origin of the god Hermes and the meaning of his name, which has always puzzled scholars. The name Tiermes is rather similar to the Greek adjective *thermós* (with the same root as the sanskrit *gharma*), meaning "hot" or "burning." Hermes, it is told, "experimented with the art of fire" (*Homeric Hymn to Hermes* 1.108) and "was the first to produce fire and the means to light it" (1.111). Thus Hermes is a very ancient god of fire. This idea is corroborated by the fact that he is mentioned with Hestia in the Homeric hymn dedicated to that goddess of the home hearth (as opposed to Hermes, who is the fire of shepherds and thieves—that is, the outside fire of nighttime bivouacs). It follows, then, that he is also the lord of both domestic and wild animals (*Homeric Hymn to Hermes* ll.569–71): Fire protects the former and turns away the latter during the night. It makes sense, too, that he is a musician god, because shepherds play their instruments around the fire. Hermes also produces noise (*Homeric Hymn to Hermes* 1.295), as a crackling bivouac fire does, while he is in the arms of his elder brother, Apollo, the sun god whose light and heat are silent. It is also very likely that this very archaic fire god, like Prometheus, was initially connected to lightning, which can produce fire when it strikes trees. It is not mere chance that the name Hermes can be compared to *chérma* ("stone," with reference to flint, from which fire arises via sparks similar to lightning) and *chermádion*, the stone ax made of flint which in Denmark is called the "thunderstone." We should note that the Lapp Tiermes is a thunder god, and thunder is clearly connected to lightning (another reason, perhaps, why Hermes is considered "noisy"). Thunder and lightning were considered the gods' omens—and the Homeric Hermes is the messenger of the gods.

the far north thousands of years ago. It has miraculously survived for dozens of centuries, perhaps much like the Pyramids have, remaining intact through the vicissitudes of human history. The world in this myth seems much more archaic than the one described in the *Iliad*. The northern, or, better still, hyperborean atmosphere pervading Greek mythology has never been so clearly manifest as it is here.

What is more, the characters in the *Hymn to Hermes* demonstrate many solar characteristics that link them to an archaic shamanistic tradition that has been preserved in Greek as well as other Indo-European mythologies. Hermes is perhaps the newborn sun who comes into the world in a "dark cave" during the solstice night. There are similar myths in Indian mythology telling of a missing child *(kumara)* who is the sun god—that is, Agni or Surya. In these tales the child is sometimes thrown into the sea in a chest, just like the Greek Perseus and the Finnish Kullervo—and like Romulus and Moses. Apollo, the solar god par excellence, is the adult sun. Likewise, the figure of the Old Man *(géron)*—the old year and the old sun—appears in the *Hymn* as well.[26] Perhaps his last echo has reached us, after many transformations, in the figure of Santa Claus.

The cows Hermes steals from Apollo are far from incidental in the story. They can be best understood in the context of the sun god's cows in the *Odyssey* whose slaughter brought a dreadful fate to Ulysses' companions. It is easy to infer, then, that Hermes' rustling of fifty of Apollo's cows symbolizes the loss of days in the solstice darkness. (We should also remember that in the original Vedic civilization, according to Tilak, cows symbolized the days of the arctic year.) We can add to this interpretation the threats of the sun god after Ulysses' men slaughter his cows: "I will go down to Hades and give my light to the dead men" (*Odyssey* 12.383). Both of these cow thievings can be seen as references to an Arctic primordial calendar in which the solar cycle, represented by Apollo, consisted of ten moons per year, given that the solstice darkness concealed the last two. These correspond to the fifty cows that are stolen from Apollo, who is represented as a cowherd in a passage from the *Iliad* (21.448).

Likewise, the number of double axes, which symbolize the moon's double waxing and waning during the month's cycle, is significant in two incidents in the *Odyssey* and the *Iliad*. In the *Odyssey* the twelve axes in the archery competition correspond to the twelve months of the year, while ten axes instead of twelve are mentioned in the archery competition in the *Iliad* (23.851). Considering that in both the *Iliad* and the *Odyssey* the poet emphasizes that the competition is under Apollo's patronage—the winner has "promised Apollo the Archer / a splendid hecatomb of lambs"(*Iliad* 23.872–73)—the fact that there are only ten double axes *(pelékeas)* may signify that the *Iliad*'s Achaeans retain the memory of an Arctic primordial calendar.

This extremely ancient system, which corresponds to the ten ax moons in the *Iliad,* has remained "fossilized" in the names of the last four months of the Roman calendar we use today: from September—that is, the seventh month (from the Latin *septem,* "seven")—to December, the tenth month (*decem* means "ten" in Latin).

In short, by returning the events narrated in Greek mythology to their original geographic context, we can find the consistent remains of a conceptual and symbolic system based on complex astronomical-theological thought that is much more ancient than the Homeric world. This primordial Arctic Indo-European civilization most probably died out because of the beginning of the decline of the climatic optimum, which likely had the strongest effect on the Arctic regions. Obliged to leave their northern home, they established cultures farther south, settling along the Baltic shores. Here they continued to preserve the idealized memory of their ancestors' paradisal land, now changed by ice into the land of the dead. After the climatic reached its end altogether, the Achaeans migrated even farther south and, having reached the warm Aegean basin, gave birth to the Mycenaean culture that retained some distant memory of the ancient gods and its hyperborean origin.

The explorations in this chapter have led us to the extreme borders of the Homeric world and have thus enriched the frame of the picture we have drawn up to now. We could conclude our work here, but as we have seen, the relocation of the Homeric poems from the Mediterranean to the Baltic cannot be considered merely a geographical change; it also opens new, unexpected hermeneutic horizons with particular reference to the fields of cultural anthropology and comparative religion. From the clues in these poems and in the immense mythological literature of the entire world—even though they cannot be considered decisive evidence—we can find traces everywhere left by primitive Indo-Europeans.

CHAPTER 14

CLIMATE CHANGE AND THE MIGRATION OF CULTURE

THE ORIGINAL HOMELAND OF THE INDO-EUROPEANS

As we have seen, the northern location of the Homeric world not only corroborates the northern origin of the Mycenaeans (as claimed by Professor Nilsson in his consideration of the archaeological evidence found at Mycenaean sites in Greece), but also lends credence to the hypothesis of a remote Indo-European civilization at very high latitudes. The connection between northern cultures and the climatic optimum and its collapse that we have explored sheds light on the age-old question of the original homeland of the peoples belonging to the Indo-European family, as well as the cause that spurred them to move to warmer lands.

Our findings here both support and are supported by the theories put forward by the Hindu scholar Bâl Gangâdhar Tilak regarding the original Arctic home of the Aryans. Tilak's two learned books, *The Arctic Home in the Vedas* and *The Orion, or Researches into the Antiquity of the Vedas*, dating from the end of the nineteenth century, have not been as well known and appreciated as they deserve to be. In *The Arctic Home in the Vedas*, Tilak expounds on the theory that the Aryans, "cousins" of the Achaeans, originally came from an Arctic region. His theory centers on the fact that the Vedas—that is, the most ancient collection of hymns in Hindu literature—show traces of a calendar typical of the Arctic regions, which includes winter darkness and the midnight sun.

In *The Orion*, using various astronomical references, Tilak shows that the Vedic hymns date back to a well-defined period when the rising of the sun at the spring equinox (which at that time was considered the beginning of the new year) corresponded to Orion's constellation. This phenomenon occurred every year from about 4000 to 2500 B.C.E. (the "Orionic period"). This configuration later changed due to the precessional motion of Earth's axis.

In short, Tilak's books—one from the geographic point of view, the other chronological—allow us to form an opinion about the location in both space and time of the original civilization that produced the Vedic hymns prior to its movement south to India, which took place more or less at the same time as the migration of the Achaeans to Greece (around the seventeenth century B.C.E. The fact that the Aryans' language was similar not only to Greek but also to Germanic and Celtic languages (and to Lithuanian!) finds accord with what has previously emerged regarding the northern origin of the Achaeans.

Significantly, the Orionic period preceded the Indo-European migration and, by a surprising coincidence, chronologically overlapped the peak of the climatic optimum, which provided acceptable living conditions even at the highest latitudes. Tilak could not, however, draw the obvious conclusion from his studies—that the original Aryan civilization flourished in an Arctic land during the Orionic period—because he was unaware of the climatic optimum. Thus, he was obliged to backdate that civilization to an unlikely very distant past, even preceding the last ice age.

Interestingly, several place-names found in the Norwegian area of the Vesterålen (where we have located the enchanted islands of Circe and Aeetes), and the lands facing them on the border between Norway and northern Sweden, seem to recall the Aryans. In the Vesterålen, the islands Hinnøya and Langøya, respectively, recall Hindi (in Hindu mythology, India was considered an island) and Lanka (the island to which Sita, heroine of the *Ramayana* epic, is carried after she is stolen from her bridegroom Rama). On the facing mainland are Lake Sitasjaure and the city of Ramsund. The roots of place-names such as Kaalas, Gangnesaksla, Vajsa, Kalixålven, Riksocokka, Jamnfjellet, and Arjeplog seem to correspond to well-known names in Indian civilization: the Kailasa (the sacred mountain of the Hindu paradise), the Ganges River, the Vasu (the eight beneficial gods of the elements), the goddess Kali (Kalixålven means the Kalix River), the seven Rikshi (the stars of the Bear), the Yamuna (a mythical river), and the Arjans, respectively. Burma, to the east of India, has a remarkable counterpart both lexically and geographically in Biarmia, the ancient name of a Russian region facing the White Sea to the east of Norway. The Suleiman Mountains of northwest India recall the Solymi Mountains mentioned by Homer in reference to Scheria, which we have located in Norway. Also in Norway, near Tromsö in the north, are two adjacent fjords known as Balsfjorden and Malangenfjorden, whose names have remained almost unchanged for more than four thousand years and nearly eight thousand miles: They can be likened to the names of the Indonesian island of Bali and the nearby Javanese town of Malang. Intriguingly, a mountain next to Malang is known as Mount Semeru (Semeru is synonomous with the name Meru), while six miles south of Malangenfjorden there stands a hill known as Sumarbakke (Sumar's Hill). Further, a branch of the Balsfjord named Ramfjorden recalls the name of the hero Rama.

It is in this area along the coast of northern Norway that the *Odyssey* locates the dreadful whirlpool of Charybdis, which we have already identified with the Maelstrom. Indian mythology retains a vestige of this feature in the myth of the whirling sea. (Mentioned in the *Mahabharata,* it is one of this system's most powerful tales.) In fact, it is difficult to understand this myth outside of its northern setting. Another Indian parallel to this part of Norway is the river Sarasvati, which "flows in the sea"—no doubt the branch of the Gulf Stream that runs along the Norwegian coast, making the climate of the Lofoten and Vesterålen Islands more habitable. This is, in short, the perfect counterpart to Homer's River Ocean.

There are other parallels, congruencies, and cross-references between northern Europe and the Aryan world that cannot be considered mere coincidences. In his *Prehistoric India*, Stuart Piggott writes:

> The entire structure of ancient Indian society and their way of waging war, to what we know of it from the most ancient Sanskrit tales, is remarkably similar to the heroic Irish tales . . . The Aryan war chariots in India were fundamentally the same as vehicles in other Indo-European areas in Mycenaean and Homeric Greece or in Celtic Great Britain.[1]

Indian literature mentions the Danavas, mythical enemies of the Aryans and perhaps analogous to the Homeric Danaans. Additionally, Greek mythology tells us that the Theban god Dionysus conquered "India." Now, Boeotian Thebes, found in today's Sweden, was near the Homeric

Thrace, which in turn was closely linked with Ares, the Homeric god of war, whose name recalls that of the Aryans. The name Thrace seems to echo Trakajit, another name of Kartikeya, the Hindu god of war. Kartikeya was also known as Skanda, which, on the one hand, is remarkably similar to the Homeric city of Scandaea (*Iliad* 10.268), and on the other, to Scandinavia itself.

Still concerning Thrace, we come across a similarly named village in Sweden, Trekilen. Here flows the river Indalsälven—that is, the river Indals, which sounds quite similar to the river Indus. We can infer, then, that the Homeric Thrace (also the home of the Norse god Thor, which extended along the western side of the Gulf of Bothnia) was a region interposed between the original Aryan world and the Achaean one, which lay to the north and the south of the Scandinavian peninsula, respectively.

It is also significant that Indian mythology mentions a land at "the ends of the earth," corresponding to the Homeric Ethiopia. In his introduction to *The Orion* by Tilak, Giuseppe Acerbi tells us that the *Mahabharata* calls it Uttarakuru, "the Utmost Land" or "the Utmost Region," known as Paradesha in Sanskrit, Pairidaeza in Iranian, Parádeisos in Greek, and Pardes in Hebraic. In his essay *Airyana Vaêjo: The Original Home of the Aryans,* Onorato Bucci writes: "In the Vedic tradition, Uttarakuru is the original homeland of the Vedic Aryans, instead of Airyana Vaêjo." Moreover,

> The Indo-Iranic sources speak of a solar cult in the country of Airyana Vaêjo, before the ice age arrived; the cult of Apollo, [which] came from the land of the Hyperboreans and, according to tradition, settled in Greece, is its amazing parallel. The Hyperboreans— who lived at the ends of the Ocean—are the counterpart of the Aryans, who themselves live in a country which is sunny for six months (or ten months, according to another version), with a mild climate and a night six months (or two months) long. Their main deity is the Sun god.[2]

As we have seen, we have found traces of the Ethiopians, "most distant of men," in Scandinavia's northernmost point, the Nordkyn peninsula, not far from the Varanger, which accords with Uttarakuru, the "Utmost Land" of the *Mahabharata*. If we also consider the location of Hades by the White Sea—where we find the very ancient rites common to Homer, the Vedas, and the ancient Roman world—the original homeland of the Indo-Europeans finally emerges from this converging information as an Arctic land that may at last be definitively identified on the map: It lay in the northernmost part of Scandinavia, the sort of "hat" atop the European continent that faces the Arctic Ocean and stretches from Lapland to the Vesterålen Islands and the Kola peninsula. The Porsanger, Nordkyn, and Varanger peninsulas, as well as the island of Mageröya and the Tanafjorden, are found at the top of this area. Five or six thousand years ago, when the constellation of Orion marked the spring equinox and the Dragon pointed out the North Pole, the primordial Indo-European civilization developed there, in the "islands in the north of the world"—from which came the mythical ancestors of the Celts—thanks to the most favorable climatic period ever experienced in the region.

We can assume that the climatic optimum affected not only northern Scandinavia, but also other regions situated around the Arctic Ocean, including the coasts of present-day Siberia, Alaska, Canada, and Greenland, not to mention countless adjacent islands. Today this area consists of millions of uninhabitable square miles, but up to four thousand or five thousand years ago, for thousands of years, it enjoyed environmental conditions that fostered human settlement. In that time, contacts by sea perhaps enabled this "Arctic Mediterranean Ocean" to develop a common civilization and maybe similar languages among its peoples, as the tale of the Tower of Babel—found in many mythologies, even in Polynesia—seems to suggest.

Greek mythology has preserved the memory of a happy primordial age before Homer's time, under the rule of Cronos, the god corresponding to the Latin Saturn and lord of the Golden Age. This mythical Age of Cronos matches the time frame Tilak identifies as the Orionic period, reflected in the fact that Orion's Greek name, Krónos, recalls the Sanskrit word Agrayana, which means "he who starts the year." Thus, the Age of Cronos was under the sign of Orion-Agrayana, which at that time marked the beginning of the year at the equinox. According to Tilak, another eloquent Hindu synonym for Orion was Prajâpati, "the god of time." It is not, then, sheer chance that the Greek word chrónos, "time," is found almost unchanged in the name of Krónos, whom the inexorable precessional motion of Earth's axis through the ages first enthroned, then ousted from the unique position held by Agrayana, "he who starts the year."

THE TWILIGHT OF THE GODS

Some time after the gradual precession of the axis concluded the Orionic period, the climatic optimum began to decline, putting an end to the happy Age of Cronos and the "kingdom of the gods." The *Younger Edda* provides us with this dramatic foretelling: "The Fimbulvetr [dreadful winter] will come, snow will fall whirling all over, there will be a terrible frost, ice and bitter winds, there will be no more Sun. Three uninterrupted winters will come at once without any summer in between."[3] These "uninterrupted winters" recall the cold summers of more recent times caused by great volcanic eruptions like the one in Tambora, Indonesia, in April 1815.

The memory of an ancient climatic collapse is actually found in the mythology of many peoples. The series of terrible winters that heralded the Ragnarok, the fateful "twilight of the gods" in Norse mythology, is mirrored by the destruction of Airyana Vaêjo, the Indo-European primordial paradise, due to snow and ice, as written in the Persian Avesta, a collection of the sacred writings of Zoroastrianism. In the Avesta, the god Ahura Mazda warns the first king of humankind, Yima, that his land will be destroyed by a series of icy winters lasting at least ten months of every year[4]—roughly equivalent to the present climate of the Arctic regions. Ahura Mazda tells Yima to keep animals and plants in a special enclosure known as Vara (a name used to indicate Yima's entire primordial kingdom) to save them from destruction. Yima is called Yama in Indian mythology, in which he is the lord of the dead. In the Homeric world, his precise counterpart is Hades, whose gloomy kingdom we have located in Lapland. Perhaps there is a relationship between the wide Varanger peninsula, lying east of Scandinavia's northernmost point, and the Iranian Vara. What is more, Avestic Varena (Varuna in Sanskrit), a region Ahura Mazda personally created, has "four corners,"[5] corresponding to the Varanger peninsula's quadrangular shape.

That the proto-Indo-Europeans were forced to leave their Arctic homeland and migrate south fits with the intuition of some nineteenth-century writers, though these authors lacked our present knowledge about climate change and even about Tilak's research. At the beginning of his famous work *The Great Initiates*, Édouard Schuré writes: "The ice of the Arctic Pole saw the beginning of the white race: They are the Hyperborean peoples mentioned in Greek mythology, men with red hair and blue eyes who came down from the North through the forests lit up by the Northern Lights . . ."[6]

Although the memory of happier days was still alive in stories of the Age of Cronos, Homer tells us that Cronos himself was ousted by his three sons, who shared the world among themselves: Poseidon "got to live always in the gray sea; / Hades got the foggy darkness; / Zeus got the wide sky in the air and the clouds" (*Iliad* 15.190–92). Interestingly, these lines seem to list the effects of the collapse of the climatic optimum when, around 2000 B.C.E., the mild Atlantic period was superseded by the Sub-Boreal one. This gave rise to more and more frequent sea and atmospheric storms, not to mention the growing desertification of the northernmost regions, now held fast in the unforgiving grip of cold and ice.

This situation is mirrored in the metaphorical features of Cronos's three sons as they appear in both the *Iliad* and the *Odyssey*: Poseidon rages over the seas with his terrible storms; Hades, the lord of the dead, lives in a desolate Arctic environment; and Zeus, in the skies, displays all the traits of a storm god with his various epithets such as Lightning Thrower *(terpikéraunos)*, Gatherer of Clouds *(nephelegerétes)*, Black Cloud *(kelainephés)*, Flinger of Thunderbolt *(asteropétes)*, and Big Thunder *(erígdoupos)*. When it snows heavily, it is said that he "is showing men his darts" (*Iliad* 12.280). It is not mere chance, then, that he is the ruler of "stormy Dodona" (*Iliad* 16.234). Homer also mentions "great Zeus' lightning / and terrible thunder when he rumbles in the sky" (*Iliad* 21.198–99). In his essay "The Original Myth in the Light of the Sympathy between Man and World," Walter Otto, the great historian of religions, compares Zeus to Tesub, the Hurrite storm god. In light of this picture, we can attempt an interpretation of a passage in Book 1 of the *Iliad* in which Zeus is temporarily imprisoned. A number of gods on Olympus have schemed a sort of palace plot against Zeus and almost immobilize him, but the sea giant Aegaeon, informed by the goddess Thetis, comes to his aid and forces them to desist:

> You, Goddess, arrived and untied him from the chains,
> by immediately calling the [giant] with a hundred hands to great
>   Olympus
> whom the gods call Briareus, but men call
> Aegaeon, who is better than his father by strength.
> He proudly sat down by Zeus,
> the blessed gods took fright at him and gave up. (Iliad 1.401–406)

This passage could derive from a mythical tale, likely already ancient in Homer's time, in which the temporary restraint of the god was perhaps a metaphor for a temporary improvement in the weather after the beginning of the decline of the climatic optimum. But after a short respite, the weather worsened and the storms returned. Metaphorically speaking, aided by Aegaeon-Briareus, the lord of the stormy seas, Zeus, the storm god, regained his authority. As we have seen, during the first half of the second millennium the final collapse of the optimum—perhaps due to Thera's terrible volcanic explosion and its effects on the atmosphere of the whole planet—forced the Indo-Europeans to move to even lower latitudes, the Achaeans from the Baltic to Greece and the Aryans from the Russian steppes to India.

Although the Russian steppes have often been cited as the original home of the Aryans, in this scenario they appear to be a secondary homeland, probably due, in part, to their position in relation to the Volga and the Dnieper, the rivers that played such an important role as trade and transit routes between north and south. As we have noted, the hypothesis that the Indo-Europeans originated on the Russian plains or the continent of Asia does not fit with the Homeric poems' and Greek mythology's characterization of them as seafaring peoples. Likewise, because archaeologists have found many ancient Mycenaean trade bases along the Mediterranean coasts and because seafaring practices generally required a good deal of time to develop within a culture, we can infer that Mycenaeans had been practicing seafaring intensely prior to their settling in Greece. It follows, then, that they had inherited a tradition dating back to a time long before their move from the north, which implies that their original land lay near the sea. As we have seen, the northern features of their architecture and their own physical traits tally with the parallels between Homeric and Norse myths, both of which have a marked seafaring nature. We need think only of the relationship between Aegaeon and Aegir or between Proteus and the marmendill; these have very little to do with the geography of the steppes.

We can presume that after the decline of the optimum, while the Achaeans were traveling down the river Dnieper toward the Black Sea, the Aryans moved down the Volga (see fig. 9.1, page 206) toward the Caspian Sea. Some of them settled in Persia (now Iran); others continued into India and Indonesia.

In support of this, we may consider the names of some peoples whose languages belong to the Indo-European family and who live in the Upper

Indus Valley, the large waterway colonized by the first Aryans when they reached India: The name of the Balti language parallels the term Baltic, and the name of the Dardi language seems related to the Dardanians, who, in the *Iliad*, are led by Aeneas, Hector's cousin. Considering that the Dardi used a round leather shield[7] identical to Hector's, it is possible to assume that some Dardanians migrated there from the Baltic area in ancient times. In a valley called Wakhan (belonging to Afghanistan) live the Wakhi, whose name may be the "missing link" between the names Achaean and Viking—which are quite similar if we consider the usual loss of the initial *v* in Greek. In the lower Indus Valley, the Sindhi live in the Sind, a district of Pakistan, and their name is homonymous with that of the Homeric Sintians.

At the beginning of the sixteenth century B.C.E.—the very time the Mycenaeans appeared in Greece and the Aryans settled in the Indian subcontinent—other Indo-European peoples were also on the move. Stuart Piggott reports:

> Around the beginning of the 16th century B.C., mountain peoples from the north invaded Mesopotamia . . . and the Cassites established a new dynasty, whose kings went by Indo-European names. They most likely came from the north or northeast and marked the beginning of the great dispersion of Indo-European language peoples toward the east . . . In the same period, another Indo-European group [known as the Mitanni] appeared along the Cassite kingdom's southwestern border . . . In the 16th and 15th centuries B.C., Indo-European names were common.[8]

Among the gods of these peoples we find names such as Mithra, Varuna, and Indra, all members of the ancient Indian pantheon.

The Hittites, who settled in Asia Minor, were also coeval with the Mycenaeans. Their Nashili language, belonging to the Indo-European family, dates back to the beginning of the second millennium B.C.E. Called Kheta by the Egyptians, the Hittites called themselves Khatti, from which came the name of their capital city, Khattushash. The term Khatti is also similar to the Homeric Ceteians or Kéteioi (*Odyssey* 11.521) and the name of the Germanic tribe called Chatti, whose territory, according to Tacitus, "begins from the Hercynian Forest" *(Chatti initium sedis ab Hercynio saltu incohant).*[9] We note that the Hercynian Forest extended to today's Assia and Thuringia, where we find the city of Kassel, called Cassala in documents dating back to the year 913 C.E.[10] If Cassala originates from the Chatti (ss and tt are interchangeable in ancient Greek), and the latter are connected with the Khatti, the Indo-European population that settled in Asia Minor eighteen hundred years before Tacitus, then the names of the ancient Khattushash and today's Kassel could be related.

In the same period, the Hyksos appeared in the Nile Delta. Recent studies carried out by Professor Jahanshah Derakhshani, of Tehran University, suggest that the Hyksos also belonged to the Indo-European family.[11] They correspond to the Haxa, who lived in Eastern Persia (also known as the Sákha and Sacae by the Hindus and Romans, respectively).

EGYPTIAN, ROMAN, NORSE, AND LITHUANIAN CONNECTIONS

The great Egyptologist W. M. Flinders Petrie, in his essay "Origins of the Book of Dead,"[12] has noted that various place-names in Transcaucasia recall the mythical geography of ancient Egypt as it appears in the Egyptian Book of the Dead, which often refers to a primordial land of the gods. Among the many instances of this, Petrie mentions Baku, a city on the Caspian Sea, which reminds us of Bekhaw, the sacred mountain of Osiris. We can also note that the name Nărte (Neith in Greek)[13] recalls the Nartees, mythical ancestors of the Caucasian Ossets. In turn, Nărte and the Nartees evoke the name of the Germanic goddess Nerthus,[14] who, according to Chiesa Isnardi, is "etymologically identical to Njord," the Norse god. The relationship between Nărte and Nerthus is strengthened by the fact that Menes, founder of the first Egyptian dynasty, sounds quite similar to Mannus, the ancestor of the Germans,[15] and to the Indian Manu, the Celtic Manannan, the Amerindian Menebus, and the Polynesian Maui, who are all protagonists in their respective mythologies. Also of note is that northern Crete of the Homeric king Minos is the country of Mannus's descendants.

In addition to parallels between the stories of Osiris and the Finnish mythological character Lemminkäinen (which we will explore in more detail in the next chapter), a relationship between Finnish and Egyptian mythology is unexpectedly confirmed by several place-names found in southern Finland, east of Helsinki. These recall both the Egyptian names and the "Egyptian-Caucasian" ones noticed by Petrie and linked to the mythical "land of the gods": Voikka (Mount Bekhaw), Teutjärvi (the god Thoth), Kymijoki (the "land of Kem," or Egypt), Kouvola (Khufu, or Cheops), Pyhtää (the god Ptah), Karhula (the city of Kher-aha), Sakkara (Saqqarah is the name of the place where the ancient pyramid of King Zoser stands), and Sokerimäki (Soker was an ancient Egyptian god). As we have said before, though it is difficult to resist the lure of conclusions drawn from these similar place-names, it is wise to avoid basing any theories solely on such parallels.

If the Egyptians came from the north, however, passing across Caucasia (many years before the Indo-European diaspora, of course), this would explain the similarities among mythical Egyptian, Caucasian, and northern names. We might also discover the origin of the puzzling animal head of the god Seth, which has never been identified among the African fauna. His strange, elongated, and slightly curved muzzle looks rather like that of a reindeer or an elk.

We are also tempted to hypothesize that the pyramids of the Nile's flat valley were actually scale models of mountains in the Egyptians' original homeland before they moved down toward the Caucasus and the Nile. In addition, the marked solar features of their relgion might be a clue that speaks in favor of their culture's northern origins.

Perhaps the ancestors of the Romans also came from northern Europe. We have noted (see chapter 8) that many ancient Latin names still seem to be echoed in the place-names of southern Finland, where we find Troy, from which the Romans claimed to come. Latin, the Romans' language, belongs to the same Indo-European family as Greek, Sanskrit, and the Germanic languages; it could have been imported into Latium by immigrants coming from the north.

Thus, it seems more than mere coincidence that there seems to be a convergence between Finnish and Roman mythology. In the former, we find "the dark waters of Manala,"[16] with Manala indicating the netherworld, and in Roman myth we find the Manalis Lapis, or the "sacred stone that has the power to bring the rain. The same name is given to the stone that closes the door of Orcus, the netherworld. If this stone were removed, the *Manes* [or] souls would leave Hades."[17] In fact, the Finnish origin of both Romans and Egyptians could also explain the parallels between the Roman deities Consus and Minerva and the Egyptian deities Khonsu and Mnevis.

An eastern Baltic origin for the Romans also fits with the fact that the Lithuanian language shows several significant similarities to Latin: Scholars have come across dozens of words that are more or less related. Additionally, regarding the countless minor divinities in ancient Lithuanian religion, Professor Frans Vyncke notes the analogy between "this plethora of spirits, whose functions are extremely marginal, and the Roman rite called *indigitamenta*."[18] As to similarities in place-names, we have only to think of the Lithuanian villages of Romainias and Romanavas, while in eastern Prussia, near Lithuania, Romuva was the most important cult site for the Baltic peoples prior to its destruction in the thirteenth century C.E. Quite a few Latin-sounding surnames are found in Lithuania (such as Maciulevicius, Vencevicius, Skarbalius), and some names of Lithuanian rivers speak of a connection: The Neris and the Viliia recall the rivers Nera and Velino, sixty miles north of Rome; Nemunas sounds similar to Lake Nemi; and the Lithuanian city of Raseiniai recalls Rasena, the name the Etruscans, neighbors of the Romans, used to call themselves.*

Interestingly, Lithuania is home to the region of Kurland (Saxo's Curetia), which we have previously linked to the mythical Homeric Curetes (a name—Kouréte in Greek—that is almost identical in sound to Quirites, the citizens of ancient Rome). Georges Dumézil underlines the distinction between the Quirites (civilians) and the Milites (soldiers) in the Roman world,[19] which highlights a connection between ancient Rome and Greek mythology—in particular, to the story of Zeus's birth. According to Greek legend, this event took place in the presence of the Curetes and strange warrior bees (*mélittai* in Greek—the Milites, or sol-

---

*A passage from Herodotus's *History* (1.94) links the Etruscans' original native land to Lydia, which could perhaps be identified with the northern Lydia of old Tantalus. Between Helsinki and Lahti there is a place called Korttia, which sounds similar to Cortona, the Etruscan city that, according to Virgil, was Dardanus's native land (and Dardanus was the progenitor of the Trojan royal family): "He, who left from here, Etruscan Cortona [*Hinc illum Corythi Tyrrhena ab sede profectum*]" (Aeneid 7.209). Not far from Korttia, Kabböle reminds us of the Kabirs, the Phrygian metalworkers linked to Dardanus. The Etruscans, also expert metalworkers (perhaps their ancestors had come to Tuscany in search of metals, specifically iron and tin), called their gods Aiser (singular Ais), a term very similar to the Aesir, the gods of Norse literature. In addition, the Etruscans portrayed one of their mythical sea monsters with a horse's head, as did the Norse, and many letters in the Etruscan alphabet are identical to Norse runes. Finally, a typical Etruscan name, Lars—as in Lars Porsena, an Etruscan king who fought against the Romans—is still a common name in Scandinavia.

diers, from which comes the adjective *military*: soldiers with their spears are parallel to bees with their sting).*

The connection between the Roman Quirites and the mythical Curetes, who attended Zeus's birth, is corroborated by the fact that in the primitive capitol in Rome, another character—the goat Amalthea— is linked to the tale of Zeus's birth. All of this implies a relationship between Rome's foundation and the birth of Zeus, which could itself have been a myth adopted by blacksmiths connected to the metalworking mysteries.

One final connection between Lithuania and the Greek world lies in the figure of Zeus himself, who seems similar to the northern god Dievas.

PEOPLE OF THE FIRE

Two places with remarkable names are found west of Tanafjorden, Norway: the Porsanger peninsula and the neighboring island of Mageröya, where lies Europe's northernmost point, Cape North. In these names we hear echoes of the Parsees and the Magi, priests of Zoroastrianism and fire worship. Their sacred book is the Avesta, the ancient Persian text that tells of a primordial homeland destroyed by cold and ice.

What is more, fire worship links the Parsees and the Magi with the Homeric Ethiopians, whom the *Odyssey* defines as "the ones of the setting Hyperion and the ones of the rising." Fire worship in Zoroastrianism incorporates a dualism of light and darkness that belies its probable roots in a primordial solar cult. In the essay *Indo-Europeans: Searching for Their Place of Origin*, Robert De Benoist underlines the close relationship between cults of the sun and fire worshippers:

> The Sun with the day-time sky was probably the great god of the Indo-European religion: The traditional formulary includes no less than five expressions applicable to it or its attributes. This solar cult most probably endured in the form of a fire cult, especially in the Vedic area . . . but also in the Roman and Germanic areas.[20]

The Magi are found not only in Persia, but also in southern Ethiopia near Lake Turkana (called Lake Rudolf until 1979), which may

---

*Intriguingly, the same metaphor is found in an Ethiopian legend: The newborn king Lalibela is covered with a swarm of bees, omens of the soldiers destined to defend him.

corroborate some relationship between the far north of Norway (Homeric Ethiopia) and eastern Africa extending to the Indo-Iranian world. Mount Meru, the most sacred mountain in Indian mythology, is known as the home of the gods, the axis of the world, the Pole's sign—but in fact, Meru is also the name of a great volcano (more than 14,700 feet high) found near Kilimanjaro in East Africa. What is more, a small African village that goes by the name of Meru is found a little farther north in the region of Tana and Tula, almost exactly on the equator.

What does all this mean? We might presume that when the climatic optimum had begun to decline in northern Europe, one branch of Indo-Europeans reached the East African coast, moved inland, and mixed with the local population. These fire worshippers gave a great active volcano the name of Meru, their sacred mountain. They were astronomers and astrologers (we recall the Magi of the gospels) who observed the motions and positions of the stars (most likely due to their ancestors' seafaring vocation). When they realized that the equator—that is, the natural counterpart of the North Pole—passed through their new land, they decided to mark it with a shrine, around which grew the present-day village of Meru, named after their mythical "polar" mountain. The precision of these people in measuring latitude is significant, though this measurement, unlike that of longitude, does not require particularly sophisticated instruments.

THE FLOOD

We now return to Caucasia, that important terminus for waterways flowing from the north and a sort of "clearinghouse" on the route to the Mediterranean, Mesopotamia, Iran, and India. Here we find Mount Ararat, traditionally considered the Mount of Salvation, where Noah's Ark was supposed to have landed. It is very unlikely, however, that the Mount of Salvation existed there among peaks higher than sixteen thousand feet! It is far more reasonable to assume that this mountain had its prototype somewhere else, in a less mountainous region, where it was high enough to save the lowlanders from being submerged in roiling waters. What is most likely is that Noah's flood is the memory of a disastrous flood that affected an area such as northern Lapland, whose territory is often marked by an uninterrupted series of lakes, rivers, and swamps. The survivors would have used the rivers mentioned earlier—the Dnieper and the Volga—to move to the Caucasus and identified Mount Ararat with the mountain of Noah. (Significantly, the name Noah recalls Noatun, the Norse "city of ships.")

The story of the Flood in the Bible echoes the Sumerian epic *Gilgamesh*, in which the hero Gilgamesh meets the old man Ut-Napishtim, a sort of Noah who has survived the Flood and lives beyond the sea. This tale is set in a typical seafaring milieu. The name given to the Mount of Salvation in *Gilgamesh*, Nisir, sounds similar to the Greek word *nêsos* (island) and to Mount Nysa, the home of Dionysus, the god of Nysa. Dionysus was associated with both wine and seafaring (according to the *Homeric Hymn* dedicated to him), as was Noah. Interestingly, in the Bible, Noah displays clear shamanistic (godlike?) features: He is in contact with God, foresees the future and the vicissitudes of his descendants, crosses the waters, and deals with heady substances. Regarding his nakedness after getting drunk, it may be comparable to the sexual ambiguity and dissoluteness typical of shamans. As Chiesa Isnardi says, the practice of *seidhr*, the shamanism of the Lapps, "involves indecency and homosexual behavior of the males."[21] It is interesting that the Lapp term *noaid*, meaning "shaman" or "he who knows," is similar to the name Noah.

Once again, names provide interesting connections among the Norse, the Greeks, the Romans, and the Egyptians: The sacred mountain of Osiris (whom the Greeks considered to be the counterpart to Dionysus) was called Bekhaw, which sounds like Bacchus, the Roman god of wine (the root of which means "hill" in some northern languages—for instance, *bakke* in Norwegian). It may be telling to compare the name Bacchus to the *baqça*, the kazakh-kirghiz shamans who, as Mircea Eliade reports, are "bards, poets, musicians, prophets, priests and doctors."[22] Also noteworthy is that following an apocryphal biblical text,[23] the mountain where Noah landed and planted grapevines was called Lubar, which is similar to Liber, another Roman god of wine. And Jean Markale tells us that Celtic mythology claims that a "drunkard" once sparked off a disastrous flood.

The famous tale of the crow that Noah first sends from the Ark[24] to find land has a significant parallel in Norse literature. According to the *Landmánabók* (The Settlement Book), a certain Floki Vilgerdharson, one of the first Vikings to reach Iceland, throws a crow from his ship to find his way toward the mainland. Perhaps we can say, then, that it was customary for these archaic seafarers to keep a kind of "compass crow" on board.

According to Genesis, Noah first sent out a crow, which did not return, and then sent out a dove. A significant detail in the *Iliad* suggests the Achaeans also kept these birds aboard ship (*Iliad* 23.852–54). At this point, we can legitimately suppose that the role of these birds was the same as that of the crows in the Viking ships and in the Ark (where the dove was held in reserve).

Another connection between the biblical tale of Noah and the northern Achaeans can be found in the Book of Enoch, one of the Apocrypha of the Hebrew scriptures: In it, baby Noah is described as having "skin as white as snow and as red as roses, and hair as white as wool."[25] This is definitely the picture of a Nordic baby!

For more on the fascinating connections between the first books of the Bible and the culture of the northern Bronze Age and what they may indicate about the origins of our civilization, please refer to the appendix.

THE DAINAS AND THE SUMERIANS

One of the important remnants of ancient Baltic culture can be found in the Dainas (pronounced in Latvian exactly like the *dynas* is pronounced in the word *dynasty*). These are ancient Latvian folksongs that relate epic, mythical, astronomical, and cultural information in verse form. They have been passed down through the millennia via oral tradition and cover all aspects of ancient Baltic life and mythology. Parallels outside the Baltic are perhaps found in ancient Mesopotamia, in the most ancient Sumerian and Akkadian hymns (for example, *Agushaya Hymn,* an ancient song text whose lines bear a strong resemblance to the unaltered text in the Dainas).[26] To support this parallel, we can point to astonishing similarities between many Sumerian and Latvian terms.[27] We can also look closely at the name of the gods' home in Hindu mythology—which, according to Professor E. H. Gombrich in *Ancient Cosmologies,* is known as Mount Meru in Sanskrit, Sineru or Sumeru in Pâli—and from it infer that the unknown original homeland of the Sumerians lay close to that of the Aryans in the extreme north, an inference supported by the fact that Sumeru in Sanskrit indicates the Arctic Pole.[28]

It is possible, then, that the Sumerians' unknown homeland was also in the north, from which they too migrated south along the large Russian rivers. This movement likely took place a few centuries before that of the barbaric, fair-haired Gutees who invaded Mesopotamia from the north and conquered the Akkadian empire just after the middle of the third millennium. (It is tempting to associate the Gutees with the Goths, who left Scandinavia in the second century C.E. to settle threateningly on the borders of the Roman Empire. The name of the Goths still endures today in the large Baltic island of Gotland and the Swedish region of Götaland.)

The possibility of a northern homeland for the Sumerians is attested to by several factors, including similarities between *Gilgamesh* and other mythologies. Some scholars, such as W. F. Albright (quoted in *Hamlet's Mill*), have noticed remarkable similarities between the Homeric nymph Calypso and Sidhuri, the innkeeper Gilgamesh meets in a fabulous garden on the borders of the "ocean of death." The main themes shared by *Gilgamesh* and Ulysses' adventure with Calypso—the protagonists' vicissitudes on the boundless ocean, the happy islands lying in the far west, the divine woman, and the promise of immortality and eternal youth— also find surprising parallels in Celtic (particularly Irish) mythology. The connection among Calypso, Sidhuri, and the Celtic legend of the women of the enchanted islands in the middle of the ocean is strengthened by the name of these enchanted Celtic women: the women of Sid. (*Sid* is the Celtic world for the afterlife.) In short, we might assume that the similarity between the root of Sidhuri's name and the Celtic word *sid* is not accidental at all. (Further corroboration of this northern connection is that on Sudhuröy, one of the Faeroe Islands, we find the place-name Seydhurdhstangi.)

Other similarity in names can be found between that of Gilgamesh and Gwalchmei, the Welsh counterpart of Gawain. The rather curious similarity between the names Chaldeans and Celts seems to corroborate the link between Gilgamesh and Gwalchmei. Perhaps furthering this connection between Gilgamesh and the north is the wonderful tree he comes across on his journey: "Its fruits are rubies . . . its blue foliage is of lapis lazuli, and it looks very beautiful."[29] It seems a sort of a "Christmas" tree, a decorated northern evergreen.

In addition to widespread references in the mythologies of Indo-European peoples to a remote, happy place and time and a subsequent climatic collapse, there are other lengendary traces of northern Indo-Europeans origins, particularly myths related to the sun, the constellations, and the moon. We shall explore these fascinating indications in the next chapter.

CHAPTER 15

SOLAR, STELLAR, AND
LUNAR MYTHS

THE ORIGIN AND DISPERSION OF
SOLAR MYTHOLOGY

An examination of the appearance of "solar" mythology in different cultures offers powerful corroboration of the Hyperborean origins of the Indo-Europeans. Solar myths are those myths that specifically focus on the daily and yearly cycles of the sun, which is considered the main god, to whom humans and the whole of creation owe their lives and prosperity. These cycles also suggest the idea of the cyclic nature of all existence and the world itself and relate to the inevitability of time's impact on human life and death and the possibility of transcending death. In addition, they include metaphorical references to a heightened sense of the contrast between light and darkness, a natural result of life in an Arctic setting in which the annual cycle of the sun involves highly differentiated seasons and the two extremes of the summer midnight sun and the winter darkness—which probably gave rise to the parallel concepts of the sun god's triumph and his death.

With reference to a deep-rooted Indo-European tradition that refers to a primitive circumpolar settlement, Jean Haudry observes in his essay "The Indo-Europeans and the Great North":

> [A] part of this tradition cannot be explained unless one starts from a geographic situation in which the year—that is, the temporal frame of human activity, especially worship—is divided into a "daytime" part and a "night-time" one, which are separated by a period of

308

dawn. A body of evidence testifies to the sense of impatience during this "dawn-time," which seems to delay the long-desired reappearance of the Sun. As regards the night-time part of the year, it is a trial that the people have to pass as if they were passing through an expanse of water.[1]

The resulting deep interest of peoples of northern origin in the contrast between light and darkness was manifested in their mythologies either as Manichean dualism or as monotheism, which often took the form of a trinity that could refer to the three different semblances of the sun (red at sunrise, white at the zenith, and black during eclipses and at night).

This may explain why God appears to Dante in the last canto of his *Paradise* in the form of "three circles of three colors and the same size," one of which is red, while the others should be white and black in symmetry with Lucifer's three faces as described in the *Inferno*. Here we find the three alchemic colors corresponding to *albedo, rubedo,* and *nigredo* (white, red, and black), which are also the colors of the pope, bishops, and priests in the Catholic hierarchy. Dumézil associates them with the three fundamental primitive Indo-European functions: priestly, warfaring, and productive. The same tricolor symbolism can be found in the goldfinch, a little bird in fashion in Renaissance art—which also had an evident interest in alchemy and esotericism—as well as in many national flags, which frequently combine red with two other colors, one of which is light and the other dark. Perhaps this connection to the sun explains why flags are raised at sunrise and lowered at sunset.

Oedipus and the Triads of Time

One of the most well-known myths of the Greeks, the story of Oedipus, provides further clues in support of the northern origin of Greek mythology and demonstrates relationships with other solar myths that no doubt share a northern origin. Before looking at how these relationships are in evidence in *Oedipus,* we must look more closely at these other solar myths and their symbols, beginning with the figure of the Theban Sphinx, a symbol of time.

In his *Greek Myths,* Robert Graves links certain composite creatures of Greek mythology—for instance, the Chimera—to the calendar. Raffaele Pettazzoni finds a similar character associated with time in the Mithraic religion. The biblical cherubim, also mentioned in the Apocalypse of John, as well as certain analogous Indo-Persian and even

North American monsters from British Columbia, probably have the same symbolic meaning. In Norse mythology we find similar monsters, such as the winged beast in the *Hrolfssaga Kraka,* which slays heroes and ravages the country during the midwinter feast. (The relationship between this monster and time is evident in the specific point in the year that it chooses for its destruction.) Interestingly, Hrolf, king of this country, is both "son and brother" of his mother,[2] which raises the topic of incest so famously portrayed in the Sophocles tragedy *Oedipus.*

In Aeschylus's tragedy *The Seven against Thebes,* the Sphinx is called "the devil destroyer of peoples." (Could there be a better definition for the destruction wreaked by Time?) We find similar metaphors in the Homeric poems: the dragon that devours nine sparrows, for instance, and the eagle that slaughters twenty geese. In Oedipus's myth, the Sphinx's link to time also appears in the riddles she asks the wayfarers: "Which creature has four legs in the morning, two at midday and three in the evening, and when he has more legs, he is weaker?" and "Who are the two sisters who bear each other?" (The answer to the former is "Man" and to the latter, "Day and Night," which are both feminine words in Greek.) The Egyptian Sphinx was in fact a solar symbol in that she was linked with the solar trinity made up of the gods Kheper, Ra, and Atum—that is, the sun in the morning, at midday, and at sunset, respectively. We come across a similar trinity concept in India, where the sun has three lights: morning light is called Vasanta, midday light is Grishma, and evening light is Sharad.[3]

Interestingly, a passage from Plutarch concerning the Egyptian religion calls to mind the Sphinx's riddle: "In Saïs, the vestibule of Athena's Temple contains the sculptures of a child, an old man, a sparrow hawk, a fish and a hippopotamus. . . . The latter represents shameless violence, because people say that after killing its father, this animal rapes its mother."[4] This reference to incest leads us back again to Oedipus, whose name means "pierced feet," from the fact that after his birth his feet were bound and then were cut on that binding. Ulysses is another who possesses solar traits and is scarred by a leg injury. Others who are similar include Wayland Smith, the Norse "Daedalus"; old Väinämöinen, the *Kalevala's* leading character; and even the Fisher King in the tales of the Grail. This could collectively refer to the tilt in the sun's course, which "limps" on its way toward winter. James Frazer mentions an ancient Egyptian rite corroborating this: After the autumn equinox, there is a celebrated feast day known as "the nativity of the sun's walking-stick," because "the large lamp sloped down in the sky every day and its light and heat decreased, so it was reckoned to need a stick to support itself."[5] The same theme is found in Indian mythology: B. G. Tilak writes that "the power of the winter Sun weakens and one can easily understand why the winter Sun is regarded as limping, old or wretched."[6]

Similar solar triads recalling the Sphinx's riddles are found in the mythologies of other cultures as well: young Lemminkäinen, adult Ilmarinen, and old Väinämöinen in the Finnish *Kalevala;* the three Magi in the Bible, who have the same age profile and who appear at the winter solstice; a very important character in Tibetan mythology, the great magician Padmasambhava, who appears as a child at dawn, an adult at midday, and an old man at dusk in a tale quoted by A. David-Néel in her introduction to Gesar's saga; and, in the *Homeric Hymn to Hermes,* the baby (Hermes), the adult (Apollo), and the old man. The other two characters who appear in the *Hymn*—Hermes' mother, Maia, and Zeus, who is the father of both Hermes and Apollo—represent Mother Earth (from where the sun rises) and the starry sky, respectively. (The famous Orphic line "I am son of Earth and Starry Sky," which probably refers to the sun's parents, is most likely from an initiation ceremony in which the initiate recognizes his divine, or solar, essence.)

This symbology is very explicit in a Gypsy tale, reported by Jerzy Ficowski, in which "King Sun flies toward the world in the early morning, when he is still a baby boy. At midday he is a middle-aged man. In the evening, when he returns home, he is a little old man who falls asleep in his mother's lap."[7]

What conclusions can we draw from all of this and how can we relate it to the tale of Oedipus? In Oedipus's story we witness the hero who defeats time (the Sphinx). In this way he achieves sovereignty and identifies himself with the sun, which is born of Mother Earth. Subsequently he kills his father—that is, the starry sky—with his brightness (thus committing an involuntary patricide), usurps his father's place, and fertilizes his mother with his own rays (here is the story's incest). Finally, in the evening he blinds himself and disappears (which perhaps explains the traditional expression "the widow's son," with reference to the sun, son of Earth, who in her turn is the starry sky's widow).

Similarly, the reference in Oedipus's myth to the Sphinx's Ethiopian origins[8] probably has a solar meaning: In the places where the Ethiopians lived—beyond the Arctic Circle—the regular alternating between day and night is dramatically suspended in summer, when the sun does not set, and in winter, when it remains long buried below the horizon.

Here is the analogy to the monster in the *Hrolfssaga Kraka* that ravages the country during the winter solstice.

The theory that the solar myths of many civilizations are connected to a northern or, better still, Arctic origin seems to fit with the fascinating hypothesis put forward by J. M. Williams in his essay "A New Theory of Celtic Festivals." Here he claims that the four main Celtic festivals—Samhain (November 1), Imbolc (February 1), Beltane (May 1), and Lughnasa (August 1)—perhaps originated in an extremely northern context, where they marked the four most important moments of the Arctic year: the beginning and the end of the solstice night (Samhain and Imbolc) and the beginning and end of the unbroken summer day (Beltane and Lughnasa), respectively. They might be, therefore, the vestigial memory of a land where the Arctic night and the midnight sun last three months—a phenomenon that does not occur anywhere in continental Europe, only in some islands such as the Svalbard, close to the North Pole. Interestingly, in relation to Williams's theory, according to a passage from "The Battle of Mag Tuired," the Celts had come from "the islands in the north of the world."

Oedipus's home in Thebes might well have been a center for sun worship, with a foundation myth and an initiation ceremony that took place in a sanctuary dedicated to the Sphinx on Mount Ficius and included the famous riddle. Sophocles has handed this down through the myth of Oedipus in which a solar initiation coincides with the royal one. Actually, Greek mythology sometimes considers Oedipus the son of Helios, the sun. When the hero defeats the Sphinx in the ritual duel on Mount Ficius, he then becomes identical to the sun and, subsequently, king of Thebes.

In that city, there may also have been a shrine that gave oracles and prophecies to the people. Here we find the prophet Tiresias, the "exoteric" and popular side of the solar cult centered in Thebes. The place-name Tyresö, near Stockholm, in the same area where Täby lies, recalls the ancient prophet and demonstrates the importance of this cult. Greek mythology hints at the exaggerated length of his Tiresias's life, which extended for seven generations. This legend could be related to the persistence of the cult and to a practice whereby the priest who inherited the oracle assumed as his title the name of its founder, Tiresias, upon taking office. In ancient times a similar practice was followed in Eleusis, home of the most famous mysteries of the Greek world, where, as Kerényi says, "the priest initiates . . . were all 'Eumolpus'—that is, the same as their mythical ancestor. 'Eumolpus' was the name of a sort of office and the Eumolpids used to lose their own name when they took office as 'Eumolpus.'"[9]

Metallurgy and Solar Mythology

Oedipus's limp is a characteristic of blacksmiths such as the god Hephaestus—a symbolic indication of the connection between solar myths and the metalworking mysteries that were centered in Thebes. Oedipus's story is somehow analogous to the myths of Theseus and Arthur (though neither of them has a limp) because each of these figures is unaware of his royal ancestry but is recognized as a king after a test (the removal of the sword from the stone, in the case of Theseus and Arthur, and the solving of the Sphinx's riddles in the case of Oedipus). As for the removal of the sword from the stone, it could be an aspect of a myth of smiths, much as Oedipus's limp is. These mythical kings of the ancient world also have technological and sacerdotal aspects; we should recall that the Roman *pontifex* was literally a "bridge *(ponti-)* builder *(fex)*.

At this point, we can see the extraction of the sword from the stone as a metaphoric reference to the skill needed to construct a sword—that is, the skill to extract it from the stone that contains iron minerals. An interesting corroboration of this is seen in an extraordinary specimen of the sword-in-the-stone motif, dating back to the twelfth century and found today in San Galgano's Cistercian abbey near Siena, in Tuscany's Metalliferous Hills. The name of the river that flows around the abbey, the Merse, is similar to Mars, the god of war, whose relationship to the symbol of the sword has been underlined by Dumézil.

Another demonstration of the relationship between metalworking mysteries and solar mythology has been found by Marcel Griaule in the mythology of the Dogon, a people who live in Mali (and to whom he dedicated his *Water God*). According to Griaule, the Dogon regard the sun as an incandescent copper pot, implying that they link the production of cast iron to the essence of the sun itself. Smiths actually gave rise to the birth of a miniature incandescent sun in their metal crucible at the climax of casting; this is the "fire from the skies" of the myth of Prometheus, which finds many similarities in Dogon mythology.

It is tempting to associate the crucible with the mythical cauldron known as the Grail, a source of wealth and power for whoever possessed it. There is a similar cauldron in the adventures of Medea, who has very marked solar features. Coincidentally, with regard to our earlier discussion of the trinity of the three solar (and alchemic) colors, there is a passage dedicated to the origins of iron in the *Kalevala* stating that this metal is born from a black milk, a white milk, and a red milk.[10] In the same passage the smith Ilmarinen uses the honey of a bee called Mehiläinen to temper the metal.[11] In addition to the similarity between the name Mehiläinen and the Greek name for "bee"—*mélitta*—we can recall that according to Greek myth, bees were present at Zeus's birth. Interestingly, the likeness between the Holy Grail and Amalthea, the goat's magical horn of plenty, is remarkable: Perhaps both of these mythical objects were linked to the same symbolism having to do with metalworking. The Grail and the horn of plenty may well be metaphors for the melting pot, the source of wealth and power from which the ancient smiths cast incandescent metal that was as shining and red-hot as the sun itself.*

All of this corroborates the importance of the solar cults, whose remains, although more or less hidden, still live in contemporary civilization: We have only to think of the enormous cachet of the psycho-analytical interpretation of the Oedipus myth, which "has caused it to win a coarse celebrity, but without any doubt is the most thoughtless and misleading,"[12] as Walter Otto outspokenly writes in his essay "The Original Myth in the Light of the Sympathy between Man and World." We have also seen that traces of these cults are possibly still to be found in some place-names scattered around the ancient territory of the Baltic Thebes, which was the site of the metalworking mysteries and, above all, of the tragic events that beset the king who was made guilty of parricide and incest by the inexorable will of Fate.

---

*In Vedic literature, according to Tilak, the word *graha* refers to a "sacrificial vessel," or, rather, a particular pot used in the rites to collect *soma*, the sacred drink that, in Indian mythology, granted immortality (under "graha" in Monier Williams, *Sanskrit-English Dictionary*). The similarity between *graha* and *grail* in both sound and concept is marked. *Soma* (*haoma* in Persian) is similar to the Finnish term *juoma*, frequently used in Rune 20 of the *Kalevala*, which tells of the mythical origin of beer. This drink is actually very important in many mythologies: The Egyptians attributed its origin to the god Ra. Considering that the Indian soma—which was mixed with curdled milk (Rig Veda 1.5.5) and honey (recalling the "Pramnian wine" mentioned by Homer)—was brown, tawny, or fawn-colored (Rig Veda 8.29.1, 9.3.9), it could be likened to a sort of beer. Romans, too, had a kind of beer, *camum* (*kámon* in Greek), which was quite similar to the Persian haoma, and a stimulating Lapp drink is called *sjöma*, quite like the word *soma*.

Scandinavian rupestrian engravings complete this picture: They often portray a ship carrying the solar disk with an armed escort. Also appearing are carvings of winged horses, associated in Greek mythology with the sun's chariot. The *Odyssey* gives us the names of these beasts, Lampus and Phaethon (Bright and Shining), "the horses that carry Dawn" (*Odyssey* 23.246). At this point, we cannot but think of the most solar of Greek myths, that of Phaeton, who drove the chariot of the sun too close to earth, thus forcing Zeus to shoot him down. His two sisters, the Heliads (meaning "sun's daughters"), wept over him by the river until they turned into poplars and their tears turned into amber, the Baltic's most precious product[13]—another reminder of the northern origin of this moving tale.

Divine Death and Resurrection

Sun worship recalls the Egyptian civilization that appeared in the Nile Valley at about the beginning of the third millennium B.C.E. after traveling from an unknown homeland. As to traces of its possible Arctic origin, we should note an amazing parallel between this Nile civilization and Finnish mythology, which can be explained by a solar key. In the *Kalevala* (Rune 14), Lemminkäinen is killed by a sea serpent, after which his body is chopped up and thrown into a river "among the dark waves of *Manala*"—that is, the nether regions. These events are remarkably similar to the Egyptian myth in which Osiris is killed by Set, or Typhoeus, the sea serpent of the Greek myths, who hacks him to pieces and throws him into the Nile.[14] As these two tales unfold, we discover other striking similarities. Lemminkäinen's mother searches for him in the river "down to the depths of Mana," where she manages to salvage the pieces of his body, which are reassembled so that he may be brought back to life. Isis, Osiris's wife, also manages to find her husband's dismembered pieces and reassemble them.

With regard to the myth of Osiris, James Frazer says that "the daily sunrise and sunset can be interpreted as a myth of sun's death and resurrection: but, if the theme was its daily death, why was [this] celebrated by a annual ceremony? Moreover, what is the meaning of the assertion that it is chopped to pieces?"[15]

Actually, the dismemberment, disappearance, and recomposition of Lemminkäinen and Osiris can be explained by reference to the sun's annual cycle in the Arctic regions. After the continuous daytime of the summer solstice, day then alternates with night (the god is "dismembered"), then comes the darkness of winter solstice, when he is thrown "into the waters" and disappears, followed by the return of alternating day and night (salvage of the pieces), and finally the restoration of the sun that never sets during the following summer (restoration to wholeness). Incidentally, the topic of the dismemberment and recomposition is often found in shamanism, which is also linked to solar worship. In short, the parallels between the myth of Osiris and the Finnish myth of Lemminkäinen—Finland being the context in which such solar phenomena actually take place—is worth studying in depth, especially considering that when the Egyptians appeared in the Nile Valley, the far north enjoyed a climate very different from today's.

In summary, then, the theme of the death and resurrection of a god that is common to so many mythologies (apart from Osiris, we can count the tales of Baldr, Adonis, Attis, Tammuz, and so on), rather than being linked with the annual cycle of agriculture, is more likely a reflection of the changes in the sun's appearance at far northern latitudes. (Interestingly, the Norse Baldr's and the Phrygian Attis's wives have the same name: Nanna.) If we consider that the great scholar Franz Cumont established that Adonis's death occurred every year on the night between July 19 and 20, when many women used to mourn his death, we can infer that this metaphor originates from the annual "death" and "resurrection" of the sun god in the Arctic regions. Those pious women in fact cried over the memory of the first sunset after two months—that is, the end of the midnight sun in the Arctic regions whence their ancestors came many years before.

The Sun and the Serpent

The fight between the sun (the god Ra) and darkness (the dragon Apophis) that is featured in Egyptian mythology is similar to both Lemminkäinen's fight with a sea serpent and Osiris's battle with Typhoeus. This theme is also found throughout Greek mythology—for instance, in the tale of the newborn god Apollo, who kills the snake Python—and in Norse sagas, in which "bold Thor by force hoists the serpent, glittering with poison, aboard ship, and strikes its horrible head with his hammer"[16] or "chopped his head off."[17] We find yet another example among the Hittites, who celebrated the myth of the battle between the storm god and the serpent on Purulli Day. In Mesopotamia, we find this concept in the fight between the god Enlil and the aquatic monster Tiamat. In the Persian Avesta and the Indian Rig Veda, Tishtrya and Indra kill Apaosha and Vritra, respectively. The Polynesian hero Maui beheads the monster-eel named Tuna, who has been persecuting a woman. In more recent European "mythology," a similar theme is found in the adventures of *Sir Gawain and the Green Knight*, an unascribed English poem dating back to the fourteenth century: At the beginning of the New Year, Gawain beheads a gigantic knight, just as the Celtic hero Cúchulainn does in "Bricriu Banquet."

We can find counterparts to these mythical figures in Norse literature as well. The *Younger Edda* dwells on the duel between the god Thor and the giant Hrungnir in which the two hit each other on the head.

In order to understand what these stories all refer to, let us return to the tale of Apollo, who kills the snake with his arrows. It is significant that in the third millennium B.C.E., when the climatic optimum was at its peak, the North Pole was not indicated by the Pole Star, as it is today, but by the constellation of the Dragon. The precessional motion of the polar axis in 2830 B.C.E. brought the star Thuban (Alpha Draconis) within only ten minutes of arc from the pole. (At present, Polaris is fifty minutes of arc away from the pole, almost a full degree.) Thus, at that time, the Dragon appeared coiled around the pole, at the center of the night sky. It was the lord of the darkness, towering at the zenith in the Arctic regions. But when the new sun, heralded by the revolving dawns, rose from the solstice night, its rays "slew the dragon." Here is the victory of the sun embodied in the Hyperborean Apollo emerging from Mother Earth over the dragon that plagued her with darkness.

We can also suppose that the omphalos, the Earth's center and navel, which was kept in Apollo's temple in Delphi, represented the symmetric counterpart of the center of the night sky—that is, the pole around which the Dragon twisted five thousand years ago. It is not by mere chance, then, that we find the dragon and the snake (also associated with the myth of lost Paradise so central to Judaeo-Christian theology) present in many mythologies, from pre-Columbian America and China to Europe, in the form of, for instance, the legend of St. George. The dragon described in *Beowulf*—"the old dawn's scourge . . . / that flies at night [*nihtes fleogedh*]"[18] has the same meaning.

Now its traces can be found in kites, whose quadrangular head and long tail imitate the shape of the Draco Constellation. (In Italian, an old name for kite is *drago*.) Another trace still lives on in an Italian tradition related to Christmas night, which coincides with the winter solstice and the birth of the new sun: The *capitone*, a large eel served at Christmas Eve dinner, recalls the terrible dragon of darkness revolving around the pole, Python-Apophis-Tiamat-Tuna, and the winged beast of *Hrolfssaga Kraka*, doomed to be defeated by the newborn sun. In short, the

Manichean theme of the contrast between light and darkness traverses not only ancient mythologies in widely varying forms, but also our present culture. A more recent literary reference, for instance, is found in Goethe's esoteric tale *The Green Snake and the Beautiful Lily*.

According to James Frazer, there is also a remarkable corroboration of this theme in an Eskimo myth: "At the end of the Arctic winter, when the sun reappears at the horizon after many weeks at Point Barrow, the northernmost point of Alaska, in the moment of its reappearing Eskimos throw the evil ghost called Tuna out of the houses."[19] The parallels between the evil Tuna, driven away by the reappearance of the sun, and the Polynesian Tuna and the Greek Python, both defeated by the newborn sun (Maui and Apollo, respectively), is quite marked.

We can also include as parallels the reference in a famous passage of the Bible: "the Lord with his sword will visit Leviathan, the winding serpent, and will kill the monster hidden in the sea."[20] Another example can be found in chapter 12 of the Apocalypse of John, which tells of the war in heaven between Michael and the dragon that persecutes the newborn baby. This motif speaks to an origin in high latitudes, where the winter solstice darkness can arouse fears that the sun will never appear again. Perhaps the Apocalypse as a whole—which is full of the metaphors of time—unfolds the "history of Salvation" as intersecting with the "history of the Dragon (the symbol of darkness fighting against the sun)," until this grand metaphor of the history of humankind ends in the triumph of the Lamb who defeats the Dragon.* Incidentally, *lamb* in Latin is *agnus* (Agnus Dei is "God's Lamb"), and *agnus* is similar to the Latin *ignis* (meaning "fire") and Agni, the great Vedic fire god. It seems, then, that Lamb-agnus is a metaphor for the sun god vanquishing the dragon, the lord of darkness.

---

*The general meaning of the Apocalypse is probably related to themes similar to those we deal with here. If we reread it from an unorthodox perspective, it appears to be full of the metaphors of time, starting from "the book that is sealed with seven seals." This could be interpreted as the book of history, composed of seven ages, the first four of which coincide with the four ages of the classical tradition before the advent of the Redeemer. They also correspond to the Four Knights, who clearly illustrate the characteristics of the ages they represent by their symbolism and the colors of their horses. The first knight, with his white horse, who appears at the opening of the first seal (Apocalypse 6:1–2), symbolizes the Golden Age connected with the philosophers. The second knight, with his red horse and his sword (the second seal), is symbolic of the Silver Age (warriors). The third knight, with a black horse and scales (the third seal), is analogous to the Bronze Age (traders who use scales). The fourth knight (the fourth seal) symbolizes the Age of Death, the Kali

STELLAR MYTHOLOGY

Just as we have seen in the myth of Apollo, we can also suppose that in a distant past, the solar and stellar myths were complementary, part of a global cosmic vision only a few fragments of which have come down to us, scattered among many different mythologies. In particular, the signs of the zodiac, the twelve divisions of the imaginary belt within which are the apparent paths of the sun, moon, and principal planets, appear in many cultures, even very distant ones. In Greek *zodiakós kýklos* means "circle of animals." The same concept is found in its corresponding Norwegian (Dyrekretsen) and Finnish (Eläinrata) terms. Marcel Griaule also finds them in the Dogon mythology in Mali. It is quite plausible, however, that this concept originated at high latitudes, where the zodiac appears as a sort of carousel of low constellations on the horizon. We also note that some of the twelve stylized signs of the zodiac—which could bear some relation to the ancient Babylonian duodecimal system traced to today's subdivision of the day into twelve hours, the hours into sixty minutes (a multiple of twelve), of the circle into 360 degrees, and the notion of "a dozen" so often used as a count—seem to be rather similar to the letters of the alphabet. We might presume, therefore, that the letters drew their origin from a prehistoric set of sacred symbols (we can imagine Norse runes) that were linked to astronomy, and, consequently, to seamanship. At a certain point, Phoenician seafarers may have started using them for trade activities, with opportune adaptations, doubling their number and disseminating them with this "profane" use beyond their "sacred" origins.

The map of the skies resembles a large fresco of mythological figures that have been "frozen" in the names of the constellations. We

---

Yuga, which attests to the influence of Indian culture on the Mediterranean at the time of the composition of the Apocalypse.

With respect to the relationship between horses and time, we can recall Homer's "horses of the Dawn" as well as Scandinavian graffiti on this subject. The last three seals are related to the three ages after the birth of Christ: the persecution (the fifth seal, the epoch of the author), the wait for Doomsday (the sixth seal), and Doomsday itself (the seventh seal). Regarding the dragon, whom Egyptians named Apophis, it may be that this was the "sea beast" associated with the number 666 in the famous riddle set in the Apocalypse (13:18). The sum of the numbers corresponding to each Greek letter of its name is 667, from which we must subtract 1 (the initial letter *a, alpha*) because the dragon's "head" has been severed from its body.

could even go so far as to say that behind the events in which they are the leading characters lie the hidden fragments of "coded" information concerning the routes of prehistoric seafarers, for whom the stars were the main "tools of the trade." Many familiar names of the stars and constellations, such as Orion, the Bear (Ursa), and the Pleiades, are found in Homer's poems, which confirms their extreme antiquity. In particular, Homer writes that Ursa (the Great Bear) "is the only one which is not subject to bathing in the Ocean" (*Iliad* 18.489): Although he is partially lowered beneath the horizon in the Mediterranean, at least during some periods of the year, this constellation, as Homer tells us, never "sets" at northern latitudes—yet another clue to the northern setting of the Homeric poems. On the subject of stars "bathing," Homer also mentions Sirius: "The late summer star, which ever so much / twinkles bright after bathing in the Ocean" (*Iliad* 5.5–6).

Stellar cults (traces of which were found even in the extremely ancient pyramid texts at the dawn of Egyptian civilization) have never ceased to influence human thought. We need only think of the continued appeal of astrology, as well as the inspiration that astronomical phenomena have always provided for poetry and literature. On this subject we can turn to the incomparable Canto 8 of Dante's *Purgatory*, indicating that this poet was inspired chiefly by gazing at the starry sky and marking its slow revolution during the night hours. This conclusion is not explicitly declared in the text but is instead revealed in the architecture of the canto itself. As the evening falls ("It was the hour when seamen turn toward desire . . ."), the brightest stars begin to appear. First, disguised as "one of the arisen / souls," the planet Venus (or Lucifer) appears, which is linked with the chorus *Te lucis ante*. Then the other stars gradually light the sky until a snake appears (which has always puzzled scholars). If we interpret this metaphor from an astronomical point of view, it becomes clear: Here the poet refers to the longest of the constellations, Hydra, the mythical serpent, which appears in the night sky in the springtime.

A passage in the *Iliad* that depicts the goddess Hera leaving Olympus on her chariot also illustrates this motion of the vault of heaven: "The doors of the sky [*pýlai ouranoû*] squeaked by themselves [*autómatai*], being overseen by the Hours, / to whom the wide sky and Olympus are confided / if the thick cloud is to be removed or lowered" (*Iliad* 5.749–51). Here this motion is as regular as the workings of a watch and is marked by the hours, corresponding to the seasons, that regulate the alternating of light and darkness (the "thick cloud" that is removed altogether or lowered during the course of the months). These archaic lines from the *Iliad* could conceal the memory of an Arctic environment in which the duality between light and darkness is far more marked than it is in lower latitudes. As to Hera's chariot, it could hint at some astronomical phenomenon—perhaps to the Moon's motion, considering that the goddess Hera is connected to astronomy in another peculiar image in the epic in which she is hanging by a golden chain "in the ether among the clouds" (*Iliad* 15.18–21).

Stellar imagery appears in the *Odyssey* as well, in which we learn that the two dogs on guard at the gates of Alcinous's palace are "immortal and ageless" (*Odyssey* 7.94)—that is, they do not belong to this world. We can find them in the skies in the two constellations near Orion, the Dogs of the Hunter (Canis Major and Canis Minor). In the Rig Veda they are "the guardians of the house and the paths lying toward the region of Yama." As Tilak reports, according to the Persian Avesta, these heavenly dogs are "yellow or white with yellow ears"; they correspond to "the golden and silver dogs" *(chrýseioi kaí argýreoi kýnes)* of Alcinous's palace (*Odyssey* 7.91).

SOLAR AND STELLAR ORION

In the constellation of Orion, the Hunter, ancient solar and stellar myths converge. Orion's double function can be explained by the fact that this constellation (probably the most beautiful in the entire firmament, given that it includes such luminous stars as Betelgeuse and Rigel) marks the beginning of the year. The myth of his love affair with Dawn and its tragic end (*Odyssey* 5.121) expresses the same concept. This myth concerned, of course, a very particular Dawn: the one that marked the equinox during the Orionic period.*

Orion, who met his death on the island of Ortygie (*Odyssey* 5.121–24), identifiable with Great Britain, and who is one of the most

---

* At Homer's time, Dawn had another partner known as Tithonus (*Odyssey* 5.1), who was obviously a star or a constellation, which is confirmed by the fact that its name is related to the Sanskrit *didhyana,* "bright." Perhaps it could be identified with Aldebaran (Alpha Tauri), the brightest star in that part of the sky where the sun rose at the vernal equinox around 2000 B.C.E. The Arab name Aldebaran, "the pursuer" or "the suitor," fits well the role of lover, which it played for a very long time. Perhaps this is why Greek mythology considers Tithonus to be extremely old—and, of course, immortal, as it is in the sky.

extraordinary characters of Greek mythology, has many parallels in other mythological systems. We can make an interesting analogy with the Green Knight in *Sir Gawain and the Green Knight:* Both men are hunters and of gigantic stature; the English poem dwells at length upon the hunting adventures of the mysterious knight, while the *Odyssey* shows in Hades "giant Orion / who hunts wild beasts on the asphodel meadow" (*Odyssey* 11.572–73). Both hunters are also hit on the head and are associated with solar symbolism.

At the end of his adventure, the Green Knight presents to Gawain a hunter's belt, a gift the poet considers so important that he proclaims it to be the ensign of the Knights of King Arthur and states that it "was called the glory of the Round Table."[21] This belt is easily found in the constellation: It is Mintaka, meaning "belt" in Arabic—that is, Delta Orionis—among the stars of Orion's constellation, and serves as the everlasting memory of a Greek and Celtic myth that probably dates back to the Orionic period, when the Indo-Europeans were still undivided.

In *Beowulf* we find a similar ensign in the mound where the dragon guards his stolen treasure. This "all-gold ensign" [*segn eall-gylden*] is "tall . . . / a great handmade wonder / weaved by skill."[22] The dragon probably represents the lord of the starry sky; its "treasure," therefore, is the whole firmament and its "ensign" is a special star or constellation. Thus *Beowulf* seems to underline the connection between Orion and the Dragon, the two constellations that must have been considered the most important at that time, given that they marked the vernal equinox (the beginning of the year) and the North Pole, respectively. In a word, Orion's belt could be rightly considered the "ensign" of the Dragon, the lord of the night.

In *The Orion* Tilak dwells at some length on the parallels among Greek, Indian, and Persian myths on this subject, especially on the belt (which he identifies with the Parsees' sacred cordon known as *kusti*). These parallels support his inference that the various branches of the Indo-European family were still undivided in the Orionic period. He also mentions that certain fancy-dress folklore festivals held on New Year's Day in England and Germany until the Middle Ages displayed the same symbolism. The timeline of the tale of the Green Knight—it takes place between two New Year's Days—also corroborates a connection with Orion.

Turning again to Homer, in the *Odyssey* Heracles is portrayed in a way that calls to mind the constellation of Orion: He stands fixed in Hades as a hunter, with his bow and arrows—"He had a naked bow in his hand and an arrow on the bowstring / and was staring grimly, always ready to shoot" (*Odyssey* 11.607–608). Heracles, like Orion, has solar features, and, interestingly, his name is similar to the Egyptian solar god Harakhte. He also wears a belt that is remarkably similar to the ensign found by Beowulf and also recalls the one Orion wears in the night sky: "A terrifying golden belt [*chrýseos telamón*] for the sword / was around his chest . . . He could not make it again or make another / the one who made this belt with such skillful art" (*Odyssey* 11.609–10, 613–14).

One of the most vivid portraits of Orion is that of him carrying the smith Cedalion on his shoulders[23] (in the Christian world, he became Saint Christopher carrying the baby Jesus). In the *Younger Edda*, Thor tells how he carried a certain Aurvandill on his shoulders in a pannier; meanwhile, one of the man's big toes broke off and was flung into the sky, where it was changed into the star called Aurvandilstá.*

A remark of Jacob Grimm's about Aurvandill (in his *Teutonic Mythology*, quoted in *Hamlet's Mill*) fits perfectly here: "The entire plot of Aurvandill's legend recalls the *Odyssey*, for example, the shipwrecked man who clings to a plank, digs a hole and holds a branch in front of himself. Even his seamless suit can be compared to Ino's veil."[24] This confirms, on the one hand, the very close correspondence between the Greek and the northern mythologies (which, as usual, are dominated by the sea and seafaring themes) and, on the other, the wealth of mythical-astronomical references from which the author of the *Odyssey* has drawn inspiration in order to build his stories and his characters.

Interestingly, the name Cedalion sounds almost exactly the same as Kurdalaegon, the mythical smith from Ossetia in the Caucasian area, where scholars have come across tales that are quite reminiscent of the Arthurian legends. The scholar Joël Grisward, in particular (quoted by Georges Dumézil), highlights significant analogies between the death of the Ossetian hero Batraz and that of King Arthur: Before dying, both of them were obliged to throw their swords into the sea, after which a miraculous event was to occur. Both the Ossets and the Celts belong to the Indo-European family. According to a passage from the Celtic "The

---

* More detail on the relationship between Orion and Aurvandill (who becomes Horvendillus, Hamlet's father, in the *Gesta Danorum*) can be found in appendix 2 of *Hamlet's Mill*.

Battle of Mag Tuired," the latter came from "the islands in the north of the world." The similarities found in legends from such distant areas may indicate that while most of the Celts moved to western Europe, some of them took the waterways toward the Caucasus.

Returning to Book 5 of the *Odyssey*, we find another thematic parallel to the empowered swords of Arthur and Batraz, both of which must be returned to specific waters after their use is fulfilled: Ulysses sailing for Scheria on his raft when the sea suddenly becomes stormy and he has to fight desperately for his life. Violent gusts and enormous waves buffet him, break the mast on his raft, and tear the sail. Just before the raft is smashed to pieces, a sea goddess appears before him in the form of a coot (a seabird called *aithuíe* by Homer). Her name is Ino Leucothoe, the white goddess, who saves him by giving him a veil *(krédemnon)* to tie around his chest. This is no common life belt, but instead leaves the wearer immortal *(ámbroton)*, preventing him or her "from suffering or dying" (*Odyssey* 5.347). The goddess tells him how to return this marvelous article: "When you touch the ground with your hands, / take it off and toss it into the wine-dark sea, / far from the ground, but you've got to turn away" (*Odyssey* 5.348–50). After landing in the mouth of the Phaeacians' river, Ulysses carries out the directions of his savior: "He took off the goddess' veil, / and threw it into the river where it met with the sea. / The strong current carried it back, and Ino at once / picked it up in her hands" (*Odyssey* 5.459–62).

In looking at these legends, we might wonder what the relationship is between the sword and the veil. Orion, whose belt holds his sword, gives us a possible answer. We might hypothesize a relationship among Orion's belt, Arthur's sword, and Gawain's belt. Therefore, Ino's veil—the counterpart of both the Parsees' sacred cordon and the Brahmans' *yajnopavîta*—is perhaps one key to understanding a mythical scheme that extends over the entire Indo-European area, from northern Europe to the Caucasus and India. The sword's (or belt's or veil's) plunge into the waters may symbolize the setting of Orion's constellation into the sea at the time when this position marked the beginning of the year.

In addition to the sword and the sword-in-the-stone motif (also found in Theseus's youthful adventures), a theme common to a number of Indo-European mythologies is that of the Wounded King who can be healed only by the same spear that has wounded him—much like Heracles' son Telephus, who is hit by Achilles' spear. Achilles, for his part, has much in common with Sir Lancelot, son of the Lady of the Lake, the counterpart to the sea goddess Thetis. The list of such analogies goes on and on. We are not surprised, then, at the fact that "in Ireland during the early Middle Ages, there were tales of abducted women *(aithid)* among the twelve main stories the poets were required to know . . . The abduction of Etaine, that is, the wife of the supreme King Eochaid Aireain, by the hero-god Mider, initiated a war."[25]

It follows that a search for the original setting (in terms of both space and time) of the Arthurian tales could be focused on contexts different from the traditional ones. In relatively recent times, some figures thought to be specifically historical have been identified with others from a much more ancient mythical substratum: The Briton king called Arthur, who dates back to the sixth century C.E., probably descends from the prototypical myths of many other heroes (Batraz, Theseus, Siegfried, and so on) who deal with a sword endowed with particular powers.

The similarities between Celtic and Greek mythology can be explained both by a common Indo-European origin and by the assimilation of legends and tales, dating back to the Early Bronze Age and maybe even before, that the Achaeans left behind in the British Isles before moving south to the Mediterranean. This theory is corroborated by the archaeological remains in Britain.

LUNAR MYTHS

Homer describes Ino Leucothoe, the goddess whose veil protects Ulysses during the storm off the Phaeacian coast, as being formerly a woman who "now, in the expanse of the sea, shares the dignity of the gods [*Nýn d'alós en pelágessi theôn éx émmore timês*]" (*Odyssey* 5.335). This line of verse—one of the most evocative in the *Odyssey*—seems to represent the echo of the last memory of an extremely distant past. Ino, called Leucothoe, the white goddess, might well have been a moon goddess worshipped by the seamen of the Bronze Age. Her magic veil could hint at a peculiar phenomenon known as the cinereous light: the dim, ashen hue hanging over the moon before and after it is new. It allows us to discern the whole lunar disk—including the part that, rather than being illuminated by the Sun, is backlit by the full earth. In fact, this cinereous light, which occurs when the sky is clear and cloudless and is so different from the brightness of the crescent, suggests a veil covering the face of our satellite. It certainly must have been considered a good omen by ancient seafarers, for it signals the end of storms.

Ino probably became Anna in Latin: Anna Perenna was a very ancient Roman goddess, according to Ovid: "Some say she is the moon, which completes the year with the months" *(Sunt quibus haec luna est, quia mensibus inpleat annum).*[26] In fact, some names for the moon in Greek and Latin (Selene and Diana, for instance) could contain the same root. The prefix of Selene probably originates from *sélas,* "splendor," the same root as the Latin *sol,* or "sun." The prefix of Diana *(dius* in Latin, *dîos* in Greek, *diviyah* in Sanskrit) has the same meaning. Therefore, both Selene and Diana might mean "bright Ino," referring to the shining moon.

Calypso was probably linked to the moon as well. Both her veil, called *kalýptre (Odyssey* 5.232), and her mantle, which is "bright as silver" *(argýpheon,* "of silvery light"—*Odyssey* 5.230), suggest this analogy. It is possible, then, that her name (in Greek, Kalypsó) means not "the concealer" but instead "the veiled (moon)." Might she have been a goddess of the moon, worshipped by the Faeroese seamen with a shrine on the island of Ogygia? If so, the poet of the *Odyssey* gave his hero the most coveted lover a man could desire—the moon goddess!

Interestingly, the name Ino is very similar to Hina, the great Polynesian goddess of the moon, hinting at the possibility that intrepid prehistoric seafarers from the far north managed to reach Polynesia via the Northwest Passage, which was not icebound at the time. The puzzling megalithic remains scattered all over the Pacific archipelagos, along with a whole constellation of tales and legends that often call to mind the myths of the Old World, seem to corroborate this idea. We need only think of the stories of the Flood and the Tower of Babel, as Professor Eugène Caillot reports in his *Polynesian Myths, Legends and Traditions.*

Here we have touched on only a few of the countless parallels among myths and legends from all over the world displaying elements of the sun, stars, or moon—all of which could point back to a far northern civilization that flourished during the early part of the climatic optimum. If we bear in mind the high level the art of seafaring reached in northern Europe, as well as the fact that the great sea routes experienced an extremely favorable period from a climatic point of view, we can legitimately presume that the first center for dispersal of solar and lunar cults, stellar myths (which were probably linked with seafaring), shamanism, and metalworking techniques was northern Europe from the Neolithic Age until the Indo-European diaspora, which increased the worldwide diffusion of that culture.

CONCLUSION

Starting with the key to the puzzle found in Plutarch's precise statement in "De facie" and developing our thoughts according to information provided by the Homeric poems, our study here has led to some perhaps startling conclusions as far as the setting of Homer's adventures and the origin of Greek civilization itself are concerned. These conclusions can be summed up as follows:

- The real setting of the *Iliad* and the *Odyssey* can be identified not as the Mediterranean Sea, where it proves to be undermined by many incongruities, but rather in the north of Europe.
- The sagas that gave rise to the two poems came from the Baltic regions, where the Bronze Age flourished in the second millennium B.C.E. and where many Homeric places, such as Troy and Ithaca, can still be identified today.
- The blond seafarers who founded the Mycenaean civilization in the Aegean in the sixteenth century B.C.E. brought these tales from Scandinavia to Greece after the end of the climatic optimum.
- These people then rebuilt their original world—where the Trojan War and many other mythological events had taken place—farther south in Mediterranean waters, transferring significant names from north to south.
- Through many generations, they preserved the memory of the heroic age and the feats performed by their ancestors in a lost homeland.

Although our study concludes here, it is in fact not conclusive: For definitive proof, it requires further archaeological corroboration, after

327

which an immense amount of investigation in all related fields awaits the experts. As we have seen, however, the striking geographic, morphologic, and climatic consistency of this new scenario lends significant support to this theory—and also happens to clear up many of the contradictions that a Mediterranean-Aegean setting has presented to Greek scholars throughout time.

We have also learned that the two poems relate to territories quite far afield. The Catalog of Ships in the *Iliad* enables us to reconstruct the Achaean settlements along the Baltic in the Early Bronze Age, while in its turn, the *Odyssey*, by means of Ulysses' wanderings, gives us a consistent picture of the information these ancient peoples had about the greater world—a world that was both fascinating and full of dangers and strange phenomena such as the "dances of the dawn" and the midnight sun, the great Atlantic tide, and the whirlpool Charybdis. These places, too, carry the distinctive marks of a northern setting.

The geographic information extracted from the entire Homeric universe finds its natural location in some main "clusters": the Ithacan world in the Danish islands, Ulysses' adventures in the North Atlantic Ocean, the world of Troy in southern Finland, and the Achaean world along the Baltic coasts. Each of these fits remarkably closely in geography, morphology, and toponomy to the worlds Homer describes as compared to the noted inconsistencies of the traditional Mediterranean locations.

As we have seen, the climatic settings of the poems, characterized by damp, foggy, cold, and unsettled weather, perfectly describe a northern environment that coincides geographically, meteorologically, and temporally with the end of the postglacial climatic optimum in northern Europe and the subsequent arrival of the Mycenaeans in the Aegean.

We have also learned that a northern setting for the epics solves many internal problems of the Homeric narrative, such as the two-day, nonstop battle between the Achaeans and the Trojans, which can be explained only by the twilit nights of the high latitudes during the summer solstice. In addition, many references in the poems clearly speak to other typically northern phenomena such as the aurora borealis and the revolving dawns.

In the course of our discussion, we have clarified many other details that have presented geographic confusion up to now: the "backwardness" of the Homeric civilization compared to that of the Mycenaeans; the presence of an ancient Hellespontian people in the eastern Baltic; the inconsistencies between the morphology of some Homeric cities and their Greek namesakes; the great inconsistencies regarding the region of the Greek Peloponnese and its presentation in Homer's work; the distance of the Trojan allies from the area of the Dardanelles; the position of Pharos in the middle of the sea; the depiction of Phthia as the land of refugees; the puzzling course of Agamemnon's fleet from Troy to Mycenae past Cape Malea, and so on.

We have found that cultural details that have long seemed strange in connection to a Greek world become understandable in relation to a northern European setting for the poems: the significance of oxen compared to other animals, for instance, and tableware made solely of metal or wood, which are abundant in the north. These and many other small, descriptive details have long perplexed scholars from Strabo's day to the present.

As we have seen, corroborating a northern setting and a connection between the Achaean and Viking worlds are the many analogies between Greek and Norse mythology. Quite a few episodes narrated by Homer are steeped in a peculiar shamanistic atmosphere that tallies with the northern environment and also attests to their ancientness. This has led us to many discoveries regarding the northern origins of mythological themes shared by many cultures in the world—which opens a great door, shut tight until now, to a new view of the Indo-European diaspora.

What of archaeology? Besides the fact that, as leading scholars indicate, the northern origin of the Mycenaeans is based on archaeological evidence found on Greek soil (which the theory here further corroborates), we should consider these discoveries:

- The similarities, dating back to the Bronze Age, between northern and Aegean artifacts
- The Bronze Age tumuli and rock carvings portraying ships that have been found exactly where the Phaeacian seafarers were settled, as determined by following Homer to the letter
- The analogies between significant Scandinavian Bronze Age remains (such as at Kivik) and coeval Aegean ones
- The resemblance between Delphi's omphalos and the Swedish round stones in the region of the Homeric Pytho, which also corroborate the links between the Delphians and Hyperboreans mentioned by classical authors

- The traces the Mycenaeans left in Wessex (England) at least three hundred years before they settled in Greece
- The German site of Nebra, where archaeologists have found a bronze disk portraying a sky very similar to that depicted in the center of Achilles' shield and some "Mycenaean" swords

From these findings, we can say that it is time to start specific archaeological investigations in the areas of Toija—in particular on the hills around the village of Kisko—and Lyø, which correspond to the Homeric Troy and Ithaca in all geographic, topographic, morphologic, and climatic respects. These represent very promising archaeological sites, as the tumuli of Perniö, so similar to those described in the *Iliad,* and the dolmen of Lyø confirm.

If the validity of our theory here is borne out by such investigation, new and fascinating horizons will open regarding the origin and prehistory of the whole European civilization, shedding light on the peoples of the northern Early Bronze Age and illuminating their life, culture, religion, and history, which have been almost totally unknown until now.

Finally, this "rediscovery" of Homer could foster a new cultural approach to the idea of European unity and could contribute to the birth of a new humanism in Western culture, which, in this third millennium, awaits humanity beyond "the fearful immense abyss" and will serve to launch us on a great adventure worthy of Ulysses: the conquest of the stars.

THE BIBLE AND THE
NORTHERN BRONZE AGE

In looking at the first books of the Bible in a new light, we could deduce that the primordial Hebrew civilization was linked to the culture of the northern Bronze Age. The details supporting this conclusion in turn corroborate the connections we have already established between the archaic Greek world and the world of the north.

The Eteians are found both in the Homeric Crete (today's Poland) and in the Bible: Maccabees 1 mentions a very strange "kinship" between the Hebrews and the Spartans,[1] who were descended from the Dorians mentioned in connection with the Eteians (*Odyssey* 19.177) on Homer's Crete. What is more, the Iardanus River flowed there (*Odyssey* 3.292), which is, perhaps, the present-day Eider, whose name recalls the river Jordan.

Another parallel concerns Joseph's dream of seven fat cows devoured by seven thin cows: It is conceptually identical to both Penelope's dream in the *Odyssey* concerning twenty geese killed by an eagle and the picture of the dragon devouring nine birds in the *Iliad*. As a matter of fact, each of these prophecies is based on a sort of kenning where the number of animals killed indicates the number of years corresponding to the prophesied event.

In both the Homeric and biblical worlds, future husbands purchased their brides, a cultural practice that also occurred in the Nordic world, as Tacitus reports: "The brides don't bring a dowry to their husbands, but the latter bring a dowry to the brides."[2]

Bearing in mind what has emerged regarding the Norse Ragnarok and the Mycenaean migration, we could infer that all the events related to Moses, in particular the seven plagues, are the last remaining memory of the effects of the explosion of Thera, which was the final trigger (heralding the true end to the climatic optimum) for the exodus from the Homeric—that is, Baltic—Egypt to Palestine. In confirmation of this scenario, it is notable that ancient Egyptian documents never mention the Hebrews or the events connected to them.

Asko Parpola[3] points out that the Hebrew name Yahve, which some scholars believe originates from Mesopotamia, finds an amazing counterpart in the Sanskrit Yahva. We can also note the similarity between the roots of Yahve-Yahva and Jove, the supreme deity of the Romans. What is more, the name of Brahma, the Hindu god who created humankind, is very similar to Abraham, the progenitor of the Hebrews. The counterparts of Brahma-Abraham in the northern world are the Norse primordial giant Brimir and the Celtic god Bran. Thus the likeness between the adjective Hebrew and the names of two countries inhabited by Celts—Iberia (the Iberian Peninsula) and Hibernia (ancient Ireland)—might not be sheer chance. Moreover, among Ashkenazi Hebrews as with the Irish, there is a high occurrence of red-haired people.

Looking further at similar sounds in names, we can consider the similarity between the names of the Chaldeans and the Celts and note that the names Tare and Aran, who were Abraham's father and brother, respectively, have Celtic counterparts. Haran, Abraham's first stopping place on his way to the Promised Land, recalls Caria (It is intriguing, too, that in Celtic literature we find Tír Tairngiri, "the Land of Promise.") As to the Cananeians and Ferezeians, mentioned in the same verse of the Bible,[4] their names recall the Homeric "Enienes and the strong Peraebians" (*Iliad* 2.749). Laban, a great sheep farmer who was Jacob's uncle and father-in-law, recalls Libya, where "flocks lamb three times in the course of a year" (*Odyssey* 4.86). And the Arabs who were descended from Abraham? They could be the Homeric Erembians, whom the *Odyssey* mentions with the Libyans (*Odyssey* 4.84).

Also significant is the similarity among Abraham's sacrifice described in Genesis,[5] the Hindu *sautramani,* the Roman *suovetaurilia,* and the sacrifice quoted in the *Odyssey* (11.131) during Ulysses' trip to Hades. As with Ulysses, Abraham's sacrifice introduces an important prophecy.

Jesse, the name of the father of David, is very similar to Esus, whose name is both that of a Celtic god and an appellation of the hero Cúchulainn. (And both Jesse and Esus seem to recall the Homeric Iéson.) Interestingly, the Bible emphasizes that David—who is nominated king by the prophet Samuel, although he is the youngest among seven brothers—is fair-haired.[6] It is worth noting that people are in such awe of Samuel[7] that he alone elected kings. This recalls the druids' influence in the Celtic world, where we can find an amazing counterpart to Samuel in Sithchenn, a Druid, blacksmith, and prophet who chooses Njall as the successor of King Eochaid after examining his five brothers. We could even dare to posit a relationship between the giant Goliath, whom David kills by a blow from a stone, and the Norse giant Giálp, whom, according to the *Skáldskaparmál*, Thor kills in the same way. There are also some striking parallels between the Hebraic Agar and the Roman nymph Egeria: Apart from the similarity of their names, they are both linked to water and fecundity, and both have an extramarital liaison with a king (Abraham and Numa Pompilius, respectively). Of course, given the link between Egeria-Agar and water, we could extend this parallel to Aegir, the Norse king of the sea, and his Homeric counterpart, Aegaeon.

Another analogy between the Bible and Norse mythology can be found in the *Younger Edda*, which tells us that in the gods' twilight there is a character known as Surt, Muspell's guardian, who "has a flaming sword . . . that radiates more light than the Sun."[8] This suggests a comparison with the passage in Genesis in which God, having driven Adam and Eve out of Eden, "places the Cherubs and the flame of the flashing sword in front of the Garden."[9]

The mythical Persian king Yima (who could also be compared with the Norse Ymir, the primordial giant in the *Edda*) was the first man to know death, which connects him with Adam, the first man of the Bible. We have previously noted Yima's connection to both Yama and Hades, who are both known as the "lord of the dead" in the Indian and Homeric contexts, respectively. Hades, also called Aidoneus by Homer, has much in common with Adonis, who in turn is linked to both a tree and the netherworld. Figuring into this picture are the so-called gardens of Adonis in the Greek classical world. Therefore, Yima-Yama-Adonis-Hades could be compared with the biblical Paradise, Adam's first home in a "garden eastward in Eden."[10]

Genesis describes the geography of Eden in a very detailed way, in part describing specifically the four rivers rising there:

> The name of the first is Pison:
> that is it which compasseth the whole land of Havilah, where
>   there is gold;
> And the gold of that land is good: there is bdellium and the onyx
>   stone.

And the name of the second river is Gihon:
the same is it that compasseth the whole land of Ethiopia.
And the name of the third river is Hiddekel:
that is it which goeth toward the east of Assyria.
And the fourth river is Euphrates.[11]

This passage contains two instances of striking geographical inaccuracy: In the area where the Euphrates and Tigris (Hiddekel) have their sources, two other rivers, identifiable as the biblical Pison and the Gihon, do not actually exist. Moreover, two of the rivers rising from Eden are said to flow through Ethiopia and Assyria, respectively—but these lie on different continents! These inaccuracies, not to mention the fact that the "land of Havilah," with its first-rate gold, is not identifiable at all, confirm that the geography of Genesis is unrelated to the actual world.

If, however, the "land of Ethiopia" in Genesis was the Homeric Ethiopia found in the northernmost part of Europe, the puzzle could be solved at once. Let us examine the river that surrounds it, today's Tana. Its source lies in the northern side of Finnish Lapland, near today's Enontekiö (meaning "which produces big rivers" in the Sami language), from which area several rivers rise.* One of these is the Ivalo River, called Avvil by the Laplanders. The similarity between Avvil and Havilah, the biblical land of fine gold, could be accidental but for the fact that this area is rich in gold, as attested to by the Gold Museum in Tankavaara,[12] a village lying near the Ivalo River. What is more, the gold of the river Ivalo-Avvil is exceptionally fine twenty-three-carat gold, just as the biblical passage claims. The bdellium, or fragrant resin, mentioned in the Bible passage is produced by conifers that are plentiful in this area, and chalcedony and jasper found there are similar to onyx in crystal composition.

Two other rivers rise from the region of Enontekiö (where the place-name Hetta, similar to Eden, is found): the Mounion-Torniojoki and a tributary of the Ounas-Kemijoki. They run south, parallel to each other, and flow into the Gulf of Bothnia at its northernmost side. In these we find the Euphrates and Tigris mentioned in Genesis. That these rivers with the territory they surround make up a sort of Finnish Mesopotamia quite like the Asian Mesopotamia is astonishing (see fig. A.1).

---

*Information about Lapland here is drawn mainly from Ada Grilli Bonini, *Iter Lapponi-cum* (Lappish Itinerary) (Bergamo: Leading Edizioni, 2000).

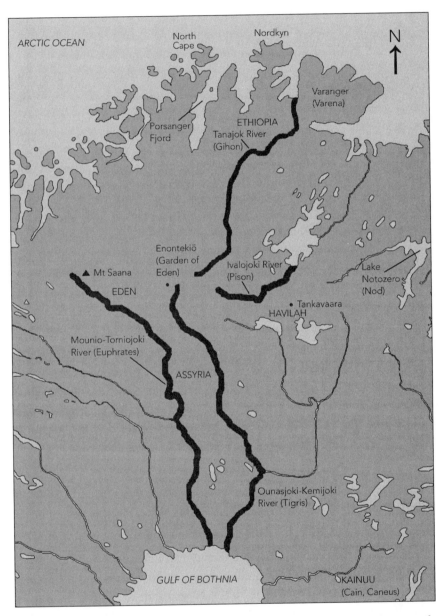

Fig. A.1. The "Edenic" features of the rivers that have their sources in the area of Enontekiö, in the north of Finnish Lapland

This could imply that northern Lapland was the region from which the Sumerians moved south to settle in the area "between the rivers" (the Greek meaning of Mesopotamia) that was very similar to the Arctic region they had left. (At this point, we might also suspect that Ur of the Chaldees,[13] from which Abraham left for the Promised Land, lay in this primordial region.)

The climatic collapse made this northern area inhospitable, which seems confirmed by a passage by Isaiah: "The Lord makes the earth empty, and makes it waste, and turns it upside down, and scatters abroad the inhabitants thereof."[14] This could be the Terre Gaste, the "waste land" of the Arthurian legend—that is, according to Jean Markale, "the desolate land, deserted by its inhabitants, deprived of cultivations, immersed in an early winter." All of this could be also compared with the Homeric passage on "the rotten home [dómon euróenta] of Hades" (especially in light of the similarity between the names Hades and Eden). It seems quite possible here that the Odyssey, the Bible, and Celtic literature all seem to refer to the same tradition.

The legendary Avalon of the Arthurian tales—probably referring to the original homeland—could recall Havilah-Avvil, thus corroborating a relationship between the Hebrew world and the Celtic one. We also note that by placing the biblical Eden in Lapland, the mythical garden lying east of Eden seems to be in the middle of a sort of four-leaf clover formed by four regions (Eden, Ethiopia, Havilah, and Assyria), which creates a picture very similar to the mythical division of Ireland, a Celtic land par excellence, where a political and religious center, Tara, was surrounded by four peripheral regions. Incidentally, the name of Eden's river, Pison, recalls Pisa, a Finnish and Lapp place-name also quoted in the Kalevala. The same root is found in Homeric terms such as pisos (watered place) and pidax (pool).

Another verse of the Bible gives us clues to geographic correspondences between the biblical world and the northen one: "And Cain went out from the presence of the Lord, and dwelt in the land of Nod, on the east of Eden."[15] Actually, on the east of Enontekiö—that is, "on the east of Eden"—in Russian territory, lie the Nota River and Lake Notozero. (An effluent from the latter is the Tuloma River, which flows into the Arctic Ocean near Murmansk, in the Kola peninsula.) In the south of this area, in Finland, we find the region of Kainuu.[16] It coincides with the territory of the Homeric Lapithae, one of whom was Caineus, grandfather of a hero who participated in the Trojan War (Iliad 2.745–46). Perhaps when the climatic optimum collapsed and the tundra made the regions beyond the Arctic Circle uninhabitable, Cain's descendants moved from the Nota basin to a more livable territory situated at a slightly lower latitude.

As we have noted earlier, it is reasonable to assume that the original site of Noah's Flood was a flat land, with isolated rises here and there, that was subject to overall flooding, such as northern Lapland. Memory of this place was later transposed to the Caucasian region, a very important crossroads of migrations from north to south. In this respect, the likeness between the name of Noah's son Shem and the Sami, the Laplanders, is significant. Interestingly, a Lappish mountain, Saana, is sacred to the Sami much as Mount Sinai is to the Jews.

But what of Ham, Noah's other son? Let us return to the Kemijoki, the Kemi River, running southward from Lapland toward the northernmost point of the Gulf of Bothnia. Behind it rises the Tana River, which runs northward toward the Arctic Ethiopia found both in Homer and in the biblical tale of Eden. This configuration is a sort of mirror of African Egypt, the Land of Kem where Ham's descendants lived: It lay along the big river extending from Ethiopia and Lake Tana (from which the Blue Nile rises).

Many other clues seem to corroborate the northern origin of the ancient Egyptians (we can also recall their solar worship and the parallels between Osiris and Lemminkäinen). Perhaps they came from Lapland as well (passing through the area of the Caucasus, where they left the traces W. M. Flinders Petrie notes in local toponymy). Both Egyptians and Sumerians, then, reconstructed their original Arctic homeland when they settled in the Nile Valley and Mesopotamia, respectively.

The Egyptian Book of the Dead mentions their original homeland as "the land of the gods."[17] A similar concept is found in both Genesis and the Homeric poems: The land where the Phaeacians lived near the gods, the region of Pieria quoted in the *Hymn to Hermes,* the seat of the Ethiopians (who were close to the gods), Mount Olympus, and Hades—all of these are found in Lapland.

There is also a Homeric reference to an original happy Eden: The *Odyssey* recalls "the Elysian plain, / at the ends of the earth," where "life for mortals is most wonderful" (*Odyssey* 4.563–65). We can find in Elysian the same root as *hell:* On the one hand, the lost land of ancestors was idealized in the memory of descendants, and on the other, it became the land of the dead. We have seen that the Elysian Fields can be compared to the Norse mythical kingdom known as Glaesisvellir (Shining Plain) or Odáinsakr (Immortals' Field) and related to "Guthmundus' garden of delights," which lay in the far north of Europe.

All the references to such themes lead to the paradisal land in which every summer repeats the marvel of the Hyperion, the midnight sun. The memory of this is perhaps found in a verse from the Apocalypse in which the new Jerusalem appears: "And the gates of it shall not be shut at all by day: for there shall be no night there."[18]

It is remarkable that the parallels between the text of the Bible and Lappish geography on the one hand corroborate the idea of the Hyperborean origin of our civilization and on the other fit perfectly with the biblical conception of the common origin of Semites, Hamites, and Indo-Europeans. We should note, however, that this collides with the old concept of the eastern origin of the European civilization—Ex Oriente Lux, or "Light (comes) from the East." This concept probably originated with the knowledge of the ancientness of the Mesopotamian civilization as well as with the misunderstanding of biblical indications regarding the location of Eden near the sources of the Tigris and Euphrates.

We have already noted, however, that this old conception was recently put into question by radiocarbon dating corrected with dendrochronology. The transfer of the origin of our civilization from east to north, then, conforms perfectly with present lore. Of course, these considerations require further investigation by specialists in the various fields they touch upon. We can consider our speculations here a starting point, rather than an end, in the search for our remote origins.

NOTES

INTRODUCTION—THE KEY TO FINDING HOMER'S WORLD

1. Michael Ventris and John Chadwick, *Documents in Mycenaean Greek*, 2nd edition (Cambridge: Cambridge University Press, 1973), quoted in Moses Finley, *The World of Odysseus* (Harmondsworth, UK: Penguin, 1979), appendix 2.
2. Finley, *The World of Odysseus*, appendix 2.
3. Ventris and Chadwick, *Documents in Mycenaean Greek*, 2nd ed., in Finley, *The World of Odysseus*.
4. Franco Montanari, *Introduzione a Omero* [Introduction to Homer] (Florence: n.p., 1992), 71.
5. Plutarch, "De facie quae in orbe lunae apparet" [The Face That Appears in the Moon Circle]. *The Books of the Moralia*, vol. 12. Translated by Harold Cherniss and William C. Helmbold. Cambridge, Mass.: Harvard University Press, Loeb Classical Library, 1957.
6. Tacitus, *Germania* 3.2, ed. L. Canali (Pordenone, Italy: n.p., 1991).
7. Strabo, *Géographie* [Geography], trans. G. Aujac (Paris: Les Belles Lettres, 1969), 13.1.27.
8. Stuart Piggott, *Ancient Europe from the Beginnings of Agriculture to Classical Antiquity* (Chicago: Aldine, 1968).
9. Federico Di Trocchio, *Il genio incompreso: uomini e idee che la scienza non ha capito* [The Undiscovered Genius: Men and Ideas Science Did Not Understand](Milan: n.p., 1997).

CHAPTER 1—ULYSSES HOMEWARD BOUND: THE ISLAND OF OGYGIA AND THE LAND OF SCHERIA

1. Adriano Romualdi, *Gli Indoeuropei* [The Indo-Europeans] (Padua: n.p., 1978), 98.

2. Karl Schuchhardt, *Alteuropa*, section 10, quoted in Romualdi, *Gli Indoeuropei* [The Indo-Europeans].
3. Under "ioeidés," in Rocci, *Vocabolario Greco-Italiano* [Greek-Italian Dictionary], 39th edition (Genoa: Società anonima editrice Dante Alighieri; Città di Castello, Società anonima casa editrice S. Lapi, 1943).
4. Hesiod, *Théogonie, les Travaux et les jours, le bouclier,* trans. P. Mazon (Paris: Les Belles Lettres, 1979).
5. Snorri Sturluson, *Vafthrudhnismal* 16 in *L'Edda, carmi norreni* [The Edda, Norse poems] (Florence: Sansoni, 1982).
6. Anton Wilhelm Brögger, quoted in Geoffrey Bibby, *The Testimony of the Spade* (New York: Knopf, 1956).

CHAPTER 2—ITHACA'S ARCHIPELAGO: DULICHIUM, SAME, AND ZACYNTHUS

1. Finley, *The World of Odysseus*, chapter 2.
2. Under "Itaca," in *Treccani Italian Encyclopedia* (Rome: n.p., 1949).

CHAPTER 3—ITHACA

1. Tacitus, *Germania* 44.2.
2. Under "épeiros," in Rocci, *Vocabolario Greco-Italiano* [Greek-Italian Dictionary].

CHAPTER 4—THE ADVENTURES OF ULYSSES

1. Strabo, *Geographie* 1.2.15.
2. Under "Querini," in *Treccani Italian Encyclopedia*.
3. Garcilaso de la Vega, *First Part of the Royal Commentaries of the Incas* 1.3, Clements R. Markham, trans. (New York: B. Franklin, 1963).
4. Snorri Sturluson, *Heimskringla* [Norse King Sagas], *Ynglinga Saga,* ed. F. Jónsson (Oslo:n.p., 1966).
5. Gianna Chiesa Isnardi, *Leggende e miti vichinghi* [Viking Myths and Legends] (Milan: n.p., 1989).
6. Roberto Bosi, *Lapponi: sulle tracce di un popolo nomade* [Laplanders: On the Tracks of a Nomadic People] (Florence: n.p., 1995), 46.
7. Under "Norvegia: Etnografia e folklore," in *Treccani Italian Encyclopedia*.
8. James Frazer, *The Golden Bough* (Oxford: Oxford University Press, 1998).
9. Snorri Sturluson, *Gylfaginning* 23, in *Edda di Snorri,* trans. Gianna Chiesa Isnardi (Milan: n.p., 1975), 161.
10. Robert Graves, *The Greek Myths* (Mt. Kisco, N.Y.: Moyer Bell, 1988), 170.4.

11. William F. Warren, *The Paradise Found* (Boston: Houghton Mifflin, 1886), quoted in B. G. Tilak, *The Arctic Home in the Vedas* (Poona: M. Tilak Bros., 1971).
12. E. Lot Falck, *Textes,* quoted in Ugo Marazzi, ed., *Testi dello Sciamanesimo* [Texts of Shamanism] (Turin: Unione Tipografica, 1984).
13. Ugo Marazzi, *Testi dello Sciamanesimo* [Texts of Shamanism], 577.
14. From the British Admiralty publication *Norway Pilot,* vol. 3A, "Offshore and Coastal Waters of Norway from Risværfjorden to the North Part of Vesterålen," 6th ed. (1982), and chart no. 2327, "Værøya to Litløya, Including Vestfjorden to Narvik" (Taunton, Somerset, UK: British Admiralty, 1982).
15. Ibid.
16. Jules Verne, *Twenty Thousand Leagues Under the Sea,* trans. Medor Brunetti (New York: Signet Classics, 2001).
17. Paul the Deacon, *Historiae Langobardorum* 1.6, Amedeo Giacomini, trans. (Udine: Casamassima, 1982), quoted in Chiesa Isnardi, *I miti nordici* [Northern Myths].
18. *Norway Pilot,* vol. 3A, "Offshore and Coastal Waters of Norway from Risværfjorden to the North Part of Vesterålen," 6th ed; chart no. 2327, "Værøya to Litløya, Including Vestfjorden to Narvik."
19. Under "mûla," in Sir Monier Monier Williams, *Sanskrit-English Dictionary* (New Delhi: Asian Educational Services, 1999).
20. Robert Graves, *The Greek Myths.*
21. Visit www.lexiline.com/lexiline/lexi52.htm.
22. Saxo Grammaticus, *Gesta dei re e degli eroi danesi* [Deeds of the Danish Kings and Heroes] (Turin: n.p., 1993).
23. Under "Carelia," in *Treccani Italian Encyclopedia.*
24. Georges Dumézil, *La religione romana arcaica* [The Archaic Roman Religion] (Milan: n.p., 1977), 562.
25. Ibid., 216.
26. Mircea Eliade, *Lo sciamanismo e le tecniche dell'estasi* [Shamanism and Techniques of Ecstasy] (Rome: n.p, 1983), 226, 335.
27. Frazer, *The Golden Bough,* 56.3.
28. *Ynglinga Saga* 32.
29. Under "histopéde," in Rocci, *Vocabolario Greco-Italiano* [Greek-Italian Dictionary].
30. Chiesa Isnardi, *I miti nordici* [Northern Myths] (Milan: n.p., 1996), 354.
31. *Helgi Saga,* "Óláfs konungs Haraldssonar" 14 (Reykjavik: n.p., 1957), quoted in Chiesa Isnardi, *I miti nordici* [Northern Myths].
32. Edgar Allan Poe, "A Descent into the Maelstrom," in *Edgar Allan Poe: Selected Works* (New York: Grammercy, 1990).

33. Poe, "A Descent into the Maelstrom."
34. Under "Thrinakíe," in Rocci, *Vocabolario Greco-Italiano* [Greek-Italian Dictionary].
35. Under "Ulisse," in *Treccani Italian Encyclopedia.*
36. Saxo Grammaticus, *Gesta dei re e degli eroi danesi* [Deeds of the Danish Kings and Heroes], 7, 9, 11.
37. Snorri Sturluson, *Skáldskaparmál,* in *Edda di Snorri,* 161.
38. Under "Hyperion," in *Webster's English Dictionary.*
39. Giacomo Tripodi, private letter, June 22, 2001.

CHAPTER 5—ULYSSES AND NORTHERN MYTHOLOGY

1. Tacitus, *Germania* 3.2.
2. Snorri Sturluson, *Grimnismal 59–60,* in *Edda di Snorri.*
3. Ibid., 3.
4. Saxo Grammaticus, *Gesta dei re e degli eroi danesi* [Deeds of the Danish Kings and Heroes], 3.4.25.
5. Ibid., 2.3.8.
6. Ibid., 1.6.10.
7. Ibid., 8.11.2.
8. Ibid., 7.1–3.
9. Ibid., 5.7.11.
10. Ibid., 9.5.6.
11. Ibid., 5.11.5.
12. Tacitus, *Germania* 44.2.
13. Saxo Grammaticus, *Gesta dei re e degli eroi danesi* [Deeds of the Danish Kings and Heroes], 9.4.21.
14. Ibid., 6.3.3.
15. Ibid., 7.11.2.
16. Ibid., 5.1.13.
17. Ibid., 7.3.1.
18. Ibid., 5.1.7.
19. Ibid., 2.6.9.
20. Ibid., 3.2.1.
21. Ibid., 5.3.2.
22. Ludovica Koch, introduction to *Gesta dei re e degli eroi danesi* [Deeds of the Danish Kings and Heroes] (Turin: n.p., 1993).
23. Saxo Grammaticus, *Gesta dei re e degli eroi danesi* [Deeds of the Danish Kings and Heroes], 3.4.10–11.
24. Ibid., 3.4.12.
25. Ibid., 1.8.18.
26. Ibid., 7.1.1–7.

27. Ibid., 7.9.14.
28. Koch, introduction to *Gesta dei re e degli eroi danesi* [Deeds of the Danish Kings and Heroes].
29. Saxo Grammaticus, *Gesta dei re e degli eroi danesi* [Deeds of the Danish Kings and Heroes], 7.9.15.
30. Ibid., 4.1.10.
31. Ibid.
32. Ibid., 3.6.10.
33. Hesiod, *Théogonie, les Travaux et les jours, le bouclier,* 1.145.
34. Rudolf Pörtner, *L'epopea dei Vichinghi* [The Epics of the Vikings] (Milan: n.p., 1996), 15.
35. *Kalevala,* eds. G. Agrati and M. L. Magini (Milan: n.p., 1988), Rune 8.
36. Mircea Eliade, *Lo sciamanismo e le tecniche dell'estasi* [Shamanism and Techniques of Ecstasy], 294.
37. Chiesa Isnardi, *I miti nordici* [Northern Myths], 532.
38. Ibid., 534.
39. Ibid., 380.
40. Stuart Piggott, *The Druids* (New York: Thames and Hudson, 1985).
41. Graves, *The Greek Myths,* 160.5.
42. Jean Markale, *I Celti* [The Celts] (Milan: n.p., 1982), 318.
43. Françoise Le Roux and Christian J. Guyonvarc'h, *Les Druides* [The Druids] (Rennes: n.p., 1982), 227–33.
44. Markale, *I Celti* [The Celts], 105.

CHAPTER 6—IF "THIS IS NOT THE SITE OF THE ANCIENT ILIUM," WHERE WAS TROY?

1. David Traill, *Schliemann of Troy* (New York: St. Martin's, 1995), chapter 11.
2. Finley, *The World of Odysseus,* appendix 2.
3. Fausto Codino, *Introduzione a Omero* [Introduction to Homer] (Turin, n.p., 1990), 16.
4. Fritz Graf, *Il mito in Grecia* [Myth in Greece] (Bari, n.p., 1997), 5.
5. Strabo, *Géographie* [Geography] 13, 1, 27.
6. Martin P. Nilsson, *The Mycenaean Origin of Greek Mythology* (New York: Norton, 1963).
7. Under "Dardanelli," in *Treccani Italian Encyclopedia.*
8. Saxo Grammaticus, *Gesta dei re e degli eroi danesi* [Deeds of the Danish Kings and Heroes], 9.4.20.
9. Karl Schuchhardt, *Alteuropa,* section 10, quoted in Adriano Romualdi, *Gli Indoeuropei* [The Indo-Europeans].
10. *Beowulf,* ed. Ludovica Koch (Turin: n.p., 1987), 2803–2808.

CHAPTER 7—WAR!

1. *Beowulf,* 499–606.
2. Saxo Grammaticus, *Gesta dei re e degli eroi danesi* [Deeds of the Danish Kings and Heroes], 7.14.2
3. Pörtner, *L'epopea dei Vichinghi* [The Epics of the Vikings], 220.
4. John Kraft, *Geology,* vol. 31, no. 2, 163–66.
5. Finley, *The World of Odysseus.*
6. Caesar, *De Bello Gallico* 4.33.
7. Ibid., 5.16.
8. Tacitus, *Germania* 14.1.
9. Under "hammer," in *Collins English Dictionary* (Glasgow: HarperCollins, 1994).
10. Pia Laviosa Zambotti, *Le più antiche civiltà nordiche* [The Most Ancient Northern Civilizations] (Milan: n.p., 1941), 226.
11. Under "amphilýke," in Rocci, *Vocabolario Greco-Italiano* [Greek-Italian Dictionary].
12. Schuchhardt, *Alteuropa,* section 10, quoted in Romualdi, *Gli Indoeuropei* [The Indo-Europeans], 98.
13. *Homeric Hymn to Aphrodite,* 196–98.
14. Pliny, *Storia Naturale* [Natural History] (Turin: n.p., 1982), 4.96.
15. Snorri Sturluson, *Gylfaginning* 9 in *Edda di Snorri.*
16. Snorri Sturluson, *Völuspá* 27–28, in *Edda di Snorri.*
17. Ibid., 239–40.

CHAPTER 8—NEIGHBORING LANDS AND ISLANDS

1. Livy, 1.1.
2. Tacitus, *Germania* 46.1–2.
3. Selma Lagerlöf, *Nils Holgersson,* quoted in Jean Markale, *I Celti* [The Celts], 527.
4. Under "aulós," in Rocci, *Vocabolario Greco-Italiano* [Greek-Italian Dictionary].
5. Karl Kerényi, *Miti e misteri* [Myths and Mysteries] (Turin: n.p., 1979), 175.
6. Graves, *The Greek Myths,* 18.1.
7. *Rig Veda,* ed. S. Sani (Venice: n.p., 2000), 1.154.3.

CHAPTER 9—CLIMATE AND CHRONOLOGY: THE NORTHERN ORIGIN OF THE MYCENAEANS

1. Under "Olocenico, periodo" in *Treccani Italian Encyclopedia.*
2. Laviosa Zambotti, *Le più antiche civiltà nordiche* [The Most Ancient Northern Civilizations], 19.

3. Piggott, quoted in A. R. Burn, *The Penguin History of Greece* (London: Penguin Books, 1985).

4. Colin Renfrew, *Before Civilization* (Harmondsworth, UK: Penguin, 1990).

5. Under "Thames River," in *The New Encyclopedia Britannica* (Chicago: Encyclopedia Britannica, 2005).

6. Tacitus, *Annales* 14.33.

7. Geoffrey Bibby, *The Testimony of the Spade*, chapter 16.

8. Laviosa Zambotti, *Le più antiche civiltà nordiche* [The Most Ancient Northern Civilizations], 223.

9. Under "Nordiche, civiltà," in *Treccani Italian Encyclopedia*.

10. Under "Bronzo," in *Treccani Italian Encyclopedia*.

11. Siegfried Fischer-Fabian, *I Germani* [The Germans] (Milan: n.p., 1985), 90.

12. See www.astro.uni-bonn.de/%7Edfischer/mirror/243.html.

13. Pörtner, *L'epopea dei Vichinghi* [The Epics of the Vikings], 7.

14. Edith Ennan, *Frühgeschichte der europäischen Stadt,* quoted in Pörtner, *L'epopea de Vichinghi* [The Epics of the Vikings], 131.

15. Tacitus, *Germania* 11.

16. *Beowulf,* 2330, 2608.

17. Ibid., 499–606.

18. Ibid., 1457

19. Tacitus, *Germania* 25.1.

20. Pörtner, *L'epopea dei Vichinghi* [The Epics of the Vikings], 105.

21. Saxo Grammaticus, *Gesta dei re e degli eroi danesi* [Deeds of the Danish Kings and Heroes], 1.1.1.

22. Bibby, *4000 Years Ago: A World Panorama of Life in the Second Millennium B.C.* (Westport, Conn.: Greenwood Press, 1983), chapter 16.

23. Tacitus, *Germania* 17.1.

24. Bibby, *4000 Years Ago,* chapter 16.

25. Under "Nordiche, civiltà," in *Treccani Italian Encyclopedia*.

26. Tacitus, *Germania* 22.1.

27. Ibid., 23.1.

28. Pörtner, *L'epopea dei Vichinghi* [The Epics of the Vikings], 207.

29. Pindar, *Pindaro: L'opera Superstite* [Pindar: The Surviving Work], ed. Enzo Mandruzzato (Bologna: Cappelli, 1980).

30. Pörtner, *L'epopea dei Vichinghi* [The Epics of the Vikings], 199.

31. Tacitus, *Germania* 5.1.

32. Under "Baltiche, lingue," in *Treccani Italian Encyclopedia*.

33. Frazer, *The Golden Bough.*

34. Karl Kerényi, *Gli dèi e gli eroi della Grecia* [Gods and Heroes of Greece](Milan: n.p., 1963), 202.

35. Laviosa Zambotti, *Le più antiche civiltà nordiche* [The Most Ancient Northern Civilizations], 20.

36. See www.usatoday.com/weather/tg/wadvfog/wadvfog.htm.

37. Tacitus, *Germania* 26.4.

38. Under "opóra," in Rocci, *Vocabolario Greco-Italiano* [Greek-Italian Dictionary].

39. Saxo Grammaticus, *Gesta dei re e degli eroi danesi* (Deeds of the Danish Kings and Heroes), 8.12.1.

40. Hesiod, *Théogonie, les travaux et les jours, le bouclier,* 157–65.

41. Pierre Lévêque, *La civiltà greca* [Greek Civilization] (Turin: n.p., 1970), 40.

42. Colin Renfrew, *Before Civilization,* chapter 11.

43. Martin P. Nilsson, *Homer and Mycenae* (London: Methuen, 1933), 76.

44. Martin P. Nilsson, *The Minoan-Mycenaean Religion and Its Survival in Greek Religion* (Lund: C. W. K. Gleerup, 1927), 19.

45. Tacitus, *Germania* 45.2.

46. Nilsson, *Homer and Mycenae,* 80.

47. Giorgio Pasquali, introduction to Martin Nilsson, *Le religioni degli antichi e i moderni* [The Religions of the Ancients and the Moderns] (Scandicci, Italy: n.p., 1993).

48. Lévêque, *La civiltà greca,* 47.

49. Nilsson, *Homer and Mycenae,* 75.

50. Pindar, *Nemean 9.*

51. Giulio Giannelli, *Trattato di storia greca* [Treatise on Greek History] (Bologna: n.p., 1983), 52.

52. Cambridge University, *Storia del mondo antico* [History of the Ancient World], vol. 2 (Milan, n.p., 1976).

53. Nilsson, *Homer and Mycenae,* 85.

54. Bertrand Russell, *History of Western Philosophy* (London: Allen and Unwin, 1946), chapter 1.

55. Renfrew, *Before Civilization,* chapter 4.

56. Finley, *The World of Odysseus,* preface.

57. Codino, *Introduzione a Omero* [Introduction to Homer], 77.

58. Fritz Graf, *Il mito in Grecia* [Myth in Greece] (Bari: n.p., 1997), 56.

59. Ibid., 52.

60. Piggott, *Prehistoric India to 1000 B.C.* (London: Cassell, 1962).

61. Alexandra David-Néel, *Vita sovrumana di Gesar di Ling* [The Superhuman Life of Gesar of Ling] (Rome: n.p., 1990), 39.

62. Geoffrey Kirk, *The Cambridge History of Classical Literature,* vol. 1, part 1 (Cambridge: Cambridge University Press, 1989).

63. Ibid., 82.

64. Hesiod, *Théogonie, les travaux et les jours, le bouclier,* 134, 374.

65. Codino, *Introduction to Homer,* 11.

66. Under "Russia: Storia," in *Treccani Italian Encyclopedia.*

67. Bibby, *The Testimony of the Spade,* chapter 16.

CHAPTER 10—THE CATALOG OF SHIPS:
THE NORTHERN ACHAEAN WORLD

1. Pindar, *Olympic* 3.25.
2. Diodorus Siculus, *Biblioteca storica* [Historical Library] (Palermo: n.p., 1986).
3. Plato, *Timée, Critias,* trans. A. Rivaud (Paris: n.p., 1970), 109a–112e.
4. Ibid.
5. Ibid., 112e.
6. Saxo Grammaticus, *Gesta dei re e degli eroi danesi* [Deeds of the Danish Kings and Heroes], 8.3.13.
7. Graf, *Il mito in Grecia* [Myths in Greece], 50.
8. Giacomo Prampolini, *La mitologia nella vita dei popoli* [Mythology in the Life of Peoples], vol. 2 (Milan: n.p., 1954).
9. Tacitus, *Germania* 46.4.
10. Jordanes, *Storia dei Goti* [The Gothic History], ed. E. Bartolini (Milan: n.p., 1999), chapter 3.
11. Saxo Grammaticus, *Gesta dei re e degli eroi danesi* [Deeds of the Danish Kings and Heroes], 5.8.1.
12. Under "Ugro-Finniche, lingue," in *Treccani Italian Encyclopedia.*
13. Tacitus, *Germania* 22.1.

CHAPTER 11—THE REGIONS OF THE PELOPONNESE

1. Leonard Palmer, *Mycenaeans and Minoans* (Westport, Conn.: Greenwood Press, 1980), chapter 1.
2. Graf, *Il mito in Grecia* [Myth in Greece], 52.
3. Saxo Grammaticus, *Gesta dei re e degli eroi danesi* [Deeds of the Danish Kings and Heroes], 7.8.2–3.
4. Snorri Sturluson, *Gylfaginning* 35, in *Edda di Snorri.*
5. Laura Orvieto, *Storie della Storia del Mondo* [Stories of the History of the World] (Florence: n.p., 1952).
6. Homer, *Hymnes,* 228.

CHAPTER 12—CRETE, THE RIVER EGYPT,
PHAROS, AND PHTHIA

1. Tacitus, *Germania* 2.2.
2. *Kalevala,* Rune 28.
3. Under "Livi," in *Treccani Italian Encyclopedia.*
4. Under "Lettonia: Clima," in *Treccani Italian Encyclopedia.*
5. Nilsson, *Homer and Mycenae,* 82.
6. Jordanes, *Storia dei Goti* [History of the Goths], chapter 17.

7. Laviosa Zambotti, *Le più antiche civiltà nordiche* [The Most Ancient Northern Myths], 209.

8. Herodotus, *History* 2.45.

9. Strabo, *Géographie* [Geography] 1.2.31.

10. Ananda Coomaraswamy, introduction to *Sir Gawain e il Cavaliere Verde* [Sir Gawain and the Green Knight] (Milan: n.p., 1986), 170.

11. Kerényi, *Gli dèi e gli eroi della Grecia* (Gods and Heroes of Greece), 294.

12. Chiesa Isnardi, *I miti nordici* [Northern Myths], 584.

13. Under "Estonia," in *Treccani Italian Encyclopedia.*

14. Under "Pskov," in *Treccani Italian Encyclopedia.*

15. Fausto Codino, in a footnote to *Iliad* 20.272, in the *Iliad,* translated into Italian by Rosa Calzecchi Onesti (Turin: n.p., 1974).

16. Chiesa Isnardi, *I miti nordici* [Northern Myths], 652.

CHAPTER 13—FINDING THE HOME OF THE GODS

1. Hesiod, *Théogonie, les travaux et les jours, le bouclier,* 776.

2. Aristoteles, Fragment 687 Rose, in Plutarch, *Il Volto della Luna* (Milan: Adelphi, 1991)

3. Plutarch, *Il volto della luna.*

4. Tacitus, *Germania* 34.2.

5. Hesiod, *Théogonie, les travaux et les jours, le bouclier,* 517–18.

6. Chiesa Isnardi, *I miti nordici* [Northern Myths], 56.

7. Snorri Sturluson, *Helgakvidha Hundingsbana* 1.116–17, in *Edda di Snorri.*

8. Plato, *Timée, Critias,* 24e.

9. Plutarch, *Il volto della luna,* chapter 26.

10. Ibid.

11. Giorgio de Santillana, *The Origins of Scientific Thought* (Chicago: University of Chicago Press, 1961).

12. Under "phrén," in *Rocci, Vocabolario Greco-Italiano* [Greek-Italian Dictionary].

13. Plato, *Timée, Critias.*

14. Diodorus Siculus, *Biblioteca storica* (Historical Library), 5.21.

15. Luigi de Anna, *Le isole perdute e le isole ritrovate* [The Lost and Found Islands] (Turku, Finland: University of Turku, 1993), 110.

16. Laviosa Zambotti, *Le più antiche civiltà nordiche* [The Most Ancient Northern Civilizations], 73.

17. Ibid., 9.

18. Plato, *Timée, Critias,* 114b.

19. Ibid., 119d and e.

20. *Kalevala,* Rune 31.

21. Ibid., Rune 37.

22. Plato, *Timée, Critias*, 114e.
23. *Second Homeric Hymn to Aphrodite*, 9.
24. Carl Robert, quoted in Jean Humbert's preface, Homer, *Hymnes* [Hymns], trans. Jean Humbert (Paris: n.p., 1967), 108.
25. Homer, *Hymnes* [Hymns], line 100.
26. Ibid., 140–41.

CHAPTER 14—CLIMATE CHANGE AND THE MIGRATION OF CULTURE

1. Piggott, *Prehistoric India to 1000 B.C.*
2. Onorato Bucci, *Airyana Vaêjo: The Original Home of the Aryans.*
3. Snorri Sturluson, *Gylfaginning* 51, in *Edda di Snorri.*
4. *Vendidad*, Fargard 2, quoted by B. G. Tilak in *La dimora artica nei Veda* [The Arctic Home in the Vedas] (Genoa: n.p., 1994).
5. Ibid., Fargard 1.
6. Édouard Schuré, *I Grandi Iniziati* [The Great Initiates] (Bari: n.p., 1973).
7. Under "Dardi," in *Treccani Italian Encyclopedia.*
8. Piggott, *Prehistoric India to 1000 B.C.*, 268.
9. Tacitus, *Germania* 30.1.
10. Under "Kassel," in *Treccani Italian Encyclopedia.*
11. See www.int-pub-iran.com/ipis05_t1.htm.
12. W. M. Flinders Petrie, "The Origins of the Book of the Dead," *Ancient Egypt*, June 1926.
13. Under "Egitto, Religione," in *Treccani Italian Encyclopedia.*
14. Tacitus, *Germania* 40.2.
15. Ibid., 2.2.
16. *Kalevala*, Rune 14.
17. Under "Manale, pietra," in *Treccani Italian Encyclopedia.*
18. Frans Vyncke, *La religione dei Balti* [The Religion of the Balts], in *Storia delle religioni* (History of Religions), ed. H. Puech (Bari: n.p., 1977), 41.
19. Dumézil, *La religione romana arcaica*, 108.
20. Robert De Benoist, "Indo-Europeans: à la recherche du foyer d'origine" [Indo-Europeans: Searching for Their Place of Origin], *Nouvelle École* 49 (1997), 98.
21. Chiesa Isnardi, *I miti nordici* [Northern Myths], 245.
22. Eliade, *Lo sciamanismo e le tecniche dell'estasi* [Shamanism and Techniques of Ecstasy], 49.
23. The Book of Jubilees 7.1.
24. Genesis 8.6–7.
25. Enoch 106.2.
26. See www.dainas.com/index.htm.

27. See www.lexiline.com/lexiline/lexi37.htm.
28. Under "Sumeru," in Monier Williams, *Sanskrit-English Dictionary.*
29. *L'Épopée de Gilgamesh,* trans. G. Contenau (Paris: n.p., 1939), 9.5.

CHAPTER 15—SOLAR, STELLAR, AND LUNAR MYTHS

1. Jean Haudry, "Les Indo-Européens et le Grand Nord" [The Indo-Europeans and the Great North], *Nouvelle École* 49 (1997), 119.
2. Snorri Sturluson, *Grottasongr* 22 in *L'Edda, carmi norreni* [The Edda, Norse Poems].
3. *Taittirîya Samhitâ* 2.1, 2.5, quoted in B. G. Tilak, *La dimora artica nei Veda* [The Arctic Home in the Vedas].
4. Plutarch, *Isis et Osiris* (Isis and Osiris), trans. M. Meunier (Paris: n.p., 1979), 32.
5. Frazer, *The Golden Bough,* chapter 5.3.
6. Tilak, *La dimora artica nei Veda* [The Arctic Home in the Vedas], 219.
7. Jerzy Ficowski, *Il rametto dell'albero del Sole* [The Little Branch of Sun's Tree] (Rome: n.p., 1985), 27.
8. Kerényi, *Gli dèi e gli eroi della Grecia* [Gods and Heroes of Greece], 95.
9. Ibid., *Miti e misteri* [Myths and Mysteries], 173.
10. *Kalevala,* Rune 9.
11. Ibid.
12. Walter Otto, "The Original Myth in the Light of the Sympathy between Man and World," *Il mito* [The Myth], ed. Giampiero Moretti (Genoa: Il Melangolo, 1962).
13. Diodorus Siculus, *Biblioteca storica* [Historical Library], 5.23.
14. Plutarch, *Isis et Osiris* [Isis and Osiris], chapter 13 ff.
15. Frazer, *The Golden Bough,* chapter 52.1.
16. Snorri Sturluson, *Hymiskvidha* 90–92 in *L'Edda, carmi norreni.*
17. Snorri Sturluson, *Gylfaginning* 48, in *Edda di Snorri.*
18. *Beowulf,* 2271–73.
19. Frazer, *The Golden Bough,* chapter 56.3.
20. Isaiah 27.1.
21. *Sir Gawain e il Cavaliere Verde* [Sir Gawain and the Green Knight] ed. Piero Boitani (Milan: Adelphi, 1986), line 2519.
22. *Beowulf,* 2767–69.
23. Kerényi, *Gli dèi e gli eroi della Grecia,* 171.
24. Jacob Grimm, *Teutonic Mythologie,* quoted in Giorgio de Santillana and Hertha von Dechend, *Il Mulino di Amleto* [Hamlet's Mill] (Milan: Adelphi, 2003).
25. Markale, *I Celti,* 73.
26. Ovid, *Fasti* 3.657.

APPENDIX: THE BIBLE AND THE NORTHERN BRONZE AGE

1. 1 Maccabees 12:20–23, 2 Maccabees 5, 9.
2. Tacitus, *Germania* 18.2.
3. Quoted by G. Acerbi in the introduction to B. G. Tilak, *Orione* [The Orion] (Genoa: ECIG, 1991).
4. Genesis 13:7.
5. Ibid., 15:9.
6. 1 Samuel 16:12.
7. See in particular 1 Samuel 16:2.
8. Snorri Sturluson, *Gylfaginning* 4, 51, in *Edda di Snorri*.
9. Genesis 3:24.
10. Ibid., 2:8.
11. Ibid., 2:11–14.
12. See www.urova.fi/home/kulta/eindex.htm.
13. Genesis 11:31.
14. Isaiah 24:1.
15. Genesis 4:16.
16. Under "Finlandia," table 2, in *Treccani Italian Encyclopedia*. See also www.kainuu.com/eng/.
17. Boris de Rachewiltz, ed., *Il libro dei morti degli antichi egiziani* [Ancient Egyptians' Book of the Dead] (Milan, n.p., 1958).
18. Apocalypse 21:25.

BIBLIOGRAPHY

Note: This bibliography has been modified from that appearing in the original Italian edition of this book. It includes many titles—especially primary sources—in their English rather than Italian translations.

Agrati, Gabriella, and Maria Latizia Magini, eds. *Kalevala*. Milan: A. Mondadori, 1988.

Aston, W. G., trans. *Nihongi, Chronicles of Japan from the Earliest Times to A.D. 697*. London: Allen and Unwin, 1956.

Beowulf. Harold Bloom, ed. New York: Chelsea House Publishers, 1996.

Bianucci, P. *Stella per stella* (Star by Star). Florence: n.p., 1997.

Bibby, Geoffrey. *The Testimony of the Spade*. New York: Knopf, 1956.

———. *4000 Years Ago: A World Panorama of Life in the Second Millennium B.C.* Westport, Conn.: Greenwood Press, 1983.

Blacker, Carmen, and Michael Loewe, eds. *Ancient Cosmologies*. London: Allen and Unwin, 1975.

Bosi, Roberto. *The Lapps*. Translated by James Cadell. Westport, Conn.: Greenwood Press, 1976.

Braccesi, L. *La leggenda di Antenore—dalla Troade al Veneto* (Anthenor's Legend—from Troad to Veneto). Padova: Signum, 1984.

Bucci, Onorato, ed. *Antichi popoli europei* (Ancient European Peoples). Rome: n.p., 1993.

Burn, A. R. *The Penguin History of Greece*. London: Penguin Books, 1985.

Bussagli, Mario., ed. *Miti dell'Oriente* (Myths of the Orient). Rome: n.p., 1976.

Bussagli, Mario, and M. G. Chiappori. *I Re Magi: Realtà storica e tradizione magica* (The Magi: Historical Reality and Magical Tradition). Milan: Rusconi, 1985.

Caillot, Eugène. *Mythes, légendes et traditions des Polynésiens* (Myths, Legends, and Traditions of the Polynesians). Paris: Ernest Leroux, 1914.

Cambridge History of Classical Literature, vol. 1, part 1, *Early Greek Poetry*. Cambridge: Cambridge University Press, 1989.

Càssola, Fabio, ed. *Inni omerici* (Homeric Hymns). Milan: Mondadori, 1994.

Castellino, Giorgio R., ed. *Testi sumerici e accadici* (Sumerian and Accadis Texts). Turin: Unione Tipografica, 1977.

Cataldi, Melita, ed. *Antiche storie e fiabe irlandesi* (Ancient Irish Stories and Tales). Turin: UTET, 1985.

Chadwick, John. *The Decipherment of Linear B*. London: Cambridge University Press, 1967.

Chapman, P. H. *The Norse Discovery of America*. Atlanta: One Candle Press, 1981.

Chiesa Isnardi, Gianna, ed. *Edda di Snorri* (The Edda of Snorri). Milan: n.p., 1975.

———. *Leggende e miti vichinghi* (Legends and Myths of the Vikings). Milan: n.p., 1989.

———. *I miti nordici* (The Myths of the Norse). Milan: n.p., 1996.

Codino, Fausto. *Introduzione a Omero* (Introduction to Homer). Turin: n.p., 1990.

Collins English Dictionary. Glasgow: HarperCollins, 1994.

Colonna, A. *Storia della letteratura greca* (History of Greek Literature). Turin: n.p., 1973.

Costa, G. *Le origini della lingua poetica indeuropea* (The Origins of the Poetical Indo-European Language). Florence: L. S. Olschki, 1998.

Dahl, Erik. *Odysseus' Pilgrimage to the Far North* (unpublished manuscript).

David-Néel, Alexandra, and Lama Yongden. *The Superhuman Life of Gesar of Ling, the Legendary Tibetan hero*. London: Rider, 1933.

de Anna, Luigi. *Le isole perdute e le isole ritrovate* (The Lost and Found Islands). Turku, Finland: University of Turku, 1993.

De Benoist, Robert. "Indo-Europeans: à la recherche du foyer d'origine" (Indo-Europeans: Searching for Their Place of Origin). In *Nouvelle École* 49 (1997).

de la Vega, Garcilaso. *First Part of the Royal Commentaries of the Incas*. Translated and edited by Clements R. Markham. New York: B. Franklin, 1963.

de Rachewiltz, Boris, ed. *Il libro dei morti degli antichi egiziani* (The Ancient Egyptians' Book of the Dead). Milan: n.p., 1958.

———. *I miti egizi* (Egyptian Myths). Milan: n.p., 1983.

de Santillana, Giorgio. *The Origins of Scientific Thought*. Chicago: University of Chicago Press, 1961.

de Santillana, Giorgio, and H. von Dechend. *Hamlet's Mill: An Essay on Myth and the Frame of Time*. Boston: Gambit, 1969.

Diano, Carlo., ed. *Il teatro greco, tutte le tragedie* (Greek Theater: All Tragedies). Florence: n.p., 1981.

Diodorus Siculus. *Historical Library*. Cambridge, Mass.: Harvard University Press, Loeb Classical Library, 1985.

Di Trocchio, Federico. *Il genio incompreso: uomini e idee che la scienza non ha capito* (The Undiscovered Genius: Men and Ideas Science Did Not Understand). Milan: Mondonari, 1997.

Donadoni, Sergio, ed. *Testi religiosi egizi* (Egyptian Religious Texts). Turin: Unione Tipografica, 1970.

Duichin, M. "Apollo, il dio sciamano venuto dal Nord" (Apollo, the Shaman God Who Came from the North). In *Abstracta* no. 39 (July/August 1989).

Dumézil, Georges. *La Courtisane et les seigneurs colorés* (The Court Lady and the Colored Gentlemen). Paris: Gallimard, 1983.

———. *Archaic Roman Religion*. Baltimore: Johns Hopkins University Press, 1996.

———. *Storie degli Sciti* (Stories of the Scythians). Milan: n.p., 1980.

———. *The Stakes of the Warrior*. Berkeley: University of California Press, 1983.

Eliade, Mircea. *The Forge and the Crucible: The Origins and Structure of Alchemy*. Chicago: University of Chicago Press, 1979.

———. *Shamanism: Archaic Techniques of Ecstasy*. London: Arkana, 1989.

Ficowski, Jerzy. *Il rametto dell'albero del Sole* (The Little Branch of Sun's Tree). Rome: n.p., 1985.

Finley, Moses. *The World of Odysseus*. New York: Viking, 1977.

Fischer-Fabian, Siegfried. *I Germani* (The Germans). Milan: n.p., 1985.

Frazer, James. *The Golden Bough*. Oxford: Oxford University Press, 1998.

Giannelli, Giulio. *Trattato di storia greca* (Treatise on Greek History). Bologna: n.p., 1983.

Gilgamesh: A New English Version. Translated by Stephen Mitchell. New York: Free Press, 2004.

Graf, Fritz. *Greek Mythology*. Baltimore: Johns Hopkins University Press, 1993.

Grande Dizionario Enciclopedico. Turin: UTET, n.d.

Graves, Robert. *The Greek Myths*. Mt. Kisco, N.Y.: Moyer Bell, 1988.

Griaule, Marcel. *Dio d'acqua* (God of Water). Milan: n.p., 1968.

Grilli, Bonini A. *Iter Lapponicum* (Lappish Itinerary). Bergamo: n.p., 2000.

Guiart, Jean. *Les Réligions de l'Océanie* (The Religions of Oceania). Paris: n.p., 1962.

Hertel, Dieter. *Troia* (Troy). Bologna: n.p., 2003.

Hesiod. *Theogony, Works and Days, Shield*. Baltimore: Johns Hopkins University Press, 2004.

Homer. *Hymns to Hermes*. Translated by Apostolos Athanassakis. Baltimore: Johns Hopkins University Press, 2004.

———. *Iliade* (The Iliad). Translated into Italian by R. Calzecchi Onesti. Turin: n.p., 1974.

———. *Iliad*. Translated by Robert Fagles. London: Penguin, 1998.

———. *Odissea* (The Odyssey). Translated into Italian by R. Calzecchi Onesti. Turin: n.p., 1977.

———. *Odyssey.* Translated by Robert Fitzgerald. New York: Farrar, Straus, and Giroux, 1998.

Italian Nuclear Asssociation (AIN) Proceedings, Rome 2001."Environmental Extremism and Scientific Information."

Jordanes. *The Gothic History.* Princeton, N.J.: Princeton University Press, 1915.

Kalevala. Edited by Elias Lönnrot and translated by Keith Bosley. Oxford: Oxford University Press, 1999.

Kanteletar. Edited by Elias Lönnrot and translated by Keith Bosley. Oxford: Oxford University Press, 1992.

Kerényi, Karl. *Figlie del Sole* (Sun's Daughters). Turin: n.p., 1991.

———. *Gli dèi e gli eroi della Grecia* (Gods and Heroes of Greece). Milan: n.p., 1963.

———. *Miti e misteri* (Myths and Mysteries). Turin: n.p., 1979.

Klepesta, Josef, and Antonín Rükl. *Le Costellazioni, Atlante illustrato* (The Constellations: An Illustrated Atlas). Milan: n.p., 1976.

Kojiki-den. Introduced, translated, and annotated by Ann Wehmeyer. Ithaca, N.Y.: East Asia Program, Cornell University, 1997.

Laviosa Zambotti, Pia. *Le più antiche civiltà nordiche* (The Most Ancient Northern Civilizations). Milan: n.p., 1941.

Le Roux, F., and C. J. Guyonvarc'h. *Les Druides* (The Druids). Rennes : n.p., 1982.

Levalois, C. *La terra di luce—Il Nord e l'origine* (The Land of Light: The North and the Origin). Saluzzo: n.p., 1988.

Lévêque, Pierre. *La civiltà greca* (Greek Civilization). Turin: n.p., 1970.

Lévi-Strauss, Claude. *The Way of the Masks.* Translated by Sylvia Modelski. Seattle: University of Washington Press, 1982.

Ligabue, G., and G. Orefici, ed. *Rapa Nui.* Venice: n.p., 1994.

Lüken, H. *Le tradizioni del genere umano* (Mankind's Traditions). Parma: n.p., 1874.

MacCulloch, J. A. *The Religion of the Ancient Celts.* Norwood, Penn.: Norwood Editions, 1978.

———. *The Hittites and Their Contemporaries in Asia Minor.* New York: Thames and Hudson, 1986.

Mandruzzato, Enzo, ed. *Pindaro, l'opera superstite* (Pindar: Surviving Work). Bologna: n.p., 1980.

Marazzi, Ugo, ed. *Testi dello sciamanesimo* (Texts of Shamanism). Turin: Unione Tipografica, 1984.

Markale, Jean. *The Celts.* Rochester, Vt.: Inner Traditions, 1993.

Mastrelli, Carlo., ed. *L'Edda, carmi norreni* (The Edda, Norse Poems). Florence: n.p., 1982.

Merwin, W. S. *Sir Gawain and the Green Knight.* New York: Knopf, 2002.

Messina, G. *Dizionario di mitologia classica* (Dictionary of Classical Mythology). Rome: n.p., 1959.

Monier-Williams, Sir Monier. *A Sanskrit-English Dictionary.* New Delhi: Asian Educational Service, 1999.

Montanari, Franco. *Introduzione a Omero* (Introduction to Homer). Florence: n.p., 1992.

Moraldi, L., ed. *Manoscritti di Qumrân* (The Qumrán Manuscripts). Turin: Unione Tipografica, 1986.

Morretta, Angelo. *Miti indiani* (Indian Myths). Milan: n.p., 1982.

New Encyclopedia Britannica. Chicago: Encyclopedia Britannica, 2005.

Nilsson, Martin. P. *Homer and Mycenae.* New York: Cooper Square, 1968.

———. *Le religioni degli antichi e i moderni* (The Religions of the Ancients and Moderns). Scandicci: n.p., 1993.

———. *The Minoan-Mycenaean Religion and Its Survival in Greek Religion.* New York: Biblo and Tannen, 1971.

———. *The Mycenaean Origin of Greek Mythology.* Berkeley: University of California Press, 1932.

Norway Pilot, vol. 3A, "Offshore and Coastal Waters of Norway from Risvær-fjorden to the North Part of Vesterålen," 6th ed. Taunton, Somerset, UK: British Admiralty, 1982.

Otto, Walter F. *Il mito* (Myth). Genoa: n.p., 1993.

Palmer, Leonard. R. *Mycenaeans and Minoans.* Westport, Conn.: Greenwood Press, 1980.

Pettazzoni, Raffaele. *La figura mostruosa del Tempo nella religione mitriaca* (Time's Monstrous Figure in the Religion of Mithras). Rome: Acc. Naz. dei Lincei, 1950.

———. *Le origini dei Kabiri nelle isole del Mar Tracio* (The Origins of the Kabirs in the Islands of the Thracian Sea). Rome: Acc. Naz. dei Lincei, 1909.

Philippe, Robert. "Ulysse est-il allé en Bretagne?" (Did Ulysses Go to Britain?). In *Planète* no. 22 (1965).

Piggott, Stuart. *Ancient Europe from the Beginnings of Agriculture to Classical Antiquity.* Chicago: Aldine, 1968.

———. *The Druids.* New York: Thames and Hudson, 1985.

———. *Prehistoric India to 1000 B.C.* London: Cassell, 1962.

Pinna, Mario. *Climatologia* (Climatology). Turin: Unione Tipografica, 1977.

Plato. *Timaeus and Critias.* Translated by H. D. P. Lee. Harmondsworth, U.K.: Penguin, 1971.

Pliny. *Storia Naturale* (Natural Histories). Turin, n.p., 1982.

Plutarch. "De facie quae in orbe lunae apparet" (The Face That Appears in the Moon Circle). *The Books of the Moralia,* vol. 12. Translated by Harold Cherniss and William C. Helmbold. Cambridge, Mass.: Harvard University Press, Loeb Classical Library, 1957.

———. *Il volto della luna* (The Moon's Face). Translated into Italian by L. Lehnus. Milan: n.p., 1992.

———. *Isis et Osiris* (Isis and Osiris). Translated into French by M. Meunier. Paris: n.p., 1979.

Porfirio. *L'antro delle Ninfe* (The Nymph's Grotto). Edited by L. Simonini. Milan: n.p., 1986.

Pörtner, Rudolf. *The Vikings: Rise and Fall of the Norse Sea Kings.* Translated and adapted by Sophie Wilkins. New York: St. Martin's, 1975.

Prampolini, Giacomo. *La mitologia nella vita dei popoli* (Mythology in the Life of Peoples). Milan: n.p., 1954.

Puech, H., ed. *Histoire des religions.* Paris: Gallimard, 1976.

Randsborg, K. "Kivik Archaeology and Iconography." In *Acta archaeologica* vol. 64, no. 1 (1993).

Recinos, Adrián, ed. *Popol Vuh: The Sacred Book of the Ancient Quiché Maya.* London: W. Hodge, 1951.

Renfrew, Colin. *Before Civilization.* Harmondsworth, UK: Penguin, 1990.

Rocci, L. *Vocabolario Greco-Italiano* (Greek-Italian Dictionary), 39th ed. Genoa: Società anonima editrice Dante Alighieri; Città di Castello, Società anonima casa editrice S. Lapi, 1943.

Rodio, Apollonio. *Argonautiche* (Argonautica). Translated by G. Paduano. Milano: n.p., 1998.

Romualdi, Adriano. *Gli Indoeuropei* (The Indo-Europeans). Padova: n.p., 1978.

Russell, Bertrand. *History of Western Philosophy.* London: Allen and Unwin, 1946.

Sacchi, Paolo, ed. *Apocrifi dell'Antico Testamento* (The Apocrypha of the Old Testament). Turin: Unione Tipografica, 1981.

Sani, S., ed. *Rigveda.* Venice: n.p., 2000.

Santangelo, P. E. *L'origine del linguaggio* (The Origin of Language). Milan: n.p., 1949.

Saxo Grammaticus. *The History of the Danes* (Gesta Danorum). Edited by Hilda Ellis Davidson and translated by Peter Fisher. Rochester, N.Y.: D. S. Brewer, 1998.

Scarduelli, P. *L'isola degli antenati di pietra* (The Island of the Stone Ancestors). Rome: Laterza, 1986.

Strabo. *Geography.* London: H. G. Bohn, 1854.

Sturluson, Snorri. *Edda.* Edited by Anthony Faulkes. New York: Oxford University Press, 1991.

Tacitus. *Germania.* Translated by J. B. Rives. New York: Oxford University Press, 1999.

Tilak, B. G. *The Arctic Home in the Vedas.* Poona City, India: Tilak Bros., 1925.

———. *The Orion*. Bombay: R. A. Sagoon, 1893.

Traill, David. A. *Schliemann of Troy*. New York: St. Martin's, 1995.

Treccani Italian Encyclopedia. Rome: n.p., 1949.

Verne, Jules. *Twenty Thousand Leagues Under the Sea*. Annapolis: Naval Institute Press, 1993.

Walker, Brian Brown. *The I Ching or Book of Changes*. New York: St. Martin's, 1992.

Wölfel, D. J *Monumenta Linguae Canariae, Die Kanarischen Sprachdenkmaler* (Remains of the Canarian Language). Graz: Akademische Druck und Verlagsanstalt, 1965.

Index